Library of
Davidson College

THE STRUGGLE OF ISLAM
IN MODERN INDONESIA

*Tanda mata
untuk sahabat²ku
di Indonesia*

VERHANDELINGEN
VAN HET KONINKLIJK INSTITUUT VOOR TAAL-, LAND- EN VOLKENKUNDE

59

THE STRUGGLE OF ISLAM IN MODERN INDONESIA

B. J. BOLAND

THE HAGUE - MARTINUS NIJHOFF - 1971

297.09
B687s

75-6672
I.S.B.N. 90.247.0781.1

PREFACE

With deep interest I have followed the Indonesian people's fight for freedom and independence from 1945 onwards. This interest has come to be centred in particular on the question of how religions, especially Islam, were involved in this struggle, and what role they would fulfil in the new Indonesia.

After having lived and worked in Indonesia from 1946 to the end of 1960, I was twice more enabled to visit Indonesia thanks to grants from the Netherlands Foundation for the Advancement of Tropical Research (WOTRO). It was during these sojourns in particular, from May to October 1966 and from February to July 1969, that the material for this study was collected, supplemented and checked.

For the help I received during these visits I am greatly indebted to so many Indonesian informants that it is impossible to mention them all. Moreover, some of them would not appreciate being singled out by name. But while offering them these general thanks I am thinking of them all individually.

In spite of all the help given and patience shown me, this publication is bound to be full of shortcomings. An older Muslim friend, however, once encouraged me by reminding me that perfection belongs only to God (*al-kamāl li'llāh*). Nevertheless, I should like to offer my apologies for errors and mistakes; I would appreciate it if readers drew my attention to them.

This treatise on Islam in Indonesia is written by someone who is, indeed, neither a Muslim nor an Indonesian, but who honestly wishes to make a contribution to mutual understanding and respect between people whose lives are determined by different cultural and religious backgrounds.

In trying to understand each other we cannot avoid asking each other questions, sometimes critical questions, perhaps even "awkward" questions. It should, however, be borne in mind that the author, as a Christian theologian, would be just as much prepared to ask such questions concerning Christianity and its doctrines, and concerning the life of the Churches and of Christians themselves.

A few remarks of a technical nature must be made here. Firstly, for the transliteration of Arabic words the system of the Encyclopaedia of Islam has been followed; where one Arabic letter has to be transliterated with two roman letters (*th, dj, kh, dh, sh, gh*), for reasons of cost they have not been underlined. However, when Arabic words occur in an Indonesian context the Indonesian transliteration of the Arabic words has often been kept.

Unfortunately, there is no uniformity in the Indonesian transliteration of Arabic words. Indonesian Muslims, however, are following more and more the system used in the new translation of the Qur'ān (see "Al-Quräan dan Terdjemahnja", published by the Indonesian Ministry of Religion, Vol. I, p. 148). Differences between the Indonesian transliteration and that of the Encyclopaedia of Islam include:

E.I. *th*	=	*ts* Ind.		E.I. $ṣ$	=	*sh* Ind.
$ḥ, h$	=	*h*		$ḍ$	=	*dh*
kh	=	*ch*		$ṭ$	=	*th*
dh	=	*dz*		$ẓ$	=	*zh*
sh	=	*sj*		$ḳ$	=	*q*.

Special attention should be paid to the difficulty that *sh* in the Indonesian transliteration stands for the Arabic $ṣād$ (in such words as *shalat* or *sholat,* and in such names as Anshary and Ash-Shiddiqy), and *th* stands for *ṭā'* (e.g. in *bathin,* Thalib, Thaha).

Arabic, Indonesian and other foreign words are printed in italics. The plural form of some common words is made by adding a roman s, thus: *ulama*s, *kiyai*s, *abangan*s, *kampung*s, etc.

Indonesian names are spelt as far as possible in accordance with the wishes of their owners (for example, using the Dutch *oe* for *u,* in Soekarno, Mohamad Roem, etc.), while the names of organizations are spelt as is usual in Indonesia (Muhammadijah, Nahdatul Ulama).

When referring to verses from the Qur'ān the so-called Eastern numbering is used. Quotations in English are often taken from the explanatory translation by Mohammed Marmaduke Pickthall ("The Meaning of the Glorious Koran").

The draft manuscript for this book was translated from the Dutch by Mrs. C. A. Franken. Its final form was established by means of consultations between the author and Mr. S. O. Robson of the editorial staff of the Royal Institute of Linguistics and Anthropology.

Oegstgeest/Leiden B. J. B.
August, 1970.

TABLE OF CONTENTS

PREFACE V

INTRODUCTION 1

CHAPTER I: THE POLITICAL STRUGGLE (1945-1955) . 7

1. Benefits from the Japanese Period 7
2. Facing up to the Problem 15
3. Looking for a Compromise 23
4. The Decision 34
5. The Fight for Freedom (1945-1950) 39
6. Strife between the Parties (1950-1955) 45
7. The Darul Islam Revolts 54
8. Religio-Political Publications 75

CHAPTER II: THE ISLAMIC COMMUNITY AMID
INCREASING TENSIONS (1955-1965) . . . 85

1. Political Developments up to 1959 85
2. The Ideological Struggle (1959) 90
3. "Guided Democracy" (1959-1965) 99
4. The Ministry of Religious Affairs 105
5. Islamic Educational Institutions 112
6. Soekarno and Islam 123

CHAPTER III: ISLAM AND THE "NEW ORDER"
(1965 and after) 135

1. The Thirtieth of September and its Aftermath 135
2. New Hope for Muslims 144
3. New Disappointments 149

CHAPTER IV: A PRELIMINARY STOCKTAKING . . . 157

1. Political Topics 157
2. Partial Realization of Islamic Law 164
3. Regional Endeavours: Atjeh 174
4. Working toward an Islamic Society 185
5. Religious Instruction and Textbooks 196
6. A Muslim "Theology of Religions" 205
7. Reformation, Liberalization, Modernization 211
8. Muslims and Christians 224

APPENDICES 243

LIST OF ABBREVIATIONS AND THEIR MEANING . . . 264

LIST OF PUBLICATIONS REFERRED TO 267

INDEX 275

INTRODUCTION

The term "Modern Indonesia" in the title of this book is intended to refer to the Republic of Indonesia which was created on August 17th, 1945. Hence, 25 years after Independence, the question may be posed as to how Islam has struggled to make its impact felt in the early history of modern Indonesia.

Now it has rightly been said, "To discuss the position of Islam in contemporary Indonesia involves the entire Indonesian situation".[1] Moreover, this history is so recent that it has not yet really become history. Anyone who has experienced some part of that history, living in Indonesia, also knows that many details were obscure even at the moment when they took place. How can one hope to reconstruct later the true background of events? Who knows the many personal rivalries, ambitions and intrigues of contemporary history which are so commonly presented to the public as fundamental matters? Moreover, how can a foreigner presume to understand the Indonesian situation, when his Indonesian informants again and again hasten to explain that for them, too, all kinds of things have been obscure?

The best that can be done at this stage is for many investigators, each working along their own lines, to attempt to describe developments in Indonesia, and in this way each to contribute a part toward a complete picture in the future. As far as the political, cultural, sociological and economic aspects are concerned, many publications have already appeared, such as those of George McT. Kahin, Ruth McVey, Herbert Feith, Bernhard Dahm, Clifford Geertz, J. M. van der Kroef and others.[2] In these studies mention is made again and again of questions concerning Islam. It is, however, both necessary and useful to pay attention to Islam in a more direct way, and to approach developments in Indonesia from the point of view of Islam, or in other words, to sketch the recent history of Islam in Indonesia.

---

[1] C. A. O. van Nieuwenhuijze, *Islam and National Self-Realization in Indonesia*, in *Bulletin d'Informations du Centre pour l'Etude des Problèmes du Monde Musulman Contemporain*, 1958, Fasc. VII, p. 80.

[2] See List of Publications Referred to.

It could be objected that it is still too early to do this. However, I would like to "steal" Clifford Geertz's remark that for the time being "sketches may be all that can be expected", and as yet no oils — "yet there is something to be said for sketches as for oils".[3]

That an attempt should be made to draw such a sketch is shown by Wilfred Cantwell Smith's famous book, "Islam in Modern History". Lengthy chapters are devoted to the Arabs, to Turkey, India and Pakistan. But in the few lines on Indonesia it is said that in the case of Indonesia "there has been a very serious disregard, both by Western students and, even more striking, by Muslims of other areas. The role of Islam in contemporary Indonesia, and of Indonesia in contemporary Islam, has still to be not only assessed but noticed..."[4]

It is interesting to see how this remark occurs again in a book by the Indonesian author Rosihan Anwar; this book is a sort of modern Muslim catechism written in the form of a discussion between Wak Hadji and Hadji Wa'ang. Speaking of the role of Islam, the former says that too few studies have been made of Islam in Indonesia. Surprised, his friend answers, "Oh, how can you say that? Just look at the list of names of Dutch scholars who have studied Islam here, and the books they have published!" But Wak Hadji maintains that Indonesia has received less attention than Egypt, Turkey, and so on, and he adds: "I once read a book by someone who writes that the role of Islam in contemporary Indonesia and of Indonesia in contemporary Islam has still to be assessed and noticed. The author of that book said that here in Indonesia there is Islamically something distinctive and fascinating and potentially very rich."[5]

W. C. Smith's abovementioned remark is a challenge to try to add something to our knowledge of the recent history of Islam in Indonesia. It must by now be more or less possible to sketch in the outlines, and to indicate the chief characteristics that are important for the Indonesian chapter of Islam in modern history.

In this endeavour we can link up with Harry J. Benda's book on developments during the Japanese occupation.[6] In his Preface, Benda

---

[3] Clifford Geertz, *Islam Observed,* New Haven/London 1968, p. X.
[4] Wilfred Cantwell Smith, *Islam in Modern History,* Princeton 1957, p. 295.
[5] Rosihan Anwar, *Islam dan Anda,* Djakarta 1962, p. 107, quoting Smith, *Islam,* p. 295.
[6] Harry J. Benda, *The Crescent and the Rising Sun,* The Hague/Bandung 1958.

remarks that his book deals with developments on the island of Java only. But he considers this limitation as not too serious a drawback. After all, "Though Islam in the other areas has undeniably played — and continues to play — a leading role in the political evolution of Indonesia, it is on Java that it has found its most important organizational expression. It is there, also, that Islamic groups have been most directly involved in the shaping of Indonesian politics in general." [7]

As a sequel to Benda, a sketch must be made of developments in Indonesia after 1945. For the time being it will neither be possible nor necessary to attempt completeness. Not every fact or occurrence, and not all aspects of the subject, can be treated. As far as possible, however, an attempt must be made to arrive at a preliminary interpretation of the developments, even though such an assessment will surely be subjective.

In order to sketch the role of Islam in modern Indonesia, attention must also be paid to the developments, problems and tendencies within Islam and the Muslim community itself. We shall therefore have to listen to what conscious adherents of Islam and well-qualified Islamic leaders say and write. In this connection, Gibb's judgement is still valid: "... it is not to the masses but to the leaders that we must look if we are to judge of the present tendencies in religious thought".[8] To this end, there are a great number of publications available in Indonesian, written by Indonesian Muslims; we intend letting these Indonesian Muslims speak for themselves by drawing on a representative selection of their publications.

This does not mean that we are going to adhere solely to a discussion of religious thought and its development, that is to say, Islamic ideas and their history. Islam is a practical religion, related to *dunyā wa ākhira* (this world and the world to come) and it includes *dīn wa dawla* ("religion" and government or "politics"). For this reason sociological studies such as those by Clifford Geertz are very important, even though theologians — both Islamic and Christian — are often suspicious of the methods and results of sociological research.

Geertz wanted to study and record the religious and cultural life of the small town of Paré ("Modjokuto") in Java, in order to make it a basis for a sketch of "the Religion of Java".[9] The distinction which

---

[7] Benda, *The Crescent*, p. 4.
[8] H. A. R. Gibb, *Whither Islam?*, London 1932, p. 372.
[9] Clifford Geertz, *The Religion of Java*, Illinois 1960.

Geertz made with regard to the religion of Java was certainly not a new one, but had formerly also been current among Javanese Muslims. This is at least true as far as the distinction between the so-called *santri* variant and the *abangan* variant is concerned (a *santri* is originally a pupil of a classical Indonesian religious boarding-school, while the so-called *abangan* variant indicates the syncretistic popular religion). It will be useful to observe the reactions of Indonesian Islamic scholars to this sociological approach, even though one may not agree with them. It so happens that Muslims use other terms for the distinction, and give a different content to them. A Muslim prefers to speak of "Islam" — orthodox or modern Islam — and its consciously faithful adherents, rather than the *santri* and the *santri* variant or the *santri* civilization. From a religious point of view the *abangan*s are those who know little of Islam and are but little concerned with the precepts of Islam, though they also consider themselves to be Muslims. Nowadays many of them would call themselves "Muslims, but not so fanatical", that is to say, not so strict; in other words, they are "statistical Muslims" (Ind. *muslim-statistik*). In any case, Muslims consider this distinction first and foremost a religious differentiation in relation to the question of whether or not one is a consciously devout Muslim. For this reason they tend to emphasize the fact that these two variants cannot be clearly divided and certainly do not indicate two separate groups. They stress that the so-called *abangan* variant of religion in Java ought to be regarded as a variant within Islam and the Muslim community. Is it not true that within every religion and every religious community the number of really practising members is fairly limited?

Muslim informants object even more strongly to the distinction which Geertz made when speaking of the *priyayi* variant of religion in Java (the *priyayi* class is the Javanese aristocracy and gentry), that is to say, the world of the *wajang* (shadow play) and Javanese mysticism. Can this sociological category, they say, be simply placed alongside the religious distinction of *santri* and *abangan*? Ought not the *priyayi* class and its behaviour, from a religious point of view, be judged on the basis of the differentiation expressed by the terms *santri* and *abangan*? Is it not possible to be a good Muslim and at the same time admire much of what Geertz counts as belonging to the *priyayi* variant of the religion in Java? The well-known Indonesian Professor Rasjidi says of himself that *abangan*-Islam and orthodox Islam are simultaneously present in him, while moreover he wants to be a modern Muslim. Speaking of *abangan*-Islam he means that he too likes *gamelan* music, the *wajang* and the *serimpi* dances, which according to Geertz's differentiation belong to the *priyayi* variant.[10]

So Geertz studied the current cultural situation in Paré in order to draw some conclusions concerning the religion of Java. As one of its aspects he also came into contact with Islam or the so-called *santri* religion. In a later study called "Islam Observed" he considers the characteristics of the world of the *abangan*s and *priyayi*s as the "mainline traditions" of Java, while the *santri* variant is termed a "countertradition", indicated as "scripturalism" and regarded as a "scripturalist interlude".[11]

In my opinion there is room for another approach alongside the sociological. That is to say, we may take as our point of departure the Islamic world of ideas and its history, in order to see how Islam functions as a living force in the new Indonesia. It will be necessary and fruitful to approach developments during the last 25 years in Indonesia from this point of view as well, and to provide some material concerning specifically Islamic activities, problems and tendencies.

As has been said, it is possible to link up with Benda's work. Speaking of the religious developments in Indonesia during the Japanese occupation from the point of view of the so-called *santri* civilization, Benda concludes: "The history of Indonesian Islam is, then, the history of this expanding *santri* civilization and its impact upon the religious, social and political life of Indonesia".[12] Benda ends his survey with the conclusion that what the Japanese left behind them in 1945 was "a more truly Islamic Java, a Java closer to the ideals of the *santri* civilization, than had existed in March 1942".[13]

This conclusion highlights some questions of primary importance with regard to the interpretation of the most recent history of Islam in Indonesia. What course did the struggle of this so-called *santri* civilization take in order to realize its ideals? Or in other words, how did Islam (orthodox and modern or neo-orthodox) strive to put Islamic principles into practice in Indonesian state and society after 1945? And in how far has that struggle been successful — that is to say, not only in resulting in an external expansion, but also in a more thorough Islamization of Indonesian society and its individual members?

---

[10] M. Rasjidi, *Mengapa aku tetap memeluk Agama Islam,* Djakarta 1968, pp. 10-11.
[11] Geertz, *Islam, passim.*
[12] Benda, *The Crescent,* p. 14.
[13] Benda, *The Crescent,* p. 187.

Furthermore, Clifford Geertz may be right when he says that Islam has not brought uniformity to Indonesia.[14] But it could be that the developments of the last 25 years tend more than ever — at least externally — toward the expansion and strengthening of a uniform Islam, through religious education and publications, the Ministry of Religious Affairs, and so on. If this assumption is correct, then, as well as through sociological case-studies, the situation will also have to be approached from the viewpoint of the "history of Islam", paying special attention to the abovementioned questions concerning the interpretation of its recent history.

In the first three chapters of this book we intend giving a historical sketch of the developments which took place during these 25 years. These years will be divided into three sections: the period of political struggle (1945-1955), the period of the internal strengthening of the Islamic community amid increasing tensions (1955-1965), and the time after September 30th, 1965, a date which marks the beginning of a third period in the modern history of Islam in Indonesia. In the final chapter, a preliminary stocktaking will be made of a number of contemporary activities, problems and tendencies in Islam in modern Indonesia.

---

[14] Geertz, *Islam*, p. 12.

CHAPTER I

THE POLITICAL STRUGGLE
(1945-1955)

1. *Benefits from the Japanese Period*

According to Benda, it is possible to differentiate three leading groups in the former Dutch East Indies towards the end of that regime. Firstly, there was the aristocracy, that is to say the *priyayi*s in Java, the *ulèëbalang*s (Ind. *hulubalang*) in Atjeh, and elsewhere the *radja*s (rajahs) and other *adat*-chiefs. They formed "the cornerstone of the Dutch colonial system for many decennia, if not centuries".[1] On the other hand the Indonesian nationalist movement was growing and took shape in many organizations. Hence in the second place we can mention those nationalists who were united in non-confessional organizations, the "secular" nationalists as Benda called them (correctly always putting the "secular" in inverted commas). Then in the third place there was the group of Islamic leaders or Muslim nationalists. In this study the last group will require much attention. Among them were intellectuals with a Western upbringing, as well as traditional *ulama*s (religious scholars or "scribes"). To the latter belonged, for example, the Javanese *kiyai*s (indicated by a capital K. before their name, just as a following capital H. shows a *hadji*). The title *Kiyai* is given by the people to "an independent religious teacher not belonging to the official scribes connected with the mosques".[2] Many of them were heads of, or teachers at, a *pesantrèn*, an institution which even now is often gratefully depicted as the nursery for Islamic leaders who resisted colonial domination.[3]

The role of the first group, the *priyayi*s, was in fact finished at the arrival of the Japanese in March 1942, the unofficial end of the former

---

[1] Benda, *The Crescent*, p. 199.
[2] G. W. J. Drewes, in *Unity and Variety in Muslim Civilization*, ed. by Gustave E. von Grunebaum, Chicago 1955, p. 309. I also refer to this essay as a general introduction to Indonesian Islam.
[3] See for example *Al-Djami'ah, Madjalah Ilmu Pengetahuan Agama Islam*, no. 5-6, Jogjakarta 1965, p. 96.

Dutch East Indies. Part of this aristocracy certainly hoped in 1945 that they would be reinstated in their former position of power.[4] And for their part, the returning administration of the Dutch East Indies hoped for renewed co-operation from this aristocracy after 1945 as well, for instance in the creation of federal states as opposed to the "Jogja Republic". But the Indonesian revolution destroyed the dreams of a new alliance between these two forces. Within the Indonesian Republic there remained a place for members of this aristocracy, providing they wanted to serve the national cause with their personal qualities and as ordinary citizens. Certainly there emerged from this group a number of intellectuals who later devoted themselves to building the new Indonesia, either as individuals or as members of a political party (generally one of the "secular" nationalist parties).

More important for the modern history of Islam in Indonesia are the second and third groups, the "secular" nationalists and the Islamic leaders. Among the so-called secular nationalists were to be found — besides a few Christians from Christian areas such as North Sulawesi (Celebes) — many *abangan* Muslims and nominal Muslims. One must not forget, however, that a number of devout Muslims also belonged to the "secular" (that is to say non-Islamic) nationalist organizations. These were people who regarded Islam in the first place as *dīn*, in the sense of a personal religion, and not as an ideological system to be put into practice in the area of *dawla* (government or politics). The latter, however, became — in all kinds of variation and nuance — the ideal of the third group, the Islamic leaders, who were united in Islamic parties and organizations.

As far as developments during the Japanese occupation are concerned, we can adopt the conclusions of Benda, who summarizes these developments as follows: "For quite some time, the Japanese seemed in fact more ready to make concessions to Islamic, rather than to nationalist, let alone *priyayi*, demands.... Only fairly late in the occupation — [that is to say, when a losing Japan began to allow preparations to be made for an independent Indonesia] — were concessions to the Muslim elite in fact paralleled, and ultimately overshadowed in importance, by increasing and decisive support to the 'secular' nationalists.... By that time, however, Indonesian Islam had been allowed to gain a position of unprecedented strength from which it could no longer be easily

---

[4] So for instance in Atjeh; cf. A. J. Piekaar, *Atjèh en de oorlog met Japan*, 's-Gravenhage-Bandung 1949, p. 247.

displaced by the nationalist leadership...." [5] So after all there was, even in the Japanese period, an obvious rivalry between both groups.

It was natural that the Japanese occupying power should try to use religion — in this case Islam — for its own wartime ends. "The Japanese considered Islam as one of the most effective means to penetrate into the spiritual recesses of Indonesian life and to infuse the influence of their own ideas and ideals at the bottom of the society. For exactly the same reasons, Christianity was chosen in the Philippines as an important vehicle for ideological penetration." [6] The way in which that took place, however, need not be retold here.[7] For our purpose the benefits which the Japanese period yielded for Islam and the Muslim community in Indonesia are more important.

Perhaps, then, two or three things may be mentioned: the creation of an Indonesian Office for Religious Affairs, the foundation of the Masjumi, and thirdly perhaps the formation of the Hizbu'llah. Much material concerning these developments can be found collected in the nearly 1,000 page long biography and collected writings of K. H. A. Wahid Hasjim.[8] Here follow some remarks on each of these three benefits from the Japanese period.

The Office for Religious Affairs (in Japanese *Shūmubu*; in Indonesian *Kantor Urusan Agama*) more or less took the place of the colonial "Office for Native Affairs". But it expanded to become the apparatus

---

[5] Benda, *The Crescent*, pp. 201-202. Benda's division between the "santri" and the "secular nationalists" has been criticized by L. Sluimers, who believes that Benda laid too much stress on Islam as a separate political force playing an independent role, while according to Sluimers the conflict which arose during the Japanese occupation was rather a conflict between conservatives and non-conservatives, cross-cutting religious boundaries (L. Sluimers, "Nieuwe Orde" op Java: de Japanse bezettingspolitiek en de Indonesische elites 1942-1943, in *Bijdragen tot de Taal-, Land- en Volkenkunde*, Vol. 124, no. 3, 's-Gravenhage 1968, pp. 336-365). In my opinion, however, the developments after 1945 tend to prove that Benda's approach is still usable, especially if we are trying to sketch the recent history of Islam in Indonesia from an Islamic point of view.

[6] M. A. Aziz, *Japan's Colonialism and Indonesia*, thesis Leiden 1955, p. 200.

[7] Cf. Benda, *The Crescent*; C. A. O. van Nieuwenhuijze, *Japanese Islam Policy in Java, 1942-1945*, in *Aspects of Islam in Post-Colonial Indonesia*, The Hague-Bandung 1958, pp. 109-160.

[8] *Sedjarah Hidup K. H. A. Wahid Hasjim dan karangan tersiar*, ed. by H. Aboebakar at a request from the Minister of Religion dated March 23rd, 1954, in memoriam of his predecessor who died in a motoring accident on April 19th, 1953; published in Djakarta, 1957; from now on referred to as "Wahid Hasjim".

which later managed all kinds of affairs formerly divided up among the Departments of Home Affairs, of Justice and of Education and Public Worship. The first senior post which the Japanese entrusted to an Indonesian in their administration was that of head of this Office for Religious Affairs.[9] This office had been headed by the Japanese Colonel Hori from the end of March 1942, but on October 1st, 1943 Hoesein Djajadiningrat was put in charge. Looking back, however, it was still more important that the man who was appointed to this position on August 1st, 1944, was K. Hasjim Asj'ari, head of the famous *pesantrèn* Tebu-ireng (Djombang, East Java), a conservative Muslim, who had, however, great authority as a *kiyai*. As he was already chairman of the Masjumi, which will be discussed shortly, the authority his name carried covered two important organizations. Through this appointment Wahid Hasjim, the son of K. Hasjim Asj'ari, got the opportunity to begin his career, for while the father continued his work in East Java his position in Djakarta was in fact held by the son.[10]

From April 1st, 1944,[11] a start was made to found regional offices for religious affairs in every residency (parts of a province). Under the leadership of people such as Wahid Hasjim and Kahar Muzakkir (not to be mistaken for the later South Sulawesi rebel Kahar Muzakkar), the foundations were laid for the future Ministry of Religious Affairs and its regional offices, a unique institution, to which special attention will be paid later on. In 1950 Wahid Hasjim became Minister of Religion in the first cabinet of the United Indonesian Republic (after the recognition of Independence by the Dutch). And it was he who organized the Ministry of Religious Affairs to an important extent, and so left his mark on it.

The second benefit from the Japanese period was the formation of the Masjumi, the name being a contraction of *Madjlis Sjuro Muslimin Indonesia,* correctly translated by Benda as "Consultative Council of Indonesian Muslims".[12] This Masjumi may be considered the successor to the M.I.A.I., the initials of *Madjlisul Islamil aᶜlaa Indonesia,* the Supreme Indonesian Council of Islam, or less correctly the Great Islamic

---

[9] Benda, *The Crescent,* pp. 126, 201.
[10] Benda, *The Crescent,* p. 273, n. 80-81; compare Wahid Hasjim, p. 331 ff.
[11] According to Wahid Hasjim, p. 597.
[12] Benda, *The Crescent,* p. 151. "Council of Indonesian Moslem Associations", George McT. Kahin, *Nationalism and Revolution in Indonesia,* Ithaca New York 1952, p. 156, and "Council of Indonesian Moslem Organizations", Clifford Geertz, *The Religion,* p. 142, are incorrect.

Council of Indonesia.[13] In 1937 this M.I.A.I. had resulted from the Al-Islam Congresses, which had been held since 1921.

The dissolution of the M.I.A.I. in October 1943 was probably considered necessary by the Japanese because this organization had been set up through the Muslims' own initiative, as a federation of Islamic organizations among whose leaders were men with a strongly anti-colonial and non-cooperative background.[14] Or in the words of Aziz, the M.I.A.I. began by being anti-Dutch (the immediate cause being the marriage law made by the colonial government in 1937), and became anti-foreign, and therefore might well become anti-Japanese.[15] On the other hand, the Masjumi which began life on December 1st, 1943, was in fact a creation of the Japanese authorities. The long list of activities and aims of the (more religious) M.I.A.I.[16] apparently had to give place to the one (more political) goal of the Masjumi: that of "strengthening the unity of all Islamic organizations", and of "aiding Dai Nippon in the interests of Greater East Asia".[17]

According to Aziz, the more obvious reason for substituting the Masjumi for the M.I.A.I. was that two of the most important Islamic organizations — the Muhammadijah and Nahdatul Ulama (N.U.) — had not joined the M.I.A.I.[18] These two were now, with all the others, included in the Masjumi, which moreover recognized individual membership. Both these associations were traditionally non-political in character. The Muhammadijah (*muḥammadīya*) came into existence in 1912 as a socio-religious association, due to the initiative of K. H. Ahmad Dahlan, who was working as a teacher at a school which gave its name to this association. The association fought for reformist principles, which, coming from Egypt, had stirred the Islamic world. On the other hand, the Nahdatul Ulama (*nahḍat al-ʿulamā*) — that is, the Awakening of the Scribes — which was founded in 1926, can be considered as a movement of *ulama*s to maintain the traditional Javanese way of life and to defend the authority of the four orthodox *madhāhib* (sing. *madhhab,* school of law). The leading positions in the new Masjumi were apparently fairly well distributed among supporters of both N.U.

---

[13] Cf. Wahid Hasjim, p. 311; Van Nieuwenhuijze, *Aspects,* p. 120; Benda, *The Crescent,* p. 90.
[14] Cf. Benda, *The Crescent,* p. 151; also Van Nieuwenhuijze, *Aspects,* p. 152 ff.
[15] Aziz, *Japan's Colonialism,* p. 205.
[16] Cf. Wahid Hasjim, p. 326.
[17] Benda, *The Crescent,* p. 150.
[18] Aziz, *Japan's Colonialism,* p. 205.

and Muhammadijah ideas.[19] Various prominent members of the Masjumi also held important posts in the Office for Religious Affairs. As has been said, K. Hasjim Asj'ari was chairman of the Masjumi; one of the vice-chairmen was his son Wahid Hasjim.

The significance of these developments has been described by Aziz as follows: "The Islamic leaders who were generally distrusted by the Dutch authority came as a closed group in direct contact with the highest governing body. The hierarchical order maintained during Dutch rule among the administrators was thus knocked down. The separation between church and state [religion and politics] came practically to an end. Islam obtained a privileged position in the political system in which, next to the secular administration, a religious apparatus had been created. The Japanese thus brought about a fundamental change in the traditional method of governing, by the increase of power for Islam" (that is to say, a change in the structure of the government by enhancing the influence of Islam).[20]

The formation of these two organizations, the Office for Religious Affairs and the Masjumi, meant in fact that an apparatus had been given to Indonesian Islam (whatever the Japanese may have intended with them) that was going to be of great importance for the future. Islam as a religious system had received an apparatus which afterwards could expand to become a Ministry of Religious Affairs — created during the second Sjahrir cabinet, March 1946 — with a network of regional offices all over Indonesia. And Islam as a political power, its wings clipped during the colonial period, would soon be able to play its part via the Masjumi, which on November 7th, 1945, was reorganized as a political party.

The third benefit accruing from the Japanese period at the end of 1944 [21] is the establishment of the Hizbu'llah ("God's Forces", or "the party of Allah" according to Sura 5 : 56; 58 : 22), a sort of military organization for Muslim youths.[22] According to Benda, the Masjumi appointed the leaders of this organization in January 1945. Its chairman was Zainul Arifin ("one of the *Nahdatul Ulama* delegates in the

---

[19] See Wahid Hasjim, pp. 351-352.
[20] Aziz, *Japan's Colonialism*, pp. 205-206.
[21] According to A. A. Zorab, *De Japanse bezetting van Indonesië*, thesis Leiden 1954, p. 107.
[22] To what extent and in which way Christian youths here and there joined the Hizbu'llah — as some rumours have it — will have to be examined more closely.

Masjumi executive"); among the leaders were Mohamad Roem, Anwar Tjokroaminoto, Jusuf Wibisono and Prawoto Mangkusasmito, later to become well-known politicians.[23] Though according to Herbert Feith the N.U. leaders led the Islamic guerilla organizations Hizbu'llah and Sabili'llah,[24] this is only true of the first chairman, and probably of the leaders of smaller military units in the fight for independence. The names just cited are associated with the Muhammadijah and P.S.I.I., rather than the N.U.

The formation of the Hizbu'llah is probably of importance because many of its members were later included in the national army. That meant that in the Indonesian army there was an important infusion of Muslim "santris". In the course of time many Christians also joined the Indonesian army (e.g. from the former colonial army). This characteristic of the army might be a difference from the navy and air force, of which both officers and men generally came from a more "secular" background (for example, education at a state secondary school, supplemented by a special training in the U.S.A.). It could well be that this difference in atmosphere even continued to make itself felt up to the events of September 30th, 1965 and their aftermath.

Weighing up the Japanese occupation, it turns out that the Muslim community made important gains. Therefore it need surprise no-one that Islamic leaders tend to paint the former colonial period very black. Right up to the latest Indonesian publications, the colonial religious policy is ascribed in particular to the influence of the Dutch Islamic scholar C. Snouck Hurgronje, who still has a very bad name among Muslims in Indonesia (with the exception of one recent example of a "rehabilitation" by the abovementioned Prof. Rasjidi, which will be reviewed at the end of this book).[25] According to general opinion, Snouck Hurgronje was "the *mufti* of the Dutch imperialists".[26] It was he who wanted to restrict Islam to being "a religion only of the mosque", and who urged the Dutch on with "What you have inherited from your fathers, defend (Ind. *pertahankanlah*), in order to keep it forever" (after a less correct Indonesian translation of some lines of Goethe

---

[23] Benda, *The Crescent*, p. 280, n. 26.
[24] Herbert Feith, *The Decline of Constitutional Democracy in Indonesia*, Ithaca New York 1962, p. 233. "Sabīli'llāh" means: (fighters in) the way of God.
[25] H. M. Rasjidi, *Islam dan Indonesia Dizaman Modern*, Djakarta 1968.
[26] M. Isa Anshary, *Falsafah Perdjuangan Islam*, Bandung 1949, p. 156.

quoted by Snouck).[27] According to oral information, others add that Snouck Hurgronje wanted to stimulate the tendency of Indonesian Islam toward mysticism, in order that Islam might become a "religion of the soul" as is Christianity in the opinion of Muslims. In my experience, in Atjeh a Dutchman is warmly welcomed, "providing you come with good intentions, not like Snouck Hurgronje who brought disaster to this area". The chief criticism of the colonial religious policy is comprised in the formula that "religion had to be an exclusively cultic (spiritual) matter and was precluded from having anything to do with affairs of state".[28]

Benda, too, points out that colonial religious policy was based on the division of Islam into a religion and a political power; in accordance with Snouck Hurgronje's suggestions, the colonial government should be neutral towards Islam as a religion (in its narrower sense), and watchful of Islam as a political power.[29] Benda suggests that "Snouck's seemingly plausible, yet facile, separation of religion and politics in Islam was, to say the least, unrealistic", because "it belied the very universalism of the faith".[30] Naturally Snouck Hurgronje was aware of this problem. But was not this sort of separation between "religion" and "politics" the only possibility — and thus the most realistic policy — that a colonial government could attempt to carry out?

It is understandable that Islamic leaders looked forward with great expectations to the independence of Indonesia. For them, the Japanese occupation had put an end to the dark centuries of colonial domination, which, being a government by infidels over Muslims, was impossible to accept or tolerate. What Islamic leaders had longed for, was basically achieved, thanks to the Japanese period: an Islam which, so to speak, had got hands and feet (an Office for Religious Affairs, the Masjumi, and the Hizbu'llah) to set itself in motion and make itself felt in Indonesian society. And this endeavour to assert itself would become the struggle of Islam in the new Indonesia.

Islamic leaders would agree with Benda that "separation of religion and politics... was at best a temporary phenomenon of Islam in decline.

---

[27] H. Ruslan Abdulgani, *Isi Kitab Sutji Al-Quräan guna membakar semangat Mahasiswa didalam suasana sekarang*, in *Al-Djami'ah*, July 1965, p. 33. The lines by Goethe, quoted by Snouck Hurgronje in *Nederland en de Islam*, p. 85, are: "Was du ererbt von deinen Vätern hast, Erwirb es, um es zu besitzen". Snouck meant: "erwirb es", try to win it in a spiritual/cultural way, through what was called an association policy.

[28] Wahid Hasjim, p. 597.

[29] Benda, *The Crescent*, pp. 23, 196.

[30] Benda, *The Crescent*, p. 29.

In an era of Islamic awakening, it could not survive for long, either in independent Muslim lands or in Islamic areas ruled by non-Muslims." [31] A reformer such as Rashīd Riḍā — in Indonesia a well-known name — also "has reaffirmed the inseparability of Islam as a religion and Islam as a political entity by stating that Islam is not fully in being so long as there does not exist a strong and independent Muslim state that is able to put into operation the laws of Islam".[32] Later on, Pakistan became a shining example for many Indonesian Muslims. But some of them realized from the beginning, and others were to discover afterwards, that putting Islamic law into practice is not as simple as holding a theory on an Islamic State. After all, "the experience of Pakistan suggests that a decree to the effect that 'This is to be an Islamic state' tends to create rather than to solve problems".[33]

Here we arrive at the heart of the problem concerning the role and the struggle of Islam in modern Indonesia. This is the question which from the very beginning thrusts itself upon us: to what extent is the idea of an Islamic State — or the functioning of Islamic law in state and society — subjectively meaningful as an ideal for believers, and in how far is it a realizable conception? That would become the burning question immediately upon the proclamation of Independence.

2. *Facing up to the Problem*

The Japanese government made a vague promise concerning Indonesia's independence on September 7th, 1944, against the time that the Allies might be defeated. On March 1st, 1945, this promise was repeated, rather more explicitly. It is not necessary to give the details here of the political developments during this last phase of the Japanese occupation and the events surrounding the proclamation of Independence on August 17th, 1945.[34] Information can be restricted to what is important for the recent history of Islam in Indonesia.[35]

---

[31] Benda, *The Crescent*, p. 29.
[32] G. E. von Grunebaum, *Modern Islam*, Berkeley-Los Angeles 1962, p. 207.
[33] Van Nieuwenhuijze, *Aspects*, p. 162.
[34] For the political facts and developments, see Benda, *The Crescent*, pp. 169-194; further Kahin, *Nationalism,* and for the developments after 1950 Feith, *The Decline*. The Indonesian source which gives facts and official documents from the period August 17th, 1945 to December 31st, 1946 is Osman Raliby, *Documenta Historica I,* Djakarta 1953.
[35] For the discussion concerning the basis of the new state, the most important Indonesian source is the work of Muh. Yamin, primarily his pamphlet *Proklamasi dan Konstitusi Republik Indonesia*, Djakarta/Amsterdam 1951;

As a reaction to Koiso's announcement of September 7th, in October 1944 the leaders of the Masjumi called on their members "to prepare Muslims for the liberation of their country and their religion".[36] One result was the aforementioned formation of the Hizbu'llah. The declaration of March 1st, 1945, resulted in the setting up of a Committee to inquire into what should be done in preparation for independence.[37] This Committee was instituted in Djakarta on April 29th. It numbered 62 members, so that it can be referred to as the "Committee of 62". The Japanese appointed Dr. Radjiman Wediodiningrat to chair the meetings.

Before this Committee held its first session (May 29th to June 1st, 1945) its members were informed by the Japanese in Indonesia — through Nishimura — that Germany had given up the struggle but that Japan would fight on alone. After pointing to "the need for careful deliberation concerning the new state's constitution", Nishimura continued as follows. "As far as the position of religion in the new government is concerned, let me say that the attitude of the Military Administration with regard to this matter could be compared to a sheet of white paper. While we very clearly appreciate the bonds which exist between the Indonesian people and Islam, the Dai Nippon authorities have not the slightest blueprint or plan concerning the place which the Islamic religion should occupy in the government, or what the relationship should be between Islam and other religions. As I already explained to you, gentlemen, the Indonesian people must realize its own ideals in

---

further the three volumes of his chaotic standard work *Naskah Persiapan Undang-undang Dasar 1945*, with texts of speeches and minutes of meetings between May 29th and August 19th, 1945, and the minutes of the meetings of Parliament and Constituent Assembly, March-June 1959 about the "return to the Constitution of 1945"; finally the additional fourth volume, *Pembahasan Undang-undang Dasar Republik Indonesia*, Djakarta 1959-1960. Unfortunately, with regard to the work of Yamin — and other Indonesian sources for political history — the question has to be put concerning the extent to which this attempt to write history springs from an interest in history, and the extent to which this writing of history has been put to the service of a special, present-day goal, a certain propaganda or political aim. Of other Indonesian sources, I mention the exact, short summaries of the most important documents in Ali Basja Loebis' pamphlet, *Undang² Dasar R.I. 1945 (Sedjarah pertumbuhan dan pendjelasan pasal²nja)*, Djakarta 1963. The most important Indonesian contribution from the Protestant point of view is W. B. Sidjabat, *Religious Tolerance and the Christian Faith*, Djakarta 1965 (thesis Princeton 1960).

[36] Benda, *The Crescent*, pp. 175-176.
[37] In Indonesian: *Badan untuk menjelidiki usaha-usaha persiapan kemerdekaan.*

establishing its new state — Nippon will only lend its aid in these endeavors..." [38]

Meanwhile Indonesian leaders had already drawn up various papers concerning independence. Muh. Yamin even quotes the text of an "Indonesian Independence Act" and a "Regulation on the Provisional Government of Indonesia", drawn up by Supomo, Subardjo and Maramis as early as 1942.[39] It is not clear whether the Committee of 62 dealt with these documents. Papers on defence, economy, finance and the educational system of the new state, however, were probably specially prepared for the meeting of the Committee.[40]

The first session of the Committee of 62 was devoted to only one subject, namely the basis for the intended Indonesian state. At the meeting of May 29th, 1945, Muh. Yamin made a speech on account of which it has been said in the post-Soekarno period that the *Pantjasila* — the Indonesian state philosophy summarized in the Five Principles — was in fact a creation of Yamin's, and not Soekarno's.[41] If the content of this speech really was the same as the text printed in the standard work of Yamin, then one would indeed have to draw this conclusion, as in this speech a number of principles and terms are used which afterwards were laid down in the Pantjasila and in the Preamble of the 1945 Constitution.[42]

In paragraph I of this speech, under the heading *Peri Kebangsaan* (Nationalism), Yamin argued that the Indonesian state should be founded not on opinions simply borrowed from other peoples, but on principles which are rooted in Indonesian civilization. Then, under the heading *Peri Kemanusiaan* (Humanitarianism/Internationalism), it is stressed that the sovereignty of Indonesia means being adopted into the

---

[38] Quoted by Benda, *The Crescent*, pp. 188-189.
[39] Yamin, *Naskah*, I, pp. 761-772.
[40] Yamin, *Naskah*, I, pp. 729-752.
[41] Cf. *Pandji Masjarakat*, one of the most influential Islamic magazines in Indonesia, ed. by HAMKA, no. 19, Djakarta, October 1967, p. 6, and also the articles by Mohamad Roem in *Pandji Masjarakat*, nos. 11, 12, 13, March-April 1967, as well as K. H. M. Isa Anshary, *Mudjahid Da^cwah*, Bandung 1964, p. 156.
[42] Cf. Yamin, *Naskah*, I, pp. 83-107. With regard to the division of this speech into 5 paragraphs and their headings — almost the same as the five principles of the Pantjasila — one cannot avoid asking whether this composition and headings were not later additions. Elsewhere the author admits that he edited his archive material somewhat before publication; cf. the following note.

family of nations. In paragraph III, *Peri Ketuhanan* (Belief in God), it is stated that belief in God belongs to Indonesian civilization, so that the state of Indonesia should have a religious basis (Ind. *akan berke-Tuhanan*). After that, in paragraph IV, under the heading *Peri Kerakjatan* (Democracy), three principles are brought forward which later reappear in the Preamble of the Constitution. They are "mutual deliberation" (*permusjawaratan/musjawarah*, taken from Sura 42 : 38) by the "representatives" (*perwakilan*) of every section of the population, carried out with "wise policy" (*hikmah kebidjaksanaan*). The last-mentioned term is explained as meaning sound, logical reasoning which should replace irrationality and pre-logical thinking. In paragraph V, under the heading *Kesedjahteraan Rakjat, Keadilan Sosial* (Public Welfare, Social Justice), explanations are given concerning the extent of Indonesian territory and concerning citizens of foreign birth, followed by only a few remarks on the welfare of the population which would be an aim of an independent Indonesia.

According to the abovementioned standard work of Yamin, he added a draft constitution as an appendix to his speech of May 29th, 1945. If that draft had the same wording as afterwards published in his book, it must be concluded that — apart from very minor changes — this draft of Yamin's appears to have become the Indonesian Constitution of 1945.[43] The article on religion (art. 29) runs as follows: (1) The State shall be founded on the Belief in the One and Only God (Ind. *Ketuhanan Jang Maha Esa*); (2) The State shall guarantee the freedom of every inhabitant to profess his own religion and to worship according to his own religion and belief.[44]

Unfortunately Yamin does not give the minutes of this first session of the Committee of 62. The speech made by Supomo at the meeting

---

[43] Cf. Yamin, *Naskah*, I, pp. 719-728. Here Yamin admits that the arrangement into articles and chapters was a later addition. What did his draft copy originally look like?

[44] The English translation given in Yamin's work (*Naskah*, I, p. 54) runs as follows: "*Sect. 1.* The State shall be based upon belief in the all-embracing God. *Sect. 2.* The State shall guarantee the freedom of the people to profess and to exercise their own religion". The translation of *Ketuhanan Jang Maha Esa* with "belief in the all-embracing God" sounds more Hindu-Javanese than orthodox Islamic. A later (and more official?) translation can be found in Yamin, *Naskah*, III, pp. 755-761. The article there runs as follows: "(1) The State shall be based upon Belief in the One, Supreme God. (2) The State shall guarantee freedom to every resident to adhere to his respective religion and to perform his religious duties in conformity with that religion and that faith".

on May 31st, however, is quoted in full.[45] From this speech it appears that the problems brought forward by "Moh. Hatta and other speakers" had centred on three questions: the question of the structure of the state (unitary or federal), the question of the relationship between state and religion, and the question of whether Indonesia should become a republic or a monarchy. The second question brings us to the heart of our subject. This part of Supomo's speech is important enough to be quoted here almost unabridged.

"The honourable member Moh. Hatta", said Supomo, "has already explained in some detail that in a unitary state of Indonesia affairs of state should be separated from religious matters. Indeed it is quite clear that there are two opinions on this question: the opinion of the members who are theologians (Ind. *ahli agama*) and who argue that Indonesia should become an Islamic State, and the other proposal advocated by Moh. Hatta, that is to say a national unitary state which separates affairs of state from Islamic affairs — in other words: not an Islamic State. Why do I say 'not an Islamic State'? The expression 'Islamic State' does not have the same significance as the formulation that 'the state is founded on the high ideals of Islam'. I shall explain the difference.

In a country organized as an Islamic State, the state cannot be separated from religion. State and religion are one, a whole. Islam is, as you know, a religious, social and political system, based on the Qur'ān which is the source of all precepts for the life of a Muslim. It has already been explained that Turkey — we look once again to other countries for examples — was a true Islamic State before the year 1924. After 1924, Turkey changed the character of the state and is no longer an Islamic State. The religion of the Turkish people is indeed Islam, but as a state, as far as the governmental system is concerned, Turkey is no longer an Islamic State. Egypt, Irak, Iran and Saudi Arabia, on the other hand — these are indeed Islamic States.

Do we want to create an Islamic State in Indonesia? I have already reminded you of the advice of the [Japanese] Government that we should not simply follow the example of other states, but must be aware of the real identity of Indonesian society... Due to its geographical situation, Indonesia has a character different from countries such as Irak, Iran, Egypt or Syria, states with an Islamic character (Corpus Islamicum).

Indonesia is part of East Asia and is a member of the Greater East Asian Prosperity Sphere. To this belong, for instance, Japan, China,

---

[45] Yamin, *Naskah*, I, pp. 109-121.

Manchukuo, the Philippines, Thailand and Burma, which are not Islamic States. Of course this fact is not yet sufficient reason for rejecting the establishment of the state of Indonesia as an Islamic State — that I would not say. But it is surely an important factor which must be remembered.

I would also remind you that in Islamic States themselves, for instance in Egypt, Iran and Irak, there have always been different opinions on the way in which the *sharī^{c}a* (Islamic law) ought to be brought into agreement with international demands, with present-day requirements, with modern thought... A very large group of people says that it is simply not allowed, but another group says: adaptation to a new age is indeed possible... Muḥammad ^{c}Abduh, whose name is widely known and who has followers here too, says: 'The *Sharī^{c}a* can of course be altered by means of *idjmā^c* or mutual deliberation, provided it does not clash with the Qur'ān and Tradition'. Others hold a still more radical opinion, such as ^{c}Alī ^{c}Abd al-Rāziḳ, who says that religion has to be separated from the law concerning state affairs. In short, within Islamic States there are opposing views with regard to the question of what the law of the land must be like in order to be in agreement with modern thought...

Supposing we create an Islamic State — then dissension will also arise in our society, and this Study Committee will probably also get into difficulties when deliberating the question. But, gentlemen, creating an Islamic State in Indonesia would mean that we are not creating a unitary state. Creating an Islamic State in Indonesia would mean setting up a state that is going to link itself to the largest group, the Islamic group. If an Islamic State is created in Indonesia, then certainly the problem of minorities will arise, the problem of small religious groups, of Christians and others. Although an Islamic State will safeguard the interests of other groups as well as possible, these smaller religious groups will certainly not be able to feel involved in the state. Therefore the ideals of an Islamic State do not agree with the ideals of a unitary state which we all have so passionately looked forward to...

Hence I propose, and declare myself to be in agreement with, the point of view of those who want to establish a *national unitary state*... which transcends all groups, and respects and is aware of the special identity of every group, both large and small. As a matter of course religious affairs will be separated from state affairs in this national unitary state, and as a matter of course in this national unitary state religious affairs will be left in the hands of the religious groups concerned. And as a matter of course everyone in such a state will be free to profess any religion he likes. Both the largest and the smallest group will feel at one with the state (in a foreign language: will 'feel at home' in his state).

Honourable members! A national unitary state does not mean a state with an a-religious character. No. This national unitary state ... will have a lofty moral basis, such as is also advocated by Islam.

For example, in the state of Indonesia citizens must be stimulated to love their fatherland, to devote themselves to and sacrifice themselves for the sake of the country, to gladly serve the fatherland, to love and serve their leaders and the state, to bow down to God, to think of God every moment. All this must constantly be promoted and used as a moral basis for this national unitary state. And I am convinced that Islam will strengthen these principles..."

On the last day of this session, June 1st, 1945, Soekarno made a famous speech which afterwards was published under the title "The Birth of the Pantja Sila".[46]

Soekarno began his address with a long introduction. He stressed that the Committee should not discuss all this too "ponderously", and should not want to arrange every detail in advance, but should clearly realize that Indonesia must be free, now, now, now! After this warming-up (it may have lasted about 20 minutes) he then posed the question: on what philosophical basis ought this free Indonesia to be built? The answer was that a philosophy of life (*Weltanschauung*) should be sought which everyone could agree on. It should not be a state just for one section, giving power to a single group, but a state which is "all for all". Therefore the first principle was nationalism (*kebangsaan*), in the sense of an awareness of being together one nation, not in the narrow chauvinistic sense of "Deutschland über alles".

The second principle should therefore be internationalism (though not cosmopolitanism, which would deny the nation) or humanitarianism (*peri-kemanusiaan*). And the third? If it should be "all for all" in the Indonesian state, then the third principle should be mutual deliberation (*permusjawaratan*), by means of representation (*perwakilan*) in order to bring about general agreement (*mufakat*). In other words, democracy.

---

[46] Yamin, *Naskah*, I, pp. 61-81. A summary based on the English translation by the Indonesian Ministry of Information (*The Birth of Pantjasila*, Jakarta 1950) can be found in Kahin, *Nationalism*, pp. 122-127. We base ours on the Indonesian text found in Yamin.

As far as the fourth principle was concerned, said Soekarno, "in the last three days I have not yet heard this principle mentioned [47] — I mean the principle of social welfare (*kesedjahteraan*), that is to say, the ideal of being free from poverty in Free Indonesia".[48] In this way the expectation of the people, linked to the coming of the *Ratu Adil* (the righteous king), would be fulfilled through realizing social justice.

As the fifth principle Soekarno named Belief in God (*Ketuhanan*), which is not only of importance for the people in general but also for every Indonesian personally, each one in accordance with his own religion, and with respect for that of others.

Thanks to a hint from a linguist, said Soekarno, he wanted to call these five principles *Pantja Sila,* the five principles or fundamentals on which the Indonesian state was to be built. It would also be possible to condense these five into three: nationalism and humanitarianism together could be called *socio-nationalism,* democracy and welfare *socio-democracy.* Together with Belief in God (*ke-Tuhanan*) the result would be the *Tri Sila.* It was even possible to comprise all this in one genuine Indonesian phrase, namely *gotong-rojong* (mutual help) — between rich and poor, Muslims and Christians, born Indonesians and Indonesians of foreign descent. The realization of these principles would demand effort — so Soekarno ended his speech — and the struggle would not end with the creation of a free Indonesian state, but would also have to be continued within that free Indonesia.

One longer quotation from this speech of Soekarno is relevant here. When speaking of the third principle, deliberation by the people's representatives, he said: "For Muslims this is the best place to promote religion. We, I too, we are Muslims — a thousand apologies, my being a Muslim is far from perfect! — but if you opened my breast and could see my heart, then what you would see is surely an Islamic heart. And this Islamic heart of 'Bung Karno' wants to defend Islam by mutual agreement, achieved by deliberation, namely in Parliament... That is the place to promote the demands of Islam... If we really are an Islamic people, let us then work as hard as we can, to see that the greatest number of seats in the Parliament which we shall form will be held by Islamic representatives... If we take it that Parliament has 100 members, then let us work, work as hard as possible, so that 60, 70, 80, 90 of the representatives sitting in Parliament will be Muslims,

---

[47] In spite of the speech by Yamin? See above, paragraph V from Yamin's speech.
[48] Yamin, *Naskah,* I, p. 75.

Islamic leaders. Then the laws which Parliament promulgates will naturally be Islamic laws. Yes, I am even convinced that only when something like this happens, only then can it be said that Islam really lives in the soul of the people, so that 60 %, 70 %, 80 %, 90 % of the representatives are Muslims, Islamic leaders, Islamic *ulamas*... Accept principle number three... And let the Muslims and the Christians work as hard as possible in Parliament. If, for instance, the Christians want every letter of the regulations of the state of Indonesia to be in agreement with the Bible, let them work as if their lives depended on it, so that a large proportion of the representatives who are members of Parliament will be Christians. That is reasonable — 'fair play'."

It may be concluded that during this first session of the Committee of 62 *the* problem which the new Indonesia was to be confronted with came into the open. It was this problem: should the official basis of the Indonesian state be formed by Islamic principles, expressed in an Islamic terminology, or would Indonesia be based on the Pantjasila and become a model of a multi-religious state, where followers of different religions (together with an increasing number of "humanists") live and work together with respect for one another?

Unfortunately, Yamin's work does not give the speeches and remarks made by Islamic leaders such as K. Bagus H. Hadikusumo, K. H. M. Mansur, Sukiman, Wahid Hasjim, Kahar Muzakkir and H. Agus Salim during this first session of the Committee of 62. The three orators — Yamin, Supomo and Soekarno — clearly made their choice for a national Pantjasila state; the most convincing was perhaps Supomo. According to Yamin the address by Soekarno aroused great enthusiasm. But did this apply to everyone? And was this really due to what he said, or only to how he said it? After the meeting, when the members began to concentrate on the "homework" which they took with them, did not some of them — in particular the Islamic leaders — notice that things seemed to be moving in a direction they had not intended?

3. *Looking for a Compromise*

A so-called Small Committee from the Committee of 62 continued the work in Djakarta after the first session.[49] Soekarno, Hatta, Sutardjo,

---

[49] This information and more that follows is taken from the minutes of the second session of the Committee of 62, July 10th-16th, 1945, as taken down by Yamin, *Naskah,* I, pp. 143-396.

Wahid Hasjim, Hadikusumo, Oto Iskandardinata, Yamin and Maramis were members of it. They dealt with the 32 proposals suggested by 40 members which were submitted in writing between June 1st and 20th, 1945; about 20 members pressed for a proclamation of free Indonesia as soon as possible.[50]

In Yamin's book we find a draft for a Declaration of Independence which ought to be mentioned here.[51] It is not clear when exactly this draft came into being. It begins with a condemnation of Dutch colonialism, while Japan is praised and thanked for its fight for the freedom and welfare of East Asia. Its concluding words later reappear in the Preamble of the 1945 Constitution, namely that now the blessed hour has come when the people of Indonesia, thanks to the mercy of God, can proclaim their independence. This fairly lengthy draft for a declaration of independence was, however, overtaken by events, and on August 17th, 1945 replaced by a proclamation consisting of only two sentences, signed by Soekarno and Hatta.

One of the points at issue in June 1945 was apparently the question of whether it might not be better to realize independence in two phases: firstly a provisional proclamation of the independent state of Indonesia under the supervision of Japan and pending Japan's defeat, to be followed by a further decision concerning the structure of the new state, to be taken in due time when freedom had been won. For such a first phase, Hoesein Djajadiningrat, Supomo, Suwandi, Singgih, Sastromuljono, Sutardjo and Subardjo drafted a provisional Constitution, which was submitted to the Small Committee on June 15th. According to that draft the leadership of the state would be entrusted not to only one person but to a Directory of three, since a truly representative body could not be elected for the time being.[52]

More important, however, was the debate which continued and intensified between the "secular" nationalists and the Islamic leaders, in contemporaneous Indonesian sources always indicated as *golongan kebangsaan* and *golongan Islam*. Now it happened that the Central

---

[50] According to Soekarno in the report which he gave at the opening of the second session of the Committee of 62 on July 10th, 1945. Cf. Yamin, *Naskah*, I, pp. 147-148.
[51] The text can be found in Yamin, *Naskah*, I, pp. 755-756. It is undated. As Yamin certainly did not give the reports and minutes of all the meetings of every committee and sub-committee, let alone informal discussions, the chronological order of the drafts cannot, as far as I can see, be fixed precisely.
[52] Cf. Yamin, *Naskah*, I, pp. 713-717.

Advisory Council met in Djakarta on June 18th, 1945.[53] A number of Indonesians who were also members of the Committee of 62 held seats on this Council. Moreover a number of members of the Committee of 62 lived in Djakarta. Therefore Soekarno, chairman of the Small Committee, called together all available members of the Committee of 62, in all 38 people. From them a group of 9 members came forward who were to look for a solution to the increasing tension between the Nationalists and the Islamic faction.

At a meeting on June 22nd, 1945, which must have been extremely difficult, these 9 leaders managed in the end to arrive at a compromise. They formulated a "gentlemen's agreement" which was intended to become the Preamble of the Constitution, or at least the working paper for the discussion on it. Some weeks later Yamin named this political document the "Djakarta Charter" (Ind. *Piagam Djakarta*).[54] Outside Indonesia little interest has apparently been taken in this document.[55] However, in retrospect it can be concluded that later discussions on the relationship of State and Islam in Indonesia were to a large extent determined by some words from this Djakarta Charter.

The text of the Djakarta Charter includes the closing words of the draft declaration of independence (which was never used in the end) combined with the closing sentence from the preamble of Yamin's draft Constitution. From a later remark of Hatta's, the reverse order of events could be deduced, that is, that after the Djakarta Charter of June 22nd, intended as a draft preamble to the Constitution, the lengthy declaration of independence was drawn up.[56] However that may be, it is important to turn our attention to the content of the Djakarta Charter. The document is difficult to translate.[57] It runs like this:

"As independence is the right of every people, any form of subjugation in this world, being contrary to humanity (*peri kemanusiaan*) and justice (*peri keadilan*), must be abolished.

Now the struggle of the Indonesian independence movement has reached the blessed hour in which the Indonesian people have safe and

---

[53] Cf. Benda, *The Crescent*, p. 190.
[54] Yamin, *Naskah*, I, pp. 228, 240.
[55] One looks in vain in Benda and Kahin, for example.
[56] For the remarks by Hatta, see the minutes of August 18th, 1945 in Yamin, *Naskah*, I, p. 401.
[57] Compare the different translations of the preamble of the 1945 Constitution in Yamin, *Naskah*, I, p. 49 and III, p. 753; also Yamin, *Pembahasan*, p. 97; further Charles Wolf Jr., *The Indonesian Story*, New York 1948, p. 165.

sound been led to the portals of the Indonesian state, which is to be independent, united, sovereign, just and prosperous.

By the Grace of Almighty God (*Rachmat Allah Jang Maha Kuasa*) and moved by the highest ideals to lead a free national life (*berkehidupan kebangsaan*), the Indonesian people hereby declare their independence (*kemerdekaannja*).

Further, in order to establish for the Indonesian state a government which will protect the whole Indonesian people and all Indonesian territory, and to promote public welfare (*kesedjahteraan*), to raise the educational level of the people, and to participate in establishing a world order founded on freedom, everlasting peace and social justice, national independence is hereby expressed in a Constitution of the Indonesian state which is moulded in the form of the Republic of Indonesia, resting upon the people's sovereignty and founded on [the following principles]: the Belief in God (*ke-Tuhanan*), with the obligation for adherents of Islam to practise Islamic law, in accordance with the principle of a righteous and moral humanitarianism (*kemanusiaan*); the unity (*persatuan*) of Indonesia, and a democracy (*kerakjatan*) led by the wise policy (*hikmat kebidjaksanaan*) of the mutual deliberation of a representative body (*permusjawaratan perwakilan*) and ensuring social justice (*keadilan sosial*) for the whole Indonesian people." [58]

The nine signatories of the Djakarta Charter were the following. There were Soekarno and Hatta, belonging to the so-called secular nationalists, as did A. A. Maramis (originating from a Protestant area); on the other hand there were Abikusno Tjokrosujoso (former chairman of the *Partai Serikat Islam Indonesia*), Abdulkahar Muzakkir (= Kahar Muzakkir, already mentioned), H. Agus Salim (the "Grand Old Man" of the former *Sarekat Islam,* which later became the abovementioned P.S.I.I.), then Achmad Subardjo (originally left-wing, but in 1945 and 1951-1952 Minister of Foreign Affairs for the Masjumi), also Wahid Hasjim — "perhaps the most prominent representative of Indonesian Islam at the close of the Japanese era", as Benda maintains [59] — and finally Muh. Yamin, who, like Soekarno, belonged to the "secular" nationalists.

In all the debates of this period this document is typified as a compromise between "the nationalist group" and "the Islamic group".

---

[58] For the original Indonesian text of this Djakarta Charter see Appendix I, at the end of this book.
[59] Benda, *The Crescent,* p. 189.

Only in recent years is the Christian group said to have been represented by Maramis and therefore mentioned as a third partner. But according to oral information this seems to be incorrect. Maramis represented the "secular" nationalists, and it is said that he too, being a non-Muslim, had his objections to this compromise, but did not want to endanger the proclamation of independence. However, it was Latuharhary (later to be governor of the Moluccas) who was considered the representative of the Christians; and Latuharhary apparently dissociated himself from looking for such a compromise.[60]

The crucial sentence in the Djakarta Charter is, of course, the stipulation that the state was to be founded on belief in God "with the obligation for adherents of Islam to practise Islamic law". In present-day Indonesia this sentence is referred to as "the seven words", *dengan kewadjiban mendjalankan Sjari'at Islam bagi pemeluk-pemeluknja*. Does this formula mean a more or less Islamic State? Does it have legal consequences, so that the government has to work for and watch over the execution of Islamic law? Should the government promulgate separate laws for the Muslims (e.g. in connection with marriage), or even see to the fulfilment of religious duties in the narrower sense of the word? Or does this formula only carry meaning as a pious stimulus for the Muslims? But if so, why does it appear in the draft of the Preamble of the Constitution? Or in other words, what has the state to do with it? Or is it only a spent cartridge as a sop to the traditional orthodox? In short, is this formula a starting point from which to work in the direction of an Islamic State, or is it only a last remnant of a lost struggle for an Islamic State? These are some of the questions which later arose and became dominant in the debate on the position of Islam in the new Indonesia.

From July 10th to 16th, 1945, the Committee of 62, in the meantime supplemented by six new members,[61] met again.

First of all, Soekarno, as chairman of the Small Committee reported on work that had meanwhile been going on. He began his address once again with an appeal for haste: in this session they had to come to an agreement on the structure of the state and on its Constitution, so that Tokyo could recognize the independence of Indonesia and install a government in Djakarta. Then Soekarno told of the initial difficulties

---

[60] Compared with Latuharhary's remarks during the second session of the Committee of 62 — to be discussed later — this oral information sounds reliable.
[61] Yamin, *Naskah*, I, p. 145.

between representatives of the two factions, and of the agreement achieved by the nine signatories of a draft for the preamble (*rantjangan preambule/pembukaan*) of the Constitution. Applause followed the reading aloud of the text of this Djakarta Charter.

On the first day of this session the form of government for the new state (republic or kingdom) was debated. On the part of the Muslims some advocated a king, as "God's representative on earth", or a republic with an *Imām* as head of state. Before this could be voted on, a moment of silence was moved and K. Bagus H. Hadikusumo recited the *Sūra al-Fātiḥa* (the first Sura of the Qur'ān). Then 55 out of the 64 members voted for a republic, while the head of the new state was to be a president; 6 votes fell for a king, 2 for "something else" — probably this meant an *imām*. Lengthy discussion followed on the extent of Indonesian territory; the morning session of July 11th was also taken up with this subject. The minutes contain interesting material concerning the debates about Malaya, North Borneo, Portuguese Timor, New Guinea and the Philippines.

In the further meetings on that day preparatory discussions were held on the coming Constitution. Yamin once more drew attention to the draft that he had already put before the Committee on May 29th. Finally the members were divided into three sub-committees: one to draft the Constitution (19 members; chairman Soekarno), one to deliberate questions of defence (22 members; chairman Abikusno Tjokrosujoso) and one to discuss economic problems (22 members; chairman Hatta). It is remarkable that the chairman, Radjiman, refused to appoint Yamin to the committee on the Constitution, without giving his reasons, at least if we can rely on the minutes in Yamin's work.

The Committee for the Constitution met under the chairmanship of Soekarno on the evening of July 11th for a preliminary discussion of the main problems in connection with the Constitution: the structure of the state (unitary or federal?), the character of the Constitution (simple, provisional?) and the draft preamble as it lay before them in the shape of the Djakarta Charter of June 22nd.

On the side of the Protestants, Latuharhary expressed objections to the words "with the obligation for adherents of Islam to practise Islamic law", as this could have considerable consequences regarding other religions, and moreover could lead to difficulties in connection with the *adat-istiadat* (customary law). Agus Salim answered that the problem of *adat*-law and Islamic law was an old one and, generally speaking, had already been solved; the adherents of other religions did not need to worry: "Their safety is not dependent on the power of the state, but on the tradition (Ind. *adat,* here: traditional tolerance?) of the Islamic community, which includes 90 % of the population".

Soekarno, as chairman, reminded them that the preamble had been arrived at with great difficulties and was the result of an agreement between the so-called Islamic and nationalist factions; the omission of this one sentence would be unacceptable to Muslims. Wongsonegoro (a liberal Javanese) and Hoesein Djajadiningrat (the first Indonesian head of the Office for Religious Affairs) also objected to these words, saying: "They may well create fanaticism, because it seems that Muslims would be forced to keep the *sharīʿa*". Wahid Hasjim denied the possibility of compulsion by pointing to the principle of mutual deliberation (*permusjawaratan*), adding that according to some people this sentence did perhaps go too far, but according to others did not go far enough. Soekarno repeated that this sentence was a compromise reached with great difficulty and, seeing that no other objections were raised, he concluded that the preamble might be taken as accepted.

Soekarno then appointed a working-committee which was to meet on July 12th to prepare a draft Constitution. To what extent Soekarno busied himself with the drafting of this Constitution is not clear. The chairman of this working-committee was Supomo; further members were Wongsonegoro, Subardjo, Maramis, Singgih, Agus Salim and Sukiman. Neither Wahid Hasjim, perhaps the most radical Muslim, nor Latuharhary who might be considered as the representative of the Christians, was included.

The draft presented by this working-committee on July 13th, 1945, is almost the same as Yamin's draft of May 29th.[62] One noticeable difference is that in this new draft, immediately after article 1 (the Indonesian state is a republic, with sovereignty of the people which is exercised by the People's Congress), the position of the President is dealt with, and only after that the position and task of the People's Congress. In Yamin's draft — as in the final Constitution of 1945 — the order is reversed, so that the People's Congress is clearly placed above the President. The article on religion is somewhat shorter and vaguer in this draft of July 13th; after the proposed preamble (= Djakarta Charter) it was apparently considered enough to put here: "The State

---

[62] The text of this draft of July 13th, 1945, is to be found in Yamin, *Naskah,* I, pp. 264-270.

shall guarantee freedom for every inhabitant to adhere to whatever religion he wants and to worship according to his own religion".

At this meeting of the Committee for the Constitution (the Committee of 19) it became obvious that a crisis was threatening. It turned out that Wahid Hasjim had indeed taken the proposed preamble as a point of departure for further provisions in the direction of an Islamic State. He suggested stipulating that only Muslims could be elected as President or Vice-President of the Republic, and that the article on religion should run as follows: "The religion of the state is Islam, with the guarantee of freedom for adherents of other religions to profess their own religion..." etc. He argued as follows: "If the President is a Muslim, the regulations will bear the mark of Islam and that will have great influence". As for Islam as the state religion, this would be important with regard to the defence of the country: "Generally a defence based on religious belief is very vigorous, for according to the teachings of Islam one may only give one's life for the ideology of religion".

Agus Salim opposed the suggestions of his co-religionist, because they would undermine the compromise between the nationalist and Islamic factions, and "if the President has to be a Muslim, then what about the Vice-President, the ambassadors, etc., and what then was the point of our promise to protect other religions?" Sukiman (who later became leader of the Masjumi), however, supported the proposals of Wahid Hasjim, saying that "it would please the people and in fact have no further consequences". Djajadiningrat and Wongsonegoro once more objected to these suggestions, as they had done earlier in the case of the "seven words"; the latter once again expressed his fear of an interpretation which would enable the state to force Muslims to keep Islamic law. Oto Iskandardinata made an intermediary suggestion: on the one hand, no stipulation concerning the President, but on the other hand a repetition of the "seven words" from the preamble in the constitutional article on religion. Supomo as chairman of the working-committee declared that the committee would adopt this suggestion, and would change the draft to cover this. A proposal by Mrs. Ulfa Santoso to include more clearly human rights in the Constitution was swept aside by Supomo as unnecessary, as the Indonesian state was founded on the people's sovereignty. Latuharhary apparently felt it was unnecessary or inopportune to repeat his objections. Apart from small corrections, the draft Constitution was then laid before the Committee of 62, which met again in pleno on July 14th, 1945.

At this plenary session of July 14th, Soekarno immediately took the floor as chairman of the Committee for the Constitution. After his report on the achievement of drafts for a declaration of independence, a preamble and a Constitution, the debate was opened by discussing the preamble (= Djakarta Charter).

The Muhammadijah leader K. Bagus H. Hadikusumo wanted to do away with the words "for adherents of Islam" in the "seven words", so that the formula would read: "The state is founded on Belief in God, with the obligation to practise Islamic law". Initially he brought forward only stylistic considerations; later he mentioned another reason, namely that a dual legislation — one for Muslims and one for others — was unacceptable. If that was the intention of the words in question, he would prefer nothing to be stipulated. Soekarno answered that the deletion of these words could give the impression "that there is no question of Muslims and hence no duty to practise Islamic law". Hadikusumo now replied that the sentence as it ran in the preamble (that is to say, the "seven words") could not be upheld, for the government could not put Islamic law into operation: "The government cannot interfere in the way people practise their religion".

From the minutes it is not clear what Hadikusumo's actual intentions were, and to what extent misunderstandings played a role. Did the drafters of the Djakarta Charter only intend to emphasize that Muslims themselves had a religious and moral duty to keep Islamic law, or would the government be involved? Did Hadikusumo read the words as stipulating that the government had to enforce Islamic law for Muslims? Was the formula capable of many meanings, in particular the very imprecise verb *mendjalankan* (keep, maintain, carry out, make operative, apply, give effect to)? Was it even intentionally multi-interpretable, as a compromise that would make it possible for the various parties and individuals to have their own interpretation?

Whatever the right answer may be, Hadikusumo was eventually silenced and gave in to Abikusno's argument that the differences of opinion on this point should not be exposed in public.

At the meeting of July 15th, Supomo explained once again his interpretation of the disputed "seven words": they did not mean that the Indonesian state would exist only for one group (the Muslims), but simply that the state would be heedful of the special identity of the largest section of the population. He repeated that these "seven words" from the preamble and from the Constitutional article on religion formed a compromise, and he gave the impression that the Committee for the Constitution (the Committee of 19) had unanimously accepted this compromise. In this connection he mentioned on the one hand the names of Wahid Hasjim and Agus Salim, and on the other the non-Muslims Latuharhary and Maramis, thus consciously or unconsciously shifting the contrast from Muslims and Nationalists to Muslims and Christians.

After speeches and discussions on other problems (citizenship, ministerial responsibility, and so on), the debate on religion flared up once again at the evening meeting of July 15th. This happened because Hadikusumo repeated his somewhat cryptic questions concerning the vexed "seven words". K. H. Masjkur aggravated the problem, saying that if Indonesian citizens had the duty to keep Islamic law, this could in fact only be carried out provided the President was a Muslim and Islam was acknowledged as the official religion of the Republic of Indonesia.

Soekarno tried to hush up the business by saying that in fact it would turn out well: the President would obviously be someone who was a Muslim. But Masjkur continued demanding clarity, not only for himself but for the whole people, he said. Finally feelings became so heated that Kahar Muzakkir, thumping the table with his fist, suggested a wholly new compromise, as he himself called it. Speaking for the Islamic faction, he demanded that everything, from the first words of the Declaration of Independence up to and including the Constitutional article in question, wherever God's Name or Islam was mentioned, should be struck out without further ado, so that nothing of this nature should remain.

The suggestion of the chairman to put the proposed preamble to the vote was sharply answered with: "Impossible, that cannot be voted on, you cannot vote about religion!" Kahar Muzakkir repeated even more explicitly his proposal that everything concerned with God's Name and with religion should be omitted. Tension became palpable — it is palpable even when reading the minutes — when Hadikusumo took the floor and began his speech with the well-known formula, "I seek refuge in God from Satan who bringeth destruction".[63] He continued as follows: "More than once it has been explained here that Islam also includes a state ideology. Hence the state cannot be divorced from Islam ... If the [Islamic] proposal is rejected ... then I am in agreement with the proposal of Abdul Kahar Muzakkir. If the ideology of Islam

---

[63] Usually: "I seek refuge in God from Satan the outcast" (or: "from the accursed/stoned Satan"); cf. Sura 16:98.

is not accepted, all right then! Then it is clear that this state is not based on Islam and therefore will be neutral. That at least is clear. Let us not accept a sort of compromise, as Mr. Soekarno calls it. As far as justice and religious duties are concerned, there is no compromise, it does not exist. Let us be clear about it — if there are objections to accepting the ideology of the Islamic community, it comes down to this: those who agree with an Islamic basis want it to be an Islamic State, but if this is not accepted, then there must be neutrality as far as religion is concerned."

The meeting was closed at midnight at the suggestion of Achmad Sanusi, who hoped "that the atmosphere of these deliberations might first cool down somewhat".

The next day, July 16th, 1945, immediately after the opening of the meeting, Soekarno took the floor. He said he was sure that many of those present, like himself, had not been able to get to sleep that night. But everyone who truly asks for directions from God receives them. And last night those directions had already begun to come. After the meeting some of the leaders of both factions — the so-called Nationalists and the so-called Islamic group — had met to look for a solution. As a result of this discussion Soekarno now wanted to appeal to everyone, especially the so-called nationalist faction, to make a sacrifice, remembering that (in Dutch) "greatness lies in sacrificing". This sacrifice would be to include in the Constitution the articles that "the President of the Republic of Indonesia must be a born Indonesian who is a Muslim", and that "the State is founded on Belief in God, with the obligation for adherents of Islam to practise Islamic law". Soekarno said he realized that he was asking a very great sacrifice from such patriots as Latuharhary and Maramis who were not Muslims. But as if in tears — again, as if in tears — he begged them to make this sacrifice for country and people.

After Supomo had made a number of proposals concerning minor editorial changes in the draft Constitution, the meeting ended in an anti-climax. Probably no-one was satisfied, yet everyone acquiesced. At the request of the chairman, everyone stood up to show that there was unanimous acceptance of the draft Constitution. Only Yamin apparently needed special encouragement to stand up too...[64]

---

[64] Yamin, *Naskah*, I, p. 396.

4. The Decision

At the beginning of August 1945, developments began to move faster and faster. On August 7th, the day after Hiroshima, the Japanese High Command in Saigon agreed that a committee should be formed in Indonesia "to make preparations for transfer of governmental authority from the Japanese armed forces to it".[65] Soekarno, Hatta and Radjiman were called to Saigon where it was agreed on August 11th that a constitutional assembly would meet in Djakarta on August 19th. On August 24th Indonesia would receive its independence from Japan.

This development was not at all to the liking of Sjahrir, the leader of an anti-Japanese underground movement in Indonesia, and some other left-wing leaders and students. Sjahrir, of course, had not been a member of the Committee of 62 or its sub-committees. From August 10th onward he had tried to persuade Soekarno and Hatta that the Japanese were on the point of capitulation, and that they themselves should take the initiative to proclaim independence immediately. But Soekarno and Hatta hesitated out of fear of a massacre, as long as the capitulation of Japan was not a fact. Until August 16th they were not convinced of the correctness of the rumours that Japan had capitulated on the 14th. Meanwhile on August 14th or 15th the Preparatory Committee, as agreed in Saigon, was set up in Djakarta. But the question arose of whether it was right to proclaim the independence of Indonesia in the name of a committee "made in Japan". Moreover some leaders preferred an anti-Japanese national leader to declare independence, in a clearly anti-Japanese formulation. But in the end Soekarno and Hatta had to take the responsibility. So on August 17th, 1945, they declared the Independence of Indonesia.

As has already been said, the new Preparatory Committee (Ind. *Panitia Persiapan Kemerdekaan Indonesia*) was set up on August 14th or 15th. Besides the chairman, Soekarno, and vice-chairman, Hatta, the Committee consisted of 19 members, among whom were many well-known names such as Supomo, Radjiman, Sutardjo, Wahid Hasjim,

---

[65] See for this and the following information Kahin, *Nationalism*, p. 127; compare Benda, *The Crescent*, p. 194. Recently Moh. Hatta tried once more to separate the truth from the myth surrounding the proclamation of Independence, in *Sekitar Proklamasi 17 Agustus 1945*, Djakarta 1969; part of this was already published in an article of Hatta's in *Mimbar Indonesia*, no. 32/33, August 17th, 1951, which is also to be found in Osman Raliby, *Documenta*, pp. 655-659.

K. Bagus H. Hadikusumo, Oto Iskandardinata and Latuharhary.[66] After the declaration of independence on August 17th, the members of this Committee were called together for an emergency meeting to be held the next morning.[67]

The minutes given by Yamin inform us that the opening was delayed for about two hours, so that the meeting only began at 11.30 in the morning. Other sources and oral information confirm this delay and explain it.[68] The point was that before the meeting could begin some members wanted to solve the difficulties which once again could lead to a clash between the Islamic leaders and the others ("secular" nationalists and non-Muslims). After the second session of the former Committee of 62 (July 10th-16th), a number of proposals for alterations to the provisional Constitution had been received. Furthermore, various influential people from outside Java had meanwhile arrived in Djakarta. Apparently the leaders in Djakarta now fully realized how difficult it would be to unite into one state the enormous area of Indonesia, with its great diversity of ethnic groups and religions. It seems that even the Japanese in Djakarta had warned Hatta that Nationalists and non-Muslims did object to certain Islamic formulas in the provisional Constitution.

On the morning of August 18th informal discussions and lobbying therefore took place between Hatta (in whom people on the Muslim side certainly had more confidence than in Soekarno) and representatives of the Islamic faction. Sajuti Melik mentions the names of Teuku Mohamad Hassan (from Atjeh) and K. Bagus H. Hadikusumo. According to first-hand oral information Wahid Hasjim was also present. These informal talks took some hours, even though people were aware that a decision had to be reached quickly and speedy action was called for. They finally came to the conclusion that in fact Indonesia only could

[66] A complete list of names is to be found in Kahin, *Nationalism,* p. 127. This list is the same as that of Yamin, *Naskah,* I, pp. 399, 427, where it is said that at the meeting of August 18th, 1945, there were 6 additional members, namely Wiranatakusuma, Ki Hadjar Dewantoro, Kasman, Sajuti Melik, Kusuma Sumantri and Subardjo. The list of an additional 5 or 6 members given in Kahin, *Nationalism,* p. 138 seems incorrect.
[67] The minutes of these meetings of August 18th-19th, 1945 can be found in Yamin, *Naskah,* I, pp. 399-473.
[68] Sajuti Melik, *Undang² Dasar '45* & *"Piagam Djakarta"*, in *Mahasiswa Indonesia,* no. 98, Bandung, April 1968. Sajuti Melik was a member of the Preparatory Committee and apparently followed the developments which preceded it at close quarters; a possible publication of his memoirs based on notes taken then could be of importance, as additional or corrective evidence to other sources, as for example Yamin.

become and remain a unity if the Constitution contained nothing that was directly connected with Islam. Therefore articles on Islam as the official religion of the state, the condition that the President must be a Muslim and "the obligation for adherents of Islam to practise Islamic law" had to be removed.

Thanks to these informal talks led by Hatta, the question of the Constitution could quickly be dealt with at the official meeting which followed. In his opening speech Soekarno urged setting aside any minor wishes, in order to get the Constitution ready that very day, and moreover to elect a President and Vice-President. He informed them that proposals had been received advocating alterations to the Constitution made by the former Committee of 62 and that, thanks be to God, due to informal talks agreement had been reached on several points.

Then Hatta was called upon to explain these proposed alterations. They concerned first and foremost the vexed "seven words" of the preamble (the former Djakarta Charter) which were to be deleted, while the expression "Belief in God" (*ke-Tuhanan*) would be amplified to "Belief in the One and Only God" (*ke-Tuhanan Jang Maha Esa*). The same changes would be made in the Constitutional article on religion (article 29). Further, the condition that the President had to be a Muslim would be omitted. As reason for these changes Hatta reminded his audience repeatedly that they had to be mindful of the unity of the whole Indonesian population. According to Hatta, representatives of the various factions had already agreed on these changes. For the rest there were only proposals for minor adjustments. Therefore it was now possible to finish hammering out the Constitution.

After this speech of Hatta's a short discussion followed, first of all on the preamble. No-one returned to the abovementioned changes, so these could be taken as accepted. A few minor changes were made, as follows. The Arabic *muqaddima* for "preamble" was replaced by the Indonesian equivalent, *pembukaan,* meaning "opening". At the suggestion of Hadikusumo a small change was made in the formula concerning the basis of the state. The sentence ran as follows: the state should be based on Belief in the One and Only God (no longer: with the obligation for adherents of Islam to practise Islamic law), "in accordance with the principle of a righteous and moral humanitarianism". Now that the vexed clause had been done away with, the words "in accordance with the principle of" had to be deleted also. Hence the sentence came to run as follows: that the Indonesian State is founded on Belief in God, a righteous and moral humanitarianism, etc. According to oral information the first formula ("in accordance with") had initially come into being in order to prevent the possibility of a too rigorous application of Islamic law. For instance, in view of a precept such as the cutting off of a thief's hand (cf. Sura 5 : 38) it had to be laid down that Islamic law would be practised "in accordance with the principle of a righteous and moral humanitarianism".[69]

At the proposal of a representative from Bali, the name *Allah* (in the expression "the Grace of Almighty God") was exchanged for the common Indonesian word *Tuhan,* originally meaning "Lord" but now felt to be the widest definition of the Supreme Being, not His specific name.[70]

After these alterations had been accepted, discussion followed on the Constitution itself. Soekarno stressed once again that this Constitution was only a "temporary Constitution", a "lightning Constitution", a "revolutionary Constitution", which in due time could be perfected by the elected representatives of the people. The discussion which followed did not produce anything of importance for the question in hand. It is only worth mentioning that at this meeting of the "Preparatory Committee" on August 18th, Soekarno was elected President of the Republic of Indonesia, and Hatta Vice-President.

At the meeting of the following day, August 19th, one of the questions to be solved was the number of Departments which were to be formed and their tasks. It was prepared by a memorandum from a sub-committee consisting of Subardjo, Sutardjo and Kasman Singodimedjo (later a well-known Masjumi leader). In this discussion Latuharhary objected to the setting up of a separate Ministry of Religious Affairs. If, for instance, a Christian became Minister of Religion, he said, the Muslims would consider it unpleasant, and vice versa. From the Muslim side, Abdul Abbas suggested that religious affairs should be part of the Ministry of Education. This proposal was accepted, after the idea of a separate Ministry of Religious Affairs had gained only 6 votes.

On August 29th, 1945, the "Preparatory Committee" was dissolved. Its members were absorbed into the larger Central Indonesian National Committee (Ind. *Komité Nasional Indonesia Pusat,* in short K.N.I.P.), a provisional parliament with an advisory task. On August 31st, 1945,

---

[69] This illustration once more strengthens the impression that some people did not take the Djakarta Charter only as a religious stimulus but indeed as a legal principle to be followed in civil and criminal jurisdiction.

[70] It is very odd that finally, by mistake, the word *Allah* did remain in the press publication which is regarded as the official publication of the 1945 Constitution, namely *Berita Republik Indonesia,* 1946, no. 7.

the first presidential cabinet came into being, succeeded by the first parliamentary Sjahrir cabinet on November 14th, 1945.

Thus the new Indonesia came into being neither as an Islamic State according to orthodox Islamic conceptions, nor as a secular state which would consider religion merely a private matter. The discussions had eventually resulted in a compromise, that is to say, in the idea of a state that wanted to recognize a religious principle, and wanted to be positive about religion in general and its various manifestations, or, according to a later slogan, a state that wanted to consider religion an indispensable contribution to "nation-building and character-building". So the Indonesion solution was not a Constitution using Islamic terms without really accepting their Islamic content, but the acceptance of common spiritual values as expressed in the Pantjasila, with its first principle of Belief in the One and Only God (*Ketuhanan Jang Maha Esa*).

This last conception has been subjected to a profound analysis by Van Nieuwenhuijze.[71] It could, however, cause misunderstanding when he calls this formula "a basically Muslim concept", that has been enlarged into a "de-confessionalized concept" to make it acceptable for non-Muslims as well. Of course, some Muslims afterwards tended to interpret this concept in an Islamic way (which is right and proper), and even wanted to make their interpretation the only possible one (which is wrong and not permissible, if one is seriously prepared to acknowledge the multi-religious character of Indonesian society). In my opinion Sidjabat was right, when he maintained, in opposition to Van Nieuwenhuijze, that the first principle of the Pantjasila "is not necessarily a 'de-confessionalized concept of Islamic God', but rather a general and neutral concept of God that gives room for everyone who worships God, without becoming indifferent in matters of religion".[72]

In other words, the first principle of the Pantjasila is neither a syncretistic compromise based on the opinion that in the end all religions are alike, nor is it a concept with only one interpretation, so that adherents of one religion could prescribe to others what their belief in

---

[71] Cf. Van Nieuwenhuijze on '*Deconfessionalized*' *Muslim Concepts,* in *Aspects,* p. 208 ff.

[72] W. B. Sidjabat, *Religious Tolerance,* p. 74. The author translated "Ketuhanan Jang Maha Esa" with "the Divine Omnipotence". Another Indonesian Christian theologian suggested "The Absolute Lordship" (Harun Hadiwijono, *Man in the Present Javanese Mysticism,* Baarn, the Netherlands, 1967). I myself would prefer to maintain the translation "Belief in the One and Only God".

God and their worship should be like, in order to be in accordance with the basis of the state. This first principle must be understood as a multi-interpretable formula and must be appreciated as providing a real possibility for people to agree while disagreeing.

5. *The Fight for Freedom (1945-1950)*

The Republic of Indonesia thus became a fact on August 17th, 1945. Some months later, however, the colonial government returned to Djakarta under the name of the Netherlands Indies Civil Administration (N.I.C.A.). The Dutch wanted a return to "law and order"; only after that would they be prepared to talk about a certain form of independence or home rule for Indonesia. Between July and December 1946 the N.I.C.A. began to set up a number of "federal states" in co-operation with certain Indonesian leaders and parts of the population in the newly occupied areas. These states then would be prepared to co-operate with the Netherlands. In this way the young Republic would be isolated in Java and some parts of Sumatra. During the so-called physical revolution (1945-1950), the existence of the Republic in Java was twice endangered by a Dutch military offensive (July 1947 and December 1948). The government of the Republic was forced to retire from Djakarta to Jogjakarta (or "Jogja") in Central Java.

The Dutch "federal states policy", together with the impossibility of destroying the Republic of Indonesia, finally resulted in the setting up of the federal "United Indonesian Republic" (Ind. *Republik Indonesia Serikat,* abbreviated to R.I.S.; in American publications usually called the Republic of the United States of Indonesia, or R.U.S.I.). Thus the Independence of Indonesia was officially recognized by the Dutch on December 27th, 1949. As early as August 1950, however, this R.I.S. was reorganized into a unitary state, again called the Republic of Indonesia (R.I.). In this way the Republic which was proclaimed on August 17th, 1945 determined the character of the new Indonesian state which was to include the whole territory of the former Dutch East Indies (until 1962 with the exception of West Irian, then Dutch New Guinea).

For a sketch of the modern history of Indonesia — and thus for the recent history of Islam in Indonesia — we can turn our attention in particular to Java. It was there that the new Indonesia took shape, in the Republic proclaimed on August 17th, 1945. What happened in and around this Republic was decisive for the new Indonesia, and not the momentary restoration of Dutch authority or the activities of the N.I.C.A.

The political developments during the first 5 years of the Republic of Indonesia ("Jogja") are dealt with at length in Kahin's standard work.[73] Naturally Kahin deals again and again with the role of Islam as organized in the Masjumi, a political party from the end of 1945. It is this side of the developments to which we want to give special attention here.

Looking back, the period of the physical revolution (1945-1950) can be characterized as the period of relative unity-in-the-struggle, a unity among Muslim leaders and factions themselves as much as between "the Muslims" and the "secular" factions. Of course there occurred a great number of incidents, and on occasion an intense rivalry and struggle for power raged behind the scenes. One of the first conflicts was that between the democratic, anti-fascist group of Sjahrir and the Indonesian National Party as had been formed during the last months of the Japanese occupation by Subardjo. The "national communist" Tan Malaka too had great aspirations for leadership. After the Renville Agreement with the Netherlands at the beginning of 1948 the government of the Republic came into conflict with the *Darul Islam* movement in West Java. At the end of 1948 an extremely dangerous situation arose, due to the Communist revolt in Madiun (East Java).

Yet in spite of all these tensions, the period of 1945-1950 can be characterized as the period of relative unity-in-the-struggle. The chief aim for everyone, also for the Muslim faction, was the defence of freedom and independence against the common enemy from abroad. For the feeling of Muslims this fight for political freedom was at the same time a struggle for the freedom of Islam. We have already quoted how in October 1944 the leadership of the Masjumi had urged its members "to prepare Muslims for the liberation of their country and their religion".[74] Likewise the fight for freedom between 1945 and 1950 was felt by Muslims to be a struggle for their country and their religion. Already on October 22nd, 1945, the Nahdatul Ulama had produced a resolution concerning the Holy War (*resolusi djihad*) to be regarded as an authoritative *fatwā* (a considered legal opinion) of the *ulama*s, as the N.U. was at that time the association of *kiyai*s and *ulama*s within the then Masjumi. In this resolution the "*djihad* for the defence of the Indonesian fatherland" was declared to be the individual duty of every Muslim, wherever he might be. The outbreak of fighting between

---

[73] Kahin, *Nationalism*.
[74] Benda, *The Crescent*, p. 176.

Indonesians and the British troops in Surabaja on November 10th, 1945 may to some extent have been provoked by this resolution.[75]

According to a publication of the Indonesian Information Service, the government of the young Republic declared on November 3rd, 1945 "that the government would be pleased to see the setting up of political parties, because political parties are capable of channelling along organized routes ideals which arise in society".[76] Kahin concluded that the real background of this development was Sjahrir's struggle against the national unitary party under Subardjo, which wanted to be the only political party. At the end of October 1945, Soekarno, Hatta and other prominent leaders had also agreed on a multi-party system. "Desirous as they all were for unity in the face of the struggle for independence, this was seen as the only way to undermine Subardjo's power and what many saw as an ominously authoritarian prospect inherent in the growth of his party." [77]

The abovementioned Indonesian publication goes on to say that in this way powers of democracy came to the fore in the form of political parties "which soon began to crystallize around three philosophies of life which were present in Indonesian society. First on November 7th, 1945, we saw the rise of the Masjumi, as the embodiment of the religious way of life, in this case, that of Islam. On December 17th, 1945, the Socialist Party was born, crystallizing the Marxist philosophy of life. On January 29th, 1946, at Kediri we could observe a fusion which afterwards resulted in the present Indonesian National(ist) Party (*Partai Nasional Indonesia*, P.N.I.), embodying the third way of life, namely nationalism." [78]

It can be said that all later parties or splinter-groups originated from the abovementioned parties or ideologies. Afterwards Soekarno's NASAKOM formula was intended to bridge the growing gap between these three pillars of Indonesian political life. NASAKOM stood for the unity of the Nationalists (NAS), the religious groups (A for *Agama*, meaning religion) and the Communists (KOM for *Komunis*). After the revolt of September 30th, 1965, Soekarno was prepared to speak of NASASOS (SOS for Socialists instead of Communists).

---

[75] Wahid Hasjim, p. 478.
[76] *Indonesisch Bulletin*, publication of the Indonesian Information Service, The Hague, March 1953 (IV, 3, p. 7).
[77] Kahin, *Nationalism*, p. 148.
[78] *Indonesisch Bulletin*, p. 7 ff.

"During the last months of 1945 there also occurred a rapid burgeoning of small parties", as, for example, the Catholic Party (in addition to the Protestant Party), the rapidly growing Communist Party and other left-wing groups.[79]

Turning to the political role of Islam, we may concentrate our attention on the Masjumi, created in the Japanese period and transformed into a political party on November 7th, 1945 in Jogjakarta. This Masjumi was intended as the Islamic unitary party. For the time being the Masjumi retained its dualistic structure dating from the Japanese period, when certain organizations as well as individuals could join it. Now, however, the emphasis shifted: the Masjumi became a political party consisting of individual members, but including also a number of non-political organizations as "extraordinary members" (Nahdatul Ulama, Muhammadijah and some regional organizations in West Java set up at Madjalengka and Sukabumi).[80]

The composition of the first Party Council (*Madjlis Sjuro*) and the first Party Executive (*Pengurus Besar*) shows that the Masjumi did include various Islamic groups. The chairman of the *Madjlis Sjuro* was Hasjim Asj'ari; one of the vice-chairmen was his son Wahid Hasjim (both from N.U. circles); H. Agus Salim (P.S.I.I.), but also Sjech Djamil Djambek (one of the "Sumatran reformers"), "and dozens of *kiyai*s and other Islamic leaders" were members. The Executive consisted of career politicians of the later Masjumi such as Sukiman, but also Abikusno Tjokrosujoso (P.S.I.I.), and furthermore Muh. Natsir and Mohamad Roem as well as Kartosuwirjo, the later rebellious leader of the *Darul Islam*.

Kahin characterizes the progressive leaders of the Masjumi as Religious Socialists, who "drew much of their inspiration from the teachings of Muḥammad ᶜAbduh"; he mentions by name Natsir, Sjafruddin Prawiranegara, Mohamad Roem, Jusuf Wibisono and Abu Hanifah. On the other hand, "the conservative older-generation religious leaders" formed its right wing, "based on the Nahdatul Ulama and the more conservative elements of the Muhammadijah". As intermediaries, he mentions Sukiman and later on Prawoto Mangkusasmito.[81] This distinction is usable

---

[79] Kahin, *Nationalism*, p. 158 ff. An analysis of the later political parties can be found in Feith, *The Decline*, pp. 122-145.
[80] This information and much of what follows can be found in Wahid Hasjim, p. 349 ff.
[81] Kahin, *Nationalism*, pp. 157-158.

with regard to "the interpretation of what Islamic social principles were and how they should be applied in Indonesia". But with regard to other problems — for example, the relationship between state and religion — the term "religious socialists" may cause misunderstanding. On such problems there may have been different opinions within the so-called left wing as well (for example, between Muh. Natsir and Abu Hanifah).

Throughout the years of struggle for freedom, the Masjumi sometimes co-operated with "secular" parties in a coalition cabinet.[82] Here too a certain dualism could not be avoided. On the one hand, the Masjumi had to agree to general, multi-interpretable formulas such as those of the Pantjasila. On the other hand, the party clearly wanted to fight for the realization of Islamic principles in state and society. However, Masjumi leaders always maintained that they wanted to fight for these principles in a democratic way, unlike the *Darul Islam* movement.

To get an impression of the opinions and ideas of Islamic leaders during the period 1945-1950, we can examine the emergency programmes and other resolutions which were passed by the annual General Assemblies of the Masjumi.[83]

At its foundation on November 7th, 1945, the Muslims were encouraged "to fight in the way of God" (*berdjihad fisabilillah*); this emergency programme was, of course, determined by the fight for independence. The programme of 1946 emphasized "the realization of the ideals of Islam in state affairs, so that a form of state can be created which is founded on the sovereignty of the people, and a society which is based on justice, in accordance with the teachings of Islam". Therefore it was necessary to strengthen and perfect the principles of the Constitution (i.e. the Pantjasila principles) "in order to realize an Islamic society and an Islamic State" (*mewudjudkan masjarakat dan Negara Islam*).[84] All the strength of the Islamic community had to be concentrated in the

---

[82] Apart from the books of Kahin and Feith, a list of all Indonesian cabinets between 1945 and 1956 and their composition can be found in the *Ensiklopedia Indonesia*, published under the editorship of T. S. G. Mulia and K. A. H. Hidding, with help from Muh. Natsir as far as Islam is concerned, 3 Vol., Bandung, no date.

[83] A résumé of the Assemblies between 1945 and 1954 is given by Wahid Hasjim, pp. 349-377. Cf. Kahin, *Nationalism*, pp. 305-311.

[84] Wahid Hasjim, p. 357. According to oral information received from some ex-Masjumi leaders the Masjumi as a party fought for an Islamic society but not for an Islamic State. The quotation seems to be in conflict with this information; we should, however, take into account the possibility that the quotation is not correct, at least as far as the use of capital letters ("Islamic State") is concerned.

Masjumi, "to defend the freedom of religion, country and people". The religion meant in this formula is, of course, Islam, which people felt to be attacked in the attacks on the Republic. Specific wishes in the social field were first and foremost the ancient prohibitions on gambling, the sale of strong drink and opium, prostitution and *riba* (interest or usury? This question will be dealt with later).

In this programme of 1946 a number of progressive demands were also mentioned: a minimum wage for labourers, the limitation of working hours, social insurance, an agricultural law to protect small farmers, and improvement of agricultural methods. The economy should be directed toward the welfare of the people, so that "the capitalist system with its obvious elements of purely individual interest would be combatted". Kahin draws attention to the fact that the Masjumi did not merely use fine words in a party-programme, but did indeed have achievements in the social field. For instance, part of the *zakāt* (alms-tax) collected by the party was applied to social reforms for the benefit of farmers and financial aid to small traders.[85]

The "Political Manifesto" of June 6th, 1947, stated: "The Republic of Indonesia, the people of which are largely adherents of Islam, shall be a state with a Constitution based on principles which are in agreement with this Religion or not in conflict with the teachings of Islam..." The Masjumi strove for "the spread of the ideology of Islam within Indonesian society, without hindering others who likewise strengthen the foundations of Belief in the One and Only God". As far as foreign policy was concerned, contact and co-operation with Islamic communities in other countries had to be increased.[86]

In the General Assembly at the end of March 1948 it was decided that the government should be urged to make religious instruction compulsory in elementary and secondary schools. A telegram was sent to the Great Mufti Amīn al-Ḥusainī, supporting him in the Palestine conflict. Kahin gives a summary of the programme drafted by the Masjumi's Party Council at the end of 1948, particularly its socio-economic aspects. He comments that "the conservative minority of the Council would put more emphasis upon Moslem education and formal religious practice than upon the socio-economic aspect of the Masjumi program".[87]

---

[85] Cf. Kahin, *Nationalism,* pp. 307-309.
[86] One can assume that among the Masjumi leaders Muh. Natsir in particular would have continuously stressed this "ecumenical" or pan-Islamic ideal.
[87] Kahin, *Nationalism,* p. 311, n. 4.

The General Assembly of December 1949 took place in the shadow of the coming recognition of Independence by the Dutch and the unification of the "Jogja Republic" with the (federal) "United Indonesian Republic" (R.I.S.). Probably as a result of these circumstances, the resolutions of this meeting breathed a quite different spirit. It is likely that the withdrawal of the Nahdatul Ulama in 1952 was caused partly by this shift. During the years from 1945 to 1950 the Masjumi apparently came to be more and more dominated by the so-called religious socialists. This meant that a clash with the conservative right wing was bound to come.

6. *Strife between the Parties (1950-1955)*

The first split in the Masjumi had already taken place in July 1947. A number of members under the leadership of Wondoamiseno and Arudji Kartawinata re-established the old *Partai Serikat Islam Indonesia* (P.S.I.I.) in order to take part in the left-wing cabinet of Amir Sjarifuddin, while the Masjumi went into opposition.[88]

More serious, however, were the tensions between the progressive left wing of the Masjumi consisting of "religious socialists" and its conservative group of *kiyai*s and *ulama*s. These tensions would lead to a break which put its mark on the struggle within the Islamic community in the new Indonesia.

The difficulties began to come into the open about the time of the recognition of Independence and the formation of the federal R.I.S. As has been said, the Masjumi programme of December 1949 breathed a somewhat different spirit.[89] The emphasis had apparently shifted from formulations concerning religious principles to a number of practical questions concerning the transition from the Republic of Indonesia ("Jogja") to the R.I.S., which would include the whole territory of the former Dutch East Indies. Such questions included, for instance, membership of the United Nations, the setting up of a Diplomatic Service, the formation of a Constituent Assembly and preparations for general elections. The programme also contained a number of socio-economic demands concerning, for example, the transformation of the colonial economy into a national economy and the care of victims of the fighting.

With regard to the Constitution of the R.I.S. — a product of the negotiations with the Dutch — it was stipulated (even before this new

---

[88] Cf. Kahin, *Nationalism*, p. 209 ff.
[89] The text of this programme is to be found in Wahid Hasjim, pp. 365-367.

Constitution took effect!) that its contents would have to be studied, and that a new Constitution would be drafted in agreement with the ideals of the people. It is a fair guess that a number of Islamic leaders genuinely believed that these "ideals of the people" would result in a more or less Islamic state. Furthermore, the position of the various "states" within the R.I.S. would have to be reconsidered. Another contribution of the Republic to the R.I.S. would be compulsory religious instruction in state schools, and the equalization of teachers of religion with other teachers. One point probably also originating from *kiyai* and *ulama* circles, concerned the "protection of the rights of women in marriages to be contracted in accordance with their own religion" (read: separate marriage laws for the Muslims as well as for the Christians and others?).

Apart from these points, the programme of 1949 did not include any formal demand to carry out the teachings of Islam in state and society. Did some Masjumi leaders realize that Indonesia included important non-Muslim areas, so that they could no longer put forward all sorts of formulas and slogans originating from conservative *kiyai*s and *ulama*s? In this Assembly at any rate the Party Council (*Madjlis Sjuro*) — with its many religious leaders — was degraded to being merely an advisory body, while the Party Executive (the "politicians") took the lead. A revealing comment from an important Indonesian source runs as follows: "This change meant that the *ulama*s withdrew and no longer developed their activities in the struggle, because every problem was henceforth considered only from a political point of view, without the guidance of religion".[90]

This comment expressed the formal reason for the withdrawal of the Nahdatul Ulama (N.U.) from the Masjumi in April 1952, and the reshaping of the N.U. into a political party. The book on Wahid Hasjim — originating from N.U. circles, like Wahid Hasjim himself — admits that this split was also influenced by injured feelings and tactical considerations.[91] The immediate cause was certainly the struggle for the post of Minister of Religion in the Wilopo cabinet (April 1952). Criticism of Wahid Hasjim's policy led to the choice of the Muhammadijah leader Fakih Usman, whereas N.U. circles continued to claim this post for Wahid Hasjim.[92]

Together with the P.S.I.I. and some smaller parties the N.U. set up a co-ordinating organization, the *Liga Muslimin Indonesia* (League of

---

[90] Wahid Hasjim, p. 478.
[91] Wahid Hasjim, p. 563.
[92] Cf. Feith, *The Decline,* pp. 233-237.

Indonesian Muslims), which, however, did not amount to much, probably because of the coming elections, which were frequently announced and then postponed, finally to be held at the end of 1955.

Just as the period of the fight for freedom (1945-1950) can be typified as the period of relative unity-in-the-struggle, so the years 1950-1955 can be characterized as the period of strife between the parties. The real issues of this struggle were as much positions, jobs and commercial interests (e.g. import and export permits for friends of the parties in power) as ideological questions. As far as the latter aspect is concerned, the Muslims clashed with the "secular" parties, in particular the Nationalists (P.N.I.) and Communists (P.K.I.). But at the same time a hidden struggle, or at least competition, arose between the Islamic parties themselves. In July 1955 the four most important Islamic parties — Masjumi, N.U., P.S.I.I. and the Sumatran *Pergerakan Tarbijah Islamijah* (Perti, the "Movement for Islamic Education") — apparently agreed to suspend all attacks on each other until the elections.[93] The P.K.I. had made a similar sort of agreement with the P.S.I.I. in April 1955, probably to prevent itself from being regarded as anti-religious.[94] The election campaign is described in detail by Herbert Feith.[95] He concludes that "the Great Debate was between the P.N.I. and the Masjumi"... while "the Communist Party did in a way constitute a third main party".

This "Great Debate" has often been simplified into the choice between a state based on the Pantjasila or a state based on Islam. Actually the Islamic parties did not succeed in convincing people that their opinions were not in conflict with the Pantjasila ideals. Both the Masjumi and the N.U. gave the impression that they were aiming at an Islamic State, whatever that might be. From the beginning of 1953 the conflict became sharper, because President Soekarno openly threw himself into the arena. In a speech on January 27th, 1953, at Amuntai (South Kalimantan/ Borneo) he said: "The state we want is a national state consisting of all Indonesia. If we establish a state based on Islam, many areas whose population is not Islamic, such as the Moluccas, Bali, Flores, Timor, the Kai Islands and Sulawesi, will secede. And West Irian, which has not yet become part of the territory of Indonesia, will not want to be part

---

[93] According to J. W. M. Bakker S.J., in *Het Missiewerk*, 1956, 4, p. 228.
[94] Feith, *The Decline*, p. 359.
[95] Feith, *The Decline*, pp. 353-366.

of the Republic." [96] For months this speech of Soekarno's was talked about. It may fairly be concluded that the definite break between the Masjumi and President Soekarno dates from this moment. The chief spokesman for the Masjumi in this matter was Isa Anshary.

Looking back, some Muslim informants are prepared to admit that the struggle for a so-called Islamic State was largely an empty, emotional battle of words for the label of the state. This certainly applied to a number of *kiyai*s and *ulama*s who were used to thinking and speaking in a religious terminology, but who were too little at home in politics to grasp the problems of modern statecraft. This type of leader played a great role in the N.U., though the Masjumi too included important spokesmen and writers who advocated a realization of Islamic principles in politics.

The difference between the Masjumi and the N.U. developed into a conflict which dominated (and probably still dominates) to a large extent the struggle within the Islamic community in Indonesia. For this reason special attention must be given to these two parties.

With regard to the Masjumi it can be said on the one hand that many of its members and leaders were modern Muslims who took Islam seriously as a religio-political and social entity. The ideals of an Islamic State or the realization of Islamic principles in politics clearly flourished within this circle. And these ideals were quite clearly formulated by some Masjumi adherents. On the other hand, however, many Masjumi leaders were modern intellectuals with a realistic view of politics as "the art of the possible". It can be concluded that under the leadership of the "religious socialists" (as Kahin called them) the Masjumi "was the Islamic party considered best able to deal with the secular problems usually associated with socioeconomic development". In order to prevent a misunderstanding of the word "secular", it must be added "that both modern and traditional Muslims believe that Islamic doctrine provides the basis for all human action".[97]

Viewed sociologically, the adherents of the Masjumi were originally to be found in particular among the urban traders and independent employers and among intellectuals descended from them. Their religion has sometimes been described as an urbanized Islam, or an Islam of areas with "a cosmopolitan, urban and commercial character developed

---

[96] Quoted by Feith, *The Decline*, p. 281.
[97] Allan A. Samson, *Islam in Indonesian Politics*, in *Asian Survey*, December 1968, Vol. VIII, no. 12, pp. 1002-1003.

through centuries of cultural contact and trade".[98] It was the same circle of "middle-class people — merchants, tradesmen, landowners, small manufacturers, school-teachers, clerks, etc." — in which reformist ideas coming from Egypt (Muḥ. ᶜAbduh, Rashīd Riḍā) first met with a response.[99] Therefore many adherents of the reformist Muhammadijah movement would be politically organized in the Masjumi.

According to the Statutes of the Masjumi, applying after August 1952, the party was based on Islam and its goal was "the realization of the doctrine and law of Islam in the life of the individual, in society and in the Republic of Indonesia as a State, directed toward that which pleases God".[100] The concrete meaning of such formulas is, however, difficult to gauge. To what extent are these formulas intentionally vague, and therefore multi-interpretable within the Islamic community itself? In how far were these phrases used in order to win over potential supporters, such as, for instance, sympathizers with *Darul Islam* ideas? On the other hand, in how far did some Masjumi leaders have in mind modern ideas of democracy and social justice — in other words, principles which are not specifically and exclusively Islamic — when they talked of "Islamic principles" as being the basis of the state?

The Nahdatul Ulama (N.U.) was of old the association (later the political party) of teachers of religion and "scribes" (*kiyai*s and *ulama*s) who had close connections with the countryside and the religious schools (*pesantrèn*s) established there. Set up in 1926, the N.U. can be considered the successor of the Nahdatul Wathan (= *waṭan*), the "Awakening of the Fatherland", founded in 1916 in Surabaja by Abdul Wahab (in 1945 a member of the Party Council of the Masjumi) and K. H. M. Mansur. The aim of this older organization was to defend the authority of the four orthodox schools of law (*madhāhib,* sing. *madhhab*) against the reformer Soorkati. It is remarkable that Mansur (who had studied in Cairo) afterwards went over to the Muhammadijah, while Abdul Wahab (who had spent some years in Mecca) played a great part in the N.U.

According to article 2 of the N.U. Statutes of 1926, the aim of this association was: "To uphold one of the schools of law of the four *Imām*s — Imam Muh. bin Idris Asj-Sjafi'i, Imam Malik bin Anas, Imam Abu Hanifah An-Nu'man or Imam Ahmad bin Hanbal — and to do everything

---

[98] Samson, *Islam*, p. 1002.
[99] Cf. Drewes in *Unity*, ed. by Von Grunebaum, p. 301.
[100] Wahid Hasjim, p. 405.

which would be beneficial to Islam".[101] Over against the modernists (*ahli bid'ah*), they liked to call themselves the *ahli sunnah wal djama'ah*, that is, the people who keep to the *sunna* (usage) of the Prophet, in community with the one great *umma* or *djamāᶜa*, in short the orthodox (in the sense of "orthoprax" [102]). Beside this official, theological characterization, the N.U. can be typified as being more moderate towards the Javanese way of life and Javanese religious practices than the "puritan" reformers. Partly for this reason the N.U. became a typically Javanese party, whereas many Javanese considered the Masjumi "too fanatical", that is to say, too rigorously Islamic.

When the N.U. entered politics in 1952, article 2 of the Statutes was formulated as follows:

"The Nahdatul-'Ulama is based on Islam and its aim is:

a. to uphold the law of Islam, in accordance with one of the four schools of law: Sjafi'i, Maliki, Hanafi and Hanbali;

b. to bring about the application of the precepts of Islam in society".[103] Also according to article 1 of the by-laws of the N.U., membership was dependent on recognition of the authority of one of the four schools of law.[104] This meant that reformists or modernists who advocated a return to the Qur'ān and Tradition in order to study these sources in an independent way as required in modern times (the so-called "new *idjtihād*") could strictly speaking not become members of the N.U., and therefore remained or became members of the Masjumi.

Probably the Masjumi tried to nullify the possible results of this N.U. propaganda for the orthodox schools of law. In December 1954 the Masjumi declared that it respected these schools of law completely, but wanted to be a political party uniting people of various opinions and schools of law.[105] Nevertheless the success of the N.U. in the 1955 elections is probably partly due to the aroma of orthodoxy spread by its defence of the four schools of law. For many voters the N.U. was emotionally the truly Islamic party, with leaders whom they could trust to maintain Islamic principles unabridged. Were not many of these leaders the teacher (Ind. *guru*) of many voters, who followed their

---

[101] Wahid Hasjim, p. 505.
[102] Cf. Smith, *Islam,* p. 20: "The word usually translated 'orthodox', *sunnī*, actually means rather 'orthoprax', if we may use the term. A good Muslim is... one whose commitment may be expressed in practical terms that conform to an accepted code".
[103] Wahid Hasjim, p. 509.
[104] Wahid Hasjim, pp. 511-512.
[105] Wahid Hasjim, p. 377.

teachers as thankful pupils (Ind. *murid*)? On the other hand, many voters might have considered the Masjumi a dubious party in many ways, as its leaders often used an intellectual language and a modern terminology which made too little contact with the traditional pious.

The resolutions and the action programme of the N.U. drawn up in 1952 give the impression that its religio-political formulations were less clearly Islamic than those of the Masjumi. Probably it was easier simply to quote available formulas, for example, those of the Pantjasila and the 1945 Constitution. For instance, the N.U. wanted "to press the government to intensify instruction in the Pantjasila to be given in an orderly and fundamental way, in particular instruction concerning the (first) pillar of Belief in God, to which clearly too little attention is being paid".[106]

According to the Action Programme of 1952, the N.U. would strive for the application of religious precepts, as interpreted according to one of the four schools of law. The N.U. wanted "a National State based on Islam, a State which guarantees and protects the fundamental rights of man, that is, the freedom to adhere to a sound religion (*agama jang sehat*) and the freedom to have and to express ideas and opinions which do not cause harm to others...". The political course of the N.U. was aimed at *As-Shulchu* (Ar. *aṣ-ṣulḥ* = peace, reconciliation, solidarity, settlement, accommodation, compromise; cf. Sura 4 : 128), as "the normal basis of contact with every kind of group as long as this is not detrimental to Islam and its struggle". Furthermore it was stated — obviously an adoption from the preamble of the 1945 Constitution — that the N.U. desired "a state upholding the rule of law (Ind. *negara hukum*) and based on the sovereignty of the people in the sense of mutual deliberation, led by wise policy executed in the representative bodies of the people..."[107]

The N.U. has sometimes been characterized as a typically government-minded party. Because of its extreme readiness to join any cabinet, it was often accused of opportunism. "The NU leaders were 'solidarity makers', wielders of symbols, both traditional and nationalistic."[108] The colour and atmosphere of the N.U. were certainly conservative when it became a political party. It gave the impression of being dominated by *kiyai*s and *ulama*s. According to Herbert Feith, "The Nahdatul Ulama

---

[106] Wahid Hasjim, p. 493.
[107] Wahid Hasjim, p. 494.
[108] Feith, *The Decline*, p. 234.

leadership included virtually no one with modern-state-type skills".[109]

It is worth recalling how Wahid Hasjim, in November 1953, explained his choice for the N.U. He admitted that originally the N.U. did not satisfy his desire to join a *radical* party; nor was the N.U. a party with many *intellectuals* — "looking for graduates within the N.U. is like looking for an ice-cream seller at one o'clock in the morning!" -- but from the beginning the N.U. somehow turned out to have an appeal for the people. "While in the course of ten years a youth movement of another Islamic group only made gains in 20 places, all close together, that of the Nahdatul Ulama came to cover 60 % of the whole territory of Indonesia." Contemplating such results, Wahid Hasjim decided to choose the N.U., because it was clear "that the Nahdatul Ulama offered great possibilities for the uplift of the Islamic community in Indonesia".[110]

The elections — in September 1955 for Parliament and in December 1955 for the Constituent Assembly — resulted in a great disappointment for the Islamic parties. Both in the spoken and written word, Islamic leaders had continuously stressed that Indonesia was a Muslim country. At least 80 %, and according to others 90 % or even 95 %, of the population were considered Muslims since they called themselves Muslims and wanted to be Muslims. Moreover, *ulama* conferences in Java and elsewhere had declared — through *fatwā*-like resolutions — that for a Muslim it was forbidden (*ḥarām*) to vote for a non-Muslim or for a Muslim who did not have the intention of putting Islamic law into practice.[111]

In spite of all this, the four Islamic parties — Masjumi, N.U., P.S.I.I. and Perti — obtained together only 43.5 % of the total number of votes at the elections for Parliament. A disinterested observer might conclude that in a country such as Indonesia it is no mean achievement if 43.5 % of the population consciously vote for an expressly Islamic party, that is, a party which "has the intention of putting Islamic law

---

[109] Feith, *The Decline*, p. 234.
[110] Wahid Hasjim, pp. 740-741. The successful youth movement referred to is the present-day ANSOR, founded in 1934. "Ansor" is the Indonesian pronunciation of the Arabic *anṣār* (*al-anṣār* were the Medinan helpers of the Prophet when he arrived at Medina in A.D. 622). The basis and aim of this ANSOR are to be found in *Anggaran Dasar dan Anggaran Rumah Tangga Gerakan Pemuda ANSOR,* Djakarta 1964. The history of ANSOR and its predecessors is sketched in Wahid Hasjim, pp. 547-559.
[111] Wahid Hasjim, p. 758.

into practice". Muslim leaders, however, seem to have taken it for granted that everyone who wanted to be called a Muslim would vote for an Islamic party.

At the elections of September 1955 the nationalist P.N.I. was returned as the biggest party, with 22.3 %. The fourth party was the Communist P.K.I. with 16.4 %, a success which many had not expected after the Communist set-back in the Madiun revolt of 1948. Numbers 2 and 3 were the Masjumi and the N.U. with respectively 20.9 % and 18.4 %. The P.S.I.I. turned out to have become a small party (2.9 %); the Perti was hardly of any importance (1.3 %). The elections of December 1955 "showed great similarity with the result of the parliamentary elections, with an over-all trend for all medium- and small-sized parties to lose votes, and for the four largest parties to gain them".[112] The numbers of votes for Parliament and Constituent Assembly, as well as an analysis of the election campaign and of its results, are given by Feith.[113] Some interesting conclusions are, for example, that the Masjumi, apart from West Java, got the greatest numbers of votes from the islands outside Java, whereas the N.U. turned out to be a typically Javanese party. Further, beside the Socialist Party, not the N.U. but the Masjumi appeared to have many adherents in the army. And as far as Java was concerned, the N.U. in East Java obtained roughly three times as many votes as the Masjumi and in Central Java twice as many, whereas in West Java (with its Sundanese, not Javanese, population) the Masjumi got three times as many adherents as the N.U.

Contrary to the expectation of many inside and outside the Islamic parties, the Masjumi support turned out to be not much bigger than that of the N.U. The explanation heard immediately after the elections was that the Masjumi had acted too much as an urban party of the better educated, with a centralized election campaign, and had certainly underestimated the personal influence of N.U. leaders (*kiyai*s and *ulama*s) in the *kampung*s and the *désa*s. That was probably what Wahid Hasjim had understood better! And to explain the success of the N.U., it has to be said that the Indonesian feeling about the relationship between teacher and pupil (*guru-murid*) was perhaps still more important than

---

[112] Feith, *The Decline,* pp. 449-450.
[113] Herbert Feith, *The Indonesian Elections of 1955,* Interim Reports Series, Cornell University, 1957.

the general connection of the N.U. with orthodoxy and peasantry that has usually been stressed.[114]

Through this election result it became apparent that the political struggle of Islam in Indonesia for the time being had failed. In the representative bodies the necessary majority had not been obtained, so that it would not be possible to realize certain Islamic principles in state and society by democratic means. Hence the year 1955 may be considered the end of the first period in the modern history of Islam in Indonesia. The attention and energy of Islamic leaders during these first ten years had in particular been directed towards politics. The struggle had been felt as a struggle for a free Indonesia which was hoped would become at least a clearly Muslim country, if not an official Islamic State. In other words, the Islamic da^cwa (the call to men to walk in God's ways) had been carried out especially in the field of politics. But from now this da^cwa would have to be more or less transferred to other fields, as free Indonesia had turned out to be *not yet* a truly Muslim country — let alone an Islamic State!

7. *The Darul Islam Revolts*

Besides the party-strife mentioned above, special attention must be paid to the revolts of the so-called *Darul Islam* movement (abbreviated D.I.). These revolts formed one of the greatest worries for the government of the Republic of Indonesia, particularly in the period after 1950.

Difficulties had already begun in 1948 in West Java, due to the reaction of Kartosuwirjo to the Renville Agreement between the Republic and the Netherlands. In 1950, in South Sulawesi (Celebes) a clash between the army and some guerilla leaders resulted in a similar rising, under the leadership of Kahar Muzakkar. At the same time tensions increased between the government in Djakarta and the province of Atjeh (North Sumatra), culminating in a rising in 1953 under the leadership of Daud Beureu'éh.

The rising in West Java came to an end on June 4th, 1962, when Kartosuwirjo was taken prisoner. On February 3rd, 1965, Kahar Muzakkar was surrounded and shot in South-East Sulawesi. The central government came to an agreement with Atjeh on May 26th, 1959, and the reconciliation was solemnly celebrated on August 17th, 1961.

---

[114] Compare W. F. Wertheim, *Indonesian Society in Transition*, The Hague 1969², p. 345.

This whole history, its background and the connection between the individual risings, could in fact form the subject for a special piece of research. Here a provisional sketch will be attempted, in as far as this is possible, as our information is still far from complete.[115]

With regard to West Java, the beginning of the history of the "Darul Islam" under Kartosuwirjo has been described by Van Nieuwenhuijze. But his abovementioned essay and some of its data can be supplemented and corrected by more recent information from Indonesian sources, in particular from Pinardi's book and the documents of the case against Kartosuwirjo.

Kartosuwirjo (full name Sekarmadji Maridjan Kartosuwirjo) was a Javanese, born on February 7th, 1905, at Tjepu (Central Java). He received a Western education at Dutch-language elementary and secondary schools. So he was not a *santri* from a *pesantrèn*. It has even been said that he never gained a real knowledge of Arabic and Islam.[116]

From 1923 to 1926 he attended the preparatory course at the "Netherlands Indies Medical School" (N.I.A.S.) in Surabaja. There he met H. Omar Said Tjokroaminoto, later a leader of the P.S.I.I., who became his fosterfather. According to Pinardi, Kartosuwirjo succeeded in beginning his medical studies in 1926, but one year afterwards he was expelled because of his political activities.[117] From 1927 to 1929 he was private secretary of Tjokroaminoto. Probably it was from this P.S.I.I. leader that Kartosuwirjo got the idea of an Indonesian state based on Islam.

---

[115] The chief publications are: Van Nieuwenhuijze, *The Dār ul-Islām movement in Western Java till 1949*, in *Aspects*, pp. 161-179; Kahin, *Nationalism*, pp. 326-331; Feith, *The Decline, passim*; Henri J. Alers, *Om een Rode of Groene Merdeka*, Eindhoven (?), 1956, pp. 240-274. Indonesian sources are: Pinardi, *Sekarmadji Maridjan Kartosuwirjo*, Djakarta 1964; Bahar Mattalioe (one-time comrade in arms, later opponent of Kahar Muzakkar), *Kahar Muzakkar dengan Petualangannja*, Djakarta 1965; furthermore there appeared small pamphlets intended to be read by the Forces, such as Zainabun Harahap, *Operasi-operasi Militer Menumpas Kahar Muzakkar*, Djakarta 1965, and Anne Marie Thé, *Darah Tersimbah di Djawa Barat*, Djakarta 1968². Further material was obtained from military archives and orally on the spot; the latter applies for Atjeh in particular.

[116] Pinardi, *Kartosuwirjo*, pp. 27-28.

[117] Pinardi, *Kartosuwirjo*, p. 21. So Kartosuwirjo did not study in Batavia (Djakarta) as Van Nieuwenhuijze believed (*Aspects*, p. 167), and it is quite impossible that "he served as president of the Batavia branch of PSII, before becoming vice-president of the central board of the party in 1924" (*Aspects*, p. 168).

After a serious illness he moved to Malangbong, near Garut, in the (Sundanese) eastern part of West Java, as his wife came from there. Together with his Sundanese father-in-law, from 1929 onward he exerted himself for the development of the P.S.I.I. in this area. When only 26 years old, he was elected general secretary of the P.S.I.I. in 1931. After the death of Tjokroaminoto (1934), the Party Congress held in 1936 elected Wondoamiseno president of the P.S.I.I., while Kartosuwirjo became vice-president.

When, during the following years, the conflict flared up within the P.S.I.I. as to whether or not they should co-operate with the colonial government, Kartosuwirjo stood on the side of non-cooperation. He wanted to carry out this so-called *hidjra* policy of non-cooperation and self-help so radically that in 1939 he was expelled from the party, and on March 24th, 1940 he founded a counter-P.S.I.I. in Malangbong with, among others, the later D.I. commander Kamran. "The Islamic ideas of theocracy which later were to form the background to Kartosuwirjo's *Darul Islam* had to some extent already been expressed in this group", says Pluvier cautiously.[118]

At that time Kartosuwirjo founded a kind of *pesantrèn* in Malangbong, called *Institut Supah* or "Suffah Institute".[119] Initially this institution was aimed at leadership training for the religio-political field. During the Japanese occupation, however, the activities of political parties were frozen. Therefore Kartosuwirjo's institution changed its character, eventually becoming a centre for the training of his later guerillas (Hizbu'llah, Sabili'llah).

---

[118] J. M. Pluvier, *Overzicht van de ontwikkeling der Nationalistische Beweging in Indonesië in de jaren 1930 tot 1942*, 's-Gravenhage/Bandung 1953, p. 117 (compare also pp. 70-75). According to Van Nieuwenhuijze, *Aspects*, p. 168, it could be said that Kartosuwirjo already "overtly preached the ideals of the *dār ul-Islām*, the Islamic state", between 1935 and 1940 in Malangbong.

[119] *Aṣ-ṣuffa* (rendered "bench", "banquette", "estrade", etc.) was probably a long covered portico in the courtyard of the prophet's house and temporary mosque at Medina. According to later traditions, in particular from ascetic and mystical circles, the "people of the *ṣuffa*" were a group of poor and pious Muslims who lived there, spending their time in study and worship (cf. W. Montgomery Watt's article *Ahl al-ṣuffa* in *The Encyclopaedia of Islam*, new edition, Leiden 1960, and his book on *Muhammad at Medina*, Oxford 1966, pp. 305-306). The word *ṣuffa* was sometimes considered the origin of the term *taṣawwuf* (sufism, mysticism). Pinardi, *Kartosuwirjo*, p. 26, translates the word as meaning inner purification, thus perhaps following the Indonesian interpretation also intended by Kartosuwirjo, who was not a *kiyai* or *ulama* interested in Islamic law, but was drawn towards mysticism and magical ideas on invulnerability, etc.

According to Alers, on August 14th, 1945 Kartosuwirjo had already proclaimed an independent Darul Islam state.[120] But after August 17th he sided with the Republic of Indonesia proclaimed by Soekarno and Hatta. When the Masjumi transformed itself into a political party on November 7th, 1945, Kartosuwirjo became a member of the Party Executive. When a cabinet was formed by Amir Sjarifuddin on July 3rd, 1947, he was even offered the (nominal) post of second vice-minister of Defence, which he refused, however. After the Dutch had begun their first military offensive against the Republic on July 21st, 1947, Kartosuwirjo called for a Holy War against the Dutch on August 14th.[121]

Thus it was taken that Kartosuwirjo and his D.I. movement supported the Republic in its fight against the Dutch, as did the units of the Hizbu'llah and Sabili'llah, which in West Java were under the leadership of his friends Kamran and Oni. As a matter of course the government of the Republic, and in particular the leaders of the Masjumi, behaved as long as possible as if Kartosuwirjo's D.I. was the regional embodiment of the Indonesian fight for freedom in West Java. Moreover, rumour originally had it that the initials "D.I." stood for the Indonesian "Daérah I", that is to say, *Daérah Satu* or "Region One", and its significance was certainly not generally known. According to Alers it meant something like a "unitary state".[122] Pinardi, however, explains that its background was a differentiation made between the various areas of the Islamic State: "Region I" was the central area of the state, completely controlled by an Islamic government and organized in agreement with Islamic law; "Region II" consisted of areas in West Java which were only partly controlled by this Islamic State, whereas in "Region III" the Islamic community could for the time being not make its power felt.[123]

As Kartosuwirjo consistently turned down every sort of compromise with the Dutch, he also refused to accept the Renville Agreement made between the Republic and the Netherlands in January 1948. Because of this he refused to pull back the groups of the Hizbu'llah and Sabili'llah behind the agreed demarcation line. In this way he clashed with the leaders of the Republic and also with the leaders of the Masjumi, which had officially accepted the Renville Agreement, albeit grudgingly. Via the creation of a *Madjlis Ummat Islam* and the appointment of Karto-

---

[120] Cf. Alers, *Rode of Groene*, p. 73 and p. 240 ff.
[121] Van Nieuwenhuijze, *Aspects*, p. 170.
[122] Alers, *Rode of Groene*, p. 243.
[123] Pinardi, *Kartosuwirjo*, p. 59.

suwirjo as *Imām* of a provisional Islamic State, the Islamic State of Indonesia (Ind. *Negara Islam Indonesia,* abbreviated N.I.I.) was apparently proclaimed a few months later. In March 1948 the Dutch federal states policy had led to the formation of the State of Pasundan in the Dutch-controlled areas (in particular in the towns) of West Java. Kartosuwirjo's troops, now "the Indonesian Islamic Army" (Ind. *Tentara Islam Indonesia,* abbreviated T.I.I.), however, controlled the larger part of the countryside, and in particular the mountainous areas of West Java.

It seems that even then the government of the Republic did not wish to consider Kartosuwirjo's action a rising against the Republic, but only a regional counter-move against the Dutch-made "State of Pasundan". Indeed Kahin notes that only by late December 1948 did the Darul Islam become openly anti-Republican.[124] It is understandable that the Republic as long as possible allowed the D.I. with its armed troops to go its own way in West Java in the Muslim struggle against the Dutch. There were many members of the Masjumi who felt an affinity for the Darul Islam ideology — that is to say, the idea that Indonesia was part of the "territory of Islam" (*dār al-islām*), and therefore should be an Islamic State — even though they rejected the Darul Islam methods. As far as the ordinary people of West Java were concerned, it may well be concluded that their co-operation stemmed more from fear of D.I. terrorism than from sympathy with the way in which the D.I. carried out the "fight for freedom".[125]

The day after the beginning of the second military action by the Dutch (December 19th, 1948) Kartosuwirjo renewed his call to a Holy War. However, this military action meant that the Republic was no longer committed to the Renville Agreement. Thus the Siliwangi Division, always one of the best regiments of the Republic, began its

---

[124] Kahin, *Nationalism,* p. 330.
[125] Compare also Van Nieuwenhuijze, *Aspects,* p. 173. The sociological approach to the background of the D.I. in West Java as given by Kahin, *Nationalism,* pp. 327-328 — viz. that the dissatisfaction among the peasantry in West Java came about because many small farmers had lost their land to Indonesian landlords in the towns during the first years after 1945 — seems somewhat far-fetched and at least in conflict with the small true following and sympathy which Kartosuwirjo apparently enjoyed even from this part of the population. Perhaps more important were other factors, mentioned by Pinardi (*Kartosuwirjo,* p. 152 ff.), for instance the disappointment and uneasiness of the population in West Java caused by the withdrawal of the national army and Kartosuwirjo's ability to make use of religious, mystical and magical beliefs among the common people of the countryside.

famous "Long March" from Central Java back to West Java, from which it had had to retire after the Renville Agreement. On January 25th, 1949 the Siliwangi Division happened to come across some of Kartosuwirjo's troops and the first incident between them occurred. After that an open clash between the government of the Republic and Kartosuwirjo's D.I. could no longer be avoided, though for some years to come a solution "in the Indonesian way" rather than by an open fight was sought.

The Masjumi leader Muh. Natsir, Minister of Information in the Hatta cabinet of January 29th till the beginning of August 1949, tried to contact Kartosuwirjo by letter on August 5th, 1949, to prevent a definite break. But it was already too late: on August 7th, 1949, Kartosuwirjo once more officially proclaimed the existence of the Islamic State of Indonesia, this time clearly as the alternative to the Republic of Indonesia ("Jogja"). It was this action and this date which later in the case against Kartosuwirjo were mentioned as the primary points in the prosecution. According to the documents of the case this proclamation ran as follows: "In the name of God, the Beneficent, the Merciful, we — the Islamic *Umma* of the people of Indonesia — proclaim the founding of the Islamic State of Indonesia. The Law to which this Islamic State of Indonesia is subjected is the Islamic Law. *Allāhu akbar, Allāhu akbar, Allāhu akbar*" (God is great).

The Constitution promulgated by Kartosuwirjo (the so-called *Kanun Azasy*, Arabic *al-ḳānūn al-asasī*) stipulated that Islamic law would be applied to Muslims, while adherents of other religions would be free to perform their own religious duties (art. 1). The highest authority in the Islamic State would be Parliament (*Madjlis Sjuro,* that is, the Council for Mutual Deliberation), but in case of emergency the ultimate power would be in the hands of the *Imām* (art. 3). He would have to be a born Indonesian, a Muslim and obedient to God and His Prophet (art. 12). In matters of principle he would be supported by a *Déwan Fatwa* (a council for giving considered legal opinions), consisting of at most 7 *muftis* under the leadership of a "Great Mufti" (art. 21), while for matters of daily administration a *Déwan Imamah* (Imamate Council) would be appointed by the *Imām* to help him (art. 22). According to art. 24 taxes would disappear and be replaced by *infaq* (compare *al-infaḳ*, the "spending of contribution" in Sura 17 : 100). Important and responsible civil and military posts would be given only to Muslims (art. 28). As a Parliament could not yet be elected, obviously all power lay from the beginning in the hands of the *Imām*, Kartosuwirjo himself, who was moreover Commander-in-Chief of the T.I.I.[125a]

In September 1949 a government committee under the leadership of Muh. Natsir was formed to look for a solution to the D.I. problem. This committee, however, could do very little.[126] Probably as chairman of this committee Natsir made a new attempt in June 1950 to get in touch with Kartosuwirjo by sending Wali Alfatah, an old friend of Kartosuwirjo's, to meet him.[127] The latter, however, let it be known that he would only receive one of the highest authorities of the Republic, and not this envoy.[128]

But Kartosuwirjo may have been hoping for an understanding with the Republic during the Natsir cabinet (September 1950 to March 1951). On October 22nd, 1950, Kartosuwirjo approached President Soekarno in a secret letter, with a copy to Prime Minister Natsir, to express his pleasure that the Republic of Indonesia had decided to become a member of the United Nations. Through this decision a choice would have to be made between the American and Russian blocs. Indonesia's policy of neutrality, then, would have to be abandoned and exchanged for an anti-Communist course. So he urged that as soon as possible a definite end should be put to Communist influence in Indonesia. On the other hand, nationalism, he said, was not an ideology comparable with Islam and Communism, and this would not be capable of saving Indonesia. Therefore they would now have to choose: either Islam or Communism! And according to Kartosuwirjo Indonesia could, of course, only be saved if Islam became the basis of government and state; in other words, if the Republic of Indonesia changed its character from a "national state" to an Islamic State.[129]

On November 14th, 1950, Prime Minister Natsir broadcast a moving speech to "the freedom fighters who have not yet returned to normal life", because they "do not yet feel satisfied with the results of the struggle for freedom, or are still standing aloof as a result of mutual conflicts during the past years of the fight for freedom". He called

---

[125a] For the Indonesian text of the *Kanun Azasy* see Appendix IV.
[126] Van Nieuwenhuijze, *Aspects,* p. 173.
[127] According to Alers, *Rode of Groene,* p. 251, Wali Alfatah left on June 8th, was taken prisoner by the Darul Islam, and on June 20th was released by Republican soldiers. Feith, *The Decline,* p. 172, gives the impression that it occurred during the Natsir cabinet, that is to say, after September 6th, 1950; likewise Anne Marie Thé, *Darah,* p. 9.
[128] According to Anne Marie Thé, *Darah,* p. 10.
[129] I have considered the text of this letter curious enough to warrant putting it in full in Indonesian at the end of this book (see Appendix II).

on them to abandon their guerilla methods and to devote themselves to the development of the new Indonesian state. In doing so, they would have every opportunity to fight for their ideals in an orderly manner.[130]

I do not know whether there was any reaction to this call. But on February 17th, 1951 a second "secret letter" was sent by Kartosuwirjo to President Soekarno, again with a copy to Prime Minister Natsir. Was this Kartosuwirjo's reaction to Natsir's efforts? Kartosuwirjo wanted to clarify and make additions to some points made in his first letter. As far as the choice between America and Russia was concerned, he was convinced that a Third World War was inevitable and imminent (he was thinking of Korea). Therefore he called once again for the extermination of Communism in Indonesia. Concerning his proclamation of the Islamic State of Indonesia on August 7th, 1949, Kartosuwirjo now explained that this proclamation was basically a holy right of the Islamic *Umma* of Indonesia, but that talks could be opened on practical questions concerning the area and borders of this state. If the government of the Republic of Indonesia was prepared to recognize officially the proclamation of the Islamic State of Indonesia (N.I.I.) as legitimate, then he could guarantee that the Republic would have a friend in life and death (that is, the N.I.I.), against every sort of danger from abroad or from within her borders. This applied in particular to Communism, which more and more endangered the country and people of Indonesia, as well as the whole democratic world. If, however, this was not agreed, then Kartosuwirjo could no longer hold himself responsible for the fate of the country and people of Indonesia, neither before the Judgement Seat of history nor before the Judgement Seat of God.[131]

One month later Natsir's cabinet fell. After a vigorous tug-of-war between the parties, a Masjumi-P.N.I. cabinet under the leadership of Sukiman (Masjumi) came into being. This cabinet promised a harder military line against the rebels until safe conditions had been restored, as had been demanded by army officers again and again.[132] Meanwhile, however, new difficulties had arisen in the South Moluccas, in South Sulawesi and in Atjeh, so that Kartosuwirjo's D.I. could for the time being continue its activities in West Java.

In the following years the Darul Islam in West Java seemed more and more to degenerate into terrorizing and plundering gangs which could

---

[130] Cf. M. Natsir, *Capita Selecta*, Bandung/Djakarta 1954/1957, Vol. II, pp. 8-10.
[131] For the text of this letter see Appendix III.
[132] Cf. Feith, *The Decline*, p. 211.

not return to normal life in society. The rise of Kartosuwirjo's D.I. can be explained from a mixture of religious and non-religious factors, an ideological background plus all sorts of political circumstances and personal interests. Some time around 1950 there may even have been co-operation between the D.I. and colonial diehards such as the Dutch Captain Westerling.[133] So in its later development this movement can certainly be counted among the *quasi*-ideological guerilla organizations which endangered the life of the Republic.[134]

Anticipating the historical sequence of this survey, the story of Kartosuwirjo can be completed here. From about 1960, Kartosuwirjo's following clearly began to decrease; many of his followers deserted or were taken prisoner. Some lost their belief in their leader when he was wounded by a bullet on April 24th, 1962, and appeared to be not invulnerable at all.[135] Finally, on June 4th, 1962 Kartosuwirjo was himself captured, having been discovered by an army patrol in a hut on the hill Geber in the district Patjet between Bogor and Tjiandjur. According to the story by Anne Marie Thé — written for the Forces — Kartosuwirjo was found seriously ill and exhausted, but he recovered when well looked after for several months. On August 16th, 1962, he was sentenced to death, on a charge of attempting to overthrow the Republic of Indonesia and having ordered the attempt to assassinate President Soekarno on May 14th, 1962. As a request for a reprieve was refused by the President, the death-sentence was carried out "somewhere in Indonesia one day in September 1962". Thus the history of the Darul Islam in West Java ended, and safety returned to the area. To quote the rather highflown phrases of Anne Marie Thé, the moral of the story is this: "No mountain is too high, no ravine too deep, no river too rapid, no forest too dense to form an obstacle for the soldiers of our army... defending the Proclamation, the Revolution and the Pantjasila... He who deviates will experience total destruction." [136]

Concerning the history of Kahar Muzakkar and his revolt in South Sulawesi (Celebes), there is less, and less trustworthy, evidence available. Nevertheless an attempt will be made to draw a preliminary sketch, indicating the questions which demand further research.

Kahar Muzakkar — his original name was La Domeng — probably came of the Buginese aristocracy and was born about 1920 in Luwu'

---
[133] Cf. Pinardi, *Kartosuwirjo*, pp. 103-150.
[134] Feith, *The Decline*, p. 81.
[135] Cf. Pinardi, *Kartosuwirjo*, p. 48.
[136] Cf. Anne Marie Thé, *Darah*, p. 16.

(South Sulawesi). For his secondary school education (which he did not finish) he was sent to a Muhammadijah school in Solo (Central Java). Married to a Javanese girl from Solo, he returned to his birthplace during the Japanese occupation. Here, however, he was *ripaoppangi-tana*, a Buginese word which apparently means that a person is ostracized and banned from the country forever by the *Datu'* (*radja* or *adat*-chief) of Luwu'. Why? Perhaps because it was in conflict with the *adat* for him to have married a Javanese woman?

Back in Java, Kahar Muzakkar became a trader. During the fight for freedom (1945-1950) he played a leading part in the K.R.I.S. (*Kebaktian Rakjat Indonesia Sulawesi*, the Service of the Indonesian People of Sulawesi). From the middle of 1946 he organized guerilla bands consisting of young men originating from South Sulawesi who sailed over in proas (Ind. *perahu*) in successive batches to fight for freedom there. According to Bahar Mattalioe, these troops of Kahar's included many ex-prisoners from Nusakambangan and Tjilatjap, well-known places of detention on the south coast of Central Java. As an answer to these guerilla activities organized by Kahar Muzakkar from Java, the notorious Captain Westerling with his colonial troops adopted a policy of revenge which — according to a generally held Indonesian opinion — resulted in about 40,000 victims in South Sulawesi.[137] Kahar himself meanwhile remained in Java, where he was involved in the battle for Malang (East Java) in July 1947, together with Bahar Mattalioe. On that occasion he insulted his later "biographer" by calling him "Bahar the Coward", an insult that the latter obviously never forgot or forgave!

After the recognition of Independence and the formation of the federal R.I.S. (December 1949) all kinds of tensions emerged in South Sulawesi, especially around Makassar, the former capital of the "State of East Indonesia". Behind these tensions lay contrasts between federalists and unionists, between regional aristocracy and Indonesian-thinking nationalists, between the former colonial army (K.N.I.L.) and the Republican T.N.I., and even between the T.N.I. and the ex-guerillas. The ex-guerillas demanded that they should be incorporated *en bloc*

---

[137] On December 19th, 1947 a representative of the Republic of Indonesia informed the United Nations that the number of victims in South Sulawesi could be estimated at 20,000-40,000. In an official Dutch report (*Rapport Enthoven*) dating from 1948, the total number of victims was said to be 3,114 (see *Nota betreffende het Archievenonderzoek naar gegevens omtrent excessen in Indonesië begaan door Nederlandse militairen in de periode 1945-1950*, 's-Gravenhage 1969, Bijlage 2, p. 17).

into the national army, and should remain together as a separate unit. The military commander for East Indonesia, Colonel Kawilarang, however, only wanted a number of selected guerillas accepted into the T.N.I. and the rest discharged. Bahar Mattalioe says that he himself wrote a letter to Headquarters in Djakarta and to President Soekarno, asking Kahar Muzakkar to be sent immediately to South Sulawesi, "because only he is able to find a solution, as he himself has created the guerilla troops and has become a symbol to them".[138] Indeed, Kahar was promptly sent to Makassar with the rank of Lieutenant-Colonel.

Did Kahar — who certainly had both the desire and the abilities for leadership — hope to play the role of "the strong man of South Sulawesi", who could now return to his area as a kind of "messianic king" in order to take the helm? Unfortunately, his coming immediately led to a clash between him and Colonel Kawilarang, as Kahar also demanded that his ex-guerillas should form a separate army unit, becoming a brigade under himself. When Kawilarang refused, Kahar left Makassar on July 5th, 1950, to join the guerillas in the jungle. This was the beginning of a long guerilla struggle, which afterwards spread from South Sulawesi to South-East Sulawesi (the area north of Kendari). In October 1950, Prime Minister Natsir said that "there are not 10,000 guerillas in South Sulawesi but a multiple of this number"; Feith speaks of 20,000 men "controlling sizable areas of the mountainous south-western peninsula of Sulawesi and apparently enjoying a significant amount of popular support".[139]

Throughout the months of October 1950 to March 1951, the central government seemed to be arriving at a compromise with Kahar Muzakkar, thanks to Prime Minister Natsir. On August 17th, 1951, preparations had been made in Makassar for a great ceremony to incorporate Kahar and 4,000 of his men into the national army, but it turned out that at the eleventh hour they had left the city, taking with them trucks, weapons, ammunition, uniforms and money. A letter was left behind saying that the army authorities had not kept their word and had not released Kahar's followers who had been imprisoned, and not transferred certain reactionary officers from Makassar.[140] Did perhaps the replacement of the Natsir cabinet by that of Sukiman (April 26th, 1951) play a role here too?

---

[138] Bahar Mattalioe, *Kahar*, p. 33.
[139] Feith, *The Decline*, p. 212.
[140] Feith, *The Decline*, p. 213.

However that may be, it seems clear that the rising in South Sulawesi initially had little to do with Darul Islam ideals. One important background factor could well be questions of prestige and resentment among Buginese-Makassarese patriots over against army authorities who came to this area from outside. The pamphlet by Zainabun Harahap makes a passing reference to the psychological factor of the differences between various ethnic groups (*suku*) as the background for this rising, for "the *suku*-feelings which were instilled by Kahar's bands had deep roots in the soul of the people".[141]

Only after the break with the central government did Kahar Muzakkar try to make contact with Kartosuwirjo, and did the rising get the ideological background of the D.I. Nevertheless, according to oral information, even then there were still Christian guerillas among Kahar's following, e.g. from North Sulawesi and the South Moluccas, who did not want to accept the unitary state forced by "Djakarta".

On January 20th, 1952, Kahar wrote a letter to Kartosuwirjo "accepting an appointment as Sulawesi commander of Kartosuwirjo's Islamic Army of Indonesia".[142] Bahar Mattalioe notes that probably on August 7th, 1953 — thus on the anniversary of Kartosuwirjo's Islamic State — Kahar's troops got the name of *Tentara Islam Indonesia* (T.I.I.), the Islamic Army of Indonesia, "preceded by the proclamation of the Darul Islam which was declared to be a part of Kartosuwirjo's Islamic State of Indonesia in West Java".[143]

This proclamation was perhaps made at a meeting in Makalua (South Sulawesi). Unfortunately Bahar Mattalioe does not mention the date and year of this meeting. And from the "Makalua Charter" which resulted he quotes only 19 of the more than 50 articles.[144] From these stipulations one could perhaps conclude that Kahar Muzakkar was a radical revolutionary, who meant well and held certain high Islamic ideals. In this Charter, Nationalist and Communist parties (P.N.I., Murba, P.K.I.) were said to be hypocritical and godless, and therefore had to be exterminated (art. 12). Islamic parties such as the Masjumi, N.U. and P.S.I.I. were considered counter-revolutionary, and had to disappear (art. 13). All feudalists who liked using titles and words such as *opu, karaeng, andi, daeng, hadji, gede-bagus, sajjid, teuku* or *raden*,

---

[141] Zainabun Harahap, *Operasi*, p. 6.
[142] Feith, *The Decline*, p. 214.
[143] Bahar Mattalioe, *Kahar*, p. 37.
[144] Bahar Mattalioe, *Kahar*, p. 38 and pp. 82-89; it may be possible to collect more complete material on this question.

had to be combatted (art. 16). Several articles were devoted to the care of victims of the revolution (widows, orphans, invalids).

As far as marriage regulations were concerned, it was stipulated, for example, that "he who opposes polygamy must be brought to trial" (art. 45). Bahar Mattalioe seizes upon this regulation to blacken Kahar's moral life and to express his pity for Kahar's second wife, a Eurasian girl named Corry van Stenus, who was a tremendous support to Kahar in his struggles between 1947 and 1965. This regulation concerning "compulsory polygamy", however, turns out to have been intended as a solution to the social problem of the widows of the war dead, and may therefore be considered an authentic Islamic solution.[145]

Finally the Charter stipulated that during the revolution the regulations concerning property would be strictly enforced; the purchase of land, factories and other capital possessions was forbidden (art. 49) — so too the use of all luxury articles and jewellery: gold, precious stones, silk materials, hair-oil, lip-stick, face-powder, and food coming from cities in the hands of the enemy, such as chocolate, butter, cheese and biscuits (art. 50).

Similar questions seem to have been broached in a pamphlet by Kahar Muzakkar, perhaps entitled "Remarks on Spiritual Questions" (*Tjatatan Bathin*), and apparently intended to combat the evils which had arisen among his following.[146] Stating that external conditions could not be improved without considering internal, spiritual ones, Kahar commanded that within 6 months, beginning on March 1st, 1955, a spiritual revolution must take place among his people and their families. To this end, all luxuries (gold rings and other jewellery, wrist-watches for private use, etc.) had immediately to be sold for the benefit of the general funds. Pressure lamps (*Petromax*) and radios for private use were also forbidden. A list of men's and women's clothing stipulated exactly what one person might own; the rest had to be given away for the benefit of those with less. Similar restrictions for a sober life were laid down with regard to the use of foreign cigarettes and luxury foodstuffs such as chocolate, butter and cheese.

Apparently Kahar acted rigorously on occasion, for example, by ordering the punishment of cutting off the hand of a thief (Sura 5 : 38) to take place in public, as a horrifying deterrent.[147] Orally obtained

---

[145] Cf. Bahar Mattalioe, *Kahar*, p. 63.
[146] Cf. Bahar Mattalioe, *Kahar*, pp. 50-57; it may not be impossible to get a copy of this pamphlet by Kahar (entitled "Tjatatan Bathin" or "Revolusi Bathin"?), although the authorities ordered all copies to be destroyed.
[147] Bahar Mattalioe, *Kahar*, p. 80.

information confirmed the fact that Kahar personally was wont to act harshly against evils and abuses. According to some informants, however, many bad elements from the urban rabble in Makassar sought refuge in joining Kahar Muzakkar's bands. It might have been these people who gave his movement a bad name by murdering, plundering and burning, while Kahar himself is said to have been of a most noble character.

I received similar information with regard to the persecution of Christians in South Sulawesi, which got much publicity outside Indonesia. In 1953, for example, it was stated that "lately alarming news came from southern Celebes, where partisans of a rebellious faction led by Kahar Muzakkar committed atrocities against Christian Toraja and attempted to convert them to Islâm by violent means".[148] Muslim informants in South Sulawesi assured me that Kahar himself condemned this sort of behaviour. One Christian informant said that he could have met leaders of Kahar's movement without any trouble whatsoever, at least in the early years.[149]

From Bahar Mattalioe's story it appears that in 1955 Kahar received a letter from someone resident in Singapore who called himself the "Minister of Foreign Affairs of the Darul Islam (Atjeh)", asking for closer contact with the movement in South Sulawesi.[150] Some months later Kahar was able to receive an authorized person from this D.I. Minister at a conference of commanders in Wanua Waru (South Sulawesi).[151]

A few years later contacts and agreements were made between Kahar's movement and the *Permesta* ("Common Struggle Movement") in North Sulawesi, one of the so-called Christian areas of Indonesia. Likewise contact existed between Kahar and the Revolutionary Government in Sumatra (*Pemerintah Revolusioner Republik Indonesia,* P.R.R.I.) pro-

---

[148] Drewes in *Unity,* ed. by Von Grunebaum, p. 308.
[149] Perhaps we should also ask to what extent such conflicts between Muslims and Christians were in fact caused by differences between certain ethnic groups of the population (*suku*) and, for example, are partly to be explained as a reaction of (Muslim) Buginese and Makassarese people against the constantly increasing influence of the (Christian) Toradja people in South Sulawesi and in the city of Makassar. To what extent did this background even play a role in the incidents of October 1st, 1967?
[150] Who was this person? Could it by chance be a certain Hassan Tiro? If not, who then was or is Hassan Tiro? According to vague information, a certain Hassan Tiro, an Atjehnese, acted as representative of the D.I. movement abroad, later on lived in the U.S.A. and acted there as "representative" of the prohibited Egyptian organization of the "Muslim Brethren".
[151] Bahar Mattalioe, *Kahar,* p. 57 ff.

claimed in February 1958.[152] New weapons and ammunition were obtained from the *Permesta*. This contact also strengthens the impression that Kahar's revolt was not in the first place a matter of principle, based on the Darul Islam ideology, but a rebellion of ex-guerillas against army authorities, combined with regional patriotism.

After 1960 troops of the national army (T.N.I.) were able to intensify their campaign against Kahar Muzakkar, who by that time had moved his headquarters to South-East Sulawesi, to the north of Kendari.[153] However, it was not until the beginning of 1965 that the T.N.I. could push on with a decisive campaign, which on February 3rd, 1965 resulted in Kahar and his bodyguard's being surrounded at a place in South-East Sulawesi near the village of Lawali on the Lasolo River. Kahar himself was shot before he could throw his hand grenade. This brought the rising in South Sulawesi to a definite end.

It seems, however, that the name of Kahar Muzakkar is still kept alive in South Sulawesi, not only among those who remember the murders, plundering and burning with horror, but also among people who are still wont to speak with deep reverence of "Pak Kahar" (Father Kahar). Even now in South Sulawesi one can meet people of good intentions who still seem to live and work in a way inspired by their contact with "Pak Kahar". Does not this reverence highlight the contrast with public opinion on Kartosuwirjo, whose memory is apparently no longer cherished in West Java?

Developments in Atjeh which in 1953 resulted in a rising against "Djakarta" were perhaps less a product of chance circumstances than the revolts in West Java and South Sulawesi. Atjeh was — and to a considerable extent still is — a closed society. The Atjehnese proudly call their area *sramòë Meukah* (Ind. *serambi Mekkah*), the "verandah of Mecca". Originally this may have been a geographical conception: the coasters with prospective *hadji*s from other parts of Indonesia called at Atjeh as last port of call in the Archipelago. Later this epithet took on the symbolic meaning of a truly Islamic area.

At the end of 1945 a kind of social revolution had taken place in Atjeh when the people, led by the *ulama*s, had settled accounts with the former "lords of the country", the *ulèëbalang*s. These were the two

---

[152] Bahar Mattalioe, *Kahar*, p. 89 ff.; exact information on these contacts cannot be culled from this source, as the author is obviously confused as to the historical order of events.

[153] Cf. Zainabun Harahap, *Operasi*, p. 9 ff.

leading groups in Atjeh. A third group, such as the "secular" nationalists in Java, hardly existed in Atjeh. Owing to the regional patriotism of Atjeh, organizations from outside — political parties as well as, for instance, the Muhammadijah — had little following there.

According to Atjehnese opinion, temporal and spiritual power originally formed a dual unity there. Temporal or worldly power lay officially in the hands of the Sultan, with the title *Tuanku,* but in fact was exercised by roughly 100 district chiefs, the *ulèëbalang*s (Ind. *hulubalang,* originally "war-lord"). The *ulèëbalang*-ship was an inherited position held by the *Teuku*s (abbr. T.), the Atjehnese aristocracy. Spiritual authority was in the hands of the *ulama*s, in Atjeh with the general title of *Teungku* (abbr. Tgk.). Corresponding to this was the dual unity of *adat*-law (embodied in the Sultan and the *ulèëbalang*s) and Islamic law (represented by the *ulama*s), which according to Atjehnese opinion could not be divorced from each other and did not conflict with each other.

The dual unity of worldly and spiritual authority was broken by the arrival of the Dutch, which was the reason for the outbreak of the Atjehnese struggle for the defence of their freedom, beginning on March 26th, 1873. At the outset the Sultan, the *ulèëbalang*s and the *ulama*s stood together against the Dutch. But on January 10th, 1903, the Sultan was captured and from then on played no role.[154] Colonial authority was established by making use of the disunity among the *ulèëbalang*s, and by fitting them into the colonial civil administration. From that time stemmed the opposition and conflict between the *ulèëbalang*s and the *ulama*s, and it was this conflict which would be decisive for further developments in Atjeh. In 1939 the *ulama*s were united in the P.U.S.A. (*Persatuan Ulama-ulama Seluruh Atjeh,* All-Atjeh Ulama Union). At the end of 1945 these initials came to be used for the slogan *Pembasmian Ulèëbalang-ulèëbalang Seluruh Atjeh,* that is, the extermination of the *ulèëbalang*s of all Atjeh!

Concerning developments in Atjeh during the Japanese occupation, we may refer to A. J. Piekaar's book on Atjeh and the war with

---

[154] According to Atjehnese records, however, the Sultan continued to be active in secret, even in captivity, and Atjeh never capitulated to the colonial powers. For example, see T. Alibasjah Talsya (beside Ali Hasjmy one of the modern Atjehnese writers and poets), *Atjeh tidak pernah menjerahkan kedaulatan kepada Belanda,* in *Sinar Darussalam, Madjallah Pengetahuan dan Kebudajaan* (an Atjehnese monthly), no. 12, March-April 1969, pp. 59-65.

Japan.[155] Regarding Atjeh he arrived at the same conclusion as did Aziz and Benda later when writing about Indonesia as a whole, namely that the period of the Japanese occupation resulted in a strengthening of the position of the *ulama*s (in Atjeh by undermining the power of the *ulèëbalang*s in the political and legal fields, for instance). According to Piekaar, this meant that Snouck Hurgronje's statement was no longer valid, namely that "the *adat* assumes the part of the mistress and the *hukōm* [Ind. *hukum*, Islamic law] that of her obedient slave".[156] Now a balance was created which could only end in conflict. And "as a result of the course of events after the Japanese capitulation, it seems that for the time being the *ulama*s have emerged from this conflict as the winners", said Piekaar in 1949.[157] Piekaar adds that it would be an over-simplification to imply that the clash was a religious conflict between *adat* and *hukum*, as political, economic and cultural factors also played a part. In any case, the *ulèëbalang*s had compromised themselves as accomplices of the colonial authorities; they were the landowners, and because they could afford to send their children to schools where they were taught in Dutch, they obtained a cultural monopoly and blocked the way of young people educated at other schools. According to Atjehnese informants, only these factors were of importance, so that it was in fact in no way a religious conflict, merely a political and social one. It is therefore understandable that the majority of the people chose the side of the *ulama*s when the conflict with the *ulèëbalang*s erupted.

After the Japanese had promised independence for Indonesia (September 7th, 1944), people in Atjeh grew more interested in what was happening in Java. "All eyes were turned to the nationalist movement in the main island, the appeasement of which was the chief reason for the Japanese premier's declaration. Java, under the leadership of Soe-

---

[155] A. J. Piekaar, *Atjèh en de oorlog met Japan*, 's-Gravenhage/Bandung 1949. Atjehnese sources with scattered information concerning the developments in Atjeh during the Japanese period and after are the following books and pamphlets: *Modal Revolusi 45*, ed. by Seksi Penerangan/Dokumentasi Komité Musjawarah Angkatan 45 Daerah Istimewa Atjeh, 1961; *Atjeh Membangun*, ed. by Pemerintah Daerah Istimewa Atjeh, 1961; *Darussalam*, ed. by Jajasan Dana Kesedjahteraan Atjeh, 1963; and finally the stencilled publication *Dewan Perwakilan Rakjat Atjeh (Dalam sedjarah pembentukan dan perkembangan Pemerintahan di Atjeh sedjak Proklamasi 1945 sampai awal tahun 1968) dan Produk-produk Legislatif*, ed. by Sekretariat D.P.R.D.-G.R. Propinsi Daerah Istimewa Atjeh, 1968.
[156] C. Snouck Hurgronje, *The Achehnese*, Leiden 1906, Vol. I, p. 153.
[157] Piekaar, *Atjèh*, p. 330.

karno, set the pace ..."; hence "during that last year in Atjeh too the seed was sown for a growing national Indonesian awareness".[158]

When at the end of August 1945 the proclamation of the Republic of Indonesia (August 17th) began to be known in Atjeh, the people, led by the *ulama*s (and a few *ulèëbalang*s who could understand the coming changes) made their stand for the new Republic. British and Dutch troops occupied the island of Sabang off the coast of Atjeh. They did not intend landing in Atjeh itself. Neither was Atjeh invaded from North Sumatra (where Medan was occupied by the Dutch and later on the "State of East Sumatra" was created). So it was in Atjeh that the colonial administration was not established anew after 1945. For this reason Atjeh afterwards got another honorific title: the *daérah modal* of the Republic of Indonesia, the "region of capital", that is, the area which spiritually and materially remained an untouched capital for the Republic during the years 1945-1950.

However, in August 1945 the Atjehnese had to face the possibility of a Dutch attempt to re-occupy their country. Allied aircraft had already dropped pamphlets with a naïve message about the liberation of Indonesia, ending with "Long live the Queen! Long live Indonesia!" [159] Apparently preparations had already been made by some *ulèëbalang*s to receive the Allied forces. Of course they hoped that their old position of power would soon be restored, so that the changes which had taken place in favour of the *ulama*s during the Japanese period would be reversed.[160] But on October 15th, 1945, the *ulama*s began to distribute a pamphlet in which the fight for the Republic of Indonesia under President Soekarno against the Dutch was declared a Holy War (*Perang Sabil*).[161] This declaration was made "in the name of the *ulama*s of all Atjeh" and was signed by four of them, including Tgk. Muhammad Daud Beureu'éh, who had held a leading position in the P.U.S.A. from the beginning.

By order of the Allies the Japanese troops remained to keep order in Atjeh till December 1945. After some incidents they were removed, but according to Piekaar a significant number remained behind and afterwards acted as instructors for the Indonesian troops.[162] After the Japanese had left, civil war broke out in earnest. Under the leadership

---
[158] Piekaar, *Atjèh*, pp. 234-235.
[159] A copy of this propaganda pamphlet has been printed from a block in the abovementioned booklet *Modal Revolusi*, p. 28.
[160] Cf. Piekaar, *Atjèh*, p. 247.
[161] Printed in *Modal Revolusi* from a block, p. 61.
[162] Piekaar, *Atjèh*, p. 250.

of the *ulamas* — in particular Daud Beureu'éh — an end was put to the *uléëbalangs*' power. Between December 1945 and February 1946, the *uléëbalangs* and their families were for the most part massacred; others were interned.[163]

Naturally the young people took an important part in this conflict. In the Japanese period they had been organized into the A.P.I. (*Angkatan Pemuda Indonesia*, Brigade of Indonesian Youth) set up by the Japanese, and into the illegal I.P.I. (*Ikatan Pemuda Indonesia*, Association of Indonesian Youth) under the leadership of Ali Hasjmy, who later became governor of Atjeh. The latter group was transformed into an army group, comparable with the Hizbu'llah in Java.

From 1947 Daud Beureu'éh was military governor of the province of North Sumatra on behalf of the Republic of Indonesia (in fact governor of Atjeh, as the other areas of North Sumatra were occupied by the Dutch). In the provisional parliament in Jogja (K.N.I.P.) there were four members representing Atjeh. But in 1948 Atjeh got its own regional administrative organization, so that it could develop independently. Financial and economic problems could for the time being be solved by barter with Malaya. As a result of the second Dutch military campaign (December 19th, 1948) a Republican emergency government, formed under Sjafruddin Prawiranegara in West Sumatra, took over the authority of "Jogja". In 1949 this government accepted Atjeh's demand to become, *de jure,* an autonomous province of the Republic, with Daud Beureu'éh as governor.[164] After the central government in Jogja had recovered its position, thanks to United Nations' mediation, it attempted to reverse this development. A sharp reaction in Atjeh, however, forced the central government to agree that Atjeh should continue to exist *de facto* as a province.

According to information gathered in Atjeh, from the beginning of 1950 left-wing factions in the *pusat* (the central government in Djakarta) carried on a campaign against Atjeh as a separate province, while left-wing papers such as *Harian Rakjat* (Medan) spread the rumour that Atjeh was preparing a rising in order to secede from the Republic. These rumours were said to have inspired the central government to appoint the Atjehnese Nazir as military commander of Atjeh. Some people in Atjeh knew this Nazir to have had Communist sympathies for a long

---

[163] See also Kahin, *Nationalism,* p. 179, n. 51.
[164] Cf. Alers, *Rode of Groene,* p. 265 ff.

time. However, a warning from Atjeh against this appointment was disregarded by "Djakarta".[165]

At the end of 1950 the problem flared up in earnest, after the government in Djakarta had decided that Atjeh should be united with Tapanuli and East Sumatra into one province of North Sumatra.[166] Governor Daud Beureu'éh then became redundant and was appointed to a post in Djakarta. But he refused to accept this and resigned from government service. The situation remained tense until 1952, without matters coming to a head. It is understandable that Daud Beureu'éh tried to prevent an open rupture as long as possible. "We must not consider him an irresponsible person who used Islam only as a political cover, while luxuriating in his own power." [167] Daud Beureu'éh may have adopted a moderate attitude for as long as the Republic was led by a Muslim or by the Masjumi, but the situation clearly changed after the cabinet of Ali Sastroamidjojo (P.N.I.) came to office on August 1st, 1953.[168]

According to information acquired in Atjeh, left-wing politicians in Djakarta had earlier in 1953 begun to spread the rumour that Atjeh was indeed organizing a rising. As a result of this rumour "Djakarta" listed 190 prominent Atjehnese who were to be arrested. In July 1953 this became known in Atjeh; later on it turned out that this list of names had probably been leaked on purpose. As these leading Atjehnese had the feeling that they might be arrested, they decided to take to the mountains on September 19th, 1953. This was the official break with "Djakarta", and the beginning of the so-called Darul Islam revolt in Atjeh.

---

[165] Piekaar, *Atjèh*, pp. 238 and 257, mentioned this Nazir, appointed by the Japanese as *ulèëbalang* of Tapa'tuan and later officer in the "people's army". Piekaar supposed that Nazir did not come from an *ulèëbalang* family. Information which I got in Atjeh supports this guess. I was told that Nazir, as an ordinary boy from South Atjeh, had had a secondary modern school education and came under Communist influence at that time; later on it was clear that he had connections with the Politburo. Via the A.P.I. youth movement of Japanese origin, he became an officer in the national army. After the unsuccessful coup d'etat of September 30th, 1965, Nazir was arrested. His family and relatives in Atjeh were for the most part murdered, although — according to an Atjehnese informant — they were probably not Communists at all. Nazir himself was sentenced to death by a military court in Medan in 1968, because he was considered to have been involved in the attempted coup d'etat in 1965.
[166] Feith, *The Decline*, p. 345.
[167] Alers, *Rode of Groene*, p. 269.
[168] Alers, *Rode of Groene*, pp. 269-270, supposes that Daud Beureu'éh still had confidence in the Wilopo cabinet (March 1952) but he makes the mistake of calling this P.N.I. leader Wilopo a Masjumi member.

Indeed, contact was made with Kartosuwirjo in West Java, even though Atjeh was certainly not thinking of being absorbed into Kartosuwirjo's Islamic State. In the years which followed, in Atjeh too — as in West Java — the central government and the national army were present in some towns and in the capital (Kutaradja, now called Banda Atjeh), whereas the countryside was largely controlled by the "rebels" under Daud Beureu'éh, certainly supported by the people.

Anticipating our chronological scheme here too, it can be said that in the years 1954-1956 "Djakarta" came to realize that a military solution to the difficulties with Atjeh was not possible. According to Atjehnese information, all the advice which the central government gathered from Atjehnese living outside Atjeh indicated that Atjeh should remain a separate province and not become just part of a province. Probably many people in the central government did not sufficiently realize how difficult it was for the population of Atjeh to form one community with the other ethnic groups of Northern Sumatra.[169]

Pressed by Parliament, Minister Sunarjo (Home Affairs in the 2nd cabinet of Ali Sastroamidjojo) visited Atjeh in October 1956. He agreed that Atjeh should be recognized as a separate province; moreover, Ali Hasjmy was appointed governor and Sjamaun Gaharu military commander. On January 27th, 1957, Ali Hasjmy was installed during another visit by Minister Sunarjo. Talks between the new governor and Daud Beureu'éh led to a cease-fire agreement in March 1957, but the announcement and enforcement of the cease-fire took a long time. In May 1959 representatives of the central government once again came to Atjeh, led by Minister Hardi. Three-cornered negotiations were opened between "Djakarta" (Hardi), the province of Atjeh (Ali Hasjmy) and the Darul Islam (Daud Beureu'éh). The outcome was that on May 26th, 1959, an agreement was signed by which Atjeh was recognized as *daérah istiméwa* (a special administrative district) with autonomy particularly in religious affairs, in questions of *adat* and in matters of education, on the understanding that this autonomy should not come into conflict with the Constitution.

It is obvious that these conditions were made by Daud Beureu'éh, and that the central government had to satisfy these demands in order to reach an agreement with Atjeh. Indeed, from the time of this

---

[169] What reactions the Bataks, as dog and pig-keeping Christians, provoke in their northerly neighbours, the strictly Islamic Atjehnese, is told in a way hardly flattering to the Bataks by M. P. M. Muskens, *Indonesië, Een strijd om nationale identiteit*, thesis Nijmegen 1969, p. 325 ff.

agreement peace returned to Atjeh. The Darul Islam troops came down from the mountains at the end of 1959 and were largely incorporated into the national army. Daud Beureu'éh, now an ordinary citizen — with a government pension as ex-governor — has devoted himself to the development of his homeland by playing a leading part in projects for the improvement of roads and irrigation. Under the leadership of Ali Hasjmy, on December 2nd, 1959, a start was made on the building of a university and students' city about four miles outside the capital, Banda Atjeh, with the significant name *Darussalam* (the Abode of Peace), another old epithet for this region.

In 1962 Kartosuwirjo was executed, and the memory of his activities in West Java now seems almost obliterated. In 1965 Kahar Muzakkar was shot, but in South Sulawesi his name seems to live on, among some people in thankful remembrance. Daud Beureu'éh, the chief man of Atjeh, survived the rising and to an important extent was able to impose his conditions for peace between Atjeh and "Djakarta". Does this mean that the problems of Atjeh have really been solved? To what extent has autonomy in Atjeh itself in fact been realized? To what extent does this solution, too, threaten to create new problems? These questions will be dealt with in the concluding chapter of this book, although even then many of them will have to be left open.

8. *Religio-Political Publications*

The attention and energies of Islamic leaders in the years 1945-1955 were concentrated on the political field. It can be taken that a large proportion of Muslim publications written during this time in Indonesian were also connected with this struggle. Probably it will prove impossible to recover and collect all the pamphlets and books dating from this period. The samples which follow here, however, look sufficiently important and representative to justify a brief characterization of their content.

One of the first publications from this period is probably the "Guide for the Holy War", written at the end of 1945 by Mohd. Arsjad Thalib Lubis in Medan.[170] The writer belonged to the strictly orthodox Shāfiʿī association *Djam'ijatul Waslijah* (more or less "Society for the Further-

---

[170] Mohd. Arsjad Thalib Lubis, *Tuntunan Perang Sabil*, Medan 1946; the second, unaltered edition is called *Penuntun Perang Sabil*, Medan 1957.

ance of Unity"), and is said to be "one of the *ulama*s and leaders of considerable calibre in Medan".[171] As a professor at the Al-Waslijah University in Medan, founded in 1958, he recently published a book on "The Unity of God according to the Teachings of Christianity and Islam", one of a whole array of publications opposing the Christian dogma of the Trinity.[172]

In the abovementioned pamphlet he first of all argues that the fight against the Dutch satisfied the conditions required for a Holy War, as (1) the fight could serve to promote Islam in Indonesia, (2) was in accordance with God's will, and (3) was directed against God's foes. In support of this claim he adduces pronouncements and *fatwa*s delivered by various Islamic organizations and *ulama*s. He goes on to explain the Islamic law with regard to the Holy War (pure intention, obedience to the leaders, prohibition on flight and cruelty, etc.), and the way in which during the Holy War one should observe one's religious duties (ablution, prayer, etc.). In solemn piety he depicts what happens to the believer who is killed in action (*mati sjahid*), and the reward he will receive. Various prayers and encouraging words are offered to the combatant. This booklet ends by pointing to the comfort of faith in God's decree (*taqdir*), which means that no-one dies before his time (Ind. *sebelum adjal berpantang mati*).

The book on "Islam and Politics" by Aziz Thaib, probably a collection of articles and speeches, seems to date from the latter part of 1946.[173] The author wants to show that Islam is not only a cultic religion, but that it offers clear-cut and practicable political principles for building a democratic, socialist welfare-state. The reader is roused to "fight in the way of God" against the N.I.C.A. heathen.[174] To stimulate his Muslim readers, the author reminds them of the hundreds of youths who have already died in this Holy War. The book ends with a chapter on training for leadership and a paper from the Department of Information on democracy according to the Constitution of 1945. Thus it offers an example of the rendering of Islamic principles in a modern political terminology.

---

[171] Wahid Hasjim, p. 210.
[172] (Mohd.) Arsjad Thalib Lubis, *Keesaan TUHAN menurut adjaran Kristen dan Islam*, Medan 1968.
[173] Aziz Thaib, *Islam dengan Politik*, Boekit Tinggi, no date; perhaps this writer, who is unknown to me, lived at that time in Central Sumatra and had something to do with the Republican Ministry of Information.
[174] N.I.C.A. = the Netherlands Indies Civil Administration, the provisional Dutch East Indies administration which returned at that time.

Much broader in conception and approach is the book by the well-known Indonesian writer HAMKA (abbreviation of *H*adji *A*bdul *M*alik *K*arim *A*mrullah) on "Religious Revolution", dating from 1946 but only known to me in the second (improved and enlarged) edition of 1949.[175] The author places the Indonesian revolution within the framework of the revolution or awakening of mankind, which in essence is a religious revolution or awakening, because religion creates real freedom, that is to say, the freedom of the spirit and soul (Ind. *djiwa*).

The first liberation of mankind was from "nature worship" for the service of God who sent His prophets and messengers to this end. Whenever the representatives of religion repressed the freedom of man, new revolutions occurred again and again, for example — a widespread idea in the Islamic world — the liberation from the domination of the Pope due to Luther. In the same way the French revolution meant liberation from the power of the clergy, and the Russian revolution meant liberation from the power of the Russian Orthodox Church. Even within Islam a revolution took place, thanks to such people as Muḥammad bin ᶜAbd al-Wahhāb, Djamāl al-Dīn al-Afghānī, Muḥammad ᶜAbduh and Aḥmad Khān.[176]

This religious revolution within Islam was the distinctive force behind the Indonesian fight for freedom, because the Indonesian revolution too was carried forward by the religious awakening: Muslims understood that they could only reach their aim through self-confidence and awareness of their own strength.[177]

The new, free Indonesia will take its place among the peoples of the world, and be conscious of its responsibility, as a people maintaining the Pantjasila ideals. Ultimately all these ideals can be reduced to the first

---

[175] HAMKA, *Revolusi Agama,* Djakarta 1949^2; the author, originally a writer, is now an influential publisher in the religious field, editor-in-chief of the magazine *Pandji Masjarakat, imām* of the Al-Azhar Mosque in Kebajoran Baru (Djakarta), and professor at the Al-Azhar University recently established there.

[176] This political awareness, linked to the reform movement in Islam, is a much loved theme in the publications of HAMKA, son of a West Sumatran teacher of religion and himself a passionate adherent of the Muhammadijah and Masjumi.

[177] Compare Sura 13:11, which modern Muslims like to quote and comment on as follows: God does not change the conditions of a people as long as that people does not itself make changes in the causes for its backwardness (Cf. *Al Qurāan dan Terdjemahnja,* ed. by the Ministry of Religion, Djakarta 1965-1969, Vol. II, p. 370, n. 768).

"pillar": the Belief in the One and Only God (*Ketuhanan Jang Maha Esa*), although in fact this belief is not to be found in one religion (Islam) only.

We must also mention here the very authoritative Islamic leader, writer and orator, the militant Muh. Isa Anshary (died 1969), according to Herbert Feith "an important political figure of radical fundamentalist conviction".[178] Born in 1916 in Central Sumatra, he lived since 1935 in Bandung (West Java), where he met and at first admired the student Soekarno. But being a devout Muslim and co-founder of a Muhammadijah branch in Bandung, he soon joined young men such as Muh. Natsir, "who had radical and modern opinions on religion".[179]

In 1949 he published his *Falsafah Perdjuangan Islam* (philosophy of the Islamic struggle), written in a compelling style.[180] He appealed for a spiritual fight against materialism, individualism, rationalism, egoism, capitalism, imperialism, etc. as essential for the fight for freedom. The true Holy War (*djihad*) meant more than the fight for freedom against the Dutch, which was merely a "little *djihad*". The "great *djihad*", however, was the fight of mankind against all sorts of passions as embodied in the list of -isms mentioned above.

Just as his friend HAMKA, the author traced the revolutionary *élan* to Islamic leaders on the reformist side, such as al-Afghānī and others. Here too the struggle of Islam is compared to the fight for freedom of the Protestants against the Pope and the Roman Catholic Church. The writer tries to explain the origin of the separation between Church and State in Europe, as well as the separation between religion and state in modern Turkey (where religion had decayed and was unsuitable for the development of the country). The author, however, does not advocate such a separation. On the contrary, he wants to call Muslims to renew Islam, to be active and to create a strong Islamic political party which will fight for the foundation of an Islamic State where people obey God's directives and strive for the well-being of society. This aim does not rest on the "negative factor" that 95 % of the Indonesian population adheres to Islam, but on the inner conviction of all Muslims that only with the help of Islam can this world be organized and improved.

---

[178] Feith, *The Decline*, p. 137.
[179] Wahid Hasjim, pp. 219-225, gives a short biography of Isa Anshary.
[180] M. Isa Anshary, *Falsafah Perdjuangan Islam*, Bandung 1949.

In an Appendix, the last chapter of the abovementioned book, the unity of religion and state is once more emphasized, because (1) Islam is not a private matter and (2) the state is the instrument to see that divine laws are put into operation, for the good of man. According to the heading, however, this last chapter was written by A. Muchlis, a pseudonym for Muh. Natsir. Its contents are the same as contained in the pamphlet on "Islam as an Ideology" which Muh. Natsir published under his own name, probably in 1950.[181] In his foreword, the author reminds the reader of Gibb's formula, which is very often quoted in Indonesian publications on Islam and given here as follows: "Islam is more than a religious system. It is a complete civilization." [182] In Indonesian publications this quotation is usually interpreted as supporting the unity of religion and politics in Islam, contrary to Christianity, which is usually characterized by Muslims as a religion only of the soul and the world to come.[183]

In this connection, the reader may be reminded of the two volumes entitled "Capita Selecta" by Muh. Natsir; part one contains articles from before 1941, and the second speeches and articles from the period 1950-1955.[184] We should also mention here Natsir's contribution in publishing and distributing an Indonesian version of a pamphlet by Leopold Weiss, alias Muhammad Asad, "Islamic Constitution Making".[185]

---

[181] Moh. Natsir, *Islam sebagai Ideologi*, with a short sketch of Natsir's life by Tamar Djaja, Djakarta, no date.

[182] This should be: "Islam is indeed much more than a system of theology; it is a complete civilization"; H. A. R. Gibb, *Whither Islam?*, p. 12. In this correct form it was quoted and translated by Natsir in 1936, perhaps for the first time in an Indonesian publication; cf. *Capita Selecta*, I, p. 3. As to the exact meaning of Gibb's words, we have to return to C. H. Becker, who stated that originally Islam was purely a religion, then after 622 (in Medina) also became a political power and during the next centuries developed into a complete civilization (especially during the ᶜAbbāsids). Afterwards, however, Islam lost its political power and in this way has continued to exist only as a religion and civilization. See his *Islamstudien*, I, Leipzig 1924, pp. 1-23.

[183] More correct and, I believe, worth considering, is Von Grunebaum's definition: "The principal difference between Islam and Christianity as sociological entities is that Islam can, but Christianity cannot, be viewed as a community of the 'nation' type" (G. E. von Grunebaum, *Modern Islam*, p. 181).

[184] M. Natsir, *Capita Selecta*, Vol. I, Bandung-'s-Gravenhage 1954; Vol. II, Djakarta 1957. Although Natsir does not have any political function at this moment, he is still an influential leader and he probably still has a part to play.

[185] Muhammad Asad (Leopold Weiss), *Undang-undang Politik Islam*, Djakarta 1954.

An interesting and important booklet concerning religious freedom within the new Republic was written in the middle of 1949 by Dr. Abu Hanifah, a well-known Masjumi member from 1945, afterwards Minister of Education in the first R.I.S. cabinet (1950).[186] In this pamphlet the writer criticizes the fears and meddling of foreigners abroad with regard to the freedom of religion in Indonesia, as had become evident from the Dutch press and the negotiations with the Netherlands on the independence of Indonesia.

The author advises these foreigners to remove the beam from their own eyes, pointing to the all-embracing power of the Church in the Middle Ages, articles in the Constitution of Scandinavian countries in favour of a certain religion or church, the existence of Christian political parties in the Netherlands and their influence in Indonesia (e.g. via the Missions), and the impossibility of a government's being really neutral towards religion. He stresses that the Indonesians are a deeply religious people with a great awareness of tolerance, and insists that Indonesia should be allowed to settle this problem itself. In the new Indonesia, then, the government will turn out to have a positive attitude towards religion in general and to the various religions. Thus freedom of religion will be upheld completely, as indeed can be proved by looking at the situation within the Republic since 1945.

About the time of the recognition of Independence, on the other hand, publications appeared in favour of an Islamic State. Even before the end of 1949 Zainal Abidin Ahmad published his book on the Islamic ideas concerning the structure of an Islamic State.[187] The starting-point of his exposition is twofold: the Caliphate as a definition of the character of an Islamic government, and the "darul Islam" as a definition of the Islamic community. These concepts are elaborated by connecting them with four principles which are considered basic to Islam: (1) the authority entrusted to the government (*amāna,* an ambiguous term used in Sura 4 : 58), (2) justice, (3) belief in the One and Only God (*Ketuhanan Jang Maha Esa*) "as implied in the command to obey God and

---

[186] Abu Hanifah, *Soal Agama dalam Negara Modern,* Djakarta 1949. The author clashed later on with the leaders of the Masjumi, in particular with Natsir, who according to him — if I am well informed — seemed sometimes more interested in Islamic and pan-Islamic questions than in political and Indonesian national problems.

[187] Z. A. Ahmad, *Konsepsi Tatanegara Islam,* Djakarta 1949; the writer seems to come from Medan, but afterwards lived in Java and was known as a friend of Natsir, Isa Anshary and other Masjumi leaders.

His Messenger", and (4) the sovereignty of the people or democracy (*kedaulatan rakjat*).

That is to say, an Islamic State would be a sovereign state, a religious state, a state upholding the rule of law, a constitutional state, a democratic state, a parliamentary state (with the *ūlū 'l-amri*, Sura 4 : 59, as the elected representatives of the people), a republican state, and a tolerant and peace-loving state (*Negara Perdamaian*).

Somewhat later there appeared a pamphlet written by an author who calls himself M. Sj. Ibnu Amatillah (a pseudonym? *Ibn amatillah* = the son of a handmaid of God), entitled "Analysis: Is it possible to base the Indonesian State on Islam?" [188] This writer recalls the book of the abovementioned Z. A. Ahmad, "who did not give a detailed design for an Islamic State, but nevertheless laid an important basis for the further unfolding of this idea". In his preface of January 1950 — immediately after the recognition of Independence — the writer asserts flatly: "Now that our national aspirations have been fulfilled and we have become free and independent, a new question arises, the question of the form of our state; and it is not impossible that here the beginning of mutual disagreement will be found".

Against those who want to introduce the (Western) forms of democracy, socialism or communism, the author makes a plea for Islam and what Islam can offer for the development of the state: the democracy of Islam rests on mutual deliberation (Sura 42 : 38); Islam recognizes the rights of man, provides valuable stipulations in the field of economics (prohibition of extortion and luxury, regulations concerning the *zakāt*), and so on.

From Atjeh, in April 1950, the well-known and still very productive Mohd. Hasbi Ash-Shiddiqy published a brief summary and explanation of "The Principles of Islamic Government".[189] In the first part, he discusses various terms from the Qur'ān and Tradition relevant to the Muslim idea of a state in accordance with Islam (*chalifat, ulul amri, darul Islam, darul harb,* etc.). In the second part, an attempt is made to show that some data of Islamic law can be used for the building of

---

[188] M. Sj. Ibnu Amatillah, *Analyse: Mungkinkah Negara Indonesia bersendikan Islam?*, Semarang 1950.

[189] Mohd. Hasbi Ash-Shiddiqy, *Dasar-dasar Pemerintahan Islam,* Medan 1950. Soon after this publication the writer was appointed professor in Jogjakarta We shall very often come across his name again in connection with other publications.

a modern Islamic nation, in particular those concerning Finance: the *bait al-māl,* "treasury", from the earliest period of Islam (based on Sura 12 : 55), is basically a "Ministry of Finance" which gets its income from all sorts of taxes, e.g. the *charādj* (land tax), various forms of *zakāt,* and the *djizja* as poll-tax from the subject non-Muslims. As far as this last tax is concerned, it is emphatically explained (as an apology?) that this kind of tax is not exclusively an Islamic one, but was also imposed by the Greeks and Romans on subjugated peoples.[190]

Thus it turned out that by the time of the recognition of Independence on December 27th, 1949, some people were searching for a more clearly delineated idea of an Islamic State to fight for. The common struggle against the enemy from abroad could not prevent various contrasts from living on within the new state. These tendencies are reflected in religio-political publications of this period.

Meanwhile the first General Elections drew near. Hence this survey of Muslim publications during the period 1945-1955 may be concluded with a few selected election pamphlets.

First of all, there is Abikusno Tjokrosujoso's pamphlet entitled "The Islamic Umma of Indonesia facing the General Elections".[191] The author has already been mentioned frequently, for instance as a signatory of the Djakarta Charter. This pamphlet was written for the *Liga Muslimin Indonesia* (P.S.I.I., N.U., Perti); it does not support any one of the affiliated parties, nor does it attack the Masjumi which was not affiliated with this League.

The Djakarta Charter of June 22nd, 1945, is printed on the first page of this pamphlet as the ideal to be striven after. The author points out how much Muslims had hoped that one of the basic principles of the state would be "Belief in God, with the obligation for adherents of Islam to practise Islamic law". Unfortunately this clause was later eliminated, as were all words pertaining to Islam.

Then the pamphlet criticizes changes which had taken place in Indonesia due to foreign influence. For example, the changeover from the first presidential cabinet at the end of 1945 to the parliamentary cabinet of Sjahrir, which was enforced by Van Mook, representing the Dutch government, and similarly the Round Table Conference, which brought the R.I.S. into being.

---

[190] In 1968 the same writer published a separate pamphlet on *Baital Mal* which will be mentioned again in the last chapter of this book.

[191] Abikusno Tjokrosujoso, *Ummat Islam Indonesia Menghadapi Pemilihan Umum,* Djakarta 1953.

The conclusion is that no stability would be achieved in Indonesia as long as the Constitution was not based on God's decrees. The pamphlet furthermore points out the suffering of the people and the lukewarm attitude of many Muslims, and expresses the hope that now, through the elections, the building of a *Baldatun Tojibatun* (*balda ṭayyiba*, a good, prosperous land; Sura 34 : 15) would be taken in hand.

A declaration of the P.S.I.I. on the basis of the state and a *fatwa* of the *ulama* conference held in Medan in April 1953 (with the names of 207 members present) follow as an Appendix. In both it is emphasized that the state has to be based on Islam, that the head of state has to be a Muslim, and that the laws being enacted have to be in agreement with the Qur'ān and Tradition.

A pamphlet with almost the same title, "The Islamic Umma facing the General Elections", apparently appeared at the same time from the hand of Isa Anshary. I have not succeeded in finding a copy of it. According to Sidjabat,[192] Isa Anshary now stated — somewhat differently from his abovementioned theme — that the coming elections would be the "great *djihad*", as opposed to the earlier fight against the Dutch which was only a "little *djihad*". This "great *djihad*" would consist in the fight for the *sharīᶜa* (Islamic law) as basis for the Indonesian state, instead of the vague Pantjasila.

Finally I refer to a pamphlet by the Action Committee of the Masjumi entitled "The Masjumi, prop and mainstay of the Indonesian Republic".[193] Compared to the pamphlets by Abikusno (P.S.I.I., N.U. and Perti) and the Masjumi member Isa Anshary, this official Masjumi publication is more politically down-to-earth in its formulations. On the one hand, this could be characteristic of the difference in approach, atmosphere and language between the N.U. and the Masjumi as already discussed. On the other hand, this pamphlet could show that the Masjumi itself did intend to fight for an Islamic society, but not explicitly for an Islamic State, as did some of its members personally (for instance, Isa Anshary).

However this may be, in this last pamphlet a bit of world history, centering on the Second World War, is given in order to illustrate the struggle between dictatorship and democracy. Then the Indonesian fight

---
[192] W. B. Sidjabat, *Religious Tolerance*, p. 66.
[193] *Masjumi, pendukung Republik Indonesia*, ed. by Pusat Komité Aksi Pemilihan Umum Masjumi, no date.

for independence is sketched and the reader is reminded of the role of the Masjumi and several of its prominent leaders during the period 1945-1950. The transformation of the federal R.I.S. into the unitary state is primarily ascribed to the parliamentary motion submitted by Muh. Natsir, general chairman of the Masjumi and the first Prime Minister of the unitary Republic.

In a concluding chapter mud-slinging of all sorts on the part of the Communists is repudiated and the reader is assured that Islam is as much anti-capitalist as anti-communist. In this pamphlet too no other Islamic party is mentioned or attacked. But it is already clear that even then the Masjumi considered the Communist Party as its greatest enemy and the greatest danger for Indonesia.[194] Ten years after the first general elections, this enmity was to lead to an explosion of proportions that no-one would have thought possible beforehand.

---

[194] To illustrate this conflict, one could recall an example taken from the election campaign: the Communist Party promised land-reform by the redistribution of land among the peasantry; the Masjumi propaganda answered: "The Communists promise us all a bit of land, but what they will give us will be too little and too late — a grave!"

CHAPTER II

THE ISLAMIC COMMUNITY AMID INCREASING TENSIONS

(1955-1965)

1. *Political Developments up to 1959*

After 1955 the political situation in Indonesia soon became very complicated and obscure. For details of the developments the reader should consult Herbert Feith's publications.[1] There follow here the most important facts and the main outlines of the events which are important for understanding the modern history of Islam in Indonesia.

The elections of 1955 had not brought victory to any one of the main streams in Indonesian society.[2] A balance of power had come about which was to make a political compromise necessary, both in Parliament and in the Constituent Assembly. The Islamic parties now tried to continue their fight for Islam in this Assembly. On a regional and local level Islamic groups managed to keep a considerable amount of influence through appointed or elected Muslim civil servants. But it can be said that on the national level, as a result of the elections of 1955, the political progress of Islam was in fact blocked. Hence from this time the attention and energy of many Islamic leaders were turned to the internal strengthening of the Islamic community and questions such as education, the publication of books and the development of the work of the Ministry of Religion.

The balance of the political parties made possible the later intervention of Soekarno. From a political point of view, the second decade of the Indonesian Republic can be characterized as the Soekarno period, that is, the period in which Soekarno gathered more and more power into his own hands, under the guise of a "guided democracy". In the course

---

[1] Herbert Feith, *The Decline*; idem, *The Indonesian Elections*; idem, *Dynamics of Guided Democracy* in Ruth T. McVey, *Indonesia* (Survey of World Cultures), New Haven 1963.
[2] See Feith's analysis in *The Indonesian Elections*.

of these ten years the public role of the Islamic factions was more and more curtailed, in particular through the banning of the Masjumi in 1960. On the other hand, the Communist Party expanded to become the best organized party and developed its influence in such a way that it became "a state within the state".

In particular two concentrations of power came more and more into the public eye, that of Soekarno and his followers (acquiring the character of a palace clique), and that of the army under General Nasution. Concerning the years 1958-1961, Feith says of these two groups: "There was close co-operation between them on a large number of matters, a good deal of complimentarity of functions, and some division of governmental areas into spheres of influence of one or another partner. But the two remained fairly sharply distinct, and there was considerable competition and conflict between them. It was in many ways a tug-of-war relationship..." [3] In their conflict with Soekarno and the Communists over the years some Islamic groups (particularly adherents of the Masjumi) put their hopes on the army, especially on General Nasution.

In order to sketch in the developments which occurred during this second decade, we must first of all itemize a number of political facts from the period 1955-1959. After that, special attention will be paid to developments in the ideological or quasi-ideological field, culminating in the Assembly meetings of 1959.

The first cabinet crisis after the general elections ended on March 20th, 1956, with the formation of the second cabinet of Ali Sastroamidjojo (P.N.I.). The Masjumi and N.U. also participated in it, and so the cabinet was very broadly based. But co-operation between all the factions and people concerned did not last long.

From October 1956 Soekarno had begun to toy with his "conception" (Ind. *konsèpsi*), which was to become "guided democracy". At the opening of the Constituent Assembly on November 10th, 1956, Soekarno said that he personally was alive to the necessity of protecting the weaker group against the power of the stronger. "This means that for the time being our democracy must be a guided democracy (Ind. and Dutch: *demokrasi terbimbing, demokrasi terpimpin — geleide democratie*), not founded on the ideas of liberalism".[4]

---

[3] Feith, *The Decline*, p. 591.
[4] Yamin, *Naskah*, I, p. 640; Soekarno's speech is here published in its entirety, pp. 631-648.

On December 1st, 1956 Hatta resigned from the vice-presidency, saying that he had originally accepted this post "on the understanding that it would be for a period of one to two years".[5] In fact, this was the end of the so-called *Dwitunggal* (Dual-Unity), which had had more symbolical meaning than foundation in real congeniality and cooperation. It is obvious that from the beginning Hatta had difficulty in working with Soekarno, as the latter had the vanity typical of a leader who cannot abide anyone by his side. Soekarno was the popular leader, who was of great importance for the period of revolution and conflict. But with his "cowboy romanticism" he wanted to carry on a permanent revolution, always warning (right up to May, 1966) that the revolution was not yet finished (Ind. *revolusi belum selesai*). Hatta, however, on November 27th, 1956, was already warning that a revolution must be canalized at the right moment. According to him, the problem was not one of ending or continuing the revolution, but the issue at stake was winning the revolution (by beginning constructive development), or losing it (by drifting into anarchy and adventurism).[6]

Hatta's resignation occasioned much uneasiness and protest, particularly in islands outside Java and in anti-Communist circles. The sympathy for Hatta strengthened the anti-Djakarta and anti-Soekarno tendencies.

At the end of 1956 the Masjumi ministers withdrew from the cabinet. The N.U. continued to hold its seats. This development intensified the tension between the Masjumi and the N.U. at the level of daily governmental responsibility. When fundamental questions came under discussion in the Constituent Assembly, however, the two parties were later going to form an Islamic bloc.

In a speech on February 21st, 1957, Soekarno explained his "conception to save the Indonesian Republic", that is to say, his way to "guided democracy".[7] He suggested the formation of a *gotong rojong* cabinet (a cabinet of "mutual help") in which every party, including the Communists, would be represented. A National Council would act

---

[5] Feith, *The Decline*, p. 524.
[6] See Hatta's speech to students in Bogor, printed in the Djakarta newspaper *Kompas* of June 30th, 1966, where Hatta replied to a remark of Soekarno's made at the installation of Air-Commander Rusmin Nurjadin at the end of May 1966. In this speech Soekarno had cautioned against someone (Hatta) who even ten years ago believed that the revolution was finished and who thus obviously did not have a revolutionary spirit.
[7] Yamin, *Naskah*, I, p. 666.

as advisory body to the cabinet. This council would be led by Soekarno himself and would be set up more by unanimity than by ballot, in particular by appointing representatives of the "functional groups" (farmers, workers, intellectuals, army, police, religious groups, etc.). The political parties had to make known their answer to this "conception" of the President's within a week. Of the larger parties, the Nationalists (P.N.I.) and the Communists (P.K.I.) declared themselves for; the Masjumi and the Catholic Party declared themselves against. Other parties gave a hesitant answer or put conditions; for example, the N.U. was against the participation of the P.K.I.

While the debate on the President's "conception" was going on, the territorial commander in Makassar, Lt. Col. Sumual, declared the State of War and Siege for East Indonesia on March 2nd, 1957. Simultaneously the so-called Charter of Common Struggle (Ind. *Piagam Perdjuangan Semesta*) was enacted there. The chief aim of this regional campaign was to see that the economic output of this area (e.g. from the export of copra) was used for the development of the area itself and not swallowed by "Djakarta" and Java. Similar solutions had been striven for in Sumatra too.

The President consolidated his position, when, following a cabinet crisis (March 14th, 1957) he declared the whole of Indonesia to be in a State of War and Siege. Between April 4th and 8th, 1957, playing the role of "citizen Soekarno" — yet at the same time being Commander-in-Chief of all Armed Forces in the State of War and Siege — he pushed through the formation of the Djuanda cabinet. I was told that he had called a number of politicians from different parties to a meeting which was clearly designed to intimidate those invited. Arriving at the meeting, they found that they had to sit opposite Soekarno and a number of high army officers. After Soekarno had explained things, they got a stencilled form on which to write down the words "yes" or "no", in answer to the question whether they were willing to take part in the cabinet which Soekarno was going to form. Two parties, the Masjumi and the Catholic Party, flatly refused. According to my information, the spokesman for the Socialist Party (P.S.I.) was prepared to co-operate; but Soekarno passed this party by and in due time pushed all the Socialists aside. Other parties sympathized with Soekarno's initiative or left the decision to those of their members who would be approached to accept ministerial office.

This intervention of Soekarno's in fact heralded the period of "guided democracy", although its beginning was officially announced only some two years later.[8] The Djuanda cabinet was largely composed of P.N.I. and N.U. members, while the P.K.I. used to give its support. This attitude of the N.U. according to some informants may be considered as "flexible", according to others "opportunistic" or springing from political inexperience. However that may be, the participation of the N.U. certainly brought it new adherents and nominal followers, but it also brought it discredit and widened the split with the Masjumi.

The period between April and November 1957 was typified by increasing tensions and incidents between "Djakarta" and the leaders of regional movements, particularly in Sumatra and Sulawesi. From regional elections in Java (June-August, 1957) it appeared that the Communist Party, with 27.4 % of the votes, had become the largest party there. At the end of 1957 political developments were accelerated by the conflict with the Netherlands over West Irian (New Guinea), and the take-over of Dutch concerns by "the workers" (first of all in Djakarta, on December 3rd, 1957). As a reaction to the chaotic situation, which seemed ripe for a Communist coup, some Masjumi leaders left Djakarta for Padang in Sumatra (Natsir, Sjafruddin Prawiranegara, Burhanuddin Harahap). In spite of this situation Soekarno left for an overseas trip of six weeks on January 6th, 1958. On February 15th, a counter-government was formed in Sumatra, the "Revolutionary Government of the Republic of Indonesia" (Ind. *Pemerintah Revolusionèr Republik Indonesia*, P.R.R.I.). Two days later, the *Permesta* movement in North Sulawesi joined this revolt.

In spite of the sympathy which these risings enjoyed from many in Java too — from anti-Communists, opponents of Soekarno and people coming from the areas concerned — General Nasution refused to make any compromise with the rebels. The fighting in Sumatra, however, was not too serious.[9] At the beginning of May the central government was again in control there. After that it was possible to stamp out the rising in North Sulawesi; at the end of July the troops of the central government held all the larger towns, although this did not put an end to guerilla activities.

---

[8] Compare the remark by S. M. Abidin in the Constituent Assembly on April 29th, 1959, that Guided Democracy, proposed by Soekarno in relation to the return to the 1945 Constitution, had in fact already been in operation for two years, that is to say, from the very day that the President took upon himself the formation of the Djuanda cabinet (Yamin, *Naskah*, II, p. 275).
[9] Cf. James Mossman, *Rebels in Paradise, Indonesia's Civil War*, London 1961.

In this way the situation throughout the greater part of 1958 was determined by the P.R.R.I. and Permesta risings. The involvement of some Masjumi leaders and prominent Socialists (Sumitro Djojohadi-kusumo) in these risings was later going to be used as an argument against the rehabilitation of these parties, even up to the post-Soekarno period of 1968.

2. *The Ideological Struggle (1959)*

The year 1959 was characterized by the struggle on a more fundamental level, resulting in the deadlock of the debates in the Constituent Assembly. Elected in 1955, this Assembly began its sessions on November 10th, 1956 in Bandung. Its task was to draft and approve the definitive Constitution for the Republic of Indonesia. The Constitution of 1945 had at the end of 1949 made room for the Constitution of the federal R.I.S., a product of the Round Table Conference between the Netherlands and Indonesia. Then this R.I.S. Constitution was hastily exchanged for a temporary Constitution when the unitary state was formed in August 1950.

The debates in the Constituent Assembly did not proceed from a draft Constitution, but in the first place fundamental principles were discussed which later on could be incorporated into the Constitution. Points at issue concerned, for instance, the form of the state (federal or unitary), parliament (one House or two) and the power of the head of the state.

After some years the Assembly had reached agreement on many details. One question, however, had developed into a main issue that caused two blocs to be formed which could not arrive at any compromise. This was the formula concerning the basis of the state, roughly speaking the old problem of a so-called Pantjasila State or something like an Islamic State (that is to say, "a state based on Islam", or "a state in which the laws are in agreement with, or not in conflict with, the Qur'ān and Tradition"). Looking back, we can ask to what extent this discussion was only a verbal combat, or in other words a struggle for the label of the state. How far did the Assembly come to a clear exposition concerning the essential content of these ideas? How much was antagonism based merely on suppositions concerning the other's intentions, and on fear of these presumed intentions?

At the beginning there were still tensions between the various Islamic parties, as from the end of 1956 the Masjumi and the N.U. opposed each other with regard to the Ali cabinet. But the Islamic parties presented a united front when faced with the non-Islamic and anti-Islamic parties, which had combined into a Pantjasila bloc. The tendency which Feith believed he could trace back even to the election campaign now became an open fact: "The Pantja Sila, previously accepted by Moslem political leaders as a symbol to which they could give at least tentative assent, now became anti-Moslem property; President Soekarno, as a vigorous defender of the Pantja Sila... came to be seen as a spokesman for one side in the struggle, instead of a non-partisan head of state".[10]

A compromise between these two blocs proved less and less possible. The problem became insoluble. It was impossible to get a majority for the concepts along "Islamic State" lines. But for the "Pantjasila State" idea, even with Communist support, the two-thirds majority laid down as necessary for the making of the Constitution was also unobtainable. For almost two and a half years many meetings were held to deal with this question, without coming any nearer to a solution.

As has been said, from 1957 Soekarno was busily working towards his "guided democracy", in both what he said and did. One may suppose that at a certain moment he had come to the conclusion that the 1945 Constitution gave the President more power than the later Constitutions, or the one which the Assembly was preparing. The 1945 Constitution could open the way to his "guided democracy", and could thus legalize his "conception". So he decided to enforce a "return to the Constitution of 1945", passing over those of 1949 and 1950 and setting aside the work of the Assembly. If this interpretation is correct, it must be concluded that Soekarno's real aim was to bring about "guided democracy" via a "return to the Constitution of 1945", and not that he was looking for a way out of the deadlock in which the Assembly found itself and then decided to force the issue by a "return to the Constitution of 1945" which then ended up in "guided democracy".[11]

The cabinet was the first body which Soekarno asked to sanction his idea. From December 5th, 1958, an "exchange of ideas" took place between the President and the cabinet. On February 19th, 1959, the

---

[10] Feith, *Dynamics*, p. 317.
[11] The way in which Prime Minister Djuanda denied the truth of this interpretation given by S. M. Abidin (Yamin, *Naskah*, II, p. 275) and Dahlan Lukman (Yamin, *Naskah*, II, p. 460) is not convincing (Yamin, *Naskah*, III, p. 287).

cabinet unanimously passed a resolution for "the realization of guided democracy within the framework of a return to the Constitution of 1945".[12]

In the 24 points covered by this resolution, among other things the opinion is expressed that the 1945 Constitution was a better guarantee for putting the principle of guided democracy into practice, and that guided democracy certainly meant democracy; furthermore, that the 1945 Constitution could guarantee a stable government for at least five years (i.e. the term of office of the President, who would appoint and dismiss the ministers). This 1945 Constitution also left a possibility for the appointment of representatives from the "functional groups" to the various Councils.

Point 9 of this resolution is particularly important for our subject. It runs as follows: "In order to meet the desires of the Islamic groups, in connection with the restoration and assurance of public safety, the existence of the Djakarta Charter of June 22nd, 1945 is recognized..." In the "Explanation" it is added that "the intention of the return to the Constitution of 1945 is the restitution of the total national potential, including the Islamic groups, in order to be able to concentrate on the restoration of public safety and on development in all fields". In other words, the Djakarta Charter was mentioned here as a friendly gesture towards Darul Islam leaders in West Java, South Sulawesi and Atjeh, and other Islamic politicians, both in Parliament and the Constituent Assembly, who sympathized with the ideology behind the Darul Islam.

As to the procedure for the "return to the 1945 Constitution", it was decided that after agreement between the President and the cabinet (sic!) the President would address a meeting of the Constituent Assembly in Bandung, urging them to accept the 1945 Constitution as the definitive Constitution of the Republic of Indonesia. The decision of the Assembly would be laid down in a "Charter of Bandung", in which stipulations would also have to be made "concerning the existence of the Djakarta Charter of June 22nd, 1945".

On March 3rd and 4th, 1959, Parliament was given the opportunity to ask questions about this resolution by the cabinet; these questions would be answered in writing by the government.[13] There was no question of Parliament's either passing or rejecting this resolution of the cabinet (read: the President). Besides expressions of agreement with the

---

[12] The text of this resolution by the cabinet and the explanation added to it can be found in Yamin, *Naskah,* I, pp. 487-508.
[13] For the minutes of these meetings see Yamin, *Naskah,* I, pp. 511-571.

opinion of President and cabinet (for example from the P.N.I. and P.K.I.), critical questions were also put. For example: will "guided democracy" still be real democracy? Has all the work of the Constituent Assembly been in vain, though its chairman had just said, on February 18th, that (1) the difficult, fundamental questions were already solved, and (2) that the content for a draft Constitution had already for 90 % been fixed? (Anwar Harjono of the Masjumi). A number of representatives of the Islamic parties asked for elucidation of the sentence about the Djakarta Charter. Did it mean that this document would possess the same legal force as the Constitution, or was it only a historical document, the existence of which was only recognized in order to use it incidentally in connection with public safety? (Anwar Harjono). Did the recognition of the Djakarta Charter carry legal weight, so that the expression "Belief in God" (*Ketuhanan*) in the preamble of the 1945 Constitution might be explained by adding the famous "seven words" from the original Djakarta Charter, so that it would read thus: Belief in God, with the obligation for adherents of Islam to practise Islamic law? And would it be possible to create on this basis a legislation which would be in agreement with Islamic law? (Achmad Sjaichu, N.U.).

As far as the written answer from the government is concerned, let us concentrate on the remarks concerning the Djakarta Charter.[14] In answer to Anwar Harjono's questions came the reply that, although the Djakarta Charter was not a part of the Constitution of 1945, it was nevertheless a historical document which possessed considerable significance for the struggle for freedom of the Indonesian people and for the drafting of the preamble of the 1945 Constitution, which was indeed a part of the Constitution.[15]

The answer to Achmad Sjaichu's questions went somewhat further. "The recognition of the existence of the Djakarta Charter as a historical document means for the government also the recognition of its influence on the 1945 Constitution. This influence therefore not only concerns the preamble of the Constitution of 1945, but also article 29 of that Constitution, which must be the basis for further legislation in the religious field."[16] "That is to say, the words 'Belief in God' in the preamble of the 1945 Constitution can be explained as 'Belief in God,

---

[14] Cf. Yamin, *Naskah,* I, pp. 573-623.
[15] Yamin, *Naskah,* I, p. 587.
[16] Article 29 runs as follows: (1) The State is founded on Belief in the One and Only God; (2) The State guarantees the freedom of every inhabitant to profess his own religion and to worship according to his own religion and belief.

with the obligation for the Islamic community to maintain its religious law', so that on these grounds a legislation for the adherents of Islam can be created which can be brought into agreement with Islamic law." [17]

On April 22nd, 1959, just before he left for a journey abroad of more than two months, President Soekarno made his speech in the Constituent Assembly in Bandung, in which he appealed for a return to the Constitution of 1945.[18] After an introduction in which he stressed that the Assembly had already been meeting for 2 years, 5 months and 12 days, that is almost two and a half years, his speech followed closely the 24 points of the resolution by the cabinet of February 19th mentioned above.

With regard to the Djakarta Charter, Soekarno said first that it was a historical document which preceded, and had had influence upon, the 1945 Constitution, and therefore he would still officially send the text of the Djakarta Charter to the Assembly. Coming to point 9 on the recognition of the existence of the Djakarta Charter for the sake of the restoration and assurance of public safety, Soekarno repeated almost literally the answer the government had given to Achmad Sjaichu's questions in Parliament, namely that the Djakarta Charter had not only influenced the preamble of the Constitution, but the whole Constitution, and therefore also the article on religion and religious freedom (article 29), which had to be the basis for further regulations in the field of religion. But the sentence which then followed in the earlier answer — that this influence meant that "Belief in God" could be explained with the addition of the "seven words" and for this reason special laws could be made for the Islamic part of the population — it was just this sentence which now was not included in Soekarno's speech!

Once again the Djakarta Charter became one of the most important issues on which some Islamic leaders brought discussions to a head at the following meetings of the Assembly, held between April 22nd and June 2nd, 1959.[19] At first only some members did so. The speech of the well-known Masjumi leader Prawoto Mangkusasmito, for example,

---
[17] Yamin, *Naskah*, I, p. 621.
[18] This extremely long speech is known under the title of *Res Publica, sekali lagi Res Publica!* ("Res Publica, once again Res Publica!"); cf. Yamin, *Naskah*, I, pp. 653-702; in English, II, pp. 199-244.
[19] A great deal of Yamin's work covers the minutes of these Assembly meetings; cf. *Naskah*, II, pp. 187-848 and III, pp. 115-625.

held on May 4th, was mainly an attack on Soekarno's idea concerning "guided democracy" and an appeal for the restoration of the *Dwitunggal,* Soekarno-Hatta, as a better way of achieving stability.[20] This "restoration" was, of course, intended to restore Hatta's influence in the government of the country, as a counterweight to Soekarno. But, for example, H. Saifuddin Zuhri (N.U., later Minister of Religious Affairs) gave special attention to the problem of the Djakarta Charter. He asked the government to stipulate that the Djakarta Charter of 1945 had legal significance for the present day and could be used as a source of law for the realization of Islamic legislation for Muslims.

It is worth mentioning that on May 5th, the representative of the Catholic Party, B. Mang Reng Say, stressed that for his party the Djakarta Charter was nothing more than "one of the historical documents from Indonesian soil which have occurred in the course of the history of the Indonesian people moving toward the proclamation of their independence", so that the Djakarta Charter "may not and cannot be a source of law" but may only be considered as a precursor, a draft, for the preamble of the Constitution.[21] The same point of view was taken by the spokesman for the Protestant Party (Parkindo), J. C. T. Simorangkir, in his speech of May 11th, 1959.[22]

A spokesman for the small Islamic party Perti requested straight out that the Djakarta Charter should be made the preamble of the 1945 Constitution and that other articles of the Constitution should be brought into agreement with it.[23] H. Abdul Malik Karim Amrullah (HAMKA) [24] launched a vehement attack on the way Soekarno had organized his campaign to put pressure on the Assembly by means of mass demonstrations. He foresaw that "guided democracy" would be the way to dictatorship. Although he was an authoritative religious leader and writer, he did not enter into the question of the Djakarta Charter. This, however, was done explicitly by Kahar Muzakkir, a Muhammadijah leader from Jogja, one of the nine signatories of the Djakarta Charter on June 22nd, 1945. He voiced the disappointment of the Islamic community, which had accepted the Constitution on August 18th, 1945, because Soekarno had promised that this Constitution could

---

[20] Yamin, *Naskah,* II, pp. 362-376.
[21] Yamin, *Naskah,* II, p. 476.
[22] Yamin, *Naskah,* II, p. 664.
[23] Yamin, *Naskah,* II, p. 537; what is meant is a return to the draft Constitution as it was on July 16th, 1945 (see Chapter I, par. 3).
[24] Mentioned in Chapter I, par. 8; for his speech, see Yamin, *Naskah,* II, pp. 544-554.

later on be perfected and brought into accordance with the ideals of the Muslims. It was, after all, from this Constitution that the important "seven words" of the Djakarta Charter had been struck out. Now the existence of the Djakarta Charter was being recalled, but alas, once again not to give it legal force, but only to appease the Islamic community. He proposed that the Assembly should go on with its work until a result was achieved that the Muslims also could accept and take responsibility for.[25] The spokesman for the P.S.I.I. also criticized the government for intending to set aside the work of the Assembly without further ado, by taking the Constitution of 1945 out of cold storage, but leaving the Djakarta Charter there as just a historical document.[26]

The climax of this debate was perhaps reached in a speech by the N.U. leader H. Zainul Arifin on May 12th, 1959.[27] According to his line of argument, the Djakarta Charter had cleared the way for the proclamation of the Republic of Indonesia, so that, strictly speaking, this Charter was the true basis of the Republic, not the altered form of it as embodied in the preamble of the Constitution of August 18th, 1945. To the many speculations concerning the famous "Light Verse" from the Qur'ān (Sura 24 : 35) he added this one: that the Djakarta Charter could be compared to the light of the lamp which, as a shining star, formed an eternal source of light for the Constitution of 1945, to illumine the dark road which the Indonesian people had already walked and would still have to follow. So he proposed that the original Djakarta Charter should be recognized as the fundamental norm for the state and for its legislation.

On May 21st, 1959, Prime Minister Djuanda replied to what until then had been brought forward in the Constituent Assembly.[28] With regard to the criticism of some members who had said that the lack of public safety and the risings were engendered not only by Islamic groups, the government declared itself prepared to omit the sentence about public safety when mentioning the Djakarta Charter. As far as the meaning of the Charter and its relation to the Constitution of 1945 were concerned, the government believed that this question had already been sufficiently explained in earlier statements by the President and in the answer in Parliament to Achmad Sjaichu, which had been handed to

---

[25] Yamin, *Naskah*, II, pp. 701-707.
[26] Yamin, *Naskah*, II, p. 836.
[27] Yamin, *Naskah*, III, pp. 149-164.
[28] Yamin, *Naskah*, III, pp. 285-329.

the Assembly. According to the government, the Djakarta Charter was a historical document that inspired (Ind. *mendjiwai*) the 1945 Constitution, especially the preamble and article 29, although the original Charter did not have legal effect in a direct way.

The fundamental norm for the state and its legislation — this in answer to H. Zainul Arifin — was, however, already laid down in the preamble of the Constitution. (In other words, the government did not intend to acknowledge the Djakarta Charter in its original setting as that norm). Moreover, the government was of the opinion that, considering the composition of the Indonesian population, the coming Parliament and People's Congress would for the greater part consist of Muslims, so that people need not fear the enactment of decisions and laws at variance with Islamic law. (This was a typical Soekarno argument from 1945 on).

In order to mould the governmental proposal into a more definite form, the Prime Minister presented a draft for a "Charter of Bandung", which would sanction the return to the Constitution of 1945. With regard to the Djakarta Charter it was laid down in this draft "that we recognize the existence of the Djakarta Charter of June 22nd, 1945, as a historical document that inspired the formulation of the preamble of the 1945 Constitution, which preamble is indeed part of this Constitution".

We may comment that the significance of the Djakarta Charter here, more clearly than before, is related to a moment in the past, that is to say the moment when the *formulation* of the preamble of the Constitution took place; for the present this Charter has only indirect significance, inasmuch as, in an altered form without the vexed "seven words", it was accepted as the preamble of the 1945 Constitution.

From May 25th to 29th, 1959, further discussions followed in the Assembly. Various speakers for the Islamic faction declared themselves dissatisfied with the answer from the government. HAMKA and Prawoto Mangkusasmito (both Masjumi) once again warned their listeners against the dangers of "guided democracy", which would surely end in a totalitarian state or a police state. They pleaded anew for the restoration of the *Dwitunggal* Soekarno-Hatta.[29]

---

[29] Yamin, *Naskah*, III, pp. 367, 447; both found that their fear was well grounded, as during the last years of the Soekarno regime they were imprisoned and only released after Soekarno's fall.

Others repeated their suggestion to give the Djakarta Charter a legal significance for the present day. The spokesman for the P.S.I.I., for example, wanted to replace the preamble of the Constitution with the original Djakarta Charter, as did K. H. Masjkur (N.U.) and the spokesman for the Perti, who, moreover, wanted to see the "seven words" of the Djakarta Charter repeated in article 29 of the 1945 Constitution.[30]

After all kinds of amendments had been suggested concerning the governmental draft for the proposed "Charter of Bandung", on May 27th, the Prime Minister once again made a speech to clarify the government's point of view.[31] This speech, however, did not reveal any new policies; the problem of the Djakarta Charter was not even mentioned.

The following day it appeared that within the Islamic bloc mutual agreement had been reached for a last effort to give legal force to the disputed "seven words" of the Djakarta Charter. At the eleventh hour the representatives of the Islamic parties — N.U., Masjumi, P.S.I.I., Perti and four small groups — moved an amendment, apparently originating from N.U. circles, to insert the "seven words" both in the preamble and in article 29 of the 1945 Constitution.[32]

After this the meeting was adjourned several times, partly in order to reach a compromise between the Islamic and other groups by lobbying.[33] These attempts, however, were of no avail. When, on May 29th, it was at last possible to vote on the amendment of the Islamic parties, it was rejected by 268 votes to 210 on the first vote. When the vote was taken again, because of an apparent mistake, the numbers against were 265 to 201 for.[34]

A day later the spokesmen for the various parties got the opportunity to give reasons for their answer to the government's proposal for the return to the 1945 Constitution, before voting. In the name of all the abovementioned Islamic parties, W. A. Rachman informed the Assembly that, although some differences in nuance were to be found among them, the Islamic parties were in agreement that they could only accept the government's proposal on the conditions formulated in their rejected amendment, and for this reason the Islamic parties would vote against the proposal.[35]

---

[30] Yamin, *Naskah*, III, p. 392, pp. 477-480 and p. 483.
[31] Yamin, *Naskah*, III, pp. 511-522.
[32] Yamin, *Naskah*, III, pp. 527-528 and p. 569.
[33] Yamin, *Naskah*, III, pp. 531-537.
[34] Yamin, *Naskah*, III, pp. 571-573.
[35] Yamin, *Naskah*, III, p. 586.

Thus the proposal for a return to the 1945 Constitution would get the support of two large parties, the P.N.I. and P.K.I., as well as the Catholics, Protestants and other small parties, but not that of the Islamic parties. In accordance with standing orders, three different kinds of voting were carried out, on May 30th, June 1st and June 2nd.[36] The result was that the government's proposal obtained successively 269, 264 and 263 votes, whereas 199, 204 and 203 votes were returned against. As a two-thirds majority was necessary for such a decision, that was, 312 votes in the last poll, the proposal was not accepted.

Now it was perfectly clear that a two-thirds majority in the Assembly was not attainable, either for a so-called "Pantjasila State" based on the Constitution of August 18th, 1945, or for something tending towards an "Islamic State" based on the "seven words" of the Djakarta Charter of June 22nd, 1945.

During a short final discussion, the speaker for one of the nationalist parties (*Ikatan Pendukung Kemerdekaan Indonesia*, I.P.K.I., the "League of Upholders of Indonesian Independence") proposed that the Assembly now dissolve itself and leave the decision concerning the Constitution in the hands of the President (outcry from the Islamic groups). A Communist representative also proposed that the Assembly dissolve itself. In this absolute deadlock, the meeting and the session of the Constituent Assembly ended on June 2nd, 1959.

3. *"Guided Democracy" (1959-1965)*

The abovementioned proposal made by the I.P.K.I. representative met with a response. On June 18th, 1959, the chairman of the P.N.I., Suwirjo, sent a telegram to Soekarno, who was at that moment in Japan, asking him for a Presidential decree proclaiming a return to the 1945 Constitution and to dissolve the Constituent Assembly.[37] They would have to wait until the President returned from abroad on June 30th. Meanwhile the P.N.I., P.K.I. and like-minded groups had made a new session of the Assembly impossible by simply refusing to attend. In this way the necessary quorum could not be achieved, so that the Assembly could not carry out its work.

After his return the President officially informed the cabinet on July 3rd that he would intervene. This took place on July 5th, 1959,

---

[36] Cf. Yamin, *Naskah*, III, pp. 591-625.
[37] *Duta Masjarakat* (Djakarta newspaper), June 19th, 1959; *Keesings Historisch Archief*, Amsterdam-Antwerpen, 1959, no. 1460, p. 14,956.

by means of the "Decree of the President of the Republic of Indonesia, Commander-in-Chief of the Armed Forces, with regard to the Return to the Constitution of 1945".[38]

The first part of this Decree consists of five considerations. Firstly, that the Assembly had not been able to achieve the necessary decision (i.e. a two-thirds majority) concerning the proposal to return to the 1945 Constitution. Secondly, that the majority of the members of the Assembly refused to attend the meetings any longer, so that the Assembly would not be able to complete its work. Thirdly, that because of this a dangerous situation for the unity and well-being of the state, the country and the people had arisen (so that, according to a later explanation, the President as Commander-in-Chief could intervene on the grounds of a state of emergency). Fourthly, that the President, supported by the majority of the people and impelled by his own conviction, now had to act in order to save the country. Fifthly, that the President was convinced that the Djakarta Charter of June 22nd, 1945 inspired the 1945 Constitution and formed a unity with that Constitution (or: "is linked in unity with that Constitution").[39]

Based on these considerations, the President decreed (1) that the Constituent Assembly was dissolved, and (2) that the return to the Constitution of 1945 had taken place. Added to this Decree was the announcement that, as soon as possible, a provisional People's Congress would be brought into being, consisting of the members of Parliament doubled by the appointment of representatives from various parts of Indonesia and representatives of certain groups of the population; furthermore a Supreme Advisory Council would be set up (both bodies were mentioned in the 1945 Constitution).

The Decree was signed "in the name of the people of Indonesia" by Soekarno as President of Indonesia and Commander-in-Chief of the Armed Forces.

For our subject the most important of the abovementioned "considerations" is the fifth and last one, which states that the 1945 Constitution is inspired by the Djakarta Charter and that these two are linked together in unity. Once more this was a compromise formula and its interpretation

---

[38] The Indonesian text of this frequently quoted Decree is to be found in Yamin, *Naskah,* III, p. 661, followed by an English translation probably originating from the Indonesian Ministry of Information.
[39] According to Yamin, the translation "is linked in unity" is too explicit an interpretation; cf. Yamin, *Pembahasan,* p. 289.

would be a subject of discussion for many years. What Soekarno himself meant has become perfectly clear from his earlier speeches, namely that the Djakarta Charter was no more than a "historical document" that had played an influential part in the formulation of the 1945 Constitution, in particular the preamble (which was the Djakarta Charter without the "seven words"). From 1959 onward the same interpretation was given by the Nationalists and other non-Islamic or anti-Islamic parties. Moreover it was their wont to stress that the relationship between the Djakarta Charter and the Constitution of 1945 was only mentioned as one of the five "considerations", which therefore did not have the legal force of the Decree itself. On the other hand, the interpretation which arose among Islamic groups was as follows: that by this Decree of July 5th, 1959, the Djakarta Charter (including the "seven words" concerning "the obligation for adherents of Islam to practise Islamic law") obtained legal significance for the present day; in other words, that the law of the land stipulated the duty of Muslims to practise Islamic law, and that, based on the Djakarta Charter, special Islamic laws could be made for the Muslim inhabitants of Indonesia.

In this conflict both supporters and opponents of Soekarno, from extreme left-wing to extreme right-wing, again and again appealed to those words and deeds of the President which agreed with their own opinions and desires. This way of arguing even continued into the post-Soekarno period, as if the fall of Soekarno was of no significance for the validity of his former words and deeds. Nationalists and friends of Soekarno liked to stress Point 4 of these considerations (that the President was right to intervene), while they interpreted Point 5 as having no legal consequences for the present day. Muslims, however, preferred to ignore Point 4 (to which they could not agree), but they clung to Point 5 and its Islamic interpretation. Thus from 1959 onward the Djakarta Charter became once more a divisive issue between two main streams within Indonesian society.

Soekarno's speech made on Independence Day, August 17th, 1959, was named his "Political Manifesto" (Ind. *Manifesto Politik*, abbreviated to *Manipol*). At the beginning of 1960 its ideas were condensed into the slogan USDEK, composed from the initial letters of:

a. *Undang-undang Dasar 1945*, the 1945 Constitution;
b. *Sosialisme (à la) Indonesia*, Indonesian Socialism;
c. *Demokrasi Terpimpin*, Guided Democracy;

d. *Ekonomi Terpimpin,* Guided Economy;
e. *Kepribadian Indonesia,* the Indonesian Identity.

At the end of 1960 Soekarno completed the state ideology of Indonesia with the NASAKOM slogan, the doctrine of the unity of the three component parts of Indonesian society, the Nationalists (*NASionalis*), the religious groups (*Agama* = religion) and the Communists (*KOMunis*). Herbert Feith said with regard to these years that "the President repeatedly fashioned new symbols of state, new formulations of the meaning of the present and the goals to be sought in the future, and these immediately dominated virtually all mass communication".[40] Apart from those already mentioned, Feith gave also the following slogans: *Gotong Rojong* (Mutual Help), Building the World Anew, and the Message of the Suffering of the People. "Their negative counterparts were 'free fight liberalism', 'Dutch thinking', 'textbook thinking', individualism, cosmopolitanism, conservatism, and reformism." [41]

Feith continues that "one other way in which the governments of the 1958-1961 period legitimized themselves was by acquiring the insignia of national power and prestige. They began the building of a steel plant. They acquired an atomic reactor. They bought a cruiser and destroyers and TU-16 long range bombers. They devoted great resources to building the stadia and hotels which would enable them to be host to the Asian Games in 1962 . . ." It can be added here that in Djakarta a beginning was made with the building of the Istiqlal Mosque (*istiķlāl* = independence) which was to be "the greatest mosque in Asia". So arose the so-called *Mertju Suar* policy, which meant that the Indonesia of Soekarno was to be a lighthouse (Ind. *mertju suar*), the beams of which would shine far out into the world.

It goes without saying that this policy of Soekarno devoured an enormous amount of money and was economically irresponsible. Some years after Soekarno's fall from power, the steel frames of unfinished sky-scrapers in Djakarta still stood rusting away as sad monuments to the *mertju suar* policy, a by-product of "Guided Democracy".[42]

---

[40] Feith, *The Decline,* p. 594.
[41] Feith, *The Decline,* p. 595.
[42] Concerning the enormous buildings which were erected in Djakarta, it must be admitted that Soekarno was a capable architect who tried to give Djakarta the appearance of a city of world standing. As a matter of fact the capital of the former Dutch East Indies was not much more than a provincial Dutch garden-city.

However, at the beginning of 1960, a large part of Parliament still had the courage to express criticism of the financial policy of the cabinet. In March 1960 the debate on the budget ended in the President's dissolving Parliament. In its place came an appointed body, composed in accordance with Soekarno's "conception" of February 21st, 1957, and including "functional groups".

Previously the Masjumi, together with the Socialist Party (P.S.I.) and some smaller groups (the Catholic Party, some leaders of the Protestant Party and even one N.U. member) had tried to throw up a democratic bulwark by forming the "Democratic League" which seemed to grow swiftly. Hatta, too, supported this Democratic League and wrote his famous article on "Our Democracy" in the Islamic magazine *Pandji Masjarakat,* which thereafter was prohibited from appearing.[43] But this League became illegal when, on August 17th, 1960, Soekarno banned the Masjumi and P.S.I. Therefore no members of the Masjumi and P.S.I. were included in the new "parliament". The N.U., however, continued to be well represented, both in parliament and the cabinet.

This disbanding of the Masjumi became a matter of bitter controversy in the post-Soekarno period. According to a statement made by Prawoto Mangkusasmito, who succeeded Natsir as chairman of the Masjumi in 1958, the Masjumi was dissolved because the party did not sufficiently dissociate itself from those leaders who were involved in the P.R.R.I. rising in February 1958; on February 28th, 1958, Prime Minister Djuanda had declared in Parliament that the leaders who had been involved would be personally punished, but not their political party as such.[44]

Herbert Feith remarked with regard to the situation after 1960 that Masjumi influence continued to be great in the Islamic community.[45] In January 1962 many former Masjumi and P.S.I. leaders were arrested. One of the greatest scandals of Soekarno's regime in its decline was perhaps the revenge on the Socialist leader Sjahrir, who from the very beginning had been critical of Soekarno's methods. His arrest and imprisonment in 1962 on political charges resulted in terrible suffering; after a stroke, and too late to save him, he was allowed in 1965 to go abroad for medical treatment. He died in Zürich on April 9th, 1966.

---

[43] Cf. Hatta, *Demokrasi kita,* reprinted as a pamphlet, Djakarta 1966.
[44] This statement of December 27th, 1966, is to be found in *Pandji Masjarakat,* no. 7, January 1967, p. 7.
[45] Feith, *Dynamics,* p. 348.

In March 1962 the Communist leaders Aidit and Lukman were included in the cabinet as ministers without portfolio. It is said that they made use of this position to travel all over the country at the expense of the state, preparing the party to assume power when the time was ripe. Also in the following years, until September 30th, 1965, many Islamic leaders were held in prison for longer or shorter periods. Between 1960 and the end of 1965 they included, for instance, the Masjumi leaders who had been involved in the P.R.R.I. rising, such as Natsir, Sjafruddin Prawiranegara and Burhanuddin Harahap, but also Asaat, Prawoto Mangkusasmito, Mohamad Roem, Isa Anshary, E. Z. Muttaqin, Junan Nasution, Kasman Singodimedjo, HAMKA and others.[46] For many Islamic leaders and others who had been openly critical of Soekarno, these were dark years of defamation, night terrors and lawlessness.

In 1963 Feith stated: "Masjumi Moslems are politically incapacitated now, or almost so, but they are actively resentful of the present state of political affairs and have an ideological basis for opposition to it, and their incapacitation could thus well be short-lived..." It did not escape the author how the tensions were growing towards an apocalyptic climax, because "there are many in almost all social groups who see the 1945 constitution and Manipol-USDEK as nostrums which have failed and gone stale. This together with the droughts, floods, earthquakes, and volcanic eruptions of 1961 and 1962, all traditional evil omens, has brought many to believe that the present *djaman* (era) may be approaching its end." [47] It is not clear whether Herbert Feith was expecting the tensions to erupt in the form of a conflict dominated by the hostility between Islam and Communism (in which the antagonism between army leaders and Communist Party would be decisive).

Others clearly pointed out the imminent clash between Islam and Communism. In July 1965, some months before the explosion, a Dutch theologian working in Indonesia wrote as follows: "Under cover of the Nasakom unity... great tensions exist, in particular between Islam and Communism. These tensions are increasing because in recent years the Communist Party has won victory after victory, and month by month has strengthened its position. No-one can foretell what explosions this sort of tension may lead to in the future." [48]

---

[46] See *Pandji Masjarakat*, no. 1, October 1966, p. 11.
[47] Feith, *Dynamics*, p. 407 ff.
[48] D. C. Mulder, *De Islam*, in *Theologische Etherleergang der N.C.R.V.*, no. 4, September 1965, p. 165.

The truth of this last sentence became clear after the unsuccessful coup d'état of September 30th, 1965, a date which marks the beginning of a third period in the modern history of Islam in Indonesia.

4. The Ministry of Religious Affairs

Many Muslims and non-Muslims believe that "religion" and "politics" are indissolubly linked in Islam. We have already quoted Rashīd Riḍā's opinion "that Islam is not fully in being so long as there does not exist a strong and independent Muslim state that is able to put into operation the laws of Islam".[49]

Some Indonesian Muslims (for example, some members of Nationalist parties such as the P.N.I. and I.P.K.I.) seemed to prefer "the way of Turkey" (the so-called secular state) or at least a clear distinction between religion and politics, or else they advocated a state with a general religious basis, where the government would recognize the positive value of religion and would therefore promote religious activities. But a larger proportion of devout Muslims (for instance, those within the Islamic parties) hoped for something like an "Islamic State", however that ideal was to be realized. As opposed to "the way of Turkey" — often considered as a betrayal of Islam — Pakistan's attempt to be an Islamic State was taken as a shining example.

In fact, however, Indonesia is obviously a multi-religious state. It has a relatively large number of Christians (probably between 7 % and 10 %), who often hold quite important positions in Indonesian society. It is impossible to put the clock back and make these people second-class citizens (as was intended in the Islamic State of Kartosuwirjo in West Java). Therefore it is just such a country as Indonesia that could be a testcase for the possibility of adherents of various religions and philosophies of life coming to a good understanding and fruitful co-operation, for the good of their country and people.

Against the background of these problems it may be said that the Republic of Indonesia, a state with a predominantly Muslim population, has aptly evaded this embarrassing alternative by creating a Ministry of Religion, which, as it is organized in Indonesia, is probably a unique phenomenon in our world, and because of this well worth our special attention.

---

[49] Von Grunebaum, *Modern Islam*, p. 207.

As has been said, the creation of an Office for Religious Affairs was one of the benefits which Islam gained during the Japanese occupation. Starting from this Office, it was possible to develop later a Ministry of Religion (or "Ministry of Religious Affairs") with regional offices spread all over Indonesia. On August 19th, 1945, the creation of such a ministry had been rejected (Chapter I, par. 4). This increased the dissatisfaction of those Muslims who had already been disappointed by the decision concerning the basis of the state, namely the Pantjasila, and not Islam or even the Djakarta Charter. So the danger grew that part of the Muslim population would consider this new Republic of Indonesia too little their own concern. It was the fairly left-wing cabinet of Sjahrir (with the important influence of Amir Sjarifuddin) which decided on January 3rd, 1946, to make a concession to the Muslims by setting up a special Ministry of Religion. The then youthful H. Rasjidi — now a well-known professor in Djakarta and at that time minister without portfolio in Sjahrir's cabinet — became the first Minister of Religion on March 12th, 1946.

According to some informants, initially there had been some discussions on whether this Ministry would be a "Ministry for Islam" (Ind. *Kementerian Agama Islam*) or a "Ministry of Religion" (Ind. *Kementerian Agama*). It became a Ministry of Religion, first with three and afterwards with four sections, for the Muslims, the Protestants, the Roman Catholics and the Hindu-Buddhists (formerly called the Hindu-Balinese religion). At present each of the four sections is run by a Director General who is directly responsible to the Minister. Until now the Minister has always been a Muslim, and naturally the Islamic section is far and away the largest. Yet in my opinion it is somewhat too strongly worded to say, with Clifford Geertz, that in spite of its various sections "the Ministry of Religion is for all intents and purposes a *santri* affair from top to bottom".[50]

It must, of course, be admitted that this Ministry was primarily set up on behalf of Islam, which was little acquainted with forms of organization for its religious affairs. Certainly many Muslims considered this compromise of creating a Ministry of Religion "too little", while others (e.g. the Christians) thought it "too much" or "unnecessary". One very sharp judgement was made by a Roman Catholic writer who said that right from the beginning this Ministry had turned out to be "a bulwark of Islam and an outpost for an Islamic State". The author continued:

[50] Geertz, *The Religion,* p. 200.

"At the beginning the Ministry was on the defensive, but soon it became aware of its power and began to develop a propaganda far beyond the possibilities foreseen in Sjahrir's compromise. When later on the Nationalist Party became permanently entrenched behind the Ministry of Information, the propaganda service of the Ministry of Religion became as powerful as that of the state." [51]

A more moderate opinion was that this Ministry would mainly be concerned with preventing or resolving difficulties between the various religions and their adherents. This more or less negative evaluation was at one time heard in Christian circles. However, I believe that gradually the positive significance of this Ministry came to the fore. That was, (1) that it offered the possibility for religion, in particular for Islam, to function as effectively as possible in state and society, and (2) that in a preponderantly Muslim country this Ministry formed a useful middle way between a secular state and an Islamic State. If I am not mistaken, over the years many Muslims and non-Muslims have moved nearer each other, in the direction of this positive appreciation. Such an appreciation in any case applies to the principle of the existence of such a Ministry, though much criticism may be levelled at how its work is carried out.[52]

It must be admitted that even after the setting up of this Ministry some Muslim groups continued the struggle for an Islamic State, in the hope that the general elections would bring a change in the position. But the elections of 1955 made it clear that the political struggle of Islam in Indonesia for the moment had reached a stalemate. It was at that time, however, that the value of the Ministry of Religion became apparent. For, although many people still refused to face the fact, it had now become clear that Indonesia would have to develop further as a multi-religious state. It was in this situation that the Muslim part of the population needed a central body which would take to heart the interests of the Muslim community.

According to Wahid Hasjim, for the Ministry of Religion the year 1955 might be considered as "the starting point or beginning of a clearer realization of its task",[53] the years preceding being the years of formation

---

[51] J. W. M. Bakker S.J., *De Godsdienstvrijheid in de Indonesische Grondwetten*, in *Het Missiewerk*, 1956, no. 4, p. 215.

[52] Compare Van Nieuwenhuijze, *Aspects*, pp. 217-243, who shows a positive appreciation, in spite of criticism of the way in which the work is sometimes carried out. In contrast to this, see Muskens, *Indonesië*, p. 288.

[53] Wahid Hasjim, p. 610 (probably taken from a speech by R. Moh. Kafrawi, for many years Chief Secretary of the Ministry of Religious Affairs).

and organization of the Ministry and its regional offices. It was, indeed, after 1955 — when it had become clear that the general elections brought no change — that many Muslims began to concentrate their attention and energy on the internal strengthening of the Muslim community and the spread of Islam. Politically speaking, the period between 1955 and 1965 could be characterized as the "Soekarno period", which in spite of "guided democracy" led to great confusion, increasing tensions and economic collapse. Also for Muslims these were, on the one hand, years of disappointment and frustration. But on the other hand, this second decade in the recent history of Islam in Indonesia can be described as a period of positive development within the Muslim community. To a certain extent interest switched from the political scene to the problems of education, religious teaching, the spread of Islam, training for leadership and the production of reading-matter. To put it in a more Muslim way, it can be said that during this second decade the Islamic da^cwa (often translated by Muslims themselves as "the Islamic mission") was not only concerned with political activities, but began to concentrate on the strengthening of the Muslim community. Hence the Ministry of Religion began to fulfil an important role.

Over the years many government regulations defined the work and scope of the Ministry of Religious Affairs.[54] Here follows the list as given in Wahid Hasjim's work.[55]
a. To make Belief in the One and Only God (*Ketuhanan Jang Maha Esa*) an operative principle in public life.
b. To be watchful that every inhabitant is free to adhere to his own religion and to worship (*beribadat*) according to his own religion and belief.[56]
c. To assist, support, protect and promote all sound religious movements.[57]
d. To provide for, give guidance to and to supervise religious instruction in state schools.

---

[54] Cf. Van Nieuwenhuijze, *Aspects,* pp. 222-231, and Muskens, *Indonesië,* pp. 282-284.
[55] Wahid Hasjim, pp. 600-601, dating from the end of 1949, when Wahid Hasjim acted as Minister of Religion. Cf. Sidjabat, *Religious Tolerance,* p. 58, probably a variant of the same list.
[56] Compare article 29, second clause, of the 1945 Constitution.
[57] The "repressive controls over new religious sects" mentioned by Feith, *Dynamics,* p. 407, were applied, for example, to the "Javanese-Sundanese Religion" in West Java, which was considered "unsound", that is to say, subversive to orthodox religion.

e. To guide, support and inspect education and teaching given in *madrasa*s and other religious institutions.[58]
f. To found training-colleges for teachers of religion and for officials of religious courts.
g. To take care of everything connected with religious instruction in the army, in hostels, prisons and wherever else it may be necessary.
h. To regulate, put into practice and supervise everything that has to do with the registration of Muslim marriages, the revocation of repudiation of a wife (*rudjuk*), and divorce through final repudiation (*talaq*).
i. To grant material help for the restoration and upkeep of places of worship (mosques, churches, etc.).
j. To provide for, to organize and to supervise everything connected with regional Religious Courts and the Islamic High Court of Justice.
k. To inspect, recognize, register and supervise religious foundations (*waqaf*).
l. To increase the discernment of the people with regard to social and religious life.

It appears from several of these points that the Indonesian state, by means of the Ministry of Religion, wanted to promote religion and religious activities in a positive way. To some extent it can be said that this programme of work was determined by the typically Muslim idea that the government of a state is concerned with the spiritual as well as the material welfare of its people — with their condition in this world and the world to come. Two formulas generally known among Indonesian Muslims are that Islam is *dīn wa dawla* (religion and government/ politics), and that Islam comprises *dunyā wa ākhira* (this world and the world to come). On the other hand, however, the first point of this programme is concerned with religious life in general, not only with Islam; and the second point is intended to be a guarantee for religious freedom and presupposes the co-existence of various religions, in other words, a multi-religious society, not an Islamic State.

In these two points the direction of Indonesian religious policy is traced out. It is a difficult path, which in a country such as Indonesia can only be found by trial and error. The ideal is to promote religious life in general, recognizing the existence of the various religions, and to do that through a positive stimulation of religious activities, without

---

[58] These *madrasa*s and other institutions are dealt with in the following paragraph.

intervening in their internal affairs, and without favouring one or discriminating against another. These ideals were to be maintained by the Indonesian government through the Ministry of Religion. Indonesian society was to be inculcated with these ideals so that they would become the common property of everyone.

Instead of regarding this Ministry as an "outpost for an Islamic State", it may be possible, with a bit more goodwill, to reach an opposite conclusion. Is it not likely that the existence of the Ministry of Religion tends to promote the idea of a multi-religious state rather than the idea of an Islamic State? In my opinion the existence of this Ministry can in due course result in an adjustment of the Indonesian population to the fact of a multi-religious society, where the adherents of the various religions have to respect each other and each other's beliefs. It should be realized what it means for some narrow-minded or closed-minded pious people (among both Muslims and Christians) to be confronted with this multi-religious situation and to have to accept it.

The positive value of having a Ministry of Religion cannot be cancelled out by all the shortcomings and mistakes, mismanagement and waste of money which in practice sometimes happen and form the debit-side to this Ministry, its regional offices and some of its officials.

As far as the other points from the abovementioned programme are concerned, that concerning religious education in state schools (point *d*) is certainly one of the most important. As has already been said, the Masjumi in 1948 urged that religious instruction be made compulsory at these schools. This point on the programme of the Ministry of Religion was due to the influence of "Jogja" in the federal R.I.S. at the end of 1949.

The Education By-Law no. 4 of April 4th, 1950, article 20, stipulated as follows: "(1) Religious instruction is given in all state schools; parents who have objections can decide whether their child will follow the lessons or not. (2) The way in which religious instruction is given in state schools will be explained in a regulation of the Ministry of Education together with the Ministry of Religion." [59] In a further regulation of July 16th, 1951, this religious instruction was fixed at two hours per week, beginning in the fourth form of the elementary school and continuing throughout secondary school. No instruction would be

---

[59] The texts of this by-law and other regulations were obtained thanks to help from the Ministry of Religion, in stencilled or typed copy.

given, however, unless a form could muster at least 10 children belonging to the same religious group.

Over the years a great number of changes and modifications were made, among others concerning religious instruction in state universities and concerning adjustments in teaching civics and morals to bring it into agreement with new explanations of the state ideology (e.g. Manipol-USDEK in 1959). Anticipating what will be said in the following chapter, it may be noted here that in the June-July 1966 session of the People's Congress various developments from the Soekarno period were jettisoned. Thus, for example, the tolerance clause about "objections" was expunged, so that religious instruction became compulsory for all, by simply providing "that religious instruction is a school subject for pupils of elementary schools up to and including state universities".[60]

In the course of the years the Ministry of Religion also stimulated or undertook the publication of textbooks for religious instruction, especially for Islamic instruction. For Protestant and Roman Catholic schools this task was left to their own religious bodies, though it took some trouble to convince the Ministry that its help was not needed. (It was likewise incomprehensible for Muslims in the Ministry of Religion that the Protestants, for instance, did not appreciate help from the Ministry to cover the cost of translating and printing the Bible).

In connection with the first point on the abovementioned programme, one should also think of the publications of the Ministry of Religion intended for a larger public. It may be admitted that these publications tended to propagate religion by propagating only Islam.

The substance of religious instruction and the content of its reading-matter will be dealt with in the concluding chapter of this book.

A very important and comprehensive task of the Ministry of Religion is the training of teachers of religion and officials for the Religious Courts. Further there can be mentioned the religious ministration to the army, later on the creation of a special service for religious ministration to the police. Particularly after the 1960 session of the People's Congress a great number of training colleges for teachers of religion were founded (for the various religious groups) and many teachers were appointed. All this was paid for by the state, through the Ministry of Religion.

---

[60] The resolutions of the People's Congress held in 1966 are collected, for example, in the pamphlet *ABRI Pengemban Suara Hati Nurani Rakjat*, ed. by Brig. Djen. Sutjipto, Djakarta 1966, two volumes.

It is not possible to describe here all the activities based on the blueprint of 1950 and its later additions, as for instance the arrangements for the annual pilgrimage to Mecca and the organization of the Afro-Asian Islamic Conference of March 1965 in Bandung.[61] The work, methods and significance of the Ministry could be made a separate subject of study. Some of its activities and the tendencies produced by its existence will be dealt with further in the final chapter of this book.

For the time being we may conclude that the Ministry of Religion has been of great significance for the new Indonesia, in particular in the period after 1955. This applies directly for Islam, but indirectly for all the religions and for their mutual relationship. As a "Pantjasila State with a Ministry of Religion", Indonesia chose a middle way between "the way of Turkey" and the founding of an "Islamic State". A "secular state" would perhaps not suit the Indonesian situation; an "Islamic State", as attempted elsewhere, would indeed tend "to create rather than to solve problems".[62] For this reason the Indonesian experiment deserves a positive evaluation. Of course one may criticize the way in which the principle of "a Pantjasila State with a Ministry of Religion" works in practice. But this critical attitude is primarily the affair of the adherents of the various religions in Indonesia itself.

5. *Islamic Educational Institutions*

After a general orientation concerning the activities stimulated by the Ministry of Religion, special attention must be paid to specifically Islamic education. For sketching these developments it is necessary to return to the period before 1955. But it was in the period from 1955 to 1965 that an intense interest arose in questions of education, in order to strengthen the Islamic community (just as occasionally happened in the colonial period, as a result of the political frustration of that time).

It can be said that after all sorts of changes and experiments a number of organizational forms became crystallized by 1965. Before sketching the confusing historical developments, let us focus on these last, fixed forms. The blueprint which government bodies and in particular the Ministry of Religion and its offices are trying to carry out shows the following types of Islamic education and instruction in Islam:[63]

---

[61] The resolutions of this A.A.I.C. are published in *Al-Djami'ah*, no. 3, May 1965.
[62] Van Nieuwenhuijze, *Aspects*, p. 162.
[63] Cf. *Petundjuk dalam Membina Madrasah*, Vol. II, ed. by Pen. MULJA, Djakarta 1966.

Firstly: the classic Indonesian *pesantrèn*, a sort of private religious boarding-school, where as far as possible an individual education is given, formerly limited to religious instruction and the observance of religious duties. Teachers and pupils form a living and working community, cultivating the land of the *pesantrèn* in order to be self-supporting. There are *pesantrèn*s of an elementary, secondary and higher level, though there are only a few of the last type.

Secondly: *madrasa dīnīya* ("religious school"), that is to say, schools which give additional religious instruction to pupils of state schools between the ages of 7 and 20. This takes place in class, about 10 hours a week, in the afternoon, at elementary and secondary levels (4 years for the former, and 3 or 6 years for the latter). After completion of a state secondary schooling, these pupils would be admitted to religious studies at an academic level.

Thirdly: private *madrasa*s, i.e. modernized *pesantrèn*s, where as well as religious instruction general subjects are offered. Usually the aim is to spend 60-65 % of the time-table on general subjects and about 35-40 % on religious ones. These schools are divided into *madrasa*s for elementary and further education, named as follows:

a. the six-year *madrasa ibtidā'īya* ("primary school"),
b. the three-year *madrasa thanawīya* (Ind. *tsanawijah*, "secondary school"),
c. the three-year *madrasa ᶜalīya* ("high school").

Fourthly: *madrasa ibtidā'īya negeri* (M.I.N.), the six-year elementary state *madrasa*, where the ratio of religious instruction to general subjects is about 1 : 2. Further education can be pursued at a *madrasa thanawīya negeri*, or (after an extra seventh year) pupils can go to a vocational school, for example, a four-year training college for teachers of religion at state primary schools, after which a further two years' training completes the course for teachers of religion at secondary schools.

Fifthly: a recent experiment has been to add to the six-year M.I.N. a two-year course in which a simple vocational training is given (trade, agriculture, poultry-raising and so on). This eight-year M.I.N. would form a complete whole for pupils who normally would return to their villages.

Sixthly: the highest theological training, at university level, has been given since 1960 at State Islamic Institutes. More will be said below about these training colleges for religious teachers at the highest level, *imām*s for ministration to the army and police, higher civil servants for the Ministry and Offices of Religious Affairs, certain positions in the Diplomatic Service and so on.

Seventhly: the minimum religious education, which every Indonesian must receive, is the religious instruction in state schools, already mentioned in connection with the activities of the Ministry of Religion.

After this official blueprint, attention must be paid to the confusing reality of the educational developments which took place in modern Indonesia. The institutions which will be discussed in succession are the Qur'ān School, *Pesantrèn, Madrasa*, an Islamic University and the Academic Theological Training Course.

a. Qur'ān School and Pesantrèn

Writers on education within Indonesian Islam generally begin with the simplest form of the so-called Qur'ān School with its training in reciting the Qur'ān, or rather in learning by heart short passages from the Qur'ān, first of all those *suras* which are used in performing the *salāt*. Generally the performance of the *salāt* and the elements of other religious duties are also taught. This old-fashioned type of school still exists. Lessons are usually given in the afternoons. But this type of education has hardly any future, although at present good recitation of the Qur'ān is being increasingly stimulated, for instance by contests for children.

A less gloomy yet far from bright future awaits the classic *pesantrèns*. Comparing them with the Qur'ān Schools, Zoetmulder says: "More important for shaping an Islamic philosophy of life and a way of life determined by Islam are those teaching institutions which formerly were to be found all over Indonesia and today still exist, albeit less flourishing, under different names... in Menangkabau *surau*, in Atjeh *rangkang*, in Java *pesantrèn* (i.e. the place of the *santris*, "pupils of a religious school"). They are boarding-schools, usually to be found a little way outside a village or town and forming their own settlement... Pupils may enter and leave whenever they like..." [64]

At a special conference on the problem of these *pesantrèns*, Muslim critics said about pupils entering and leaving that "many of those who

---

[64] Waldemar Stöhr and Piet Zoetmulder, *Die Religionen Indonesiens*, Stuttgart 1965, p. 292 ff. (my translation).

enter a *pesantrèn* only do so in order to share in the beneficent influence (Ind. *berkat,* literally "blessing") of the leader, the *Kiyai*".[65]

Zoetmulder ends his remarks on the *pesantrèn* system by stressing that these institutions are indeed less flourishing nowadays. "Although these schools still exist, they have largely lost their appeal in this time"; trying to adapt themselves in the present day, "the question is not *whether* the methods of teaching will be changed and *whether* also secular subjects will be introduced, but *to what extent* they want to do this in these schools, originally intended for religious education".[66] It can be added here that the teaching of non-religious subjects even in many modernized *pesantrèns* or *madrasas* is still too little to be able to compete with modern state and private schools.

One may then, as Indonesian Muslims themselves do, speak of a "crisis of the *pesantrèns*". In the abovementioned conference or seminar there was much discussion on the question of whether the *pesantrèn* idea should be given up, and if not, how the *pesantrèn* should be reorganized so as to meet with modern requirements. An emotional defence of this classic institution was that during the colonial period it produced a great number of freedom-fighters who refused all compromise with the colonial government.

b. *From Pesantrèn to Madrasa*

The Indonesian manual which contains much information on the history and development of Islamic education in Indonesia up to about 1960 is the work of the well-known Mahmud Junus.[67] The author attempts to give a survey of the types and institutions of Islamic teaching since the coming of Islam to Indonesia, a survey of the subjects given and the methods used, the textbooks, famous teachers, etc. The first part of his book deals with Sumatra, the second with Java, the third with the other islands, while the fourth deals with the unity in this great diversity which has been achieved thanks to the work of the Ministry of Religion.

---

[65] *Seminar Pondok Pesantrèn Seluruh Indonesia,* in *Al-Djami'ah,* no. 5-6, p. 83. Compare what Clifford Geertz says about the African *marabout* and his *baraka* (*Islam Observed,* p. 43 ff.).

[66] Stöhr-Zoetmulder, *Die Religionen,* p. 294 (my translation).

[67] Mahmud Junus, *Sedjarah Pendidikan Islam di Indonesia,* Djakarta 1960 (1379 H.).

According to Mahmud Junus, it can be said that in about 1900 education in the *pesantrèn*s was given in a very old-fashioned way.[68] The Qur'ān and other religious books were read out by a teacher and memorized by the pupils. From 1900 onward the influence of famous Indonesian teachers (*Sjèchs*) in Mecca became noticeable in Indonesia, as many *hadji*s from Indonesia had gone to study for years in Mecca, in order to be able to pass on their knowledge as a *kiyai* in their *pesantrèn* in Indonesia. Originally a subject was usually taught with the help of only one book (for example, the "Tafsir Djalalain" as a Qur'ān commentary). After 1900 it became usual for teachers and pupils to use more than one book (for instance also the commentary of al-Baiḍāwī).

From 1900 onward all sorts of renovations began to take place, first of all in outward appearance, by the founding of a new type of *pesantrèn*, built as a school and therefore called *madrasa*. In these *madrasa*s instruction was given in classes, using benches, tables and a black-board. These changes may seem to be unimportant, but their significance becomes clear if we remember that they were part of the conflict which had arisen in Menangkabau (West Sumatra) between the *kaum tua* (old guard) and the *kaum muda* (younger generation). The debates started on questions such as whether it was allowable or not to wear Western trousers, shirts with collar and tie, and so on; later, for instance, the use of a motorcycle became a point of fierce controversy. In the new *madrasa*s the curriculum broadened, but for the time being instruction was still restricted to religious subjects and orientated toward Mecca.

Little by little, but accelerating after 1930, the modernization of the *madrasa*s won ground, in particular through the use of books from Egypt (Cairo) and by the addition of secular subjects (or, to use the Indonesian word, "general knowledge"). Even today the ratio between the religious and general subjects in these *madrasa*s is still the object of much discussion and differs considerably in the various institutions.

The critical attitude of government bodies toward these *pesantrèn*s/ *madrasa*s is based on two objections. One objection is that these institutions still offer too little of the general subjects, so that it is very difficult for their pupils to pass on to state schools for a secondary or higher education. The second objection, more cautiously expressed, is

---

[68] Cf. Mahmud Junus, *Sedjarah*, p. 45 ff.; according to Mahmud Junus the names *surau* and *rangkang* still occur, but the word *pesantrèn* has already become a common Indonesian word. Officially the term *pondok pesantrèn* (*santri* hostel) is used.

that these institutions are still strongly orientated toward the Arab centres (Cairo, Mecca) at the cost of an orientation toward Indonesian problems, which is necessary in these times. This second criticism is to be heard not only in Ministry of Education circles (as this Ministry in Indonesia is often led by "secular" nationalists), but is also made by modern-minded officials of the Ministry of Religion.[69]

It is impossible to give here a survey of all the various types and names of these *pesantrèns/madrasa*s, their time-tables and textbooks, the associations and foundations sponsoring these institutions (among others, Nahdatul Ulama, Muhammadijah and the "Persuatan Islam Bandung-Bangil", founded by the late Ahmad Hassan and now led by his son A. Qadir Hassan). All this can be found in Mahmud Junus' manual.

One of the most famous *madrasa*s at this time is perhaps the so-called "Modern Pesantrèn" (*Pondok Modèrn*) at Gontor near Ponorogo (East Java).[70] As far as I can see, the word "modern", however, seems mainly to be used because of the modern buildings and some modern methods of teaching. A booklet on Islamic doctrine written by one of the leaders does not reveal a renewal in theological thinking.[71] The aim of this institution is to develop "a high character, a broad knowledge, a sound body and independent thinking". With the help of visiting teachers from Al-Azhar in Cairo, pupils are taught to speak Arabic in such a way that some of them could continue their study in Cairo without difficulty. Former pupils of this *madrasa* are, for instance, Idham Chalid (once Minister of Religion and Chairman of the N.U.) and Nurcholis Madjid, chairman of the Islamic Student Association (H.M.I.), whose name we shall have to mention again in the final chapter of this book.

The Indonesian government is, of course, concerned with these *madrasa*s by granting subsidies which depend on certain conditions. Nevertheless, trustworthy statistical information concerning the whole of Indonesia is difficult to obtain. According to Mahmud Junus, the statistics for 1954 revealed that at that time the government subsidized more than 13,000 primary, 776 secondary and 16 higher *madrasa*s. Including non-subsidized institutions, the total number of *pesantrèn*s and *madrasa*s in 1965 was estimated at about 22,000.[72]

---

[69] Concerning the contrast between these two Ministries, cf. Muskens, *Indonesië*, p. 291 ff.
[70] See Mahmud Junus, *Sedjarah*, p. 216, and *Pandji Masjarakat*, no. 26 (March 1968?), pp. 27-29.
[71] I. Zarkasji, *Usuluddin* ('*ala madzhab Ahli-ssunna wal Djama'ah*), Gontor/Ponorogo, no date [9].
[72] *Al-Djami'ah*, no. 5-6, September-November 1965, p. 46.

c. An Islamic University

Muslims in Indonesia have always looked for ways of building up a complete system of Islamic education, from the simple *pesantrèn* up to an Islamic university. According to Mahmud Junus, under his guidance the first Islamic College was opened on December 9th, 1940, in Padang (West Sumatra).[73] It comprised two faculties, of Theology (*Sjari'at/Agama*) and of Education and Arabic studies (*Pendidikan dan Bahasa Arab*). The aim of this institution was the training of *ulama*s. Probably on a higher level, an Islamic University was founded in 1951 in Djakarta (*Perguruan Tinggi Islam Djakarta*, later *Universitas Islam Djakarta* or U.I.D.), led by Professor Hazairin.

The story of the Islamic University of Jogjakarta offers a good example of the development of Islamic universities in general. For the description which follows, information culled from Mahmud Junus' manual could be supplemented from the commemorative volume published in celebration of the first ten years of the Islamic university concerned, and from oral information acquired on the spot.

Jogja(karta) is one of the most important university cities of Indonesia. Students come to this city from all over Indonesia, partly because living costs are lower and student lodgings better than in Djakarta or other cities. The history of the Islamic University, at present situated in Jogja, goes back to the beginning of 1945, when the Masjumi decided to set up an Islamic University (*Sekolah Tinggi Islam*) in Djakarta. A preparatory committee under the leadership of Hatta, later to become Vice-President, worked out the plans. Originally the purpose of this institution was the training of well-educated *ulama*s, "that is to say, people who have made a broad and thorough study of Islam and have achieved an adequate standard of general education, as demanded by present-day society".[74] The study would take two years, leading up to a bachelor's degree, and another two years for a sort of master's degree, qualifying for a doctor's degree after having written a thesis. The curriculum was largely taken from the Faculty of Theology (Higher Section) of Al-Azhar University in Cairo, as drawn up in 1936, before Al-Azhar founded faculties of medicine, engineering, agriculture and commerce.[75]

Matriculation was open to holders of a certificate from a former Netherlands Indies secondary school, but also to those who had finished a *madrasa ᶜalīya*. Both categories generally needed a preparatory course

---
[73] Mahmud Junus, *Sedjarah*, p. 103.
[74] Mahmud Junus, *Sedjarah*, p. 251.
[75] A. M. Mohiaddin Alwaye, *Al-Azhar University*, Cairo 1966, pp. 8-11.

of one or two years, the former to supplement a knowledge of Arabic and religious subjects, the latter to reach a higher standard in general subjects. As a future career for graduates, the following posts were mentioned: teachers of religion at every sort of school, officials at religious courts, in the Civil Service and in the offices of religious affairs.

With the co-operation of the Japanese it was possible to open this institution on Radjab 27th (*Mi^{c}rādj*), 1364 H., i.e. July 8th, 1945, in Djakarta. In December 1945, however, the buildings in Djakarta were requisitioned by the Allied Forces under General Christison, so that for the time being the university had to be closed. On April 10th, 1946 the re-opening took place in Jogjakarta, in the presence of President Soekarno, with a speech by Hatta as president of the board of governors.[76]

At the beginning there were two courses of study offered, Theology (*Ilmu Agama*) and Social Studies (*Ilmu Masjarakat*). But in November 1947 it was decided to transform this institution into the Islamic University of Indonesia with four faculties, Theology, Law, Education and Economics (later also Technology). Thus the same development as in Al-Azhar, Cairo, took place here; for centuries a theological training college, in recent times Al-Azhar had added other faculties, with the intention of teaching these other sciences on the basis of religious principles and in a religious spirit.

On January 22nd, 1950 a number of Islamic leaders and *ulama*s also founded an Islamic University in Solo, about 40 miles from Jogja, with a similar preparatory course, explicitly on behalf of *pesantrèn* and *madrasa* pupils. On February 20th, 1951 these institutions in Jogja and Solo were united under the name "University (later *Universitas*) Islam Indonesia" or U.I.I., which from then on had branches in both cities.

The original aim, then, was to give prospective *ulama*s a good education, but eventually the emphasis shifted to the non-religious or "secular" faculties (technology, economics, medicine, etc.). This development, however, meant that the Islamic University would have to compete with the state universities as, for instance, was the case in Jogja, where a private non-Islamic college, founded in March 1948, developed into Gadjah Mada University, which from December 19th, 1949 took on a national character as a state university. This Gadjah Mada University certainly became a serious "rival" to the U.I.I.

---

[76] This speech and more information about this University is to be found in *Buku Peringatan University Islam Indonesia,* published on the occasion of its tenth anniversary, celebrated on 27 Radjab 1374 H. (= March 22nd, 1955).

The establishment of "secular" faculties within the U.I.I. also meant that in the end the preparatory course for pupils of the *madrasa*s had to be closed, due to the state regulations concerning the standard of education required for matriculation. This was a new blow to the future of the *pesantrèn*s and *madrasa*s and a great disappointment to the Muslim community, which wanted to stick to this ideal. In an attempt to find a solution, various *pesantrèn*s later founded their own "university", as a continuation of their highest classes (*ᶜalīya*). As an example of this type of college the "Universitas Hasjim Asj'ari" in Tebu-ireng (Djombang, East Java) can be mentioned. Founding such a (private) university is, however, easier than achieving an acceptable standard of education and getting recognition from the government based on satisfactory standards. As far as I know, the aim of this kind of private "*Pesantrèn* University", however, is in fact restricted to the training of *ulama*s.

For a proper understanding of the Indonesian situation and atmosphere, it may be recorded that generally some dozen Christians are to be found among the students of the Islamic Universities of Jogja and Solo. According to some informants, the professors are helpful and show understanding for their difficulties in studying typically Islamic material with its Arabic terminology.

d. *Academic Theological Training*

Meanwhile a remarkable development threatened this Islamic University in Jogja from quite a different direction. On August 12th, 1950 the Faculty of Theology (the original reason for its foundation) had been separated from the U.I.I., taken over by the government and on September 26th, 1951 officially re-opened under the name *Perguruan Tinggi Agama Islam Negeri* (P.T.A.I.N.), the "State Islamic College", under the supervision of the Ministry of Religion. Seen in a wider context and from a Muslim point of view, this curtailing of the U.I.I. can be considered as something positive, because in this way the government could do more for the promotion of Islam than a private Islamic University. Furthermore in Jogja a kind of college for Muslim jurisprudents was founded (*Perguruan Hakim Islam Negeri*, P.H.I.N.). In 1957 in Djakarta yet another new type of training was created, an *Akademi Dinas Ilmu Agama* (A.D.I.A.), that is, a "Government Academy for Religious Studies", intended to be a training college for officials of religion in government service (e.g. the Ministry of Religion) and for religious instruction at state schools.

In 1960 the final form for a theological training on an academic level seemed to have been found. The P.T.A.I.N. and A.D.I.A. were united to form an *Institut Agama Islam Negeri* (I.A.I.N.), i.e. a State Islamic Institute, also under the supervision of the Ministry of Religion. This development may turn out to be of great importance for the future of Islam in Indonesia. Probably this I.A.I.N. offers a possibility for training in religious leadership such as the Muslim community in Indonesia has never possessed before.

The I.A.I.N. started with two divisions or "faculties" in Jogjakarta and two in Djakarta. In both places this I.A.I.N. quickly expanded into an institution with four faculties; within each faculty the three-year course can be supplemented by a specialization of two years. The four faculties are the following. Firstly, *Uṣuluddin* (or "Ushuluddin", Doctrine or Systematic Theology), comprising the more speculative aspects of Islamic studies, such as philosophy, mysticism, comparative religion and missionary work (*daᶜwa*). Secondly, the *Sjariᶜa* faculty, emphasizing the more practical aspects of religion, such as jurisprudence, exegesis, knowledge of Tradition, etc. Thirdly, *Tarbija*, the faculty of education, i.e. the training for teachers of religion. Lastly, the *Adab* or Humanities, for specialization in the history of Islam and particularly Arabic (this language is, of course, also taught in the other faculties).

From the beginning the I.A.I.N. in Jogjakarta also started a preparatory course of two years. In 1968 it was decided to substitute for this preparatory course the final three-year course of a six-year secondary school. So now pupils from a three-year secondary (state) school continue their preparation with a three-year course at the I.A.I.N. in order to be admitted to the "theological studies" at this institution.

This new type of Islamic theological training at university level has made great advances. From Djakarta and Jogjakarta associated colleges were soon established in other cities. Starting from one or two faculties, they expanded into a complete I.A.I.N. with four faculties. Now cities such as Surabaja, Makassar and Banda Atjeh each have an I.A.I.N. with more than 1,000 students, while the I.A.I.N. in Jogja has even more than 3,000 students. The majority of them only finish the three-year course, without the two years' specialization. Through contact with Al-Azhar in Cairo, the I.A.I.N. in Jogja had from the beginning a number of visiting professors from Egypt at its disposal. During recent years there has also been co-operation between Al-Azhar and other I.A.I.Ns in Indonesia.

As is the case in Indonesian universities in general, quite a number of women students also study at these I.A.I.Ns. In some faculties they form 30-40 % of the student number. Social contact between male and female students is easy, even on the campus of the I.A.I.N. in Atjeh, which may be considered a strictly Islamic area. With this progressive attitude towards co-education, Indonesia is probably well ahead in the world of Islam. Yet it is typical for the style of life at these I.A.I.Ns that female students wear Indonesian dress and thus clearly — perhaps too ostentatiously — set themselves apart from their colleagues at other universities, who generally wear "Western" clothes.

It is impossible to describe all the forms of Islamic education and the institutions concerned, for example the training for officials at the religious courts and the training for teachers of religion at an intermediate level. The subjects and books for several types of these religious institutions will be dealt with in the final chapter of this book. The intention here has been to delineate recent developments which have taken place in the field of Islamic education.

As far as the programme of this education is concerned the developments can be summarized as follows:

a. Originally all the emphasis fell on religious education, given in *pesantrèn*s at an elementary level, later on also at secondary and higher level.

b. The first Islamic Colleges also stressed the study of religion and the training of *ulama*s.

c. These Islamic Colleges expanded into Islamic Universities, including also "secular" faculties, with the intention of studying non-religious subjects on a religious basis.

d. In the end, it was the study of religion which was separated from these Islamic Universities and concentrated in the I.A.I.Ns.[77]

With regard to organizational problems, the following summary can be made:

Firstly: The *pesantrèn*s, including those in the form of modernized *madrasa*s, are in difficulties because the parents of the pupils want them to link up with institutions of further education. It is easier for children to move up the educational ladder if they begin in state schools or private schools of a similar standard. After 1945 state education in

---

[77] With the exception of the last stage, a similar development occurred at Al-Azhar in Cairo.

Indonesia assumed enormous proportions, but there is still a shortage of schools and teachers. The more the government is able to fulfil educational commitments (new school buildings, teacher-training colleges, etc.) the more the interest in *pesantrèn* and *madrasa* education will decrease, unless these institutions are radically reformed.

Secondly: Partly because the pupils of *pesantrèn*s and *madrasa*s were not sufficiently qualified for entrance to state universities, private Islamic universities were founded. This did not prove to be a solution, because these Islamic universities are also committed to various regulations in order to get their diplomas recognized by the government. Because of this, an attempt is being made to keep to the principle of *pesantrèn* education either by supplementing it with vocational training, in order to create a course which is complete in itself, or by founding a private "Pesantrèn University".

Thirdly: Islamic universities also have many difficulties, on the one hand due to the transfer of the course in theology to the I.A.I.N., on the other hand caused by the state universities, which in general have better equipment than the far smaller private Islamic universities. Reasons of principle play but a small part in the decision of parents to send their children to Islamic universities. It is often overcrowding at the state universities that turns the scale in favour of an Islamic education.

In an anecdotic way — hence distorted, yet with a grain of truth — one informant sketched the present-day developments as follows: "Some pious villagers still send their children to an old-fashioned *pesantrèn*. The head of the *pesantrèn* sends his children to a modern *madrasa*. The teachers there have their children attend a state secondary school in order to continue at an Islamic university. The professors at an Islamic university try to get a place for their children at a state university. And the professors at a state university send their children to study — abroad."

6. *Soekarno and Islam*

At the end of this chapter, which covers the "Soekarno period", we have to realize that a study on the recent history of Islam in Indonesia will have to answer the question: what role did Soekarno play in this history? In how far was it he who determined the future of the new Indonesia as a multi-religious state, based on the Pantjasila, with a positive policy of freedom of religion and the promotion of religion? Or was Soekarno only the embodiment of the religious feelings of a great part of the Indonesian people, in particular in Java? Did he not voice the feelings of many others, who were not able, or had not the courage, to express all sorts of probably "heretical" opinions in such a candid or bold way as Soekarno used to? To what extent may "Soekarno's Islam" be considered also to be a manifestation of Islam, i.e. a form of *abangan-Islam,* in this case the Islam of a mystical, artistic intellectual, yet a typically Javanese *abangan*? Some Islamic theologians said that Soekarno was a typical Javanese syncretist, and that "syncretism is the archenemy of religion". However, all agreed that Soekarno had a deeply religious nature.

Insofar as Soekarno is a representative of a sort of Indonesian or Javanese religiosity, it is certainly useful to attempt to understand more about his opinions. It is not my concern to make any judgement on Soekarno's personal belief. It is a good Muslim rule to abstain from making a judgement on someone's inner intentions: *wa'llāhu a^clam,* God knows best! But we must listen to Soekarno in order to understand his Javanese interpretation of Islam and his attitude towards the opinions of more orthodox and traditional Muslims.

For a contemporary of Soekarno's who has heard and seen him speaking, it is easy to understand that even during his life all kinds of interpretations of the Soekarno phenomenon had become current.[78] One got the impression that Soekarno himself enjoyed, with a certain vanity, playing the elusive figure, for example when he said of himself, "There are those who say: Soekarno is a Nationalist; others say: he is not a Nationalist any more, he is a Muslim now. And there are yet others who say: he is neither a Nationalist nor a Muslim, but a Marxist. There are even a few who say: he is neither Nationalist, nor Muslim, nor Marxist, he's a man with his own opinions ... What is this Soekarno? Is he a Nationalist, a Muslim, a Marxist? Dear readers, Soekarno is a mixture of all these 'isms'." [79]

In his speech on August 17th, 1960, Soekarno declared himself proudly to be "possessed (*kerasukan*) by the romanticism of the revolution". It may turn out that these words are the best starting-point

---

[78] Cf. Bernhard Dahm, *Sukarnos Kampf um Indonesiens Unabhängigkeit,* Mannheim 1964; here taken from the Dutch translation, *Soekarno en de strijd om Indonesië's onafhankelijkheid,* Meppel, no date, p. 12 ff.
[79] Quoted by Dahm, *Soekarno,* p. 184.

for discussing "Soekarno and Islam". Concerning the period before 1934 Dahm has pointed out that Soekarno did not really confess the Islamic faith. Soekarno had, indeed, even in that period "a basic sympathy toward religion", but "what he knew of Islam was acquired knowledge for the sake of convenience, largely taken from Lothrop Stoddard's 'The New World of Islam'; and he was more intrigued by 'the new world' than by Islam itself".[80]

Probably this last sentence may be taken as a key to the problem. It appeared that Soekarno was continuously searching for an explanation of the backwardness of Islam in the modern world. While in exile on the island of Flores, he once wrote that "the Islamic world became backward because so many people followed weak and false Traditions". These Traditions "were largely the origin of the decline of Islam, the old-fashioned features and impure elements of its doctrine". In order to prove his opinion, he wanted to study the Traditions, in particular the "Saḥīḥ" of al-Bukhārī, because, on the authority of "an English Muslim" he assumed that even al-Bukhārī's collection contained unreliable Traditions.[81] This collection of al-Bukhārī was, however, at that time not available in a language which Soekarno knew, so that this study could not be undertaken.[82]

Some time later the *fiḳh* (Islamic jurisprudence) became the scapegoat, because, according to Soekarno, the *fiḳh* was concerned with a religious law which "for more than a thousand years had determined the day-to-day life of a Muslim"; this law, therefore, had become "a hangman of the spirit and soul of Islam". "Islam has remained a thousand years behind the times." Soekarno criticized the *kiyai*s and *ulama*s, the casuistry of Muslim jurists. Not the letter, but the spirit!

---

[80] Dahm, *Soekarno*, p. 166. The first edition of Stoddard's book appeared in New York in 1921. Stoddard's intention was to show that the world of Islam was awakening, thanks to leaders such as al-Afghānī and Muḥ. ᶜAbduh. In this way he also opened the eyes of some Muslims to the condition of Islam and its possibilities for renewal. At Soekarno's insistence, just before his fall from power, this book was translated into Indonesian and published under the title *Dunia Baru Islam*, with a foreword by Soekarno, dated January 1st, 1966. The translation committee added a final chapter on modern Islam in Indonesia (pp. 295-332).

[81] Dahm, *Soekarno*, p. 169.

[82] According to the Indonesian *Shahih Buchari*, Djakarta Vol. I, 1964[6] and Vol. II, 1966[2], the translation and publication was begun in 1937 in instalments; the revision for a second edition (Vol. I, 1952) was apparently stimulated by the Ministry of Religion (Minister Wahid Hasjim).

Amīr ᶜAlī's book "The Spirit of Islam" (or at least its title) played a great role in Soekarno's attitude towards orthodox Islam.[83]

The formula which in the end was to carry the greatest weight and would continuously be repeated by Soekarno was that the backwardness of the Muslim world is the result of the *taḳlīd* mentality, that is to say, the acceptance of belief on the authority of others, without question or objection, in fact the acceptance of precepts that Muslim scholars of the four orthodox schools of law had laid down a thousand years ago. In accordance with well-known Egyptian reformist opinion, the decline of the Muslim world is thus ascribed to the closing of the *Bāb al-Idjtihād* ("the gate of personal effort"), i.e. the prohibition on individual reasoning based on an inquiry into the Qur'ān and Tradition by scholars of our own time. In Bencoolen (Bengkulu, Sumatra), where Soekarno had been taken by the colonial government in 1938, he came into contact with the reform movement and became a member of the Muhammadijah, where he found opinions at least partly acceptable to him.

However, Soekarno probably wanted to give a more radical interpretation of "the spirit of Islam" than many reformers. On the one hand, the point on the reformers' programme concerning the "purification" of Islam from all superstition would not have interested him much. On the other hand, Soekarno could be called a true liberal. He was certainly more interested in the new world than in Islam. In his interpretation of Islam, he always emphatically repeated the slogans of Muslim apologists, such as "Islam is progress", "no religion is more rational than Islam", "Islam insists on scientific research", "the science of Islam is knowledge of the Qur'ān and Tradition plus general knowledge", "the Qur'ān and Tradition must be interpreted with the help of general scholarship", and so on.[84]

What Soekarno envisaged was certainly not a "return to the Qur'ān and Tradition" in the way the *salafīya* reformers wanted to return to the pure belief of "the ancestors" (Ar. *aslāf*, sing. *salaf*). For Soekarno, the revolutionary, there was no "return". Islam had to catch up its thousand years of backwardness. "Not back to the early glory of Islam, not back to the time of the caliphs, but run forward, catching up with time (chasing time), that is the only way to get glory again."[85] Does

---

[83] Cf. Dahm, *Soekarno*, pp. 170-178.
[84] A small collection of sayings by Soekarno is given in Solichin Salam, *Bung Karno dan Kehidupan Berpikir Dalam Islam,* Djakarta 1964.
[85] Salam, *Bung Karno,* p. 91. When speaking of "catching up with time", one must realize that the Indonesian expression *ketinggalan zaman* (obsolete, out of date) literally means that something is "left behind by time".

not Soekarno's criticism sound like "Turkish" criticism of the Arab glorification of the past? [86]

This critical attitude toward a return to the past may well explain Soekarno's opposition to the idea of an Islamic State. He was afraid that in that case "one would continuously have to take into account a veto from a council of *ulama*s, who would always appeal to orthodox, traditional precepts". That was why he wanted, as he once said, "to accept the challenge of democracy" and "to accept the separation of religion and state". On that occasion he added (seriously or to soothe the Muslims?): "But we shall inflame the whole people with the fire of Islam, until every representative in Parliament is a Muslim, and every parliamentary decision is imbued with the spirit and soul of Islam".[87] Soekarno probably so feared the influence of conservative *kiyai*s and *ulama*s that it is to be doubted whether he really hoped for such a strengthening of the position of Islam "that 60 %, 70 %, 80 %, 90 % of the representatives will be Muslims, Islamic leaders, *ulama*s".[88] A *conditio sine qua non* for such a Muslim country — not to mention an Islamic State — would, for Soekarno, have been that Islam would have to be radically renewed, in agreement with his own idea of "the spirit of Islam".

What then was "Soekarno's Islam"? What was "the spirit of Islam" according to Soekarno's interpretation? Let us listen to Soekarno himself, by quoting extensively from two characteristic speeches from his later period. We shall have to be patient with Soekarno's verbosity, but in so doing one gets a better impression than by quoting only short passages which are supposed to contain the essence of his ideas (the method of Solichin Salam and more or less that of Dahm).

On the occasion of receiving his 24th honorary doctor's degree (from the I.A.I.N., Djakarta) on December 2nd, 1964, Soekarno made his famous speech entitled *Tjilaka Negara jang tidak ber-Tuhan* (Woe to the State without God).[89] The title was intended to emphasize that not only the citizens ought to be personally religious — turning to his audience, Soekarno addressed some of them by name: "(Su)Bandrio, you've got to be a believer, understand?", and in the same way he called

---

[86] Compare Smith, *Islam*, p. 164 ff.
[87] Quoted by Dahm, *Soekarno*, p. 191.
[88] Salam, *Bung Karno*, p. 69, from Soekarno's speech "The Birth of the Pantjasila", Yamin, *Naskah*, I, p. 61 ff.
[89] *Tjilaka Negara jang tidak ber-Tuhan*, published in *Al-Djami'ah*, special issue, January 1965.

to Leimena, Nasution and Arudji Kartawinata — no, not only the citizens, but the state as such must recognize God. In this speech Soekarno spoke as follows:

"If you ask whether Bung Karno believes in God, then I will answer: Yes, I believe in God... From my boyhood, my very boyhood, I was brought up by my parents to believe in God. My father was a Muslim, or rather, as I once said, the Muslim-ness of my father, what shall I say — it was in fact half-and-half Islam (Ind. *Islam-islamanlah*). He certainly stood nearer to what people call the Javanese religion.

And my mother, well, she came from Bali. She was a Balinese. When a young man, my father met a beautiful Balinese girl. Sukemi was my father's name. Sukemi met a Balinese girl called Njoman Rai, Ida Aju Njoman Rai. And when Sukemi met Ida Aju Njoman Rai, then, in accordance with God's will, these two fell in love, as it's called.

So they became husband and wife, and God made this Sukemi-Ida-Aju-Njoman-Rai his instrument (Ind. *dapur,* literally "kitchen") to bring Soekarno into the world. It was God who did it. Sukemi and Ida Aju Njoman Rai were used by God as instruments ("a kitchen") to give me birth.

Well, as a young boy, I used to hear from my father: Kusno — later Soekarno, as a boy I was called Kusno — Soekarno, as for me, I was only a sort of instrument, and your mother too, Soekarno, a sort of instrument, used by God to give you birth. So, don't forget, Karno, don't forget: The One who made you was God! Even though my father was really only a half-and-half Muslim!

Forgive me for talking like this. I say this, following the norms of Islam. Indeed, measured by the norms of Islam, strictly speaking, he was only a half-and-half Muslim. So, certainly, his religion was Islam, but mixed with much Javanese religion. And my mother, her religion was Hinduism mixed with a lot of Buddhism.

But both of them, my late father and my mother, considered themselves only as instruments. And it seems to me that this opinion is quite correct. An instrument — that was why from my boyhood onwards I was reminded by my father and mother: Don't forget that we, your father and your mother, were so to speak only instruments, but He who made you was God (*Allah s.w.t.*). My father called Him 'Gusti Kang Maha Sutji', my mother spoke of 'Hyang Widi'. In this way: Don't forget Gusti Kang Maha Sutji...; Karno, don't forget Hyang Widi...

When I was older and became the Leader of the people — that too by God's mercy — I often reflected on the condition of Islam. Well now,

Islam seems to have had an ebb and flow.[90] How did this happen? Before, there was a rising tide; Islam was like a lighthouse; everybody looked at it, impressed, with pride, with admiration! Later, there came an ebb tide for the Muslim community — first a flood tide, then an ebb — when other peoples considered Muslims as a group of no importance, as 'inferior'. How did this happen?

Well, in order to examine this, I freed myself from the ordinary way of thinking and rose into the higher sphere of history.[91] ... And this is what I want to tell you, students:[92] if you really want to understand the truth of Islam, if you want to understand why formerly Islam had a flood tide ... but also an ebb ... free your mind from obvious, conventional thinking. If I may put it so — don't take exception to it, please, it's just to make it clear, to help you understand it, as an illustration! — if in a minute I use a certain word, don't take it as an insult, no, it's meant for you to understand it better — you, students of the I.A.I.N., you must not study Islam and try to make Islam flourish with, as it were, the spirit — sorry! — the spirit of the *pesantrèn* (Ind. *djiwa-pesantrèn*). Do you understand what I mean? *Not, as it were, with the spirit of the pesantrèn!* [93]

No, free your own mind from the sphere of thinking in the *pesantrèn*. Rise up in space, as I did, and look outwards! And don't only look to Saudi Arabia, to Mecca and Medina, but look to Cairo, Spain, look around the whole world; look at history, at the past, the past history of the peoples of the world, not only that of the people of Indonesia and the Arabs, but the history of mankind!

Only then will you be able to make what are called comparative studies, in your case, the study of comparative religion, 'to compare', compare the one to another.

---

[90] Cf. Smith, *Islam*, p. 166, on Ḥālī's poem "The Flow and Ebb of Islam".
[91] With regard to this metaphor of "rising up" and a little later that of *miᶜrādj* (literally "ladder"), it must be remembered that this ceremony took place in connection with the celebration of *Miᶜrādj*, the feast of the Prophet's "ascension" or "journey into Heaven". Compare Sura 17:1, which, according to the translation by Moh. M. Pickthall, "relates to the Prophet's vision, in which he was carried by night upon a heavenly steed to the Temple of Jerusalem, whence he was caught up through the seven heavens to the very presence of God". In each heaven the Prophet talked with one of the earlier messengers of God. Compare the way in which Soekarno is going to speak of his encounters with "the leaders of America".
[92] I.e. of the I.A.I.N., the State Islamic Institute.
[93] That Soekarno shocked many *kiyai*s with this criticism of the *pesantrèn*s became apparent at the abovementioned "Seminar" held in July 1965 in Jogjakarta; cf. *Al-Djami'ah*, no. 5-6, Sept.-Nov. 1965, pp. 9, 53, 73, 81, 109.

Free yourself from the spirit or atmosphere or climate of the *pesantrèn*. Once more, my apologies, I do not mean to insult. I myself have released myself from this 'material' world which gave me no satisfaction, no gratification, and have ascended the *Miᶜrādj*, the *Miᶜrādj* of the mind, dear friends. The *Miᶜrādj* of the mind ... 'the world of the mind' ... That's to say, I used to read books written by people from all over the world ... There I met the thinkers, the thinkers of all peoples.

I read that Islam is a universal religion, a religion which is understandable for all people and to which all peoples of this world should adhere.[94] But (I thought): is it really true that Islam can be realized in America? It is said, Islam is the universal religion, isn't it? Therefore I wanted to get to know the American spirit, and so, 'in the world of the mind', I went to America ... Read books ... And in this 'world of the mind' I spoke, as it were, with the Leader of America George Washington, with the Leader of America Thomas Jefferson, with the Leader of America Adam Smith, and so on ... So I began to understand: Aha, so this is the American people! And (I concluded): Yes, indeed! Islam can be brought to life among the American people ..."

(In the same rhetorical vein, England, France, Germany, Italy, Russia, Japan and India pass in revue. After a repeated warning against the spirit of the *pesantrèn*, Soekarno reasserts his pet theme, that the closing of the *Bāb al-Idjtihād* was the cause of the decline of Islam. Finally he compares living in the *pesantrèn* spirit with a stay in a musty *gudang* (closed room), to wind up as follows:)

"Open up! Open the door, open the window! Yes, more yet: once you're out of that stuffy place, rise up, rise up, up into space, and look at things from above, see what the history of earlier Muslim communities was like, and what is the way that we to-day must take — that's to say, 'what is behind us, and what is before us' — in order to see what we should do to build a glorious future, a glorious time to come."

On August 3rd, 1965 Soekarno received an honorary degree (his 26th) from the Muhammadijah University in Djakarta, with a speech entitled *Tauhid adalah Djiwaku* ("To declare that God is One, is my soul", or "I confess the Oneness of God in the depths of my soul").[95] So here Soekarno was among reformers, who want to free Islam from every sort

---

[94] It should be borne in mind that Soekarno on this occasion was being made honorary doctor in *Ilmu Ushuluddin Djurusan Daᶜwah*, something like "Systematic Theology with a specialization in Missiology"!

[95] *Tauhid adalah Djiwaku, Amanat P. J. M. Presiden,* Djakarta 1965.

of superstition (for instance, visiting the graves of "saints" and asking for their intercession), in consequence of the confession of God's Uniqueness.

To begin with, Soekarno spoke of the new translation of the Qur'ān which was to appear, because, Soekarno said, we ought to be able to understand our religion, "for religion is not only concerned with feelings, but also with reason, reason, understanding, (Latin) *ratio, ratio* and once again *ratio*!" After this introduction he touched upon the *adat*, a risky subject in these circles, to go on to speak precisely about visiting graves!

"Now then, ... it is indeed a superstitious custom to visit graves in order to ask for something. To tell the truth, I do something like that also. But every time I visit my mother's grave at Blitar, or my father's grave at Karet here in Djakarta, to tell the truth, I don't ask my father for something, I don't ask my mother at Blitar for something, I only ask my father and mother that they will help me when I ask something of God, the Praiseworthy and the Exalted.

For example — I am going to do something important, let's say, I am going to the second Afro-Asian Conference in Algiers. Then I ask: father, I ask you to pray to God that I shall have success in Algiers. So, too, with my mother at Blitar... For according to the teachings of our religion, the dead can hear you, the dead can listen. Therefore it is recommended, when we visit a grave, to utter the greeting: *as-salāmu ᶜalaikum* ("peace be with you"), you within the grave!...

Well, now, allow me to speak in the following way about how I confess God's Oneness... I am someone whose mother used to follow the Hindu-Balinese religion... My father, what shall I say? He was a Muslim, but his Islam was the Islam of Javanese mysticism... I grew up and became the Leader of your movement. I was thrown into the prison of Sukamiskin by the Dutch government, and ended up in a cell 2.50 meters long by 1.50 meters wide. Small, I can tell you... I was even put in a cell for 'solitary confinement'.[96]

In these circumstances I began earnestly to meditate on the Divine Being... What is that 'God'? (Ind. *Tuhan itu apa?*). What is He like?... Thank God (*Sjukur alhamdulillah*), although in prison I was not allowed to read any political books, I could always ask for religious books to be sent: the Qur'ān and a translation of the *Hadith* (Traditions), and the Bible... and as has just been said by the promotor,

---

[96] That is to say, without neighbours.

Professor Baroroh, books by Becker and Hartmann and Isaq Bey and Snouck Hurgronje.[97] ... I read and compared, read and compared, everything with a view to the question: who is God or what is He like? ...

So, is God a Being (*zat*) on a throne up there? A Being in space, what people call 'a personal God'? If He lives only up there, God is limited. Isn't that so? ... Just as if God had only twenty attributes, then this God would be limited ... The Bhagavad-Gītā says — I'm not concerned with whether that song is true or not — the Bhagavad-Gītā says: 'I am in the fire, I am in the heat of the fire; I am in the moon, I am in the rays of the moon' ... Yes, even 'I am in the smile of a girl'. 'I am in the clouds, I am in the procession of clouds which proceed together. I am in the darkness. I am in the light. I am without beginning and without end'.

This agrees with my opinion. So then, where is God? Is God up there only, only, only there, in the seventh heaven, only in the seventh heaven? ... I am a monotheist. But I am a pantheistic monotheist. Pantheism means: I feel — feel! — this God everywhere. He is up there, and also over there, in the moon too, and in the sun, also in the stars, in the mountains too, and in the fire, and also in the heat of the fire, in the ants, too, yes, in everything, everything ... but He's One, One. Like, in a rough example, like ether. Penetrating everything.

I believe that nothing happens in this world without God's knowing. But I do not accept that God, well — sits somewhere up there and looks down below, so to speak, thinking: 'I can see you, Chairul Saleh, what are you doing there? I can see you, Jo Leimena, what are you doing there?' [98] ... I repeat, if God sits only up there, then He is limited. But God is 'without end, limitless, without any limit'. But He's One, One! ...

And so, Professor Baroroh, that's my opinion of God's Oneness. Whether it is right or not, I must leave to your judgement. Perhaps my opinion of God's Uniqueness is different from that of other people. Whether it is right or not, God knows best (*wa'llāhu aᶜlam*) ... I leave it to God, the Praiseworthy and the Exalted, the Creator of the Universe, Allah, Praiseworthy and Exalted, who is One, the Only."

---

[97] The speech by Prof. Baroroh Baried ("the first Indonesian woman who conferred an honorary degree on President Soekarno") is also published in the booklet mentioned above, under the English heading "For a fighting Moslem Hero, there is no journey's end".

[98] The ministers mentioned were apparently present at this ceremony.

Such are Soekarno's words. He could chat in such an informal, friendly way — presenting sometimes un-orthodox religious views — that many who saw and listened to him fell under his spell. It is evident that he had a good grasp of the art of choosing the right words to appeal to as many as possible. It is not surprising that in the heyday of Soekarno's regime all the various groups and parties attempted to annex him or his words. Both Muslims and Communists could make use of certain opinions and slogans of Soekarno, that "mixture of all 'isms' ". People were often prepared to trim their opinions to fit Soekarno's wishes, for example the Communists in their "acceptance" of the first pillar of the Pantjasila (Belief in the One and Only God), the Muslims in the "acceptance" of Soekarno's Guided Democracy (by translating the term *ūlū 'l-amri* from Sura 4 : 59 with "your leaders" and interpreting it by using the singular, "our leader").[99]

Much honour was bestowed on Soekarno by Muslims too, not only by giving him honorary degrees, but also, for example, titles such as "Faithful Member and Great Support of the Muhammadijah", or, much earlier, *Wālī al-Amri Darūrī bis-Sjauka,* probably to be rendered: "the ruler who at present is in power (and has to be obeyed according to Sura 4 : 59)".[100] How seriously should all this be taken? After Soekarno's fall, several of these honours were withdrawn by the Muslims. Perhaps, looking back, it could be regarded as a mutual flirtation which was carried out with a smile, in the sense of *tahu sama tahu* (like knows like).

Soekarno will live on in history as the leader of the Indonesian revolution. His grave at Blitar may become a kind of place of pilgrimage for many Indonesians, especially in Java. In the future, Indonesian Muslims too will probably again acknowledge Soekarno as one of the creators of Indonesia. For the time being, however, one of the Muslim

---

[99] Cf. the speech by the Minister of Religion, K. H. M. Wahib Wahab on January 10th, 1962, who gave this Qur'anic support for the Muslims' obedience to Soekarno's order for the liberation of West Irian; the necessity of obedience for the Christians was shown by quoting Matthew 22:21 (see *Mutiara Hikmah,* published by the Ministry of Religion, no. 330-1962, p. 41 ff.).

[100] According to Father Bakker, this "recognition" was a decision made by a number of N.U. *kiyais* and *ulamas* at a conference in March 1954 (J. W. M. Bakker S.J., *Godsdienstvrijheid,* p. 226); the author rendered the meaning of the title concerned as follows: the head of an Islamic State which for the time being has to be recognized and obeyed. The Arabic *shauka* occurs in Sura 8:7 in the meaning of armed force.

poets of the "Generation of 1966", Taufiq Ismail (pseudonym Nur Fadjar), has denounced the Soekarno cult in the following "Prayer":[101]

> Our Lord,
> We have been disgraced by collective sin;
> For years we built up this cult,
> With various motives,
> Silencing our consciences.
> Forgive us,
> Forgive.
> Amen.
>
> Our Lord,
> Too lightly
> Have we used Your Name,
> For years in this country.
> May You be willing to receive us again
> Into Your service.
> Forgive us,
> Forgive.
> Amen.

---

[101] Taufiq Ismail, *Doa*, in his collection *Tirani*, Djakarta 1966, p. 25; see also *Pandji Masjarakat*, no. 2, October 1966, p. 3, where part of this poem is used as a motto for an editorial under the heading *Taubat Nashuha* ("Sincere Repentence", cf. Sura 66:8).

CHAPTER III

ISLAM AND THE "NEW ORDER"

(1965 and after)

1. *The Thirtieth of September and its Aftermath*

In 1963 Herbert Feith pointed out that the internal tensions in Indonesia were coming to a head; another observer indicated in particular the increasing tensions between Islam and Communism.[1] Part of the Islamic community was put out of action by the proscription of the Masjumi and the arrest of important Islamic leaders. But even without a strong organization, the Muslim community formed a latent power which could move into action at any moment. On the other hand, the Communist Party (P.K.I.) was certainly the only well-organized party, and as such was a "state within the state".

The army has to be mentioned here as the most important third power. Within the army there was a strong Muslim influence (in particular from adherents of the Masjumi), while Christian influence was also relatively strong. The army officers had for years played the role of guardian of the Pantjasila ideals, as much against the left (Communists) as the right (e.g. the Darul Islam movement). Some army units — for instance, within the Diponegoro Division in Central Java — had certainly been considerably infiltrated by Communists. But the senior officers of the armed forces (at least those of the army) were fiercely anti-Communist. General Nasution in particular had for years been fighting Communist influence within the army. On certain occasions he appeared to be in agreement with Soekarno, but in fact there was a continuous tug-of-war between Nasution and the President, for instance in appointing or dismissing left-wing army officers.

Soekarno's Guided Democracy was in fact based on a policy of divide-and-rule, in spite of the official NASAKOM principle. This policy of Soekarno's certainly did not include any promise or solution for a future

---

[1] See the end of Chapter II, par. 3.

without Soekarno. However, I have the impression that it was hardly expected that one of the power groups (e.g. the Communists) would attempt a coup d'état before Soekarno's death; similarly the growing number of Soekarno's opponents (e.g. among the military and the Muslims) could not risk an attempt to remove him from power, because of his remaining popular support. So everyone bided his time. It was, however, generally believed that when Soekarno died there would not only be a personal tussle for the succession, but also an open clash between the various power groups. Many years before 1965 it was even possible to hear people in Indonesia saying that they hoped "the clash" would come soon, as otherwise the consequences would be even more catastrophic. Thus people anxiously awaited Soekarno's death. Symptomatic of the tension were the rumours about the President's illness which emerged again and again, sometimes with spicy details. Was not, after all, the tragedy of Soekarno's life that the great hero of the fight for freedom had outlived his reputation?

In the night of September 30th, 1965, the storm broke, due to the action of Colonel Untung, the Commander of the Palace Guard in Djakarta. A number of generals were surprised in their sleep in the early morning of October 1st and horribly murdered. They were accused of belonging to a "Council of Generals" preparing a military coup d'état. The "September 30th Movement" was said to have prevented this. On the morning of October 1st, the establishment of a "Revolutionary Council" was announced, which would safeguard the state and the life of the President.

But a day later the action of Untung and whoever was behind him appeared to have failed, thanks to the swift intervention of General Soeharto, chief of the office for the "army's strategic reserve". This office was concerned with the stationing and movement of troops, but was not itself a fighting unit. Was this probably the reason why Soeharto's name did not occur on the list of generals to be arrested? A second mistake made by Untung's men was that they let General Nasution escape. His escape was of great importance, first of all psychologically (perhaps even for Soekarno's wavering attitude), and later on also politically.

I do not consider myself either competent or obliged to attempt a complete analysis of the events and their background. Here follow only a few remarks, insofar as they are relevant to the subject of this book.

To begin with, two strongly contrasting opinions may be put forward.

One simple explanation is that Untung's action was just an attempt at a coup d'état by the Communist Party (P.K.I.) under the leadership of Aidit and supported by sympathetic army officers. At the other end of the scale the "October 1st Movement" — as President Soekarno and his following liked to call it — is considered to have had very little to do with Communism, let alone the leadership of the P.K.I., but "was essentially an internal Army affair, stemming from a small clique in the Diponegoro Division, which attempted to use both Soekarno and the PKI leadership for its own ends"; according to this analysis there were even certain "idealistic motivations" within this group (e.g. resistance to corrupt Djakarta circles and "a return to the spirit of Jogja", as it was in the first period of the Revolution), although these motives were "far less important than resentment, ambition, puritanism and unanchored radicalism".

The first of these explanations is generally maintained in Indonesia among all anti-Communist groups, including religious circles. The second — eagerly accepted outside Indonesia by critics of this anti-Communism — was chiefly based on "A Preliminary Analysis of the October 1, 1965, Coup in Indonesia", originating from a famous American university and dated January 10th, 1966.[2]

In favour of the first explanation it has to be admitted that the Untung action was also considered a Communist action by Communist groups themselves, in particular in Central Java, and anyway the Communists and their press relations had heavily compromised themselves by their initial reactions on the morning of October 1st. Moreover, the unsuccessful Untung action was clearly connected with conflicts of far wider dimensions: "The brief 'civil war' of late October, though precipitated by the events of October 1st, represented the logical culmination of deeply-felt hostilities and hatreds between a far wider range of

---

[2] This document of about 160 pages was initially "strictly confidential", that is to say with regard to its origin, not its contents. Its preface says: "Feel free to use [the material in] it as you wish in publication, but please do not refer in any way to this document". By now, however, this document has become well-known enough, also in Indonesia, and it is quite generally admitted to be both one-sided and obsolete. In the Dutch weekly "Vrij Nederland" of April 25th, 1970, the formerly Indonesian Professor E. Utrecht mentioned this document as the "Cornell Report" written by two specialists on Indonesian affairs, B. R. O'G. Anderson and Ruth T. McVey, and intended to be used only within Cornell University circles.

groups and ideologies — right and left, Islam and Communism, landlord and landless, *santri* and *abangan*, *prijaji* and peasant".[3]

On the other hand, the opinion that the Untung action was simply an attempt by the Communist Party to seize power has been modified by more subtle analyses. Some, for example, believe that it was a plot hatched by a number of individual Communists and fellow-travellers together with a number of officers from outside Djakarta, while the P.K.I. leaders themselves would have preferred to wait and see. Others believe that the P.K.I. had to join in at a certain moment, owing to particular circumstances. Yet others maintain that at any rate the Untung action, had it succeeded, would in the end have resulted in a Communist government. A recent Dutch publication concluded: "Who exactly it was who inspired the coup of the night of September 30th to October 1st... will probably always remain an unresolved question: a group of frustrated officers with the knowledge of the P.K.I., or the P.K.I. with the help of these officers".[4]

For the time being John Hughes [5] arrived at the conclusion that the P.K.I. was indeed directly involved in the coup, although the question remains as to whether the P.K.I. took the initiative or only joined in when the sign was given by someone else, whoever that may have been. Moreover, the various groups took part in the coup for different motives: the Communists because they believed that circumstances forced them to, though it was probably a little too soon for them, and the army officers concerned (Sujono, Supardjo, Omar Dhani) because some of them were fellow-travellers or joined in because of military ambitions or opportunism. Soekarno himself, according to Hughes, may at least have known that something was going to happen, and it would not have been displeasing to him to know that certain generals would be silenced. This does not mean that Soekarno had given direct orders or that anyone had officially or straightforwardly asked for his assent. "In Indonesia, things are not done that way." [6]

---

[3] See for this and the preceding quotations *A Preliminary Analysis*, pp. 8 and 63. These contrasts are also dealt with in a Dutch publication by the Indonesian sociologist Basuki Gunawan, *Kudetá, Staatsgreep in Djakarta*, Meppel 1968.

[4] Muskens, *Indonesië*, p. 250.

[5] John Hughes, *Indonesian Upheaval*, New York 1967.

[6] Hughes, *Upheaval*, p. 114. It could be useful to compare the events surrounding September 30th, 1965 with the Madiun affair of 1948. According to Alers, even the Communist rising in Madiun was not ordered by the leaders of the party, but simply "broke out". Alers' conclusions were as follows. The plans of the former P.K.I. leader Musso were not aimed at a

Recently Donald Hindley gave a "tentative reconstruction", which can probably be considered a correction to the preliminary analysis contained in the abovementioned Cornell Report.[7] This reconstruction can be summarized as follows. It was obvious that Soekarno's death would lead to a clash between the Communists and their many enemies (army officers, Muslims, certain intellectuals, bureaucrats and even the majority of P.N.I. members). In the middle of 1965 the Communists realized that they would lose in such a clash. In August Soekarno's health suddenly seemed to be much worse. Subandrio, Minister of Foreign Affairs, who apparently played an obscure role, recalled the P.K.I. leader Aidit from China, together with a team of Chinese doctors. "Aidit had to assume that if Sukarno was removed from effective leadership, then the army generals would at once launch an attack against the unprepared party. The September 30 Movement was conceived to avert this threat." Although "a definitive analysis of this movement may never been written", it may be concluded that "the September 30 Movement, as finally conceived, was not a coup to establish a communist government". Of the 45 members of the Revolutionary Council proclaimed by the insurgents on October 1st, 1965, "only about five would be communists or known communist associates, none of them PKI leaders". In this way "the general tenor of political life would have shifted to the left — without provoking a massive anti-communist reaction". In other words, the immediate aim of the coup was not to establish a Communist government, but to save the Communists from the destruction which would threaten them on the death of the President, and in this way the Communist Party could have continued to strengthen its position gradually, also after the death of the President, until in due time the party was indeed ready to take over power.

---

coup d'état but primarily at limited changes in the government, through forced changes in the cabinet, after which the assumption of power could be prepared in stages. Djokosujono broadcast at that time: "The Madiun affair is not a coup... it is not an attempt to overthrow the Republic, but is merely an attempt to eliminate colonial and feudal elements" (Quoted by Kahin, *Nationalism*, p. 298). Musso, however, was a bad organizer, in spite of his training in Moscow, and did not have control over his friends (e.g. Djokosujono and Sumarsono). In the end the whole P.K.I. was involved in an affair which could only be regarded as an attempt at a coup d'état, and which was crushed as such. Cf. Alers, *Rode of Groene*, p. 15, n. 1 and pp. 185-197.

[7] Donald Hindley, *Alirans and the Fall of the Old Order*, in *Indonesia*, Cornell 1970, no. 9 (April), pp. 23-66.

However that may be, inside Indonesia the Untung action was called *Gerakan Tigapuluh September* (September 30th Movement), abbreviated to G-30-S or (with an abbreviation intended to remind one of Hitler's Germany) indicated as *Gestapu* (from "*Ge*rakan *S*eptember *Tigapu*luh"), combined with the initials of the Communist Party, thus: "Gestapu/P.K.I.". All traditionally anti-Communist circles in Indonesia are in agreement that the rising, anyway, was in essence a Communist affair. The question of whether or not there really existed a "Council of Generals" (or at least a close contact between a number of anti-Communist senior officers) is sometimes answered by pointing out that it would have been incomprehensible if the army — just as the Communists — had *not* made certain preparations in order to be ready when "the moment" came. That moment was generally expected to coincide with the death of the President. So it can be concluded that the "time-bomb", which for years had been ticking away in Indonesia, went off too early, whatever the reason for this may have been.

This long awaited explosion took on proportions which no-one would have believed possible. To begin with, the events brought about an attempt to exterminate Communism and the Communists and probably anyone whom one could score off, thanks to this political label. The reports on the number of victims vary between 80,000 and 500,000; some even speak of one and a half million.[8] A further result was that, *de facto*, power came into the hands of the army, while President Soekarno was gradually pushed aside.

As far as the discussion on the number of victims is concerned, Hughes remarks that "it is tragically academic whether 100,000 or 200,000 or 500,000 people lost their lives in the blood bath. For whichever of these figures is most nearly accurate, any one of them makes the Indonesian massacre one of the ghastliest and most concentrated bloodlettings of current times." [9]

The problem of how this slaughter, which in particular took place in November and December 1965, could have come about is almost as obscure as the number of victims. It has been said that the clashes in various areas occurred between varying groups: in Central and East Java, for instance, between on the one hand Muslims and the other hand Communists or every *abangan* and nominal Muslim who could be accused of having left-wing sympathies (e.g. the left wing within the

---

[8] Cf. J. Verkuyl, *Momentopnamen van de huidige situatie in Indonesië*, in *Wending*, June 1967, p. 217; also Hughes, *Upheaval*, p. 184 ff.

[9] Hughes, *Upheaval*, p. 189.

P.N.I.) or having had connections with left-wing organizations (e.g. certain trade unions or artists' organizations); in Hinduistic Bali, members of the P.N.I. attacked P.K.I. members.[10] In some places soldiers apparently took the lead or incited the population to kill their enemies, in other places they restrained the people; Soeharto himself is said to have urged restraint.[11] In some districts of Java a complete vacuum in authority occurred, as it was not clear which army unit was on whose side. A situation of mass-hysteria arose, in which each took the law into his own hands, sometimes with the feeling that it was a question of kill or be killed (or, for instance, the feeling that one would have been killed, should the Communist coup have succeeded).

To push all this onto the responsibility of the Soeharto government — as is sometimes done outside Indonesia — is to make a simplification which does not sufficiently take into account the confused situation in Indonesia during those months. The authority of the new leaders — in particular Soeharto and, more in the background, Nasution — was extremely unstable at that time. They had to grope their way very carefully to discover who was who and how sympathies and relationships lay among the population as well as within the army. They still had to behave as if they were acting on the authority of Soekarno, for Soekarno was still President and apparently made mischief and intrigued against the new leaders in every sort of way. As late as May 1966 Soekarno installed a new air-commander and took the opportunity to fulminate against Hatta, who at that moment seemed to be gaining authority again. Even some months later Soekarno's prestige and his opposition to the new leaders were still so great that I was able to see P.N.I. students in Jogja demonstrating and using as a chant, "Say what you will, the *Marhaenists* will win".[12]

The change from the *ORLA* (= *Orde Lama,* the "old order" of before September 30th, 1965) to the *ORBA* (= *Orde Baru,* the "new order"), took place by means of close co-operation between the army and

---

[10] Cf. Verkuyl, *Momentopnamen,* p. 217.

[11] Hughes, *Upheaval,* p. 194.

[12] Even in the years before the Second World War *marhaenis* was a favourite name of Soekarno's for the proletarian peasants and other have-nots. Soekarno liked calling his brand of Indonesian socialism "Marhaenism". "Marhaen" was apparently the name of a poor Sundanese peasant, whom Soekarno had once met long ago. See Soekarno's *Dibawah Bendera Revolusi,* Vol. I, 1963², p. 167 ff. and p. 253 ff.; cf. also Cindy Adams, *Sukarno, An Autobiography as told to Cindy Adams,* New York 1965, p. 62.

the youth movements of the so-called "Generation of 1966". These youths were united in the *KAMI* ("*K*omité *A*ksi *M*ahasiswa *I*ndonesia", the Action-Committee of Indonesian Students) and the *KAPPI* (Action-Committee of the "*Pa*ra *P*eladjar", secondary school pupils). Within the *KAMI* it was particularly the H.M.I. (*Himpunan Mahasiswa Islam,* the very strong Islamic Students' Association, with unofficial relations with the Masjumi and other modern Muslim organizations) and members of the Catholic Students' Association which played an important part. From the beginning of 1966 these students began to demonstrate in the streets, partly spontaneously, partly with the scene set by others, whoever they may have been. At first they protested against all sorts of abuses, rising prices, corruption, etc. Over the months the campaign developed into protests against Soekarno, with insults of a sort no-one would have believed possible before. The co-operation between the army and the students sometimes threatened to lead to a clash — e.g. with regard to the position of Soekarno — as the young people wanted quicker and more radical action than the new leaders considered possible.

It was not until March 11th, 1966, that the new leaders considered the time come to demand Soekarno's signature to a letter in which the President "commanded" General Soeharto to take all the steps necessary for the safety and stability of state and government, protecting Soekarno as "the President, Chief-of-Staff, Great Leader of the Revolution and Mandatory of the People's Congress". The interpretation of this letter, too, led to a long tug-of-war between the President and the new leaders: was it only a temporary authorization of the President given to his subordinate, General Soeharto (since February 21st officially chief-of-staff of the army), or was it in fact a definite transfer of authority? Only a year later, on March 12th, 1967, did Soeharto become Acting-President, and again a year later, on March 27th, 1968, officially become President for a term of five years. In Indonesia things are done that way!

For the time being, the New Order was sanctioned in a session of the Provisional People's Congress (*Madjelis Permusjawaratan Rakjat Sementara,* M.P.R.S.) held in June-July 1966 (the use of the word "provisional" originated from the 1945 Constitution, indicating pending regulations based on general elections). According to the 1945 Constitution the People's Congress embodied the sovereignty of the people and therefore the President officially was subordinated to this Congress. After the period of Soekarno's Guided Democracy, this trump could now be played. This took place in the meeting of the People's Congress, first of all by authorizing Soekarno's letter of March 11th to Soeharto, which move was called "a wise policy". The next step was to elect General Nasution as chairman of the People's Congress. Further decisions in this session were concerned with the general elections, the position of Soekarno as "Mandatory" of the People's Congress (to stress that the President received his mandate only from the Congress and was thus responsible to this body), the revision of all sorts of measures, regulations and political doctrines dating from the period of Soekarno's Guided Democracy, the proscription of the Communist Party, financial and economic reconstruction, the importance of education (with religious instruction as a normal subject), in short, the repudiation of the "old order" of the Soekarno period. This period was now considered as "lost years... in which no attempts were made to tackle the structural problems of Indonesia in a realistic way",[13] or, in the bitter words of one of my Christian friends, "years which were like a bad dream".

One of the most awkward problems for the new leaders — and a source of much criticism of their policy — must finally be mentioned here. I refer to the fact that as a result of the Communist witch hunt after September 30th, 1965, there are still a large number of people detained in camps and prisons. These detainees were divided into three groups. Category A were brought to trial. Of Category B many were deported to a distant island for "re-indoctrination", in order to be released in due time. Roughly two-thirds, however, belonged to Category C, that is, the "minor offenders". They are the people who had probably belonged to one or other Communist or left-wing organization. Over a period of time some of them were released, but some were again detained on suspicion of renewed activities.

For many years it seemed that the government was not able to resolve this problem. To what extent was there a real danger of a resuscitation of Communism, which naturally could not have been completely exterminated? The chief reason, commonly heard, was that society, and in particular the Muslim community, was not prepared to receive these Communists again. A well-informed army officer told me: "Viewed in retrospect, it would have been better if we had released the majority of the prisoners straight away during the first months. But at that moment we considered the time inopportune. Yet in fact we have got ourselves more and more entangled, because the longer we hold them, the more difficult it is to release them and integrate them into society". Indeed, this too is Indonesia!

[13] Cf. Verkuyl, *Momentopnamen*, p. 218.

All these years the government has seemed to be afraid of risking its authority by trying to persuade people that an end must be put to the "Gestapu/P.K.I." affair. Religious leaders — both Muslims and Christians — seemed to fear arousing the antipathy of people and the extremists within their own circles if they publicly demanded that this inhuman situation should be brought to an end. One of the few whom I heard advocating mercy was the well-known writer Bahrum Rangkuti, now *imam* in the Indonesian navy. In a Friday meditation (on Thursday evening) on television in July 1966 he said that one may hate and resist Communism as a system, but towards the people, the Communists, the prisoners, one must be merciful, for God is *ar-Raḥmān ar-Raḥīm,* the Beneficent, the Merciful.

2. *New Hope for Muslims*

Once the army had overcome Colonel Untung and his supporters, the slogan became "total extermination of the Gestapu/P.K.I.". In this slogan an Indonesian verb was used which could be understood both literally and figuratively (viz. *kikis habis,* wipe out, sweep away, exterminate, finalize).

In Muslim circles the conflict was primarily felt as a struggle between the Islamic community and the "Gestapu/P.K.I.", or, even more simply, between Islam and Communism. This controversy had already arisen in the colonial period (in particular after 1921) and had afterwards become acute in the new Republic. On the part of the Communists there was always agitation against "religious capitalists". The ownership of land by a number of *kiyai* families (e.g. in East Java) was a useful theme to provoke poor peasants to turn against "the *hadji*s". Actually it has to be admitted that every religion, Islam included, tends to defend the established order and to look askance at movements toward revolutionary changes in the structure of society. During the Communist rising in September 1948 in Madiun, a number of prominent Muslims were murdered, particularly civil servants and school-teachers.[14] On the other hand, Muslims were wont to combat Communism as atheism and hence the archenemy of religion. In connection with the Madiun revolt in 1948 even Soekarno said that the Communists had abandoned the Pantjasila principles; "and in particular they have deviated from the belief in God and carry out actions which are in conflict with this principle, because they no longer believe in God".[15]

---
[14] Cf. Kahin, *Nationalism,* p. 300; Muskens, *Indonesië,* p. 177.
[15] Quoted in Dutch by Gunawan, *Kudetá,* p. 42.

The fight against Communism and the Communists could therefore traditionally be considered an aspect of the *djihād,* the "Holy War" against the enemies of Islam, God's foes. Referring to the murder of the generals on the morning of October 1st, 1965, a Muslim informant unconsciously recalled almost literally Soekarno's words of 1948, when he said: "On October 1st, 1965, we saw how far people can go who no longer have any religion!" One might also ask how far men sometimes go who do have a religion. Yet if a foreigner in Indonesia asks critical questions concerning the massacre of 1965, he will probably get the answer: "You foreigners don't realize the stress and lawlessness which we in Indonesia, especially the Muslims, had experienced in the years leading up to it".

With regard to the conflict between Muslims and Communists, it is commonly said that in East Java it was chiefly the ANSOR youth movement which undertook the extermination of the "Gestapu/P.K.I.". Non-Muslim informants often added that this occurred at the instigation of "the *hadji*s", who were usually anti-Communist not only as Muslims but in particular as landowners. This indictment may contain a grain of truth. It is, however, incorrect to speak in general terms of "the *hadji*s" as a social group. At best it can be said that among the landowners in East Java there are indeed a number of *kiyai*s or *kiyai* families. Moreover, it is thanks to these *kiyai*s from the *pesantrèn*s and *madrasa*s that the Nahdatul Ulama (N.U.) is far and away the largest Islamic party in East Java. Now the ANSOR can be considered the youth movement connected with this N.U.[16] So statistically it is obvious that in East Java the ANSOR and N.U. members were in the forefront of the actions to exterminate the "Communists". This does not mean that they were more anti-Communist than other Muslim groups.

An influential Muslim told me that in Java (perhaps in Central Java) a *fatwā* of the Muhammadijah chairman had been of great significance in the extermination of the "Gestapu/P.K.I.", because in this *fatwā* it was stated that their destruction ought to be considered a religious duty. This informant was probably referring to the statement issued at an emergency meeting of the Muhammadijah held on November 9th-

---

[16] ANSOR (from the Arabic *al-anṣār,* the Medinan helpers of the Prophet) is not a student organization as Muskens supposes (*Indonesië,* p. 251). The student association closely allied to the N.U. is the *Perhimpunan Mahasiswa Islam Indonesia* (P.M.I.I.), much smaller and of less significance than the H.M.I. mentioned above.

11th, 1965, in Djakarta.[17] From this period there are more statements known, made by Muslim leaders who declared this conflict to be a "Holy War". This Muhammadijah statement, however, can be taken as an authoritative example.

Under the heading *Ibadah dan Djihad* (Religious Duty and the Holy War), this statement explains that the action on September 30th, 1965, is to be regarded as an extension of the Madiun Communist rising of 1948. Officers such as Untung, Latif, Supardjo, Bambang Supeno and others are said to have been involved in the Madiun Affair. Therefore this time a decisive follow-up ought to be carried through in order to prevent a third Communist attempt at a coup in the future. The statement continues as follows:

"Therefore it was right for the Muhammadijah, together with [the leaders of] its youth movement, during an emergency meeting in Djakarta, November 9th-11th, 1965, trusting in God (*tawakkal*), to make this pronouncement: THE EXTERMINATION OF THE GESTAPU/ PKI AND THE NEKOLIM IS A RELIGIOUS DUTY.[18] ... This religious duty is not (only) recommended (*sunnat*) but obligatory (*wadjib*), even an individual obligation" (*wadjib ᶜain*, i.e. an obligation which is not only to be fulfilled by the Muslim community in general, so that, for example, it can be carried out by a certain body on behalf of this community, but an obligation for each Muslim personally) ... "And because this action and this struggle must be carried out by consolidating all our strength — mental, physical and material — therefore this action and this struggle are nothing less than a HOLY WAR (*DJIHAD*). This Holy War, according to religious law, is not (only) recommended, but obligatory, even an individual obligation..." Finally it is stated — in accordance with Islamic law — that when carrying out this *djihad* "destructive excesses, defamation, revenge, etc. must be prevented".

It is not explicitly stated what interpretation the (modern) Muhammadijah at that moment gave to the term *djihad*. But the conclusion drawn by an average Muslim as well as his enemy can easily be guessed. It is, however, hard to assess to what extent this *fatwā* had a result similar to that which the earlier "*djihad* resolution" had on events in Surabaja in November 1945.[19]

---

[17] Published in *Suara Muhammadijah*, no. 9, November 1965.
[18] "NEKOLIM" is a Soekarno abbreviation for "neo-colonialist imperialists"; they, too, were not forgotten in this statement!
[19] See Chapter I, par. 5.

Whatever the proper explanation may be of the events of September 30th, 1965 and thereafter, to the Muslim way of thinking it was a "holy war" against atheistic Communism, the archenemy of religion. One of my principal informants characterized the destruction of the "Gestapu/P.K.I." as *the* great victory of Islam in Indonesia". It is not surprising that afterwards many Muslims wanted to claim the victory wholly for Islam.

The foreword which a translator wrote for the Indonesian edition of Mawdūdī's book "Towards Understanding Islam" may serve as an example of this flush of victory.[20] It runs as follows: "Once more the banners of the truth of Islam flutter in the procession of the Indonesian people marching on their way to complete the revolution. Once more the dynamic spirit of Islam has appeared amid a people who had been squabbling among themselves over the truth of each other's ideology. Once more the truth is proved of what God has said in His Holy Book, that what is true shall be true for eternity, and that what is vain shall perish. The doctrine of Marxism/Communism is only a creation of the human mind... and evidently brings no harmony to life but breeds chaos and confusion in the life of society. The doctrine of Marxism/Communism and similar teachings, however, were forbidden in Indonesia in 1966 by order of the People's Congress... People are now constantly wondering: what and where is the real mainstay of our souls? The answer is: to grasp and acknowledge again the strength and glory of the metaphysical doctrine which cannot be called in question. This is Islam, which has shown the superiority and solidity of its point of view, not to be laid low by the power of the theories of all the theorists in the whole world..." And so forth.

It can perhaps be said of the translator, as has been said of Mawdūdī himself, that "He presents Islam as a system, one that long ago provided mankind with set answers to all its problems, rather than as a faith in which God provides mankind anew each morning the riches whereby it may answer them itself".[21]

But the new government seemed to be less enthusiastic than this translator. Its caution is seen in the initial "freezing" of the activities of

---

[20] S. Abul Ala Maududi, *Menudju Pengertian Islam*, Djakarta 1967, translated by Amiruddin Djamil. For this Sayyid Abū 'l-ᶜAlā' Mawdūdī and his group (in some ways comparable to the Egyptian *Ikhwān* and the Indonesian *Darul Islam*) see W. C. Smith, *Islam*, p. 233 ff.

[21] Smith, *Islam*, p. 235.

political parties. In the same cautious way, Islamic leaders such as HAMKA, Isa Anshary and Burhanuddin Harahap were only gradually released from prison. On August 14th, 1966, I was present at a service of thanksgiving (*tasjakkur*) held in and around the Al-Azhar mosque in Kebajoran-Baru (Djakarta) and led by HAMKA. Only then had the last Islamic leaders returned from imprisonment. Great enthusiasm reigned, though even on this occasion veiled criticism of the government was not lacking. To a crowd of about 50,000 people the following leaders were successively presented: Sjafruddin Prawiranegara, Asaat, Prawoto Mangkusasmito, Mohamad Roem, Kasman Singodimedjo and finally Muh. Natsir — cheered as formerly Soekarno had been — in other words, the entire top leadership of the former Masjumi.

More than one speaker demanded the "rehabilitation of Islam" after its oppression in the times that had passed. Prawoto ended his speech by stressing that an "overall rehabilitation" (*rehabilitasi multikompleks*) would have to include the Muslim community's being given back the means for their struggle (*alat perdjuangan*).[22] In a mosque it is considered improper to mention names of movements and parties within the one Muslim community, but this speaker was obviously referring to the rehabilitation of the *Masjumi* as a political party. The hope was not fulfilled. Developments after September 30th, 1965, also held disappointments for the Islamic community.

It may nevertheless be concluded that the events of 1965 have resulted in a far stronger position for Islam in Indonesia, at least on the surface. Initially it seemed that the developments could be heralding the beginning of a new phase in the modern history of Islam in Indonesia. "The clash" had come and appeared to have resulted in victory. Oppression and menace had gone. One could breathe again. One could say and write what one wanted to. Muslim newspapers and magazines were allowed to reappear. And religion was in favour as never before.

Freedom of religion has also often been stressed since 1965, but with this restriction: that such freedom does not include the freedom to be non-religious, let alone anti-religious. A former Minister of Religion, Idham Chalid (N.U.) compared religious freedom to the freedom exercised in clothing, saying that this did not include the freedom to be a nudist! [23] So it came about that after Soekarno's fall his slogan of 1964

---

[22] Cf. *Pandji Masjarakat*, no. 1, October 1966, pp. 11-13 and p. 30.
[23] Quoted in *Suara Muhammadijah*, Febr.-March 1966, p. 35.

once more became topical: the Indonesian people as well as the Indonesian state *"must* have a God and a religion" (*harus ber-Tuhan dan harus beragama*). It is understandable that many religious leaders considered this development a reason for new hope.

3. *New Disappointments*

A considerable shift has taken place in Indonesian politics since 1965. After all, the most important left-wing groups have officially left the scene, due to the proscription of the P.K.I. and the elimination of former left-wing leaders within the P.N.I. The vacancy is said to have been filled by the army; and if an army is given an inch, it takes an ell. Yet Hughes was perhaps right when he concluded that Indonesian foreign policy had not simply switched from left to right.[24] Nor was it correct to regard the new government of Indonesia as just another of the present-day right-wing dictatorships by a military junta.

In situations like this there is, of course, a danger of sliding in that direction. In 1967 an observer wrote "that there are undoubtedly some military commanders who would prefer some kind of military junta".[25] The emergence of a new pressure-group (now a military one) trying to fence in the new leaders is an obvious danger in such a situation. Moreover, in out-of-the-way areas it is easy for the military to misuse their power. But, on the other hand, criticism of the government and military commanders is certainly still possible, in spite of some restrictions laid down in new press-laws. And this freedom is used with a mixture of sarcasm and humour which is proof that Indonesian democracy is not dead.

Unfortunately, the political parties in Indonesia still lead a languishing existence. After 1965 the new leadership of the P.N.I. had great difficulties in re-orientating the party. The former Socialist Party of Sjahrir did not get a successor. The replacement of the Masjumi by a new Islamic party remains problematical, as long as certain ex-Masjumi leaders have to remain onlookers. Soekarno's Guided Democracy hindered the emergence of a new generation of politicians. Among young intellectuals one meets people with a political education but lacking political experience. It is understandable that the new government hesitated to welcome a resuscitation of all former political parties, because this could result in new strife between the parties, particularly

---

[24] Hughes, *Upheaval*, p. 291.
[25] Verkuyl, *Momentopnamen*, p. 219.

in view of the coming elections. Party politics would absorb the energy, time and money that should be used on national reconstruction. But there is a growing conviction that political life and the activities of political parties will have to be stimulated if democracy is to function properly.

In this connection it may be worth recalling a rumour which I remember was current during the October 17th affair in 1952, when the army (including Nasution) apparently wanted to dissolve Parliament. Some prominent leaders at that time were said to have warned against military intervention, saying that "it is easy to establish a military dictatorship, but there will be no way back to democracy". The Soeharto government now faces the difficult job of proving that, after the necessary seizure of power by the army in 1965, there is still a way back to genuine democracy.

Let us now, within the framework of this survey, make a special examination of Islam in Indonesian politics during recent years.[26] The burning question in Muslim circles during the years since 1965 has been that of the rehabilitation of the Masjumi. The proscription of this party in 1960 had caused some of its adherents to join other Islamic parties, although most of them continued to feel themselves members of the (temporarily) forbidden party. Some former Masjumi members and others seemed to have turned to the P.S.I.I., which in recent years may have got a fairly large following. The N.U., too, may have drawn many new members and, partly as a result of this, probably shifted to a more progressive policy. In some areas the Sumatran Perti may have strengthened its position at the cost of the former Masjumi. Other Masjumi members "immersed themselves in religious or cultural activities" (e.g. founding private universities), or "remained silent".[27] It can be added that from about 1955, and in particular after 1960, some ex-Masjumi leaders entered the business world. For example, a Batik Co-operative Society and a match factory in Central Java and a number of printing-houses in Djakarta may be mentioned here. This, too, was considered to be part of the internal strengthening of the Islamic community, which Muslims hoped in good time would result in a stronger position for Islam.

---

[26] *Islam in Indonesian Politics* was the title of an important article by Allan A. Samson, in *Asian Survey*, December 1968, Vol. VIII, pp. 1,001-1,017, from which a number of the following facts and data are taken.

[27] Samson, *Islam*, p. 1,004.

On December 16th, 1965, a "Co-ordinating Body of Muslim Activities" (*Badan Koordinasi Amal Muslimin*) was formed, uniting 16 Islamic organizations which wanted to work toward a rehabilitation of the Masjumi. Among the supporters were also a few army officers who, according to Samson, were hoping to see the power of the N.U. restricted, realizing that the more modern-minded Muslims could no longer be counted out. (Perhaps it should be noted, however, that some senior officers were modern Muslims who felt a sympathy for Muhammadijah and Masjumi ideas).

After the elimination of Soekarno from active politics (from the moment of the "command" to Soeharto in the letter of March 11th, 1966) the ex-Masjumi leaders expected that the Masjumi would soon be allowed to begin its activities again, on the assumption that they were the very people who had resisted Soekarno's Guided Democracy. From June 1966 onwards, many Islamic organizations, and in the first place the Muhammadijah, openly began to advocate the return of the Masjumi. How this took place at the huge "thanksgiving service" of August 14th, 1966, has already been described.

On December 21st, 1966, a statement from the army officers was issued which was largely directed against Soekarno, in order to prevent further activities and intrigues on his part. This statement, however, at the same time stressed that the army "would take firm steps against anyone, whichever side, whatever group which will deviate from *Pantja Sila* and the 1945 Constitution as which has already been done by the Communist Party Revolt in Madiun, *Gestapu,* Darul Islam... and Masjumi-Socialist Party of Indonesia...." [28]

Thus the fate of the old Masjumi was sealed. The fact that Masjumi leaders were involved in the P.R.R.I. rising of 1958 appeared to be used as an argument for continuing the proscription. Was that the real and only reason? Some believe that the government did not want to see the rehabilitation of the Masjumi because of this party's leanings toward an Islamic State.[29] In my opinion, however, these leanings are not a specific characteristic of the Masjumi. Could it be that this indictment was spread by certain anti-Masjumi circles, while the real motives of these circles were not matters of principle at all? [30]

---

[28] Quoted or translated by Samson, *Islam,* p. 1,005, from a source which he does not mention.
[29] Cf. Verkuyl, *Momentopnamen,* p. 222.
[30] Samson quotes an anti-N.U. informant, according to whom the N.U. later on started a rumour campaign with a similar accusation directed at the new Islamic party which took the place of the Masjumi (*Islam,* p. 1,012).

However that may be, the Masjumi followers now had to choose another way. Thanks to the "Co-operative Body", it was decided on April 7th, 1967, to found the *Partai Muslimin Indonesia* (initially abbreviated P.M.I., afterwards also *Parmusi* or *Partai Muslimin*), the "Party of Indonesian Muslims". This new party was obviously intended to be the continuation of the Masjumi under another name. The government agreed, but certain army officers objected to an active participation of important ex-Masjumi leaders in the new party. Samson believes that Acting-President Soeharto at that time would have liked to meet the wishes of the new party, but did not want to have difficulties with the army officers.

On October 24th, 1967, Natsir decided to resign from the leadership of the new party. The provisional executive at that moment consisted of 30 members, 9 of whom were adherents of the Muhammadijah. On February 5th, 1968, Soeharto let it be known that no single ex-Masjumi leader was allowed to hold a leading position in the new Partai Muslimin.[31] They would have to wait till the general elections had taken place (which one month later, in March 1968, were postponed to 1971). This decision was a very great disappointment to the former adherents of the Masjumi. Would this new party have a chance to win the sympathy of Muslims, without ex-Masjumi leaders such as Natsir and Prawoto taking part in its activities?

Tension reached a climax at the first Congress of the new party, held from November 4th to 7th, 1968, in Malang (East Java).[32] It became clear that the well-known Mohamad Roem would become chairman of the party. But at that very moment a telegram from the government in Djakarta reminded them that the attitude of the government toward this question was unchanged. In other words, even Mohamad Roem was unacceptable to the government as chairman of this new Islamic party.

This interference of the government provoked stormy reactions in the Muslim newspapers and magazines. Hatta, too, expressed cautious criticism.[33] In 1969 even some non-Masjumi informants called this attitude of Soeharto and the army officers towards Mohamad Roem inexplicable, because this ex-Masjumi politician, originating from Java, certainly had nothing to do with the P.R.R.I. rising in 1958. In him the

---

[31] In *Pandji Masjarakat*, no. 35, November 1968, Prawoto Mangkusasmito gave information on this meeting with Soeharto held on February 5th, 1968.
[32] See *Pandji Masjarakat*, no. 35, November 1968; Samson's article was apparently written before that Congress.
[33] Cf. *Pandji Masjarakat*, no. 35, p. 9.

new party would have had a capable and moderate leader. With his leadership this party would probably have attained a great following and, like the Masjumi in former times, would likely have become the largest Islamic party. Such a party would probably also appeal to modern-minded youth, e.g. from the circles of the Islamic Student Movement H.M.I.

We shall have to wait and see whether the Partai Muslimin under its present leaders, and despite its many internal tensions, can prove attractive to the people. The Muhammadijah openly urged its members to support the new party. Its first chairman was Djarnawi Hadikusumo.[34] He was a teacher and chairman of the political study committee of the Muhammadijah. We shall come across his name again as the author of theological pamphlets concerning Christianity. General Secretary of the party became Anwar Harjono, who wrote a doctor's thesis in 1968 on Islamic law as the all-embracing and righteous law.[35] Both appear to have a great interest in Islam as a religio-political system, but unlike Mohamad Roem they have little political experience, let alone being able to look back on a political career.

Apart from this conflict concerning the former Masjumi, other developments occurred which also ended in a feeling of disappointment among the Muslims; Samson even spoke of "a growing frustration in the Islamic community".[36]

One example of these disappointing developments is the renewed but barren struggle to give the Djakarta Charter of June 22nd, 1945, an official status. According to Samson, N.U. members as well as Partai Muslimin followers "pressed for legalization of the Djakarta Charter as the preamble to the 1945 Constitution" during the session of the People's Congress in March 1968,[37] but without success. The Islamic parties, according to Samson, still seem unable to influence national political decisions; in their disappointment they cling to "the myth of the numerical majority", in "the belief that if only everyone in Indonesian society could express his will, Islam would be in the majority",

---

[34] A son of K. Bagus H. Hadikusumo, ex-chairman of the Muhammadijah, who took part in the discussions surrounding the proclamation of the Republic (see Chapter I, par. 3-4).
[35] Anwar Harjono, *Hukum Islam, keluasan dan keadilannja*, Djakarta 1968. One of the propositions in this thesis runs: "Politics is the art of the possible plus X (X = God's eternal Decree)".
[36] Samson, *Islam*, p. 1,014.
[37] Samson, *Islam*, p. 1,012.

for "it is only a minority that is thwarting the will of the majority".[38]

In this connection the question may be posed of whether Muslims once again (as in 1955) are putting their hopes on the coming elections for Parliament and the People's Congress. After the upheaval of 1965-1966 these elections were announced for 1968. But during 1967 government and Parliament could not agree on regulations for these elections. Hence it was decided that they should be postponed, but were to be held before July 5th, 1971. At the end of 1969 the necessary agreement was reached. According to oral information, the most important conditions would be the following. Firstly, the fundamental principles of the state will no longer be under discussion and therefore may not appear in party programmes or in the election campaign (in other words, a new discussion on a "Pantjasila State" or an "Islamic State" must be avoided). Secondly, the same number of representatives must come from outside Java as from Java (to prevent new regional difficulties). Thirdly, of the 460 members of Parliament 100 will be appointed by the government; of the 920 members of the People's Congress 307 will be appointed (among whom will be the 100 appointed members of Parliament); these appointed members will represent the so-called functional groups (army, police, intellectuals, etc.); the most important of these is, of course, the army. Fourthly, participation in the elections is only allowed for political parties registered before the end of 1969 (thus, for example, a new Socialist Party, let alone the Communist Party, cannot participate).

These elections certainly promise to be interesting, and it will be especially interesting to see where the votes go of those who once voted Socialist or Communist. As in 1955, it may be expected that the elections will take place in an orderly way, without much intimidation or other irregularities. But due to the restrictions mentioned above, the coming elections probably cannot bring radical changes. Supposing that the Islamic parties once again (as in 1955) hope for victory on the basis of a nominal majority of Muslims, then these elections too may end in disappointment.

At the beginning of 1969 various Muslim acquaintances said that one of the most disheartening problems of recent years was the tension between Muslims and Christians. Unfortunately the provocative behaviour of sects such as the Jehovah's Witnesses and the Seventh Day Adventists is often considered typical for "the Christians" in general.

---

[38] Samson, *Islam*, p. 1,013.

The obvious apostasy of nominal Muslims to Christianity, particularly in Java, has probably added to the trouble. These questions will be dealt with in the final chapter of this book.

Yet another problem can be mentioned, which is connected with the "Five-Year Plan for Development" (Ind. *Rentjana Pembangunan Lima Tahun*, abbreviated to REPELITA or PELITA), intended for the years 1969-1973. This also includes paragraphs concerning the promotion of religious activities: grants for the building of mosques and churches, the printing of the Scriptures, facilities for religious instruction, and so on. But it is laid down that all this will have to be carried out "within the limits of what is possible". This will probably mean that Soeharto's government will be forced to restrict various kinds of expenditure, e.g. on behalf of the annual pilgrimage to Mecca, which has always been very much in favour with Indonesian Muslims but consumes a great deal of foreign currency.[39]

In connection with the Five-Year Plan the question can sometimes be heard of whether the Muslim community would not withdraw and dissociate itself from the present government and this Plan, in particular those Islamic groups which felt disappointed because of the new government's attitude toward Islam. At the beginning of 1969 I twice heard a sermon given on Friday in a mosque; both times the duty of Muslims to exert themselves for the realization of the Five-Year Plan was stressed. Did these sermons show enthusiasm to participate in the government's programme, or rather the existence of a tendency toward apathy? Samson concludes his article as follows. "Developmental efforts in Indonesia make cooperation between all meaningful groups essential. Although Islam is not a powerful enough political force to exercise predominant influence, it is too powerful to be disregarded... Given modernist Islam's orientation to development, no sustained developmental effort can succeed without its support. A governmental policy that disregards Islamic desires may result in a conservative and rigid reaction from the Islamic community which will nullify the present Islamic adaptation to modernization. The Islamic community possesses genuine interests which must be fairly considered. Anything less courts economic stagnation and religio-political calamity." [40]

---

[39] Cf. the pamphlet *REPELITA, Pendjelasan Presiden Soeharto Didepan BP-MPRS 29 Pebruari 1968,* Djakarta 1968, p. 30. Compare Muskens, *Indonesië*, p. 288.
[40] Samson, *Islam,* p. 1,017.

More symptoms of hope as well as of disappointment could be mentioned, but they will be reserved for the final chapter of this book.

At the end of this historical survey it can be concluded that after September 30th, 1965, a "third period" in the recent history of Islam in Indonesia began — a period which seemed to hold great opportunities and possibilities for the spread of Islam and the expansion of its influence on Indonesian society. But alongside an initial optimism, a feeling of disappointment soon arose, because things did *not* go as had been hoped.

CHAPTER IV

A PRELIMINARY STOCKTAKING

In the first three chapters a historical survey has been given of developments in Indonesia since 1945 and the role of Islam as a constituent of contemporary political life in Indonesia. Against this background a preliminary stocktaking can be made of the most important activities and problems of the Islamic community in present-day Indonesia. This means that we shall be dealing with those activities and problems which nowadays are topics of discussion among Indonesian Muslims and in Muslim publications. Reflecting on those activities and problems, we may then be able to perceive some characteristic tendencies of Islam in modern Indonesia.

1. *Political Topics*

After the suppression of the "September 30th Movement" of 1965, the contrast between Islam and Communism became one of the most topical subjects of discussion. On this question, the well-known Professor H. M. Rasjidi wrote a pamphlet which can be taken as a typical example.[1] After a historical introduction, the elements of Marxism are described and criticized: the dialetic philosophy, historical materialism, Marx's opinions on economics, the state, revolution, class warfare, religion and ethics. The author stresses that Communism was able to emerge in the materialist, capitalist Western world, which had not yet seen the light of Islam. That held for Marx and Engels too. They were atheists (Arabic *mulḥid,* apostate, unbelieving). What is written in Sura 45 : 23-26 applied to them exactly. They believed that the heaven of a classless society could be established on this earth. Islam, however, considers the life to come as the real life (Sura 29 : 64 and 93 : 4). That does not mean that we may turn away from this world and be interested exclusively in the life to come (see Sura 28 : 77).

---

[1] H. M. Rasjidi, *Islam Menentang Komunisme,* Djakarta 1966, based on a lecture to *ulama*s in Djakarta, November 29th, 1965.

Communism did not arise as a mass-movement of poor workers, but as a philosophy which was made possible by three centuries of increasing secularization, i.e. the setting aside of religion. This philosophy can only be overcome by a doctrine radically opposed to it, the doctrine of Islam. The ex-premier of Syria, the late Faris al-Khouri, once chairman of the Security Council of the United Nations and himself a Christian, agreed that only Islam could stop Communism in Indonesia.

The events of September 30th, 1965, showed the Communists in their true colours; they killed a number of army officers and had already made preparations to massacre religious leaders. After the victory over the Communists and the proscription of the Communist Party, the spiritual vacuum must be filled by Islam, the religion of 90 % of the Indonesian people. The precepts of Islam ought to be put into practice, especially those concerning social justice (e.g. by the *zakāt* and other alms). Muslims must exert themselves by performing good works for the welfare of society, so that Communism will get no chance to revive.

In an appendix to this pamphlet we find the text of Soekarno's letter of March 11th, 1966, in which authority was handed over to General Soeharto as well as the text of Soeharto's order for the dissolution and proscription of the Communist Party (March 12th, 1966) and the text of the order to other parties and organizations not to receive ex-Communists into their fold (March 14th, 1966).

As has already been said, the extermination of the "Gestapu/P.K.I." was considered by Islamic leaders as *the* great victory of Islam in Indonesia. To what extent did the hope revive that perhaps the ideal of an Islamic State could now be realized? It soon turned out, however, that the army would resist every group, including right-wing ones, which deviated from the Pantjasila as the basis of the Indonesian Republic. It was already becoming clear in 1966 that the army would not allow any new discussion on the idea of an Islamic State. Moreover, Islamic leaders themselves were said to have become aware that the unity of Indonesia could only be ensured on the basis of the Pantjasila. In military circles it could be heard that certain Christian areas (Tapanuli and North Sulawesi) were "strategically dangerous", that is to say, they were so far-off that a rebellious or separatist movement could easily arise, should an Islamic State be proclaimed. One of my most important informants put it this way: "The founding of an Islamic State is impossible; now we have really accepted the Pantjasila as the basis of the Republic; the problem which we are now facing is: how shall we imbue the Pantjasila with the teachings of Islam?"

In this situation Muslims turned once again to the Djakarta Charter of 1945 and its famous "seven words". In the years prior to September 30th, 1965, this Charter was already being pushed forward in various publications.[2] Apparently a new discussion on the Djakarta Charter in the June-July session of the People's Congress of 1966 was prevented because it was spread about in the lobbies beforehand that the army would not allow such a debate. A new attempt was made during the session of February-March 1967, when the only point on the agenda was the deposition of President Soekarno and the appointment of General Soeharto as Acting-President. But the attempt to add some Muslim demands to the agenda — e.g. that the President must be a Muslim and the state should be based on Islam — was rejected.[3] As has been said, according to Samson, once again "legalization of the Djakarta Charter as the preamble to the 1945 Constitution" was pressed for in the session of March 1968.[4]

After 1965 it has often been stressed by Muslims that the "seven words" of the Djakarta Charter hold good only for Muslims, so that non-Muslims do not have to worry about it. Furthermore, it is often said that a legalization of the Djakarta Charter would definitely not result in an Islamic State. One informant put it as follows: "Actually we do not talk any more about an Islamic State, but at best about an Islamic society; such an Islamic society can be attained by the realization of Islamic law or certain elements of it in Indonesian society, on the basis of the Djakarta Charter".

The struggle to realize the $shari^ca$ (Islamic law) in Indonesia was originally regarded as a struggle for a formal proclamation of an Islamic State, by deciding first that "This is to be an Islamic State".[5] It appeared mainly to be a dispute about formulas, words, a label, a banner. Supposing such a proclamation had been carried through, then it would have turned out — as in Pakistan — that the real problems became manifest afterwards, i.e. when trying to make Islamic law operative in state and society.

---

[2] For example, Achmad Sanusi, *Islam, Revolusi dan Masjarakat*, Bandung 1965; H. A. Notosoetardjo, *Peranan Agama Islam dalam Revolusi Indonesia*, Djakarta 1964; H. Aminuddin Aziz, *Islam dan Tjetusan Revolusi Indonesia*, Djakarta 1963 (on behalf of the Executive Board of the N.U.).
[3] Verkuyl, *Momentopnamen*, pp. 219-220.
[4] Cf. Chapter III, par. 3.
[5] Cf. Van Nieuwenhuijze, *Aspects*, p. 162.

In recent years a shift has taken place in the opinion of many Muslims. They wanted to make a start from another angle, so to speak from below, not by the proclamation of a theoretical Islamic State but by striving for a practical application of certain precepts of the *sharī^{c}a* in society, proceeding from the "seven words" of the Djakarta Charter. What these "seven words" would actually involve is usually not very clearly defined. According to some, the "obligation for adherents of Islam to practise Islamic law" would include religious duties in a narrower sense (*ibādāt,* such as prayer, fasting, etc.). According to others, this clause has to result in the government's promulgating special laws for the Muslims (e.g. marriage laws) in agreement with the *sharī^{c}a*.

Many Islamic leaders stress that actually it is no longer necessary to debate the question of the legalization of the Djakarta Charter. They argue that this document was already sanctioned by President Soekarno's Decree of July 5th, 1959 concerning the return to the 1945 Constitution. In the "considerations" of this Decree it was laid down that the Djakarta Charter "inspired the 1945 Constitution and is linked in unity with that Constitution". In other words, according to many Muslims, the significance of the Djakarta Charter was already officially recognized on July 5th, 1959. Thus it was indeed possible to make special laws for the Muslim part of the population on this legal basis. To this end Parliament could now pass further resolutions with a normal majority of votes. The difficulty of obtaining a two-thirds majority, as occurred formerly in the Constituent Assembly, would thus be avoided.

A more moderate comment was given by Mohamad Roem in a Commemoration Day Lecture at the Islamic University in Medan in February 1967.[6] He stressed that Muslims are obliged to keep Islamic law, whether or not the Djakarta Charter was included in the preamble of the 1945 Constitution or in President Soekarno's Decree. "This obligation holds good for everyone who calls himself a Muslim." It is "an obligation not in a 'legal' sense, with legal consequences which could be enforced but an obligation in the religious sense. It depends on the person concerned, to what extent he keeps Islamic law. In this respect he will have to answer to God ... The Djakarta Charter possesses permanent significance, not in a legal sense, but all the more so in a spiritual sense." In other words, according to Mohamad Roem, whether

---

[6] The text of this speech can be found in *Pandji Masjarakat,* nos. 11, 12, 13, March-April 1967; concerning the Djakarta Charter, see in particular no. 13, pp. 8-9.

Muslims keep Islamic law or not has actually nothing to do with the government; in this sense the Djakarta Charter is of no legal consequence; but the permanent religious significance of the Djakarta Charter, mentioned in the Decree of 1959, is that Muslim citizens are explicitly reminded of their responsibility to God to keep Islamic law.

Of course there are also Muslims now — particularly outside Islamic parties and organizations — who fear that an actual legalization of the Djakarta Charter could lead to the "fanaticism" against which Hoesein Djajadiningrat and Wongsonegoro had warned on July 11th, 1945.[7] Many Muslims and nominal Muslims, especially in Java, eagerly quote in this connection the words *lā ikrāhā fī 'd-dīn* (there is no compulsion in religion; Sura 2 : 256) to justify their lukewarm attitude. Muslim theologians, however, are apt to point out that these words only concern the Muslim attitude toward non-Muslims. Islamic law, however, is incumbent on anyone who calls himself a Muslim; and according to many Islamic leaders this would be applicable to 90 % of the Indonesian people. It may be this kind of "fanaticism" that nominal Muslims are afraid of. Moreover, "compulsion" may not officially be exerted by the authorities, but it might well be carried out in the form of an inevitable social control from the Muslim community, especially in a strictly Islamic area.

In any case it can be stated that in the ideological dispute on the basis of the state — "Pantjasila" or "Islam" — a gradual shift has taken place insofar as Muslims no longer strive openly for the proclamation of an Islamic State (whatever that might be). The question is now being approached from a different angle, by trying to put into operation certain "elements" of Islamic law, partly through legal regulations by the government, proceeding from the "seven words" in the Djakarta Charter of 1945.

In connection with these topics, attention should be paid to certain publications in Indonesian. For instance, the Indonesian translation of a pamphlet by M. F. Hoballah (Al-Azhar, Cairo) on Democracy and Islamic Law is of interest.[8] According to this author, the four fundamental sources of Islamic jurisprudence are the Qur'ān, Tradition, *Kiyās* (analogy, parity of reasoning) and *Idjtihād* (the use of individual reasoning, based on one's own examination of the religious sources).

---

[7] Cf. Chapter I, par. 3.
[8] M. F. Hoballah, *Demokrasi dan Hukum Islam*, Surabaja 1966.

The Qur'ān and Tradition only give some general principles for politics (e.g. the "mutual deliberation" from Sura 42 : 38). The third and fourth sources are proof that much is left for man himself to decide. In other words, the democracy of Islam is extremely flexible; there are only a few fixed, eternal principles, but as far as the rest is concerned, the form of the state and questions of legislation are left to human reasoning.

Before 1965 the Indonesian author Moh. Sjafaat had already written in a similar vein on Democracy and the Teachings of Islam.[9] This writer, however, put more emphasis on the excellence of Islamic principles above all others for the construction of a democratic state. Moreover, he had to suit the "democracy of Islam" at that moment to Soekarno's Guided Democracy.[10]

The Egyptian professor, the late ᶜAbd al-Ḳādir ᶜŪda, whose writings enjoy considerable authority in some Indonesian circles, was much more rigid. His book on Islam and Legislation has already been translated, while another, on the application of the sharīᶜa to economics, is being prepared by Professor Kahar Muzakkir of the Islamic University in Jogjakarta. ᶜŪda, a follower of the Egyptian Ikhwān al-Muslimūn, objected strongly to all "human law-giving", as Islamic law provides precepts for every aspect of life and society.[11]

As regards earlier publications, there is apparently a new interest in Ibn Khaldūn's writings. An anthology from his Muḳaddima ("Prolegomena") has already been published in Indonesian, while a complete translation in six volumes is in course of preparation.[12] Osman Raliby translated special passages from Ibn Khaldūn on society and state.[13] This interest is apparently bound up with the conviction that one need not look to the West for a sociological approach to topical problems,

---

[9] Moh. Sjafaat, *Demokrasi dan Adjaran Islam*, Bandung 1963.
[10] Compare K. H. Idham Chalid, *Islam dan Demokrasi Terpimpin*, Surabaja (1961?), a Commemoration Day lecture at the N.U. University by the then Minister of Religion.
[11] Abdulkadir Audah, *Islam dan Perundang-undangan*, Djakarta 1959[1], 1965[3]. According to the foreword by the translator, the author took an active part in the revolution against King Farouk's regime (1952); he was then commissioned to draft a new Egyptian constitution, but as a result of defamation of character he was executed by hanging on December 8th, 1954. See, however, Encyclopaedia of Islam, new ed., III, p. 1069.
[12] Ibn Chaldun, *Filsafat Islam Tentang Sedjarah, Pilihan dari Muqaddimah*, Djakarta 1962. The complete *Muḳaddima* edition is being prepared in an Indonesian translation by Mukti Ali.
[13] Osman Raliby, *Ibnu Chaldun tentang Masjarakat dan Negara*, Djakarta 1963.

as relevant sources can also be found in Islamic history. Among these are the works of Ibn Khaldūn (1332-1406), considered by Muslims as the "father of sociology".[14]

In 1964 a translation of al-Fārābi's *Al-Madīna al-Faḍīla* (the ideal state) appeared by Z. A. Ahmad, who himself had already published a book on the ideal of an Islamic State.[15] Earlier publications which once more drew attention are, for instance, the English-Indonesian pamphlet "Pakistan, the Struggle of a Nation" and the translations of two booklets by Muhammad Asad, alias Leopold Weiss, "Islamic Constitution Making" and "The Principles of State and Government in Islam".[16] This author also tends to emphasize that Islam is very flexible with regard to these questions and that many forms of an Islamic State are possible, each one adapted to a certain country, for, apart from a few principles and moral precepts, the details of an Islamic government can be left to the modern *idjtihād* of people in a certain age and area.

When studying the content of some of these publications, the question can be put as to whether it might in fact be possible for Muslims, nominal Muslims and non-Muslims to agree on principles such as indicated by Hoballah and Muh. Asad. The discussion, however, frequently remains enmeshed in formal terms and slogans. Of course there are still traditional *ulama*s who believe that Islamic law offers a complete recipe which can be applied in our age without any difficulty (perhaps because in fact they themselves do not see the problems of modern life). But is it not possible that others, speaking of "Islamic principles" such as democracy and social justice, actually mean the same thing as certain nominal Muslims and non-Muslims? In other words, to what extent is political discussion in Indonesia threatened by a sterile verbalism?

It is perhaps useful to note that in Indonesian Muslim publications — in contrast to Western books on Islam — generally the term "theocracy" is not used for the Islamic idea of a state. The word *theokrasi* is mostly used in an unfavourable sense, that is to say, to refer to a government controlled by priests or a state in which the religious leaders dominate

---

[14] It may be noted that among the many private universities in Djakarta there is also an "Ibn Khaldun University" (furthermore, for example, a "Muhammadijah University" and even a "Djojobojo University").

[15] Zainal Abidin Ahmad, *Negara Utama (al-Farabi)*, Djakarta 1964; Ahmad, *Konsepsi*.

[16] *Pakistan, the Struggle of a Nation*, by Roesli DMB, Solo 1956; Muhammad Asad, *Undang-undang Politik Islam*, Djakarta 1954; idem, *Azas^2 Negara dan Pemerintahan didalam Islam*, Djakarta 1964.

the ruler (as, for example, the Pope in the Middle Ages). It is not this sort of "theocracy" which is considered characteristic of an Islamic State, but the realization of the *sharī^{c}a,* which according to modern Muslims first and foremost stresses the principle of "mutual deliberation". The Indonesian author T. M. Usman el-Muhammady is an exception to this rule; by piling up Western terms and formulas, which make his writings difficult to read, he does not hesitate to use the term *theokrasi Islam* as well.[17]

2. *Partial Realization of Islamic Law*

As was said in the above paragraph, many Islamic leaders no longer strive for an official Islamic State, but now want to begin from another angle, by infusing society with Islamic precepts and thus working toward a gradual Islamization of the country. Moreover, nowadays many of them no longer speak of "Islamic law" in general, but only of a partial realization of it, i.e. of certain "elements" (Ind. *unsur-unsur*) of Islamic law, through regulations made by the government. Traditionally priority is given to the area of family law, including regulations concerning marriage, divorce by repudiation and the law of inheritance.

In a comparison between jurisprudence in Egypt and Indonesia, Notosusanto, professor in Jogja, suggested in 1953 that in Indonesia one Civil Code for all citizens, irrespective of origin and religion, should be made, with the exception, however, of marriage law. In this field separate regulations for the various religious groups would have to be made, while a new law should also be made for groups who did not yet have their own marriage regulations (e.g. Buddhists).[18]

But here too problems immediately arise when theory is to be put into practice; some examples are the position of *adat* law with regard to Islamic law[19] and the differences between the various traditional schools of law (*madhāhib,* sing. *madhhab*). One of my informants, a Muslim scholar, said: "Of course we all want the realization of Islamic law, but

---

[17] T. M. Usman el-Muhammady, *Pembangunan Djiwa-Negara dan Kebudajaan Islam* (*Kultuur, Politis dan Sociologis*), Djakarta 1951[1], 1953[2]; cf. pp. 161-162.

[18] Notosoesanto, *Sedikit tentang Peradilan Perdata di Mesir,* Jogjakarta 1953 (?), p. 13.

[19] See J. Prins, *Adat en Islamietische Plichtenleer in Indonesië,* Bandung 1960[4] (thesis Leiden 1948) and note the remark made by J. Schacht, *An Introduction to Islamic Law,* Oxford 1964, p. 62: "... custom and customary law have coexisted with the ideal theory of Islamic law, while remaining outside its system, in the whole of the Islamic world".

which one?" (i.e., according to which school of law?). With regard to the application of the *sharīᶜa*, he mentioned five groups of scholars:

a. Those who exclusively want to stick to the Shāfiᶜī school of law, probably a diminishing number of older *ulama*s, who, however, are still powerful, particularly in the religious courts;
b. A group of scholars who are also prepared to make use of the three other schools (Ḥanafī, Mālikī, Ḥanbalī) when their regulations are to be preferred to those of the Shāfiᶜī school;
c. Those who, moreover, want to use certain opinions held by earlier (now extinct) schools of law, e.g. concerning a literal or symbolical interpretation of some verses of the Qur'ān;
d. Those who adhere to the "new *idjtihād*", "as for example Hasbi Ash-Shiddiqy and Professor Hazairin and in fact most members of the Muhammadijah, although this association has never made an official pronouncement on the question";
e. Even more extreme is the group of those who want to go back to the Qur'ān as the only source of religious law, and leave the decision to the individual in all cases which are not provided for in the Qur'ān.

This informant was inclined to draw the negative conclusion: "If it is up to ourselves to arrive at solutions, the Muslim community will never reach an agreement".

After the questions of family law, regulations concerning the collection and use of the *zakāt* (alms-tax) have to be mentioned. In 1969 a student of an Islamic university explained the matter in this way: "At present we do not talk about an Islamic State, but only about the realization of some elements of Islamic law, in accordance with the Djakarta Charter; the sequence of elements of Islamic law which we want to see regulated by the government depends on the situation and the tactics to be followed at a certain moment: first of all, for instance, marriage legislation, later on perhaps the *zakāt*, then the extension of the cognizance of religious courts, e.g. with regard to questions of inheritance and *waḳaf* (pious foundations), and so on".

During the conferring of a doctor's degree on Anwar Harjono (the first General Secretary to the new Islamic political party) at the Islamic University of Djakarta, he complained that in the colonial period Islamic regulations concerning marriage and inheritance could more or less be carried out, whereas at the moment it was not possible to agree even on a new marriage law. He had studied the Qur'ān and Tradition, in order to discover those Islamic precepts which could be realized in society at this time. He was prepared to consider the opinions of the four *Imam*s of the official schools of law important material, but stressed that according to these *Imam*s themselves it was not wrong to develop new ideas, based on the Qur'ān and Tradition. One of the propositions in his thesis runs as follows: "The precepts concerning *zakāt, wakaf* and *hiba* (donation) ought to get priority in legislation, as a contribution to achieving more quickly a just and prosperous Indonesian society".[20]

As far as the *zakāt* is concerned, President Soeharto made a remarkable move in 1968. On October 26th he urged his Muslim countrymen to show that they were able to take concrete steps in the direction of progress, by making generous contributions when paying this religious tax. He declared himself prepared to see to the collection of *zakāt* and called on the Muslims to send him their money-orders for this purpose. The President himself opened the *zakāt* account with a gift of 100,000 Rp., and certainly many large sums flowed in. In order to prevent misunderstanding, it was afterwards explained that the sum collected would not be used to cover the national debt, but would be allotted to social and educational purposes (e.g. Islamic orphanages and educational institutions).[21]

With regard to other "elements" of Islamic law which Muslims want to see regulated by the government, the only concrete attempt was the draft of a new marriage law, on the preparation of which a government appointed committee had been working for many years. Until then there had been only marriage regulations dating from the colonial period. According to these regulations the marriage of Muslims had to take place under the supervision of the *Penghulu* (the head of the mosque personnel) in his position as state registrar of marriages. Problems connected with Muslim marriages and divorce by repudiation were solved by jurisprudence, based on the *fikh* books (i.e. on the doctrines) of certain Islamic scholars, in the case of Indonesia those belonging to the Shāfiʿī school. A "secular" wedding at a registry-office was always rejected by the Islamic leaders. This meant in fact that everyone who was considered a Muslim had to marry in an Islamic way. Even those who considered themselves Hindus or Buddhists married this way; they accepted Muslim

---

[20] Anwar Harjono, *Hukum Islam,* p. 274; cf. *Pandji Masjarakat,* no. 24, pp. 6-7, where a short biography of Anwar Harjono is also given.
[21] According to information in the Indonesian daily *Djakarta Times* of 26-10-1968, 27-11-1968, 16-12-1968.

marriage ceremonies as a formality which simply could not be avoided, as other possibilities did not exist. Amongst the Communists in the years prior to September 30th, 1965, it had become usual to marry at one of the offices of the party. Thus within some mystical Javanese groups (the so-called *aliran kebathinan*) marriage also took place according to their own rules, even with the use of their own marriage certificates.[22]

The draft laid before Parliament on September 7th, 1968 was not yet a complete marriage law, but only a "bill of the fundamental principles of marriage". These principles included the age of the partners, rights and duties of husband and wife, rights and duties of parents and children, community of goods obtained after the wedding, and so on. The procedure proposed was to accept first these "fundamental principles" and then draft separate marriage laws for groups of people belonging to different faiths. The closing articles of this bill were therefore the most important ones. "The marriage contract for Islamic, Catholic, Protestant, Hindu-Buddhist and other communities (*umat-umat*) and for mixed marriages will be regulated in separate laws" (art. 38). "Conditions in this law do not nullify what will be stipulated in the special marriage laws for the separate religious groups" (art. 39).

The bill was debated in Parliament in October-November 1968, and defended by the Ministers of Justice and Religious Affairs. One of the points energetically discussed was the problem of polygamy. Article 3 of the bill ran as follows: "1. In principle marriage is monogamous; 2. Exceptions can be made when permitted by the law which regulates marriage contracts for the group concerned". In other words, in the marriage law to be made for Muslims polygamy could be accepted, albeit with certain limitations and on certain conditions. In the debate on polygamy it was mainly the female members of Parliament who took part.[23] On the one hand this principle was criticized as being out of place in a modern state. Many agree that polygamy will gradually disappear as a result of modernization, so that it would be better for the time being to stick to the old regulations than to make a new

---

[22] So, for example, within the "Original Javanese Religion of the Republic of Indonesia" (Ind. *Agama Djawa Asli Republik Indonesia,* abbreviated A.D.A.R.I.) and within the "Budha Djawi" sect, two of about 40 groups which formed a subject of research for students of the I.A.I.N. at Jogja, under their lecturer K. Kamil Kartapradja. The results of this fieldwork were stencilled for private use: K. Kamil Kartapradja, *Aliran-aliran Kebathinan di Indonesia,* 2 Vol., Jogjakarta 1968. Cf. Vol. II, pp. 161 and 236.
[23] *Djakarta Times* commented (28-10-1968): Only the women seem to be interested in a marriage law, the men probably only in marriage.

marriage law in which polygamy is still recognized.[24] On the other hand, however, it was just some female representatives of Islamic parties who defended polygamy, saying, for instance, that countless children would not know who their fathers were, should polygamy be prohibited.[25]

One of the objections to the proposed principles — although less explicitly debated — may have been the remaining link of the wedding to a certain religious institution and the lack of an alternative possibility for a "secular" wedding. The Islamic marriage law, to be made later, would be applied to all those who statistically could be considered Muslims (90 % of the population?), and a Christian marriage law to the Christians; in both cases those who otherwise never entered a mosque or a church would have to be married with a religious ceremony.

All things considered, it became clear that in Parliament there was too much resistance to these fundamental principles which were to precede a new marriage law, so the proposal did not come to the vote, but was withdrawn by the Ministers concerned in order to be perfected. As far as I know, this means that it has been put into cold storage. This, then, was the disappointing result of one attempt to put into official practice just one element of Islamic law.

In connection with family law, attention must be paid here to the work of Hazairin, professor of *Adat* law and Islamic law in the University

---

[24] Concerning the question of polygamy, an interesting book was edited by Solichin Salam, *Menindjau Masalah Polygami*, Djakarta 1959, based on an inquiry in which 200 specialists were asked for their opinions. Articles by 26 of them were included in the book, as well as some statistical material concerning marriage, divorce and polygamy in Indonesia during the years 1951-1957. To give some impression of the figures I quote the following examples. During 1957 the mosque officials in West Java registered 302,506 marriages, 172,472 divorces and 11,474 revocations of repudiation; this produced registration-charges to an amount of 8,024,370 Rp. (at that time worth about 250,000 U.S. dollars, probably an important source of income for the mosque staff). Figures for polygamy in the same year and concerning the same province are as follows: two wives, 20,796; three, 626; and four, 82. Statistics for the year 1956 and concerning the whole of Indonesia show a total number of 390,063 divorces; 123,734 occurred at the instance of the husband, 88,295 at the instance of the wife and 178,034 at the instance of both partners. Reasons given for these divorces were as follows: economic difficulties (118,020), dereliction of duty (87,378), incompatibility (84,809), physical reasons (51,741), taking a second wife (39,228), differences of political opinion (7,951), other reasons (936).

[25] *Djakarta Times*, 26-10-1968.

of Indonesia in Djakarta.[26] His opinions are a good illustration of the attempt to begin "from another angle", not by striving for a formal proclamation of an Islamic State but by aiming at a partial realization of Islamic law for Muslim citizens.

Hazairin has specialized in family law, in particular the laws of inheritance. He has come to conclusions which are rejected by many conservatives but may nevertheless become of great significance through his pupils, among whom are many lawyers and judges. Summarized briefly, his opinions are as follows.

Hazairin strongly criticizes the so-called "reception theory" (*theorie receptie*), "which was created by the Dutch colonial authorities to hinder the progress of Islam in Indonesia". What he means is the limitation of the competency of the religious judges to disputes which from of old were considered by the population as falling under religious jurisdiction. According to Hazairin, this policy of the colonial government meant that "Islamic law was not considered law; Islamic law could only be recognized as law if it had already become *adat* law" (i.e. if a "reception" or assimilation had taken place of Islamic provisions into the social life of a certain ethnic group). "This diabolical theory meant that people could sin against the precepts of the Qur'ān and the *Sunna* (normative custom) of the Prophet (e.g. sexually), but went unpunished as long as their behaviour did not conflict with the *adat*. This is not acceptable for a Muslim. The Islamic law as such must be recognized as law." According to Hazairin, this was agreed by the signatories of the Djakarta Charter of 1945.

To prevent misunderstanding, it must be added that Hazairin is one of the most radical adherents of the "new *idjtihād*". According to him, Indonesian society differs sharply from Arab society within which Islamic jurisprudence developed. Since 1950 Hazairin has become more and more convinced that the Qur'ān is adverse to any unilateral organized society, i.e. a society consisting of clans following a matrilineal or patrilineal system of kinship. He therefore felt free to advocate the

---

[26] Cf. the short remark on Hazairin's work in Prins, *Adat*, pp. 89-90. Hazairin's most important publications on these questions are the following: *Ilmu Pengetahuan Islam dan Masjarakat*, Djakarta 1951; *Hukum Islam dan Masjarakat*, Djakarta 1952¹, 1963³; *Hukum Kewarisan Bilateral menurut Qur'ān dan Ḥadīth*, Djakarta 1958¹, 1964³; *Hendak Kemana Hukum Islam?*, Djakarta 1960; *Ḥadīth Kewarisan dan Sistim Bilateral*, Djakarta 1962; *Hukum Kekeluargaan Nasional*, Djakarta 1962¹, 1968²; the lastmentioned publication, 2nd. edition, contains an extensive working paper with a draft for a possible new law of inheritance.

creation of a genuine Indonesian school of law (*madhhab Indonesia*) alongside the four mediaeval schools, an idea which has also been put forward by Hasbi Ash-Shiddiqy. According to such an Indonesian *madhhab,* family law and in particular the law of inheritance could proceed from a "*bilateral-parental* system". This would not be in conflict with the Qur'ān and Tradition. (With regard to religious duties in a narrower sense, i.e. duties to God or *ibādāt,* the Shāfiᶜī school could be maintained). According to Hazairin, the significance of the Islamic universities and other institutions of advanced Islamic education is that they can produce the necessary *mudjtahid-baru,* i.e. the scholars who, using the "new *idjtihād*", will come to a new interpretation of Islamic law as needed in modern Indonesia.[27]

In 1963 Hazairin defended his opinions in a public debate against Mahmud Junus and Toha Jahja Omar.[28] Mahmud Junus in particular is a well-known adherent of the four orthodox schools or, in fact, the Shāfiᶜī school of law.[29]

As mentioned above, Hazairin also wants to stick to the clause in the Djakarta Charter concerning "the obligation for adherents of Islam to practise Islamic law". According to Hazairin, these "seven words" do not refer to acts of worship (*ibādāt*), let alone official supervision of their performance, but refer to questions with which every government always and everywhere is concerned, in particular marriage, divorce and inheritance. In these cases Indonesian legislation must proceed from Islamic family law, expounded by an Indonesian *madhhab,* and declare those regulations to be valid for and to be maintained by Muslim citizens. If Christians wanted to, they could ask for Christian or Biblical precepts to be made law for the Christian community in Indonesia. According to Hazairin, these ideas have nothing to do with an Islamic State. An Islamic State can only be founded by Muslims. The Indonesian people does not consist only of Muslims, and even the Djakarta Charter was also signed by one non-Muslim. So Hazairin's aim is not an Islamic State but only a rejection of the so-called "reception theory" which hindered the development of Islamic jurisprudence. That theory now has to be replaced by the application of certain "elements" of Islamic law for Muslims, interpreted by an Indonesian *madhhab* and based on the "new *idjtihād*".

---
[27] Quotations from Hazairin, *Hukum Kekeluargaan,* p. 4 ff.
[28] *Perdebatan dalam Seminar Hukum Nasional tentang Faraid,* Djakarta 1964.
[29] Cf. Mahmud Junus, *Hukum Perkawinan dalam Islam, menurut mazhab: Sjafiᶜi, Hanafi, Maliki dan Hanbali,* Djakarta 1956¹, 1964³; idem, *Turutlah Hukum Warisan dalam Islam,* Djakarta 1958¹, 1962².

Together with Hazairin, the name of Hasbi Ash-Shiddiqy has been mentioned above. The latter recently published a booklet entitled *Baital Mal* (the "treasury" or "Ministry of Finance").[30] The author wants to show that Islamic law contains all kinds of elements necessary for the organization of the revenue and expenditure of the state. After a few words on the historical background of this *bait al-māl* — created by Umar, the second Caliph, and based on Sura 12 : 55 — sixteen types of revenue or tax are listed. Moreover the flexibility of Islamic law is stressed by stating that the *ūlū 'l-amri* (Sura 4 : 59, read: "Parliament") is free to make the necessary fiscal laws, providing they do not conflict with the revealed law. Number 10 on the list is the *djizja* (poll-tax) which according to Islamic law is to be paid by "those who have been defeated in war and have surrendered, but who want to keep their old religion and refuse to accept Islam".

When reading this pamphlet one wonders whether the author only wanted to make a historical contribution, or whether he believes that all these elements of Islamic law are still relevant to modern Indonesia. If even the *djizja* is considered of importance, should we not conclude that the author apparently advocates an Islamic State?

In an interview I had with Professor Hasbi he vigorously denied such an interpretation, adding the following explanation. "You cannot turn the clock back! Non-Muslims in Indonesia are recognized as full citizens like any others. This cannot be ignored. As you know, I am a supporter of the "new *idjtihād*" and even advocate the creation of our own *madhhab*. That is to say, in Indonesia we have to proceed from the Indonesian situation, and can only use those elements of Islamic law which are suited to modern Indonesia. Muslims who, for example, live in Holland ought to look there for an interpretation of Islamic precepts which suit the situation there. It is for this reason that I not only speak of an Indonesian *madhhab* — like Hazairin — but of national *madhhab*s, suited for us in Indonesia, for Muslims in Holland, and so on."

These then are some ideas of Hasbi Ash-Shiddiqy, who certainly enjoys considerable authority in Indonesia as an *ulama,* just as Hazairin does as a scholar.

This paragraph can be concluded with a few remarks on the religious courts, which are concerned with day-to-day questions of Islamic law (e.g. with regard to marriage and divorce or repudiation). The following

---

[30] Cf. Chapter I, par. 8.

data are chiefly based on publications and oral information from Professor Notosusanto of Gadjah Mada University in Jogjakarta.[31]

In comparison with the former *millet* system in Egypt, Indonesian jurisdiction was less complicated. Before 1956 there existed in Egypt an Islamic Court and separate *millet* councils for each religious community (*millet* or *milla*) alongside the ordinary courts of law. But alongside the ordinary courts in Indonesia there were only separate courts for Muslim affairs, not for other religious communities. In the colonial period these so-called religious courts (= Islamic courts) were supervised by the Ministry of Justice. After 1945 the Republic kept the old legal system and almost the whole content of the former legal codes. On March 25th, 1946, however, the religious courts were transferred to the Ministry of Religious Affairs. Looking back, it must probably be said that this change was a mixed blessing; the danger arose of the courts becoming controlled by conservative opinion when the Ministry was controlled by conservatives.

On June 8th, 1948 the Republican government promulgated a law on the re-organization of jurisdiction in a direction similar to developments in Egypt after 1956.[32] The proposal for this change apparently came from certain circles in the Islamic University of Indonesia (U.I.I.) in Jogjakarta. According to this bill, religious jurisdiction would become part of the ordinary courts of law. Within these courts a special "religious chamber" would be created for religious (= Islamic) questions. The chairman would be a qualified lawyer — obviously a Muslim — and he would be assisted by two *ulama*s. They would be appointed by the President, after being nominated by the Minister of Religion in agreement with the Minister of Justice.

Unfortunately, this law was never enforced, probably due to the political situation. Also after the recognition of Independence this law remained shelved. Its aim was to free the religious courts from conservatism and the exclusive influence of Shāfiʿī *ulama*s, as religious judges were (and are still) not trained at universities, but at institutions of a lower standard (*Pendidikan Hakim Islam Negeri*, P.H.I.N., i.e. a "Government Course for Islamic Judges"). At this level students are at best able to examine only Shāfiʿī *fikh* books. Moreover, this training and

---

[31] Notosusanto, *Peradilan Agama Islam di Djawa dan Madura*, Jogjakarta 1953; idem, *Sedikit tentang Peradilan Perdata di Mesir* (already mentioned); idem, *Organisasi dan Jurisprudensi Peradilan Agama di Indonesia*, Jogjakarta 1963.

[32] Notosusanto, *Peradilan*, pp. 13-14.

the appointment of teachers fall under the authority of the Minister of Religion, who also appoints the judges of religious courts. This means that everything depends on the progressive or conservative attitude of the Minister concerned. A Minister belonging to the Nahdatul Ulama (N.U.) might appoint exclusively so-called *madhhab* people, i.e. defenders of the authority of the four traditional schools of law or, in fact, followers of the Shāfiʿī school.

With regard to the organization as well as the jurisdiction of religious courts, little change has taken place in modern Indonesia. The former colonial regulations concerning the "religious councils" and the "Court for Islamic Affairs" — promulgated in 1882, 1909, 1926 and 1937 for Java and Madura, and in 1937 for South Kalimantan — remained fundamentally unchanged. The regional "religious councils" are now called *Pengadilan Agama* (Religious Court) or *Mahkamah Sjariʿah* (Court of Islamic law); the former "Court for Islamic Affairs" is now called *Mahkamah Islam Tinggi*, the High Court of Islamic Justice.

For the other islands religious jurisdiction was regulated by a new law in 1957. The list of matters falling under the jurisdiction of religious courts seems to include more than the old regulations for Java and Madura. But according to Notosusanto, the *adat* law still has priority over Islamic law in the new regulations, so there is in fact no question of an extension of the field of religious jurisdiction. The Indonesian High Court of Justice found in 1960 that "throughout Indonesia as far as inheritance is concerned priority has to be given to the *adat* law, which in areas where the influence of Islam is strong has already assimilated some elements of Islamic law to a greater or lesser extent..."; therefore, "as far as inheritance is concerned, the right to give verdicts belongs to the ordinary court of law".[33]

One problem which may be touched upon here is that a religious court is only authorized to act when both the plaintiff and defendant are Muslims. Thus the question arises of who then is a Muslim or when someone is to be considered a Muslim. Notosusanto gives four successively stricter definitions.[34] Firstly, anyone reckoned among the Muslims in the general opinion of his fellow-citizens, who himself says or does not deny that he is a Muslim and, for instance, has contracted marriage and wants to be buried in the Islamic way can be considered a Muslim. Secondly, anyone who willingly and sincerely pronounces the two sen-

---

[33] Notosusanto, *Organisasi*, p. 34.
[34] Notosusanto, *Peradilan*, p. 27 ff.; *Organisasi*, p. 28 ff.

tences of the Islamic profession of faith, i.e. I confess that there is no god but God and that Muhammad is His Messenger, can be considered a Muslim. Thirdly, someone is only considered a Muslim if he not only pronounces the Islamic profession of faith but also appears to have some knowledge of the tenets of Islam. Fourthly, someone is only considered a Muslim if he has not only some knowledge of Islam but also performs his religious duties, in particular prayer and fasting. Religious courts in Indonesia generally rely on the first and second definitions.

As a preliminary conclusion it can be said that Islamic leaders in Indonesia are striving for the realization of some elements of Islamic law in state and society, but that in fact not much progress has yet been made. The struggle for a formal proclamation of an Islamic State has failed. Likewise the attempt to start from a different angle and to put Islamic principles into practice in at least some sectors of social life has turned out to be more difficult than was expected.

3. *Regional Endeavours: Atjeh*

Outside Atjeh it is often said that the people of Atjeh are in fact trying to create an Islamic State within the Republic of Indonesia. According to some informants, Atjeh could well become a "pilot project" for the realization of Islamic law in other parts of Indonesia as well. According to others — including some Atjehnese informants living in Java — the attempts being made in Atjeh can only be made in Atjeh, because for the time being Atjeh is still a closed society where the modern world has as yet hardly penetrated.

Coming from Java, one gets the impression that Atjeh is indeed a "special area" or "special territory" (*daérah istiméwa*), as it is called administratively. Atjehnese are indeed Muslims. Among the almost two million inhabitants there are a small number of non-Atjehnese (for instance, among the civil servants and traders), some of whom are Christians. Furthermore, according to oral information, there are roughly 5,000 inhabitants of Chinese birth left in Atjeh, after the Chinese foreigners had to leave the area some years ago. Recently about 2,000 of them chose to become Muslims, while 1,000 wanted to become Christians. Atjehnese informants are wont to emphasize that in Atjeh too a complete freedom of religion is maintained. But for an Atjehnese himself, being an Atjehnese is equivalent to being a Muslim; it is simply inconceivable that a real Atjehnese could adhere to a religion other than Islam.

Atjehnese society does possess an Islamic character. Atjeh is probably the only part of Indonesia where people normally greet each other with *salām ᶜalaikum* (Arabic *as-salāmu ᶜalaikum*, "peace be with you"). "Prayer is a part of the lives of most Atjehnese men; they seem actually to pray five times daily." [35] On Fridays at noon the noise of daily life in the town of Banda Atjeh is replaced by the praises of God and common prayer in the mosque. When discussing religion a visitor is struck by the fact that people in Atjeh are so to speak Muslims as a matter of course and in an unselfconscious way, whereas in Java one sometimes gets the impression that many Muslims are more or less on the defensive, probably on account of the struggle against the old Javanese religion, rising secularism and Christianity. Harmony of life, founded on religion, seems to be undisturbed in Atjeh.

When asking the Atjehnese in Atjeh whether they intend making their area a kind of Islamic State on a provincial level, one receives roughly the same answer as one would elsewhere: "We do not intend to establish an Islamic State, but we want to expound Islamic law for Muslims here and make some elements of it practicable for them". Here too these attempts are said to be based on the Djakarta Charter of 1945 with its famous "seven words". Informants usually added that they were still studying general principles at the moment, and had not yet arrived at details for daily life. Moreover, they probably had to wait for approval from "Djakarta" before certain decisions could be put into practice.

Yet it may be said that there is a difference between the way of thinking of Islamic leaders in Atjeh and in Java, or rather that there is a certain similarity between the former way of thinking among Muslims in Java and the way in which people still approach matters in Atjeh now. Some Islamic leaders in Java originally dreamed of a proclamation of an Islamic State, after which they would have to realize this ideal in daily life. In the same way apparently the Atjehnese first of all fought for a recognition of Atjeh as a "special area" and are still trying to consolidate the position of Atjeh as an autonomous province, in order to make this status of Atjeh a starting-point for defining afterwards what it actually means to be the "verandah of Mecca" where Islamic law is to be put into practice.

---

[35] James Siegel, *The Rope of God,* Berkeley & Los Angeles 1969, p. 104; compare the article by the same author, entitled *Prayer and Play in Atjeh,* in *Indonesia,* Ithaca New York, April 1966, p. 6.

If one attempts to summarize the scattered information gleaned from Atjehnese sources and interviews with Atjehnese informants, developments can be sketched as follows.

As a result of the compromise between Atjeh and "Djakarta", the province of Atjeh was recognized as a special administrative territory on May 26th, 1959. This took place in an announcement by Minister Hardi (Home Office), based on a decision by Prime Minister Djuanda, after a discussion in the cabinet in February 1959.[36] This decision was taken "in order to obtain a greater guarantee for the improvement of safety and development" in Atjeh, and "as a stimulus for the realization of as great a degree of autonomy as possible"; this autonomy would in particular be realized in the fields of religion, *adat* and education. On August 17th, 1961 the return of peace to all Atjeh was solemnly marked, and Atjeh was declared to have been restored from *darulharb* ("area of war") to *darussalam* ("area of peace").[37]

Some months later, from December 19th to 23rd, 1961, the regional government of Atjeh organized a public consultation (*musjawarah*) to discuss a programme for the reconstruction and development of Atjeh. This programme was probably drawn up by the energetic governor Ali Hasjmy. After some corrections it was accepted and published in January 1962.[38]

It may perhaps be concluded from article 5 of this programme that the formal status of Atjeh at that time was still a point at issue between Atjeh and "Djakarta". According to that article, the status of Atjeh as a "special administrative area" (as decided on May 26th, 1959) would still have to be authorized either by law or by a decree of the President. As far as I know, this authorization has never officially been given.

In article 11 of the programme a list was given of the activities which ought to be transferred from the central government to the regional authorities in Atjeh; this summary was more precisely dealt with in articles 13 to 42. To begin with, regulations were mentioned concerning religious affairs, the supervision of religious instruction, the promotion of religious information and the organization of religious courts. For fundamental religious questions, the creation of a regional *Madjlis Iftā'* was announced in article 39. This was to be a council for giving expert

---

[36] See the stencilled publication *Dewan Perwakilan*, p. 33; the complete text of the resolution is published in *Atjeh Membangun*, p. 69 ff. and can also be found in *Kehidupan Beragama di Daerah Istimewa Atjeh*, ed. by "Secretariat DPRD-GR", Atjeh 1967, p. 85 ff.
[37] *Dewan Perwakilan*, p. 33.
[38] Cf. *Atjeh Membangun*, pp. 17-44.

advice (*fatwa*s) concerning questions on which differences of opinion might exist within society. With regard to education, Atjeh wanted the competency of the central government to be transferred to Atjehnese authorities, from the founding of kindergartens (Ind. *taman kanak-kanak*) to the management of secondary schools. In the exposition of the details it was suggested that one of the subjects to be taught in primary schools should be the Atjehnese language.

Also with regard to other fields it was stipulated that real substance had to be given to the autonomy of Atjeh, e.g. with regard to decisions on questions of exports and imports, the use of foreign currency, admission of immigrants into Atjeh, the organization of co-operatives, regulations concerning ports, the intensification of agriculture, stockbreeding and fisheries, the development of health services, the promotion of sport by improving equipment and training instructors, and the promotion of tourism by drawing attention to the history of Atjeh, its culture and its natural beauty.[39]

From 1962 onwards a number of decisions were made to bring about the realization of this Atjehnese development plan. In the field of religion some visible results are eagerly shown to the visitor. The great mosque in Banda Atjeh has been enlarged and beautified; it now has five domes (formerly three), two minarets and a very large courtyard. In the extensive grounds of the new university and students' city Darussalam, where the "Sjiah Kuala University" has been set up with faculties of economics, technology and agriculture, there has also been founded a State Islamic Institute (I.A.I.N.) called "Ar-Raniry".[40] For the time being it is accommodated in a former secondary school, but a huge I.A.I.N. building is nearly finished. Half a mile further on, in a corner

---

[39] As far as history is concerned, it is worth mentioning that a search was made for the grave of the famous Sultan Iskandar Muda (1607-1636). It is said that the Dutch either never discovered where it was or wanted to keep its place a secret, because the Atjehnese used to say: "Atjeh cannot remain subjected by someone as long as the bones of Iskandar Muda remain in Atjeh". During the Japanese occupation the exact place was given by the old Potjut Meurah — mentioned in Piekaar, *Atjèh,* pp. 68 and 227 — who in her youth had participated in ceremonies at this grave, before the colonial government built its office on this site. Some years ago the building concerned was pulled down and a massive monument built on the supposed burial place of Iskandar Muda.

[40] The "Universitas Sjiah Kuala" is named after Abdur Rauf of Singkel, later called the "Sjaich of Kuala", a 17th century teacher of religion in Atjeh. The I.A.I.N. is called after Nuruddin ar-Ranīri, a champion of "orthodox" mysticism in 17th century Atjeh.

of Darussalam, the *pesantrèn* "Pantekulu" has been built.[41] It is a *pesantrèn* in the old style, which will produce *ulama*s for the countryside, where graduates of the I.A.I.N. may be considered too modern. In another corner of Darussalam there stands a women's mosque. It is said that in the countryside a great number of mosques and *mushalla*s have also been built (the word *mushalla* = *muṣalla* is now commonly used for a small building or room where people can perform the *ṣalāt*).

On April 7th, 1962, the military commander of Atjeh declared himself in agreement with the wish of Islamic leaders to make certain elements of Islamic law obligatory for Muslims in Atjeh. On August 15th, 1962, the regional representative body followed with a resolution to apply elements of Islamic law to the Muslims (*akan melaksanakan unsur-unsur Sjariᶜat Islam bagi pemeluk-pemeluknja*); a committee would be set up to draft regional regulations to carry out this resolution; the central government in Djakarta would be asked to make laws in which certain religious principles would be officially defined, in order to prevent deviations (that is to say, in order to make these deviations punishable?).[42]

In the years following, various decisions were made to prepare for executing the abovementioned decisions. But for the time being not much more could be achieved than decisions and resolutions to prepare new regulations. In the capital Banda Atjeh a spacious building arose which was to be the "Office for the Realization of Elements of Islamic Law" (*Biro Pelaksanaan Unsur-unsur Sjariᶜat Islam*). The suggestion of 1962 to create a *Madjlis Iftā'* apparently resulted in the foundation of a *Madjlis Ulama* in 1966. This "Council of *Ulama*s" was to advise the regional government on religious affairs, either at the request of the authorities or on its own initiative. Vice-chairman and one of the most important younger members of this Council is Ismail Muhammad Sjah (abbreviated Ismuha), principal of the I.A.I.N.

After September 30th, 1965, topical questions were, for example, the extermination of Communism and the revision of President Soekarno's

---

[41] Tgk. Tjhik Panté Kulu was a 19th century *ulama*, writer and poet, whose Atjehnese poem on the Holy War (in Indonesian, *Hikajat Perang Sabil*) is said to have inspired the Atjehnese to persevere in their fight for freedom against the Dutch for more than 50 years. Cf. Tgk. M. Hasballah Saleh, *Tgk. Tjhik Pante Kulu, Tokoh Penjair Perang Terbesar Didunia*, in *Sinar Darussalam*, no. 5, pp. 76-80.

[42] *Dewan Perwakilan*, pp. 129-131.

position. In June 1963 the regional representative body had passed a resolution in which God was thanked for the decision of the People's Congress in Djakarta to appoint President Soekarno as president for life; but on September 28th, 1966, this resolution was withdrawn.[43] The composition of the regional representative body was of course reviewed, as after September 1965 the P.K.I. and P.N.I. delegates were dismissed. In December 1966 of the 43 members eight belonged to the Perti, seven to the P.S.I.I., six to the N.U., two to the I.P.K.I. (in Atjeh led by a member of Muhammadijah) and one to the Protestant Parkindo; the "functional groups" were represented by 16 members, and the young people (the so-called "Generation of 1966") by three.[44]

On September 23rd, 1967, the regional representative body accepted a "Memorandum concerning Religious Life in Atjeh", in which measures were demanded against certain activities of Christian groups.[45] This Memorandum opened with considerations such as the following. The people of Atjeh have for centuries been so deeply devoted to Islam that this area was given the honorific name "verandah of Mecca". Islam inspired the people of Atjeh in the fight for independence against colonialism. Even Snouck Hurgronje advised the colonial government to realize that the people of Indonesia adhered to Islam and that their social and cultural inadequacy could not be used as an argument to allow Christian missions to operate in areas such as Atjeh (article 177 of the Netherlands East Indies Statute Book). Article 29 of the Indonesian Constitution of 1945 did indeed recognize the freedom of every inhabitant to practise his own religion. But according to this Memorandum this did not mean that religious propaganda of another religion within an Islamic community such as Atjeh ought to be allowed. Such propaganda would mean an attack on the principle of tolerance and would endanger law and order, as this sort of propaganda would hurt Muslim feelings. Since May 26th, 1959, autonomy in Religion (Islam), *Adat* and Education had been given to Atjeh. The authorities and the people of Atjeh proved to be tolerant toward adherents of other religions, as long as they did not behave in a demonstrative, provocative and aggressive way. It was, however, unacceptable that within an Islamic community such as Atjeh a religion other than Islam could be propa-

---

[43] *Dewan Perwakilan*, p. 97.
[44] *Dewan Perwakilan*, p. 28. Before the banning of the Masjumi this was probably the strongest party in Atjeh; it will be interesting to see how many votes the new Partai Muslimin gets in the coming elections.
[45] Its text can be found in *Kehidupan Beragama*, pp. 3-7.

gated and spread by public meetings, the distribution of books, pamphlets and leaflets, house to house visiting, the building of places of worship in the very midst of Muslim villagers, let alone the use of verses from the Qur'ān for the propagation of that religion.[46]

Based on all these considerations, the regional representative body of Atjeh concluded: (1) That for this area a policy should be followed as intended in article 177 of the old Statute Book; (2) That the propagation and spreading of a religion other than Islam by the distribution of books and the handing out of leaflets should be forbidden; (3) That it should be forbidden to propagate another religion by using verses from the Qur'ān; (4) That the Islamic community should be urged not to send their children to schools which were based on a religion other than Islam; and (5) That the governor of Atjeh should be empowered to take the necessary steps to carry out these decisions.

Another important meeting was that of the *ulama*s from all Atjeh on November 21st-26th, 1967.[47] This congress decided that the *Madjlis Ulama* was to be a body to advise the regional government and to consult with it on questions concerning religion and society; that the *Madjlis* was to be an authoritative body for giving *fatwa*s; that the *Madjlis* was to be the instrument for promoting unity within the Islamic community, and that the Islamic parties and organizations had to obey the decisions and *fatwa*s of the *Madjlis*. With regard to the *zakāt*, the congress decided that the regional authorities should make regulations so that they themselves could organize the collection of the *zakāt*.

---

[46] In connection with the remark about the building of places of worship amid the Muslims, reference must be made to the conflict concerning the building of a Methodist church in Meulaboh, West Atjeh, in April 1967. The questions put in Parliament by J. C. T. Simorangkir (Parkindo) concerning this conflict and the government's answer can be found in *Kehidupan Beragama*, pp. 33-41. As to the verses from the Qur'ān used for propagating another religion, verses, of course, are meant which deal with Nabī ᶜĪsā (Jesus), sometimes misused as a starting-point for Christian propaganda. It is, however, difficult to believe that Christians in Atjeh would dare to do such a thing. Probably this criticism is based on information from Djakarta about the campaign of a certain C. E. Moseley, an American Adventist, held from August 27th to September 1st, 1967, in the Senajan Stadium in Djakarta. It is said that in preparation for this campaign leaflets were distributed in which no less than 15 verses from the Qur'ān were used. See *Pandji Masjarakat*, no. 18, September 1967, pp. 6-7.

[47] Minutes of this meeting seem to be unavailable; its final resolution has been published in *Sinar Darussalam*, no. 3, pp. 117-125. Some of its results can also be deduced from articles in *Sinar Darussalam*, no. 9, December 1968, pp. 46-63.

On October 7th, 1968, during a visit to Atjeh, the Minister of Religion gave his blessing to the existing *Madjlis Ulama,* explaining that he considered its organization, function and status to be right, and also approving the resolution concerning the collection of the *zakāt*.[48]

Meanwhile President Soeharto had visited Atjeh from August 30th to September 1st, 1968.[49] This visit was to create the opportunity for both sides to get to know each other. According to some informants, however, this visit was also intended to eliminate the fear that "Djakarta" and Atjeh would once again drift apart, for instance, because Atjeh might go too far in realizing its autonomy or taking decisions in conflict with the Indonesian Constitution.

In his address after the Friday prayer in the great mosque of Banda Atjeh, the President emphasized that Indonesia was a unitary state, based on the 1945 Constitution and the ideals of the Pantjasila. He asked whether Indonesia, especially the Islamic community which included 90 % of the population, exerted itself sufficiently for the maintenance of this unity. He warned against controversy as well within the Islamic community itself as between the various religious groups. The President reminded his audience of his attempts to achieve genuine religious tolerance.[50] He warned them against whispering campaigns by those who (like the Communists) wanted to sow the seeds of dissension, for instance by making a problem of foreign support received by other religions; he assured them that the government would examine this question objectively.[51] The President believed that the Islamic community in Indonesia, 90 % of the inhabitants, had no need to fear that another religion could destroy Islam. But the Islamic community ought to be aware of its responsibility to make good Muslims of those who,

---

[48] *Sinar Darussalam,* no. 9, December 1968, pp. 62-63.
[49] For a report of this visit, including the text of speeches, etc., see the stencilled publication entitled *Presiden Soeharto Ditengah-tengah Rakjat Atjeh,* ed. by the Reception Committee, dated Atjeh, September 2nd, 1968.
[50] Cf. the text of Soeharto's speech at the Inter-Religious Consultation held in Djakarta on November 30th, 1967, after incidents between Muslims and Christians in Makassar. See *Al-Djami'ah,* May 1968.
[51] Reference is here made to the question put in Parliament by Lukman Harun on June 10th, 1967, in which the government was asked to make an inquiry into financial aid and staff given to the Indonesian churches by foreign Missions. The text of the question and the government's answer were published in *Kehidupan Beragama,* pp. 13-32. Cf. also *Pandji Masjarakat,* no. 18, September 1967, p. 6.

for example, were only Muslims in that they could recite the *shahāda* (the Islamic profession of faith), as is necessary at a marriage ceremony. In comparison with foreign aid to other religions, the President stressed the amount the Islamic community could do, if even half of them contributed a reasonable *zakāt*. And so he urged self-correction instead of fear.

At every opportunity during this visit to Atjeh the President stressed the unity of all Indonesia. In an explanation of the Five-Year Development Plan, he called good contact between Atjeh and Djakarta an absolute condition for the success of the plan. People in Atjeh too had to realize that notwithstanding genuine autonomy the regional authorities had to carry out the policy of the central government. The President gave similar answers to written questions posed by delegates of the various political parties in the regional representative body. To the question of whether he gave credit to rumours that a rising was brewing in Atjeh, he answered that he could not believe that Atjeh would betray the Pantjasila and the 1945 Constitution. When asked whether he agreed with the Atjehnese desire to be really Islamic, and if so, how this should be brought about, he answered that in Indonesia any religion could develop without hindrance; this held good for Islam as well as for other religions.

Soon after President Soeharto's visit to Atjeh, the fourth session of the regional representative body was held, from November 5th to 11th, 1968.[52] The congress of *ulama*s, held in November 1967, may well be considered as a preparation for these meetings of the representative body. They were entirely devoted to the question of the realization of Islamic principles in Atjehnese society and resulted in the acceptance of Regulation No. 6/1968, concerning "The Realization of Elements of Islamic Law".[53]

According to the Explanatory Memorandum, this Regulation was intended to give substance to the special character of Atjeh as the "verandah of Mecca". In its first article it is stated that the term "elements of the Religious Law" refers to "the teachings of Islam as God

---

[52] The complete minutes of this session are available in a stencilled publication, edited by "Secretariat DPRD-GR", entitled *Sidang Ke-IV Dewan Perwakilan Rakjat Daerah Gotong-Rojong Propinsi Daerah Istimewa Atjeh 1968*.

[53] The text of this Regulation and the Explanatory Memorandum are to be found in the abovementioned minutes, pp. 365-370 and in *Sinar Darussalam*, no. 9, December 1968, pp. 47-58.

has ordained for mankind, including both the area of belief and the area of behaviour". After a summary of all the "elements" concerned (art. 2), articles 3 and 4 stress the duty of the regional authorities, the *Madjlis Ulama* and the population to practise Islamic law in personal life and in the life of family and society. Of those who adhere to a religion other than Islam it is expected that they will respect these endeavours for the realization of elements of Islamic law and will cooperate in promoting them.

In article 5, concerning spiritual life and doctrine (*'aqidah/keimanan*), it is stipulated that Muslims are obliged to strengthen the belief in God and the love of Islam in the life of the individual, of the family and of society, while the authorities and the *Madjlis Ulama* are pledged to oppose unbelief and atheism. According to article 6, every Muslim is obliged to worship (*'ibadah*); the authorities and the *Madjlis Ulama* will try to see that every Muslim does indeed carry out this duty. Furthermore, the authorities will see to the maintenance of Islamic precepts for various transactions, such as, for instance, trade, recovery of debts, pawning, terms of lease, power of attorney and family law (art. 7). Questions of ethics and morals (*achlaq*) are dealt with in article 8; in order to combat a decline in morals, supervision will be exercised over (women's) clothing, publications, art, dancing, and so on. According to article 9, education, art and culture must be in harmony with the spirit of Islam; Muslim children must be prevented from receiving an education in conflict with this spirit.[54] Every Muslim is free to work for the spread and development of Islam (*dakwah Islamijah*), provided his work furthers the unity of the Islamic community (art. 10). As far as finance is concerned, it is stipulated in article 11 that the regional authorities together with the *Madjlis Ulama* will form and run a *Bait al-Māl* as a separate fund for the benefit of Islam and the Muslims. Article 12 deals with social life (*kemasjarakatan*), stipulating that the authorities and the *Madjlis Ulama* will exert themselves for the creation of real Islamic brotherhood (*uchuwah Islamijah*) in society. Under the heading *Sji'ar Islam* it is stipulated in article 13 that the authorities have to stimulate

---

[54] As far as education is concerned, the Atjehnese are striving for an integration of religious instruction (originally given in the *pesantrèn*) and general education as given in state schools. The Commemoration Day lecture which Ibrahim Husein gave on October 10th, 1965 at the I.A.I.N. in Banda Atjeh was devoted to the problem of "giving substance to the special character of education in Atjeh". It was published in *Al-Djami'ah,* no. 5-6, Sept.-Nov. 1967.

the celebration of Islamic feasts and everything connected with the sublime sacred things or ceremonies of Islam.[55]

From the closing articles it appears that this Regulation will be followed by further directives for practical use, for example, concerning the infringement of this Regulation and its punishment (imprisonment for up to a maximum of six months or a fine of up to 10,000 Rp.).

It is not necessary to report the discussions held in the regional representative body before this Regulation was accepted. Once or twice a representative touched on the possibility of difficulties when the Regulation was put into operation (for instance, in connection with some differences between the four orthodox schools of law). But in general there was great unanimity concerning the aim and character of this Regulation.

The only representative of the Protestant group, Sormin Siregar, declared for the Parkindo that he would leave the decision to the Muslim representatives, as he did not feel it right or proper for a Christian to participate in discussions regarding the religious life of the Islamic community. Yet he wanted to appeal to the regional authorities not to forget the 45,000 Protestants and the 15,000 Roman Catholics living in Atjeh. He wanted to stress that this Regulation should not be misused in order to trouble the adherents of another religion. One amendment he wanted to suggest was the following. According to article 4, it was expected of non-Muslims that they respect these endeavours for the realization of elements of Islamic law and co-operate in promoting them. However, as this realization was entirely a matter for the adherents of Islam, he would like to suggest that it only be stipulated that non-Muslims be expected "to respect Islam and the Islamic community".[56] As far as I know, there was no reaction to this suggestion and so it was not adopted.

---

[55] The word *sji'ar*, assimilated into Indonesian from the Qur'ān, is rarely used and is said to be almost untranslatable. Apparently the word reminds an Indonesian Muslim of all "sublime sacred things" or "ceremonies" of Islam in general. In the Qur'ān the word *shiᶜār* occurs four times in its plural form *shaᶜā'ir*. The new Indonesian translation of the Qur'ān uses the Indonesian plural *sji'ar-sji'ar* in 2:158, with a note that Al-Ṣafā and Al-Marwa belong to "the symbols and places which are concerned with obedience to God"; the same translation is used in 5:2, where it is noted that the word is connected with ceremonies and places of the pilgrimage; in 22:30 the word is translated with "that which is sanctified by God"; in 22:36 — referring to the sacrificial animals — *sji'ar-sji'ar* is used again, this time without further comment.

[56] Sormin Siregar's speech can be found in the minutes, *Sidang Ke-IV*, pp. 117-118.

I do not know how much progress has so far been made in putting this Regulation into practice. Is perhaps the passing of the Regulation one of the points at issue between Atjeh and "Djakarta"? However that may be, this formal question is probably not of vital importance for daily life in Atjeh. With regard to the performance of religious duties by Atjehnese Muslims, the social controls within a society such as Atjeh in fact have the same effect as legal stipulations. Moreover, legal provisions can only sanction what already exists within a certain community and has met with a response there. Now it must simply be concluded that Atjeh *is* indeed a special area — at least for the time being — and that it might be possible to carry out something there that is impossible elsewhere. On the other hand, it is understandable that the central government is afraid that Atjeh could create a precedent. Apparently in some small districts elsewhere in Indonesia people tend to imitate the Atjehnese way. Permitting such regional endeavours could end in a disastrous dissolution of the Indonesian unitary state.

As far as Atjeh itself is concerned, the future will show whether and for how long Atjeh will remain a closed society, where religion to a large extent keeps together and controls society. It may be supposed that great changes will also take place in Atjeh within this generation, changes in the direction of further modernization and individualization. Various symptoms indicate that in Atjeh too these changes cannot be resisted. More and more young Atjehnese are going to study at a university, in Atjeh and elsewhere, even in foreign countries. On the campus of Darussalam there is easy social contact between male and female students; they are going to choose themselves their own boyfriends and girl-friends, their husbands and wives. The cinema in Atjeh too attracts the people; censorship may restrict imported sex-films, but this means that the cinemas are dependent on films full of violence. In the course of time Atjeh will be included on the routes of world traffic; it will become part of the so-called modern world, and be penetrated by it. So the question may arise as to whether the future of religion does not depend primarily on defending its communal character as a cultural, social and political system, but on promoting the personal religious life of its individual adherents.

4. *Working toward an Islamic Society*

According to some informants, the Masjumi had never actually been striving for the creation of an official Islamic State, but at best for an Islamic society. Be that as it may, it can be concluded that with the passing of time the term "Islamic society" became more frequently used, as it became less opportune to talk of an "Islamic State". When I inquired of my informants what exactly the objectives of the struggle for an Islamic society were, the answers I collected were as follows. It means (1) the attempt to have Islamic principles imbue Indonesian society; (2) the promotion and strengthening of the *uchuwah Islamijah*, the Islamic brotherhood; (3) making visible the impact of Islam on public life; (4) spreading an Islamic style of life; in short (5) the furthering of everything that could give Indonesia the colour of a Muslim country, in accordance with the fact that far and away the majority of the inhabitants are Muslims.

The problem faced by the Muslim community of Indonesia is, of course, that nominally 80-90 % of the population adhere to Islam, but that there is an enormous gap between theory and practice. The discrepancy between the number of nominal and the number of practising adherents of a religion is certainly not a specifically Muslim feature, but applies likewise to other religious communities. There is no point in foreign non-Muslims trying to fix the percentage of "real Muslims" in Indonesia, based on figures and guesses concerning the number of "practising Muslims". What criteria can be used? And how can one judge of another's intention?

It has been said, for example, that according to Wahab Wahib, Minister of Religion in 1960, no more than 10 % of the Indonesian population were practising Muslims; furthermore, research in Java had shown that in villages where the inhabitants called themselves Muslims sometimes 0 %, at best 15 %, performed the duty of prayer (*ṣalāt*); in 1967 the *zakāt* was paid by 14 % of people in Jogjakarta, in Djakarta by 30 %; *Ramaḍān* (the month of fasting) was observed by 12 % in West Java and by only 2 % in Central Java.[57] For those reasons it was concluded that of people who seem to follow Islam only 10 % could be considered true Muslims. With regard to the Muslim view that 90 % of the Indonesian people adhere to Islam, the author of the paper quoted above added: "Actually this juggling with numbers is turning against

---

[57] According to Muskens, *Indonesië*, pp. 266-267, who quoted these and many other data from *Herder Korrespondenz* (or *Herder Correspondence*) and from unpublished writings by the Indonesian contributor to this Roman Catholic journal.

Islam itself, for it means that according to the Muslims all those who are known as former P.K.I.-members, corrupt people, etc. belong to their ranks. This view is not to the credit of the image of Islam."

In answer to this sort of criticism it may be argued that Indonesian Muslims too are well aware of the problem. The point is, however, that basically they want also to include the "nominal Muslims", or *abangan*s or whatever they may be called, as members of the Muslim community (in the same way as Christian churches often assume that all baptized members are once and for all to be considered Christians).

In March 1968 Moh. Hatta, the former Vice-President, shocked many Muslims when he said in a sermon in the mosque in Bandung that the Islamic community in Indonesia probably comprised only 60 % of the population; what Hatta meant, however, was merely a result of the following subtraction: about 10 % of the Indonesians are said to be Christians, another 10 % can be considered Hindus, Buddhists and "Animists", and furthermore there are perhaps 20 % who are Communists and cannot be considered Muslims; so there remains 60 %.[58]

A more remarkable view was voiced by Rafik in an article published in the Islamic magazine *Pandji Masjarakat,* under the heading "Analysis of the Real Potential of the present-day Islamic Community".[59] In his opinion the general belief that the Islamic community included 90 % of the Indonesian people ought to be corrected. He wanted to admit that a great deal of the 90 % were only formal, passive Muslims. The existence of a nucleus of active Muslims would be far more important. A criterion could be whether or not one participates in the activities of Islamic parties or other Islamic organizations. The author criticized the dissension within the Islamic community, while referring to the situation within the Roman Catholic and Protestant parties, where supporters and opponents of Soekarno did not combat one another.[60] He urged self-examination and the purging of the Islamic community, and blamed the behaviour of some so-called leaders as being in complete defiance

---

[58] Cf. D. Bakker, *Daᶜwah, Missionarische Mobilisierung des Islams in Indonesien,* in *Evangelische Missions-Zeitschrift,* August 1969, p. 128, n. 40. My interpretation of Hatta's remark is based on an interview with him on April 23rd, 1969. Cf. H. B. Jassin, *Heboh Sastra 1968,* Djakarta 1970, pp. 60 and 67, who apparently did not know how Hatta had arrived at his conclusion.

[59] Rafik, *Analisa Tentang Potensi Ummat Islam Sekarang,* in *Pandji Masjarakat,* no. 32, Sept. 1968 (?), pp. 15-16.

[60] Probably this refers to the conflict between adherents of the N.U. and the former Masjumi.

of Islam, because among them there were swindlers, corrupt people, gamblers and owners of nightclubs with striptease dancers. As long as the Islamic community was deceived by the figure of 90 %, and did not come to examine and purify itself, it would again and again have to suffer defeats. The author concluded that being a community of less than 90 % did not matter. It would be more realistic and more important to be involved in creating a nucleus of active Muslims, to whom God — as in the time of the Prophet — could grant victory. The author wanted to consider such a "small band", *fiatan kalilah* (= *fi'atan kalīlatan*, cf. Sura 2 : 249) as the real potential of the Islamic community in present-day Indonesia.

An important aspect of the creation of such a nucleus is, of course, leadership training, which will be further dealt with in the next paragraph. The point here is, however, that at the same time Islamic leaders continue to look to the masses, the 90 %, in order to Islamize the nominal Muslims and Indonesian society in general.

To begin with, the importance of the Ministry of Religion may once again be stressed. The existence of this Ministry was to prove the positive attitude of the Indonesian state towards religion. Its first aim would be to make the *Ketuhanan Jang Maha Esa* (Belief in the One and Only God) an operative principle in the Indonesian state. According to the Muslim interpretation the furtherance of this "Belief in the One and Only God" meant, of course, the furtherance of Islam, in particular through the Islamic section of the Ministry of Religion (just as, according to another interpretation, other sections of that Ministry could give support to the activities of Christian churches).

The Ministry of Religion, then, stimulates and supports in various ways the activities of the Islamic community. This support consists, for example, of financial aid for building mosques and other Islamic places of worship all over the country. Furthermore, the Ministry stimulates obedience to precepts of Islamic law such as fasting; the beginning of *Ramaḍān* is in fact fixed by calculation (*ḥisāb*) and there actually seems no longer to be discussion on the problem of *ḥisāb* or *ru'ya* (the observance of the new moon), although some Muslims privately still keep to the method of observation in order to check the date officially fixed by the Ministry.

The Ministry also regulates the religious feasts and promotes their celebration. For example, the celebration of *al-ᶜīd al-kabīr* (the "sacrificial feast" during the pilgrimage), to which formerly hardly any attention had been paid in Indonesia,[61] is now promoted by local committees formed by the authorities. According to my informants, during this feast in 1969 a number of buffaloes were publicly slaughtered in Jogjakarta in front of the great mosque, while families at home slaughtered more sheep than ever before, for themselves and their neighbours.

The Ministry with its offices spread all over Indonesia also promotes the payment of the *zakāt* and assists in its collection. The rather high percentage of 30 % in Djakarta, as mentioned above, may partly be due to the influence of the authorities on the civil servants in the departments and government offices in Djakarta. It is rather difficult to abstain, if one is reminded of one's religious duties by one's superior.

The fact that in particular at the centre of government, Djakarta, religion and religious duties are officially held in high esteem typifies one aspect of the Indonesian situation which has to be considered. There is not only a social control within the community of a Muslim *kampung* or *désa*, but also something like a "religious *dirigism*" by the government, that is to say, the government to some extent directs, regulates and promotes all kinds of religious activities from above, through its official bodies, with the Ministry of Religion at the top. This "religious *dirigism*" is not only founded on the Muslim view of the unity of religion and state, but also on Soekarno's doctrine that Indonesia and every Indonesian must have a God and a religion, while freedom of religion nowadays does not include the freedom to be non-religious, let alone anti-religious. Moreover, only those religions are recognized that are represented in the Ministry of Religion (that is to say, not the remaining tribal religions). Partly thanks to all these factors, religions in Indonesia seem to be flourishing more than ever before. To what extent may religious people be misled by this flourishing state of affairs? Do they realize that beneath the surface, in Indonesia too, secularism, lack of interest and estrangement from religion are perhaps slowly but surely increasing?

For the furtherance of religion, in particular Islam, a great number of pamphlets aimed at the general public have been published and distributed by the Ministry of Religion. This applies, for example, to speeches by President Soekarno and the different Ministers of Religion, as well as to other authors. These publications cover the meaning of Ramaḍān; the place of woman in society; Islam as the universal religion; the significance of the Qur'ān for the renewal of man; religious

---

[61] Compare Th. W. Juynboll, *Handleiding tot de kennis van de Mohammedaansche Wet*, Leiden 1930⁴, p. 112.

ministration to people in prisons and hostels, to transmigrants, or the police; the importance of religion for "nation building and character building"; appeals for a return to the moral standards of Islam; and so on.[62]

Here too an observer is inclined to ask a number of questions. For instance, will not the religious communities, including Islam, rely too heavily on government aid, especially financial help, and that mainly for religious purposes in the narrower sense of the word? Could this policy not result in the religious communities — the Islamic as well as the Christian — becoming more and more introverted, when religion seems to be promoted in this way for the sake of religion itself? Even insofar as religious activities are directed at society in general, the intention seems to be to make society more religious in the narrower sense of the word, i.e. to have people observe religious duties such as prayer and fasting. The question could, however, be put as to whether in present-day Indonesia it may not be even more important to stress that religion has to be a source of inspiration for changes and developments in the socio-economic field. In other words, does our world have to be made interested in the problems and development of religion, or does religion first and foremost have to be made interested in the problems and development of our world? Finally one could ask to what extent "religious *dirigism*" could form an obstruction to the development of initiative by the various religious communities themselves.

With regard to the last question, however, we can also discern much private initiative within the Muslim community itself. Various observers have noticed that during the last decade the term *dakwah* (Ar. *daʿwa*, call, invitation) has become one of the most frequently used words in Muslim circles.[63] To give a short definition: "In the religious sense, the *daʿwa* is the invitation, addressed to men by God and the prophets, to believe in the true religion, Islam"; cf. Sura 14 : 44.[64] In Indonesian publications the term *daʿwa* is sometimes explained with expressions such as "Islamic propaganda" or "Islamic Mission" (Ind. *Missi*), sometimes even with the Dutch word for Mission, e.g. "Zending Islam Indonesia".[65]

---
[62] See the List of Publications, under "Departemen Agama".
[63] Cf. the abovementioned article by D. Bakker, *Daʿwah*; also Jacob Vredenbregt, *De Islam in het moderne Indonesië*, in *Oost en West*, December 1968, pp. 6-10.
[64] *The Encyclopaedia of Islam*, New Edition, Vol. II, Leiden 1965, p. 168.
[65] An organization in Medan (North Sumatra); see photo in the German mission magazine *In die Welt für die Welt*, Aug.-Sept. 1969, p. 13.

After 1965 Muslims have more and more realized that the Islamization of Indonesia would in fact mean the Islamization of Java, and that this was a question of now or never. One of my principal informants said in 1966: "The question of whether we succeed in making the masses in Java true Muslims will be decisive for the future of Islam in Indonesia". To hope for succeeding in this may sound rather optimistic or even naïve to people in the West who believe that they live in a post-religious era. Islamic leaders, however, stress that these millions in Java have not drifted away from Islam, nor have they become secularized or indifferent to religion, but rather have never really been Islamized or even become acquainted with real Islam. According to the Muslim point of view these millions still have Islam ahead of them, not behind them. It is only a small, though growing, elite of intellectuals who have in fact dissociated themselves from Islam or become secularized; part of the proletariat in the cities may have become indifferent to religion, and, of course, a much bigger group of people are lukewarm toward or ignorant of religion.

It can be said that during the past centuries most of the Indonesian islands have nominally been incorporated into the world of Islam, but that the problem of a more thorough Islamization has been tackled in a resolute and organized way only in the 20th century. The reformist movement in Indonesia took shape in the founding of the Muhammadijah in 1912.[66] It was this movement in particular that restored self-respect to a new generation of Muslims. "The Muhammadijah has brought the truth home to us that we may be proud of being Muslims"; "the Muhammadijah wanted to create a generation of Muslims with hearts full of belief and heads full of knowledge." One of the main points of the reformist movement was the purification of Islam from all sorts of superstitious beliefs and practices, in other words, a real Islamization of people who nominally had already been incorporated into the world of Islam. Therefore education and information played a great part in the activities of Islamization. The slogan was, as it were: teach the people who want to be called Muslims what it means to be Muslims.

Right up to recent publications the Islamic community has been urged "to Islamize the Muslims" (Ind. *mengislamkan orang Islam*). "It is not yet necessary to call non-Muslims to Islam (*mendakwahi*). First call the Muslims to Islam, so that they do not use the term 'Muslim' too lightly, but will become true Muslims." [67] By using all modern media, the press,

---
[66] A recent Indonesian study on this organization is Alfian, *Islamic Modernism in Indonesian Politics: the Muhammadijah Movement during the Dutch Colonial Period (1912-1942)*, thesis Madison, Wisconsin 1969, 2 Volumes.
[67] Sidi Gazalba, *Integrasi Islam, Ilmu dan Kebudajaan,* Djakarta 1967, p. 279.

radio, television, popular leaflets and where possible films, attempts are being made to bring Islam home to the people. During recent years mosque attendance has apparently increased considerably. Here and there attempts are being made to create new forms of religious, cultural and social education, e.g. by using the mosque for meetings with an address and discussions early in the morning, immediately after morning prayer. Such meetings are said to be attended "by army officers as well as bètjak drivers and also by women"; the lastmentioned are sometimes segregated from the men only by a small aisle. In this way an attempt is being made to add a new function to the mosque, so that it is not only a place of prayer but also a centre for all kinds of other activities.[68]

Originally the daᶜwa was chiefly performed through tablīgh (preaching). The Muhammadijah had a special Madjlis Tablīgh (a "Mission Council", so to speak) and had at its disposal many muballighs (Muslim "missionaries"). Although the Muhammadijah carried out important social and educational work, the greatest emphasis was laid on preaching, i.e. the spread of Islam by the spoken and written word. Many other organizations were inspired by this kind of activity of the Muhammadijah.

A great number of pamphlets of this kind, published by private initiative and aiming at the general public, could be listed. As a sample I refer to a pamphlet by the well-known ulama A. Hassan of Bangil (East Java) containing the report of a debate with an atheist, who finally had to acknowledge that Hassan had convinced him of the existence of God.[69] When reading such a pamphlet one wonders, however, whether people in Indonesia could really be convinced by "proving" God's existence with a discussion ending in the question of which was first, the chicken or the egg.

From the list of publications given at the end of this book I want to mention here pamphlets concerning the celebration of the birth of the Prophet (e.g. by Djaᶜfar Amir), the descent of the Qur'ān (Moh. Hatta), the Prophet's "ascension" or "Journey into Heaven" (Muchtar Jahja, Moenawar Chalil) and a large number of books on Muslim

---

[68] Cf. Sidi Gazalba, Mesdjid — Pusat Ibadat dan Kebudajaan Islam, thesis Djakarta 1962. The author is himself closely associated with activities in the Al-Azhar mosque in Kebajoran-Baru (Djakarta), where services are held on the first floor, while the ground floor is used for a medical centre, university lectures, an office for funeral arrangements, the offices of the magazine Pandji Masjarakat, and so on.
[69] A. Hassan, Adakah Tuhan?, Surabaja 1956¹, 1965².

etiquette (Ind. *etikèt*) or social behaviour (Aboebakar Atjeh, A. Hassan, Marzuki Imron, Nj. Nurlela). Pamphlets on marriage, family life and sexual instruction can also be classed in this category, as they are intended to promote an Islamic style of life (Hasbi Ash-Shiddiqy, Kahruddin Yunus, and others).

In all these ways the "Islamization of Muslims" has been carried out. Religious leaders, however, began to realize that the word *tablīgh* was too limited to cover all the activities needed for a true Islamization of the people. About 1960 the word *daʿwa* (Ind. *da'wah* or *dakwah*) came into use and gradually this word is superseding the word *tablīgh*. In 1965 the *Madjlis Tablīgh* of the Muhammadijah was changed into a *Madjlis Da'wah*; one who practises *daʿwa* is now often called a *dāʿī* instead of a *muballigh*.

Indeed it can be said that "*daʿwa* has become the key word for promoting Islam in Indonesia and for the clarification of ideas concerning Islam, particularly among those groups of the population who are generally indicated with the collective noun *abangan* ..." [70] The same author points out that the *daʿwa* is not only aimed at unsophisticated people, but also at the intellectuals. At a congress held in 1968 the aim of *daʿwa* was formulated in the phrase *meng-ulamakan sardjana dan men-sardjanakan ulama*, i.e. to make *ulama*s of the intellectuals and intellectuals of the *ulama*s.

In the course of time it came to be stressed more and more that *daʿwa* meant the propagation of Islam not only by preaching and publications, but also by deeds and activities in all areas of social life, in other words that *daʿwa* had to be a comprehensive Islamization of society. In 1963 Mukti Ali stated that Islam had to follow the example of Christian *daʿwa*, which consisted of "preaching, teaching and healing".[71]

An important publication on the meaning of *daʿwa* was S. Sanusi's thesis, published in 1964, a book which may be called a modern Muslim missiology.[72] The author wanted to use the term *daʿwa* not only "in the general sense of a sermon, address, lecture, or for transmitting doctrines orally, but ... in the sense of bringing about what is good and fighting what is wrong"; in other words, *daʿwa* means "*ishlah* (Ar. *iṣlāḥ*), that is, the improvement and development of society". According to this Muslim missiology the essence of *daʿwa* can be comprehended in the

---

[70] Vredenbregt, *De Islam*, p. 8.
[71] Quoted by D. Bakker, *Daʿwah*, p. 122, n. 9.
[72] Shalahuddin Sanusi, *Pembahasan Sekitar Prinsip Daʿwah*, Semarang 1964, pp. 8 and 75.

oft-quoted expression based on the Qur'ān: *al-amru bi 'l-maᶜrūf wa 'l-nahyu ᶜani 'l-munkar*, usually abbreviated in Indonesian publications to *amar maᶜruf, nahi munkar*, that is, "urging what is reputable and restraining from what is disreputable" (cf. Sura 3 : 104, 110, 114; 7 : 157; 9 : 71, 112; 22 : 41).[73]

Another recent publication, by Toha Jahja Omar, intended as a textbook for *daᶜwa*, however, adhered mainly to *daᶜwa* as preaching. In a similar way Isa Anshary defined *daᶜwa* primarily as *tablīgh* and the *dāᶜī* as a *muballigh* (rendered by the author with *Tukang Seru*).[74]

On May 9th, 1967 an Indonesian Islamic *Daᶜwa* Council (*Dewan Daᶜwah Islamijah Indonesia*) was founded by adherents of the Muhammadijah and the former Masjumi, under the leadership of Muh. Natsir, formerly chairman of the Masjumi and Prime Minister. As the Masjumi continued to be prohibited, the close relationship between the Muhammadijah and the Masjumi nearly resulted in the Muhammadijah's becoming a political party. But after all the leaders preferred to maintain a clear distinction between politics and *daᶜwa*, with the result that the new "Partai Muslimin Indonesia" took the place of the Masjumi, whereas the Muhammadijah decided explicitly to remain an organization for *daᶜwa*.

Muh. Natsir's opinions concerning the programme of the *daᶜwa* organization, as expounded in one of his speeches, can be summarized as follows. (1) Methods and techniques must be evolved to make the *daᶜwa* work more effectively, e.g. by improving the training of the *dāᶜī*s. (2) *Daᶜwa* must be intensified with tangible contributions in the socio-economic field, particularly for the relief of poverty. (3) Close co-operation between traditional Islamic institutions such as *pesantrèns* and *madrasa*s must be achieved in order to raise the level of education. (4) Co-operation must be stimulated between all kinds of Islamic institutions and organizations as well as between Muslims personally.[75]

Among the many *daᶜwa* organizations which arose special attention should be paid to the *Pendidikan Tinggi Daᶜwah Islam* (P.T.D.I.), a kind of "extramural instruction for Islamic *daᶜwa*", founded in 1963 in Central Java, but transferred to Djakarta in July 1965. Among the

---

[73] Translation quoted from Richard Bell, *The Qur'ān*, Edinburgh 1960².
[74] Toha Jahja Omar, *Ilmu Daᶜwah*, Djakarta 1967; K. H. M. Isa Anshary, *Mudjahid Daᶜwah*, Bandung 1964.
[75] Cf. Vredenbregt, *De Islam*, p. 8. See also Muh. Natsir's stencilled publication *Fungsi Daᶜwah dalam rangka Perdjuangan*, Jogjakarta, (1968?).

leaders of this organization are senior officers of the army (General Sarbini and General Sudirman), of the police (General Sutjipto Judodihardjo) and the navy (Commodore Sukmadi). In every province activities were to be led by a "Co-ordinating Body"; in every district of a province a "Senat P.T.D.I." would be established, while in the villages there would be "commissariats" and local "study groups".[76] In West Java the Co-ordinating Body publishes a monthly magazine.[77] There too an important pilot project has been started, involving the development of the village Tjiaro near Nagrek, in the eastern part of West Java. After a solemnly celebrated agreement with the villagers (about 5,000 people), from 1967 onwards 173 teams have been engaged in 23 projects such as education and information, founding a library, building a mosque, improvement of irrigation, agriculture and fishing, the laying out of an experimental garden plot, reafforestation of hills, etc.

When asked why the military in particular are involved in these *da ͨwa* activities, informants said, (1) that initially these officers had wanted to concentrate their activities on ex-service men, because many of them had been influenced by left-wing leaders; (2) that these army officers were aware of the danger of Communism and wanted to fight it by means of *da ͨwa* (this argument does seem to have been used by General Sarbini when the P.T.D.I. was founded); and (3) that after 1965 some officers wanted to restrain militarism by interesting servicemen in the *da ͨwa* and socio-economic development of the country.

A similar experiment to stimulate modernization in village life was begun in Tjiampéa, about 8 miles south-west of Bogor. Muh. Natsir may be considered its most important supporter. Its centre is an "Agricultural Pesantrèn" called *Darul Fallah* (= *dār al-fallāḥ*, the "house of the farmer"). Its pupils, young men about 14-20 years old, receive the usual religious instruction as well as a training in cattle-breeding, poultry-keeping, the use of a small motor-plough, the use of a sickle for cutting rice, and so on.[78]

---

[76] For extensive information concerning this P.T.D.I., see D. Bakker, *Da ͨwah*, p. 132 ff.

[77] *Madjalah Bulanan Séri Da ͨwah Islam*, Bandung, since 1968.

[78] As an example of a clash between popular belief and attempts at modernization, I was told that initially the villagers protested against the use of a sickle instead of the traditional rice knife (*ani-ani*), which is connected with their belief in the rice goddess, Déwi Sri. Their objections were said to be overcome by arguing that Déwi Sri did not like to see the rice standing ripe in the *sawah* for such a long time simply because of old-fashioned methods of harvesting; "You can't say that Déwi Sri doesn't exist, can you?"

Bakker concluded: "It is encouraging to see that the da^cwa has not ended up in a flow of words, but intends tackling the whole of life in a practical way through a comprehensive approach which begins at the roots of village life, in order to make a positive contribution to the essential development of the Indonesian state at the present time".[79]

It can therefore be said that modern da^cwa plays an important part in working toward an Islamic society, and at the same time can make a useful contribution to the socio-economic development of the Indonesian state.

One might ask to what extent these two aspects can be separated. Is it possible that in the course of time a shift of emphasis will take place, for instance from the first ideal (an Islamic society) to the second need (the socio-economic development)? Supposing the efforts to Islamize the Javanese masses do not in due time result in a truly Islamic Java, will Muslims continue to work for the development of their country without aiming at an Islamic society? In other words, will they continue to make these efforts, inspired by their religion and thus willing to serve their fellow-men, setting aside the question of whether or not these masses become truly converted to Islam?

5. *Religious Instruction and Textbooks*

The Ministry of Religion is in charge of religious instruction in state schools, inclusive of the training, appointment and payment of religious teachers, setting the curriculum, and as far as necessary the preparation of manuals and textbooks. At state schools two hours of religious instruction per week have to be given, beginning in the fourth class of the primary school, continuing throughout secondary schools and including two years at the university.

After the changeover to the "New Order", attendance at religious instruction became in fact compulsory, although some people warned against compulsion. An editorial in a newspaper stemming from army circles called it evidence of fanaticism to stipulate that parents would be fined if they refused to let their children attend religious instruction; the writer stressed that it would depend chiefly on the teacher and his way of teaching whether religious instruction was attractive and would have any result.[80] The then Minister of Elementary Education, Moh.

---

[79] D. Bakker, *Da^cwah*, p. 136.
[80] *Angkatan Bersendjata* (Djakarta), June 29th, 1966.

Said, also emphasized that religious instruction ought to be given in a way different from other subjects; if pupils regarded religion as something which had to be learned by heart (like other subjects) in order to go up into the next form, then they would sooner dislike religion than love it.[81]

Initially religious instruction at state schools met with great difficulties. In elementary schools, for example, children learned the basic elements of the Islamic faith and religious duties, but teachers at secondary schools often simply repeated the same themes in the same way. And it was, of course, still more difficult to find teachers capable of giving religious instruction to university students. Temporary solutions were, for example, that these lectures were given by a well-known writer who knew how to captivate the students (Djakarta) or by a lecturer from the faculty concerned, e.g. a lecturer in medicine for giving religious lectures to students of the medical faculty, and so on (Jogja). Now it has become possible to appoint graduates from an I.A.I.N. to give religious lectures at universities. The problems connected with these religious lectures were dealt with in two "seminars", held in 1962 and 1965 under the leadership of I.A.I.N. professors. Representatives of all officially recognized groups (Muslims, Protestants, Roman Catholics and Hindu-Buddhists) took part in the seminar of December 1965.[82]

It is, of course, almost impossible to avoid superficiality in religious instruction, particularly in primary and secondary schools. In the case of doctrine, there is a danger of intellectualism, by presenting scholastic definitions as a set of truths to be accepted. In the case of religious duties (for instance, prayer) instruction is threatened by formalism, as it is difficult to transmit more than external forms and formulas. It may be useful to recall a remark by Clifford Geertz, though made in a different context, that "formalism or intellectualism, it really comes down to about the same thing: holding religious views rather than being held by them".[83]

---

[81] *Gotong Rojong* (Djakarta), June 29th, 1966.
[82] The stencilled report in two volumes (133 and 235 pp.) was published by the Department of Higher Education, under the title *Seminar Pentavipan Kurikulum Pendidikan Agama Pada Perguruan Tinggi*. The origin of the term *pentavipan* is *tavip*, a contraction of "*Tahun Vivere Pericoloso*" — the year of living dangerously — which was the title of Soekarno's speech on August 17th, 1964. So *pentavipan* means that the educational curriculum had to be brought into accordance with that phase of the Indonesian revolution.
[83] Clifford Geertz, *Islam,* p. 17.

Several Muslim leaders do realize that religious instruction in schools does not automatically create devout believers, but most informants seem to be rather optimistic about the results. Religious instruction is often considered the most effective way to Islamize the people of Java and to realize an Islamic society. Others hold that religious instruction will result in belief penetrating the individual soul, in accordance with the Muhammadijah ideal of Muslims "with a heart full of belief and a head full of knowledge". However that may be, with regard to religion one informant commented, "unknown, unloved"; and referring to the situation in Western countries, he added: "Here we want to prevent a generation from growing up without any knowledge of religion whatsoever".

The curriculum for religious instruction in state schools, beginning in the fourth class of the primary school, includes four subjects: elements of belief (*keimanan*), morals (*achlak*), religious duties (*ibadat*) and reciting the Qur'ān.

As far as the elements of belief are concerned, the manuals stipulate that religious instruction must begin by strengthening the conviction that God exists. In the first year furthermore God's attributes are dealt with, often in the classical way of explaining the "twenty attributes". Subjects for the following years are: belief in the Messengers, the Holy Books, the Angels, the Last Day and God's Decree. It is noteworthy that religious instruction in nursery schools (e.g. of Muhammadijah) as well as the university begins with providing the "proof" of God's existence. In its simplest form, the teacher starts from the fact that the table in the classroom must have been made by somebody; by way of the trees, nature, the world, sun, moon and stars, he arrives at the "cosmological proof" of God's existence as the basis for belief in God the Creator. In the seminar of December 1965 mentioned above, Muslim and Christian theologians obviously agreed on this starting-point. In religious circles I have met with hardly any doubt on the value of such a theological "proof".

The subject "Morals" includes matters such as obedience to parents, love of one's country, the feeling of responsibility, behaviour at home, in the street, in class, in the mosque, in a house of mourning, towards non-Muslims, and so on. Some of the textbooks look rather sentimental, for example when a picture of a little boy reading a book is captioned with "The child who is thankful to God — his eyes he uses to read and his hands to hold a book".

Instruction in religious duties is concerned with the performance of prayer, including the necessary Arabic formulas, the meaning of Islamic feasts, precepts for *Ramaḍān* and the payment of *zakāt* at its end, and finally the pilgrimage to Mecca.

In the second half of the fifth class the Arabic alphabet is taught, followed by reading the Qur'ān and learning a few passages by heart, particularly some well-known short *sura*s.

It is impossible to summarize and to describe all the manuals, textbooks and readers which are available for religious instruction. While referring to the List of Publications, the following examples may pass in review.

For elementary schools Mahmud Junus wrote one of the most popular series of textbooks on belief, morals and religious duties.[84] The author is an elderly *ulama* and rather conservative. These books are attractively illustrated, though partly in the abovementioned style. The well-known Hasbi Ash-Shiddiqy also wrote a simple book on Islamic belief.[85] As far as their substance is concerned, these books do not differ much from the classic Muslim "catechism" by Ṭāhir al-Djazā'irī, Al-Djawāhir al-Kalāmīya (gems of doctrine), first published in Damascus in 1895.[86] Many editions of this booklet have been published in Indonesia, in Arabic and in Indonesian, and it is still used in conservative circles. The Indonesian textbooks mentioned above try to offer this material in a more modern form.

This applies also to some textbooks for secondary schools, e.g. a pamphlet on Islamic belief written by Munir Rusli and Nur Asjik.[87] A textbook by Muaz Ali shows a more modern approach.[88] This author starts with a short history of religion, leading up to Islam, followed by a discussion of the most important religious duties and some remarks on the present moral crisis and how to combat it. He concludes with discussing the meaning of terms such as belief ("to accept the truth in your heart"), Islam ("obvious surrender"), unbelief, apostasy, etc. The

---

[84] Mahmud Junus, *Keimanan dan Achlak, Marilah Sembahjang, Puasa dan Zakat, Hadji ke Mekka,* Djakarta, since about 1950.
[85] M. Hasbi Ash-Shiddiqy, *Peladjaran Tauhid,* Medan 1954.
[86] For a Dutch translation of this catechism, see G. F. Pijper, *De Edelgesteenten der Geloofsleer,* Leiden 1948.
[87] A. Munir Rusli and H. M. Nur Asjik, *Peladjaran Tauhid,* Djakarta 1964; Nur Asjik is a son-in-law of the Atjehnese leader Daud Beureu'éh.
[88] Muaz Ali, *Agama Islam,* Djakarta 1964 (published by Tintamas, considered one of the more progressive publishing houses).

publications of Ustadh Dja{c}far Amir, coming from Muhammadijah circles in Central Java, are probably popular in Muhammadijah secondary schools.[89] As far as the history of Islam is concerned, an outstanding manual has been written by Latif Osman.[90]

It may be more important to turn our attention to more scholarly Muslim publications, which have appeared in great numbers in modern Indonesia, especially for the training of skilled *ulama*s and religious teachers.[91]

The first book to be mentioned here, intended to be widely used, is the new, more or less official, publication of "The Qur'ān and its Translation", Arabic and Indonesian in two columns. After a resolution of the People's Congress in 1960, a foundation for "the translation of the Holy Book, the Qur'ān" was set up by the Minister of Religion in 1963. Two translation committees, mainly consisting of I.A.I.N. staff in Jogjakarta and Djakarta, have since then been working on this translation, exchanging their drafts. In August 1965 the first volume appeared, with a foreword by President Soekarno. It consists of an introduction of 148 pages (including a justification of "translating" the Qur'ān, because understanding its content is more important than only reciting the text) and a translation of Djuz 1-10 (i.e. Sura 1 to Sura 9 : 93). Volume II appeared in 1967, with forewords by the Acting-President General Soeharto and the Chairman of the People's Congress, General Nasution; this volume contains Djuz 11-20, i.e. Sura 9 : 94 to Sura 29 : 44. The third and last volume appeared in 1969, likewise with forewords by Soeharto, Nasution and some Ministers concerned.

Within the circle of these Qur'ān translators a new Qur'ān commentary is also being planned. Preliminary discussions seem to be concerned with problems such as how to speak now of heaven, hell, *djinn*s,

---

[89] For the books of Dja{c}far Amir, see the List of Publications. "Ustadh" or "Ustaz" is a title given to an authoritative scholar or teacher in the field of religion. So it is not a proper name, as one might conclude from Clifford Geertz, *The Religion*, p. 139.

[90] A. Latif Osman, *Ringkasan Sedjarah Islam*, Djakarta 1951[1], 1965[15].

[91] In order to give an idea of the number of published works, one could mention that a catalogue of the Islamic bookshop Alaydrus (Djakarta) listed in 1966 about 750 titles of books and pamphlets which were at that time on sale. Apart from scores of books and pamphlets on the Qur'ān, the following categories may be mentioned: Islamic history, culture and jurisprudence (49), the life of the Prophet (34), morals (39), doctrine (58), woman, marriage, the family (46), and philosophy and mysticism (39).

and so on (in other words, the problem of "demythologizing" old conceptions of religious truths).

Meanwhile about two-thirds of the Qur'ān commentary *An-Nur* (The Light, cf. Sura 24) by Hasbi Ash-Shiddiqy, planned to appear in 30 volumes of about 200 pages each, has already been published. The author is considered a scholarly *ulama* with original ideas (remember his opinions on a national *madhhab,* instead of sticking to the four old schools of law). The character of this commentary is sober and scholarly. A careful explanation is given of the meaning of words and sentences as well as an explanation of the historical situation that caused certain revelations to be sent down (based, of course, on the Tradition and not to be confused with a Western critical approach to the history and text of Holy Books). Conclusions on its application to our present-day life are left to the reader to draw for himself.

This sober character is one of the differences from another Qur'ān commentary, written by H. Abdul Malik Karim Amrullah (HAMKA), which is also in course of publication. It is called *Al-Azhar* after the mosque in Djakarta, which wishes to be a centre of modern Islam in Indonesia. This commentary was largely prepared during the years in which the author was imprisoned by the Soekarno regime. It too will be published in 30 volumes, three of which have already appeared. It is apparently intended to be more widely read than Hasbi's commentary. Its character is more edifying, occasionally with an apologetic and polemic trend (for instance against authors who are considered representatives of Christianity), just as the Islamic magazine *Pandji Masjarakat* edited by HAMKA.

Besides these commentaries there are various introductions to the study of the Qur'ān (Hasbi Ash-Shiddiqy, Nur Idris and others) and several books dealing with favourite *sura*s, such as the first and the twelfth.

A general introduction to the study of Islam is the voluminous manual *Al-Islam* by Hasbi Ash-Shiddiqy. Equally lengthy works are the biography of the Prophet by Zainal Arifin Abbas (1938[1], 1959[3]) and Munawar Chalil. Books on the culture and philosophy of Islam have been written by Oemar Amin Hoesin.

Hasbi Ash-Shiddiqy has also written a history of, and introduction to, the study of the Tradition. A simpler manual for studying this subject has been published by H. M. Kasim Bakry. The latter also wrote a manual on Islamic criminal law as well as a manual on the history of Islamic jurisprudence, sharply criticizing the centuries of *taklīd,* when people had to "clothe with authority" the four mediaeval schools of law.

A promising book on the "roots" of jurisprudence was *Usul Fiqh*, written by A. Hanafie (I.A.I.N., Jogja), who unfortunately died in the prime of life as a result of an accident in 1966. Beside the "roots" which are considered valid in the Shāfiʿī school, he also referred to methods of reasoning used in other schools, such as for instance *istiḥsān* (literally "approval", i.e. a discretionary opinion in breach of the usual *kiyās* or "deduction by analogy", cf. Sura 39 : 18) and *istiṣlāḥ* (taking the public interest or human welfare into account). From his cautious criticism of al-Shāfiʿī's objections to *istiḥsān*, it may be concluded that the author wanted to advocate the use of these controversial principles. Obviously he also urged the "new *idjtihād*", even calling it a "duty" (not just a "right") of modern scholars to arrive at certain legal decisions based on their own studies of the Qur'ān and Tradition. On the other hand he agreed that ordinary laymen could maintain the "right of *taklīd*", defined as "following the opinion of someone else, without knowing his source or his argumentation". It may be concluded that Hanafie's book offered important starting-points for wide and modern development and interpretation of Islamic law in our time.

One authoritative informant, however, did not consider a discussion on these "roots" or principles of jurisprudence so very important. In fact, he said, we do not first have to decide on the "roots" or sources of jurisprudence in order to achieve legal decisions which may lead to modernization. Jurisprudence and the making of laws do not create or stimulate new rules for human behaviour, but can only follow and sanction new developments. All kinds of modernization are taking place, whether we want them or not, and we cannot turn the clock back. Therefore the only value of the "roots" of jurisprudence is that they can officially legitimize these modernizations after they have already taken place.

In the field of doctrine there seems to be almost as little new discussion in scholarly books as in popular publications. Dogmatics is often considered theological speculation and therefore a luxury in circumstances where the practical realization of Islam in the daily life of society is of primary importance. Moreover, dogmatics is usually dealt with as a set of doctrines which were definitely settled centuries ago. Therefore these doctrines have to be expounded and accepted without too much discussion and questioning. The principle of *bi-lā kaif* (i.e. without asking "how" exactly things must be understood), first and foremost connected with belief in God, apparently tends to dominate the whole field of doctrine. How difficult it is to speak in a non-traditional way about God and the Prophet without insulting pious people can be shown, for example, by the court case against H. B. Jassin, who had advocated freedom of imagination in literature in connection with a short story written by Kipandjikusmin. In this story the writer described the Prophet's descending again to our planet in order to examine the sinful condition of our world today, in particular Indonesia, which has resulted in so few people entering Heaven in recent years.[92]

Apart from some general introductions for a wider public (pamphlets by M. A. Badawy, T. M. Usman el-Muhammady and H. Abubakar Atjeh), perhaps the only important books on doctrine to be mentioned here are the publications of Taib Thahir Abdul Mu'in (I.A.I.N., Jogja). As a textbook for students he initially published a short summary (*Ichtisar Ilmu Tauhid*). His later Systematic Theology (*Ilmu Kalam*) is more extensive, though not going beyond 300 pages. In its historical introduction, the "history of the growth of the belief in one God" is dealt with. The author touches upon nature worship, the ancient religions of Egypt, Persia, etc. and the revealed religions (Judaism and Christianity). These religions are mainly dealt with in the light of the Qur'ān, as a "theology of religions" so to speak. Christianity is hence only treated as a pre-Islamic religion; its dogmatic development is only sketched up to the rise of Islam, giving the impression that Nestorius and the Syrian Jakobites are still relevant. However, compared to the average apologetic and polemic publications, this author shows a more serious attempt to understand the meaning of certain Christian doctrines and formulas, for instance the symbolical meaning of the title "Son of God". In the second part of his book the author explains the elements of the Islamic creed, largely with quotations from the Qur'ān and Tradition. According to this book too dogmatics is a summary of ageless doctrines rather than a topical discussion on the problems and belief of modern man. Only the problem of *Ḳadar* and *Ḳaḍā'* (both concerned with God's eternal decrees and their realization in time) gets special attention in the third part of the book. But the author confines himself to offering a compromise between the opinions of the *Djabrīya* (who denied the freedom of will) and the *Muʿtazila* (who emphasized human responsibility).

As a manual for the study of mysticism the "Introduction to the Study

---

[92] See H. B. Jassin, *Heboh Sastra 1968, Suatu Pertanggunganjawab*, Djakarta 1970. An almost complete record of the court's sessions is to be found in the literary monthly *Horison*, August 1970 ff.

of Mysticism" by H. Abubakar Atjeh may be mentioned. His book offers a survey of the history of mysticism and mystical orders as well as a discussion of the essence and phenomena of mysticism.

The theological journal of a standard similar to the publications mentioned above is *Al-Djami'ah,* published by the I.A.I.N. at Jogjakarta since January 1962. This journal has apparently laboured under many difficulties, such as a lack of money and copy, but nevertheless it is worth while to pay attention to this attempt to publish a kind of academic Islamic journal.[93]

Finally it may be noticed once again that many Islamic publications by foreign authors, both classical and modern, are being translated into Indonesian and are published or in preparation. Some of them are specially intended for students of Islam, for instance the works of Ibn Khaldūn, ᶜŪda and Mawdūdī already mentioned above. Here I add the names of al-Bukhārī (*Al-Ṣaḥīḥ*), al-Ghazzālī (*Iḥyā'*, in preparation), Muḥ. ᶜAbduh (*Risālat al-Tawḥīd*), Rashīd Riḍā (only a few passages from *Al-Waḥyu 'l-Muḥammadī*), Ṭaha Ḥusain (his autobiography and *Al-Waᶜd Al-Ḥakk*) and publications from Al-Azhar circles in Cairo, such as writings by Mahmoud Shaltout, Muh. Ghallab and Ahmad Shalaby.[94]

The above survey may suffice to illustrate that Islamic scholars in Indonesia have indeed produced a great quantity of reading-matter. This production is certainly only the first phase of what has to be done. At this first stage manuals and other textbooks had to be supplied for educational purposes. As a matter of course, in a developing country such as Indonesia religious studies — like others — consist largely of collecting what is known and what is considered to be established truth. The question may be put as to whether here too the next phase will be for research and study to be directed towards the unknown as well, and for critical questions to be asked concerning established truth.

---

[93] The Arabic *al-djāmiᶜa* means a university or college; the name of this journal is taken from the Arabic translation of *Institut Agama Islam Negeri* (I.A.I.N.), used as a sub-title: *Al-Djamiᶜah Al-Islamijah Al-Hukumijah.*
[94] The lastmentioned was for some years a Visiting Professor at the I.A.I.N. in Jogjakarta. His book on Christianity (*Perbandingan Agama, bahagian Agama Maséhi*), more polemic than scholarly, did not prove an important contribution to developments in Indonesia and must be considered out of date.

6. A Muslim "Theology of Religions"

According to some Christian theologians, Churches and Missions are at present in need of a new "theology of religions", that is to say, an evaluation of non-Christian religions from the Christian point of view, or in other words an evaluation based on the Gospel of Jesus Christ or on the Bible as the document of God's revelation.

It could be said that Islam has had a kind of "theology of religions" from the very beginning. This Islamic "theology of religions" differs in one basic aspect from tendencies within Judaism and Christianity. The latter both tend to exclusiveness, either because of a nationalistic interpretation of being the chosen people, or because of the doctrine concerning Christ as the only way to salvation. Islam, however, began by thinking "inclusively": the Prophet was sent to confirm the message of his predecessors because these messengers also called people to belief in the One and Only God (cf. Sura 21 : 25). It is true that during the life of the Prophet a sharp antithesis began to arise between the Muslims and the Jews and Christians. This development resulted in a kind of ambivalence towards "the people of the Book" (Jews and Christians). This ambivalence can be defined as a co-existence of feelings of agreement and of disagreement towards these religions and in particular towards Christianity; it often depends on circumstances whether the positive or the negative attitude becomes dominant. But all the conflicts, right up to the present day, have not done away with the basis of the Muslim "theology of religions", namely the conviction that Jews, Christians and Muslims are bound together by belief in the same God, who once spoke through Moses, later through Jesus and finally through Muhammad.

In Indonesia, and in particular in Java, this "synthetical" way of thinking is strengthened by a genuine, indigenous tendency to tolerance. Moreover, the significance of the Ministry of Religion may once again be stressed in this connection. In spite of all practical shortcomings, the existence of this Ministry tends to stimulate the feeling that within Indonesian society various religions have to exist side by side. Western, non-Muslim scholars like to explain Indonesian tolerance as stemming from Javanese syncretism with its doctrine that fundamentally all religions are alike. Speaking of the principle of Islamic tolerance, a Javanese informant once hastened to add that he was, of course, not only a Muslim but also a Javanese, in other words a Javanese Muslim. With regard to modern developments in Indonesia the question could perhaps be put as to whether there is not an increasing influence of

Javanese Muslims within the Islamic community in Indonesia (through an increasing number of Javanese leaders and scholars), at the cost of the former non-Javanese leadership in Indonesian Islam. If indeed such a shift is taking place, it could perhaps also have consequences for religious tolerance.

Acknowledging the significance of a "Javanese tolerance", we should, however, not forget that Islam itself has a "theology of religions" which emphasizes not only the finality of Islam, but also to a certain extent respect for, and a positive attitude toward, other religions, or at least toward Judaism and Christianity.

Such a "theology of religions" is, however, not the same thing as "comparative religion". The latter is the scientific study of the origin, development and interrelations of the different religious systems of mankind; unlike a "theology of religions", it must try to understand another religion from its own sources, supplemented by a study of the living belief of its present adherents, while an evaluation of that religion based on the observer's own religious tenets has to be suspended as far as possible.

If I am not mistaken, there is one Indonesian publication which falls somewhere between a Muslim "theology of religions" and "comparative religion". It is a pamphlet by A. Mukti Ali (I.A.I.N., Jogja), which could be considered basically a "theology of religions" as referred to above, but is entitled "Comparative Religion" (*Ilmu Perbandingan Agama*), and in fact shows some features of a comparative religion as indicated above.[95] It is worthwhile to review this pamphlet at some length.

In his introduction the author stresses that comparative religion does not have an apologetic character; on the contrary, it must be possible to have sympathy for the religion and belief of someone else. This does not mean that one has to put aside one's own conviction in order to arrive at "objectivity". In our study of religions as well as in other sectors of social life our attitude has to be an attitude of agreeing to disagree. Comparative religion is a positive method to understand how God from the beginning has given directives to mankind and how man has reacted to God's revelations. Comparative religion is therefore concerned basically with the relation between God and history. It is not concerned with the question of truth. This question can be left to the philosophy of religion.

---

[95] A. Mukti Ali, *Ilmu Perbandingan Agama*, Jogjakarta 1965.

After a survey of the methods of comparative religion, the author sketches its history, both in the West and in the world of Islam. He admits that among Muslims the study of religions has often been practised as apologetics. In a survey of authors who wrote on other religions, he first of all mentions ᶜAlī ibn Sahl Rabbān al-Ṭabarī (d. A.D. 854), who indeed attacked Christianity, but not too fiercely, and produced a list of verses from the Bible which predict the coming of the Prophet Muḥammad. Then Ibn Ḥazm (d. 1064) is mentioned; having discovered 78 contradictions in the New Testament, he proved that the Bible must have been falsified by Jews and Christians and cannot be the original revelation. Furthermore the author refers to al-Shahrastānī (d. 1143), Aḥmad al-Ṣanhādjī Ḳarafī (d. 1235) and Ibn Taimīya (d. 1328) — the last two writing in answer to Paul al-Rāhib, the 12th century bishop of Sidon [96] — then Ibn Ḳayyim (d. 1350), followed by later Indian authors such as al-Hindi (19th century) and the great apologists of our age Muḥ. ᶜAbduh, al-Afghānī and finally Amīr ᶜAlī, whose book "The Spirit of Islam" (1891) is still widely read and whose way of arguing is still popular with present-day Muslim apologists everywhere. The author concludes this survey by stating that among Muslims comparative religion has not yet actually been developed as it ought to be, but still has to find its way.

In the third chapter the various schools of thought in Western comparative religion are dealt with. Special attention is given to evolutionism and its rejection by Father Wilhelm Schmidt. Apparently the author feels attracted by Schmidt's idea of so-called "primitive monotheism" (*Urmonotheismus*) which could, of course, suit the starting-point of Muslim "theology of religions", i.e. that mankind from the very beginning believed in the One Supreme Being. The author stresses that Schmidt's ideas are not simply based on Roman Catholic doctrines or on the Bible, but on anthropological research. With regard to Muslim authors he states that Muḥ. ᶜAbduh as well as Rashīd Riḍā and Muḥ. Iqbāl were indeed prepared to acknowledge evolution in the progress of God's revelation — from "national prophets" who spoke in such a way that people of their own age and society could understand, up to the final and universal Prophet for all people and all ages — but did not apply the notion of evolutionism to man's conception of God and the rise of belief in the One and Only God.

---

[96] For a recent study on the writings of Bishop Paul of Sidon, see Paul Khoury, *Paul d'Antioche, Évêque Melkite de Sidon* (*XIIᵉ s.*), thesis Leiden 1965.

Chapter IV sketches the history of Oriental studies or Orientalism in the West, where interest in the world of Islam initially arose due to the Crusades and Turkish expansion. Afterwards these studies were closely connected with Western colonialism and imperialism. This connection is considered the greatest difficulty for Western scholars to arrive at mature Orientalism (other shortcomings are, for instance, a too limited specialization either in Arabic or in sociology). Western scholars cannot be neutral or objective, as long as colonialism and imperialism are still alive. Even Gibb (one of the few Islamic scholars respected among Muslims) according to Mukti Ali betrays the fact that he is influenced by obsolete views when he quotes MacDonald's remark on the "precise pathology of Muhammad's psychology" in the foreword of his "Modern Trends in Islam".

With regard to the attitude of Indonesians to the West, the author indicates the dualism caused by Dutch educational policy. This policy resulted in some Indonesians simply taking over everything from the West, while others rejected everything to do with Western civilization. Muslim intellectuals will have to overcome this dualism. Therefore the author advocates the development of Western studies or "Occidentalism" within the Muslim community in Indonesia, as a counterpart to Orientalism in the West. In this way Indonesian Muslims will be able to enter into a dialogue (Ind. ber-"*dialoog*") with the Western world. This "Occidentalism" ought to be developed as soon as possible, the I.A.I.N. taking the initiative.

Thereupon the author sums up what a Muslim should bear in mind when studying religions other than his own. (1) A Muslim must not forget that the source for his knowledge of other religions is primarily the Qur'ān, though those religions' own sources must also be studied. (2) Various historical facts mentioned in the Qur'ān, but for a long time denied by non-Muslim scholars, are now being confirmed by archeological research. (3) Many Scriptures of other religions do not give solutions for social life, but the teachings of the Qur'ān are directly concerned with society. (4) The Qur'ān shows a pure, ethical monotheism; for the understanding of other religions it is essential to study this monotheism of the Qur'ān. (5) Islam is — like Hinduism, Buddhism and Christianity — a missionary religion; adherents of other religions, however, must be approached in a spirit of respect and with a feeling of sympathy. (6) It is a great mistake to search only for the weaknesses of other religions; the strength of a religious system cannot be discovered by looking at its errors, but by studying that which is right and true or at least partially true. The strength of Hinduism, for example, lies in the pantheistic "that art thou", of Buddhism in the extinction of man's desires, of Judaism in the conception of God's absolute holiness and the belief in God's covenant with Israel as His chosen people. The strength of Christianity lies in the belief that the eternal, transcendent God became immanent through His incarnation in Jesus, who through his crucifixion and resurrection grants forgiveness of sins, eternal life and salvation to all mankind. Finally, the strength of Islam lies in the unconditional belief in the One and Only God, in His sovereignty and transcendency, and the rejection of incarnation in any form. (7) Muslim missionaries (*muballighs*) must not be affected with a spirit of hate and contempt, but must be acquainted with the teachings of these other religions and, moreover, be able to show in a positive way what Islam has to offer towards a solution of social problems.

The author emphasizes the need to tackle social problems and warns against negative apologetics. Muslims must not look back to a glorious past (Diponegoro and other Indonesian heroes), but must be involved in the present-day struggle for realizing Islam in society (*masjarat-kan Islam*), realizing its social principles (*sosial-kannja*) and making Islam function (*fungsionil-kannja*).

In the final chapter the author summarizes the significance of comparative religion as follows. (1) This study can prove a great help in understanding the inner life and thoughts of mankind. (2) It is useful for discovering similarities between Islam and other religions, and for indicating those aspects of Islam which are superior to other religions, and furthermore for showing how pre-Islamic religions prepared mankind for the coming of Islam. (3) It is, however, still more important to create sympathy and a feeling of responsibility toward those who do not yet know the truth of Islam. (4) Comparative religion can be dangerous if it is carried out in a wrong way, so that it weakens the position of Islam; in that case a new kind of apologetics would be needed in order to defend Islam; but comparative religion can also have good results and strengthen the Islamic offensive. (5) When studying other religions, we can arrive at a better understanding of our own religion and in this way our faith will be deepened. (6) Technological progress has made our world so small that we are facing new problems in human relationships; comparative religion can help us to solve these problems. (7) Contact with other religions can help us understand other terminologies and simplify our own, so that our terminology no longer confuses the common man. (8) The greatest result of comparative religion will be the conviction of the universality, the sufficiency and the finality of Islam. (9) Perhaps Arnold J. Toynbee ("An Historian's Approach to Religion", 1956) was right when he said that the three religions which have sprung from the same source (Judaism, Christianity and Islam) tend to exclusiveness and intolerance, but there are nevertheless signs of a development which promises a better future: improving methods of research and co-operation between the various social sciences will provide us with a wider and deeper understanding of religion; we shall discover the marvellous riches which are to be found in every religion, and in this way we shall arrive at mutual respect.

The author emphasizes that with comparative religion one can overcome all sorts of prejudices as well as an emotional and polemical attitude toward other religions. Besides various differences, comparative religion also shows the similarities between religions, such as (1) belief in a transcendent Being that is holy and differs from anything else, the ordering principle in creation (Tao, ṛtam, Logos), personified as Jahwe, Varuṇa, Ahura-Mazda, Allah, Vishṇu, Krishṇa, Buddha, Kāli, or Kwan-jin. (2) This Being is considered the *summum bonum* by everyone and is sought everywhere, in mysticism, Buddhism, Christianity and also in Islam. (3) This holy Being is beneficent and merciful toward mankind and the world. (4) The way to God and to salvation — by continuously remembering Him and by ethical self-discipline — is the way of sacrifice. (5) The performance of religious duties is not only aimed at achieving salvation in the world to come but also well-being here on earth, the "Kingdom of God" according to Judaism and Christianity, and *ḥasana fī 'd-dunyā* ("good in this world") according to Islam.[97]

If religion wants to fight for humanitarianism, it must promote co-operation between adherents of the various religions. Comparative religion has an important role in pursuing this ideal: it creates mutual understanding, respect and appreciation; it removes the feeling of distance between East and West and promotes the feeling of unity among mankind. The famous lines of Kipling's poem are outdated: "Oh, East is East, and West is West, and never the twain shall meet". And the lines suggesting that the difference will be done away with "When two strong men stand face to face" could suggest a kind of balance of power to prevent East and West from warring. Comparative religion, however, can make a contribution to arriving at a truly safe world, where people enjoy order and happiness based on religion and morals.

---

[97] Cf. Sura 2:201; 7:156; 16:41, 122.

More profound than Kipling's lines are those of Goethe:

> Gottes ist der Orient,
> Gottes ist der Okzident,
> Nord- und südliches Gelände
> ruhn im Frieden seiner Hände.[98]

Still more profound are the words of the Qur'ān (Sura 2 : 115), which can be translated as follows: Unto God belong the East and the West, and whithersoever ye turn, there is God's mercy, for all-embracing is God's mercy and He is all-knowing.[99]

We may conclude that Mukti Ali advocates a dialogue on a high level, by means of comparative religion, between qualified representatives of various religions. This is, of course, a most important matter.

A "meeting of religions", however, is not only a question of words and theories, let alone of theological discussions on strictly religious problems. According to Mukti Ali, it also includes practical co-operation. So the "meeting" or "dialogue" between adherents of various religions is also a question of daily life, of being involved together in current problems of the world in which we live. This aspect will have to be kept in mind when passing on to the following paragraphs.

7. *Reformation, Liberalization, Modernization*

Three Indonesian terms frequently used at present are *reformasi, liberalisasi* and *modernisasi*. They refer to a renewal that is still at work and has not yet become a fixed theory or school of thought such as "reformism", "liberalism" or "modernism".

The three terms are often used indiscriminately, without a definition of what each of them means. If we try to differentiate them, the term "reformation" could be connected primarily with the movement for renewal dating from the beginning of this century and led by Muḥ. ᶜAbduh in Egypt. Its aim was to awaken Muslims and raise Islam out of its conservatism and to cleanse it of non-Muslim impurities. This

---

[98] In English: To God belongs the Orient, To God belongs the Occident, Nothern lands and southern lands are kept safely in His hands.
[99] The term *wadjhu 'llāhi* (literally, the face of God; Pickthall gives "countenance") is interpreted by Mukti Ali as *rahmat* (grace, mercy). The new official Indonesian translation of the Qur'ān retains *wadjah Allah*, adding in an explanatory note that God's power embraces the whole cosmos, so that man cannot flee from Him.

reformist movement advocated a return to the original Islam to free it from the shackles of the mediaeval schools of law. The term "liberalization" can be used primarily to refer to this release and therefore indicates chiefly a process in the human mind. This "reformation" and "liberalization" together can be considered as paving the way to a necessary "modernization", i.e. a change in established patterns of life in order to meet the demands of modern times.

In his booklet on Modern Islam in Indonesia Mukti Ali has indicated the significance of the shift which took place at about the beginning of this century with regard to influences from abroad on Indonesian Islam.[100] From that time onward the Arab countries clearly took the place that India had occupied in former centuries, and according to Mukti Ali, this meant that pure, orthodox Islam has been gaining ground in Indonesia, while remnants of "animism" and Hinduism have been combatted, particularly by the reformist Muhammadijah movement founded in 1912.

The influence of the Arab countries initially made itself felt through contact with Mecca, but since about 1930 Cairo has definitely come to the fore. Muḥ. ᶜAbduh and Rashīd Riḍā are still honoured in Indonesia as *the* great reformers of Islam in our age; and there is still a close relationship between Indonesian Muslims and Al-Azhar in Cairo.

Indonesian founders of the reformist movement are still honoured in many recent books and leaflets. The reader may be referred to an article by H. Abdul Malik Karim Amrullah (HAMKA), translated into German.[101] The author speaks first of all of Tahir Djalal ad-Din al-Azhari from Central Sumatra (who studied in Cairo in about 1892), whom he considers a precursor of the Indonesian reformist movement. He then deals with three "Sumatran reformers", Abdul Karim Amrullah (his father), Muh. Djamil Djambek and Abdullah Ahmad. As far as Java is concerned, the author writes on Ahmad Soorkati (the reformist leader of Al-Irsjad, an association of Arabs living in Indonesia), K. H. Ahmad Dahlan (the founder of the Muhammadijah) and Ahmad Hassan of the famous Bangil *pesantrèn*.

---

[100] A. Mukti Ali, *Alam Pikiran Islam Modern di Indonesia,* Djakarta 1964.
[101] Cf. HAMKA's article, *Wie der Islam nach Indonesien kam* — which offers more than its title suggests — in Rolf Italiaander, *Die Herausforderung des Islam,* Göttingen 1965, pp. 146-168; more extensively in HAMKA, *Pengaruh Muhammad Abduh di Indonesia,* Djakarta 1961 (originally a lecture given at Al-Azhar University in Cairo when receiving an honorary doctor's degree on January 21st, 1958); also HAMKA, *Ajahku,* Djakarta 1950.

It is of course K. H. A. Dahlan who is generally considered *the* great reformer of Islam in Indonesia. Publications on his life and work show a deep reverence for this reformist leader.[102] As has already been said, the foundation of the N.U. in 1926 can be regarded as an answer to these reformist endeavours, as the N.U. wanted to defend the authority of the four orthodox schools of law as well as a genuine Javanese style of life. Many informants assured me that the old conflicts between "reformers" and "orthodox" are now buried. The old points at issue are now said to be no longer relevant. Others stress that various ideas originating from reformist circles have now been commonly accepted. This applies in particular to practical questions of modernization in daily life, from the use of "Western"-style dress and modern transport to the calculation of the first day of *Ramaḍān*. But recent discussions on subjects such as family law and the law of inheritance (caused by Hazairin's outspoken publications) may indicate that old conflicts and controversies have not yet altogether disappeared.

The question which for a long time was considered the most fundamental difference between reformers and orthodox was the reformers' struggle for the "new *idjtihād*" (personal effort to answer modern problems from one's own study of the Qur'ān and Tradition), whereas the orthodox wanted to defend the obligation of *taḳlīd* (to acknowledge the authority of the mediaeval schools of law and the verdicts they had passed). Nowadays there is in fact very little public discussion on this problem. Does it mean that the "people of *idjtihād*" have won the day? In fact the most important authors, teachers and professors belong to the people who want to engage in "the fight for the reformation and modernization of Islam".[103] Modern Muslims are accustomed to

---

[102] See, for example, Solichin Salam, *K. H. Ahmad Dahlan, Reformer Islam Indonesia,* Djakarta 1963. Its concluding chapter consists of quotations from foreign publications praising Dahlan and the Muhammadijah (Van Nieuwenhuijze, Vlekke, Kahin, Wertheim, Gibb, W. C. Smith, Pijper, Kraemer, Berg, Drewes and others). On the other hand (p. 55 ff.) some Christian missionaries are mentioned who had to acknowledge Dahlan's superiority in their debates with him (for instance Father F. van Lith S.J. and Rev. D. Bakker Sr.), while other visitors are said not even to have had the courage to enter into a discussion with Dahlan (for instance "Pastoor Dr. Zwijmer", i.e. Samuel M. Zwemer). The name of Hendrik Kraemer, who apparently was on very good terms with K. H. A. Dahlan, is not mentioned in this connection.

[103] According to its sub-title, *Pandji Masjarakat* aims to be the magazine for "the fight for the reformation and modernization of Islam". After this magazine was banned, it was succeeded in 1962 by *Gema Islam,* which has a somewhat more cultural character. From 1966 onward both magazines

ascribing the backwardness of the Muslim world to the *taklīd* mentality caused by the "closing of the gate of *idjtihād*". Thus "taklidist" has become a term of abuse which in a revolutionary country such as Indonesia is regarded as just as insulting as "conservative". Hence hardly anyone has the courage to defend publicly the obligation of *taklīd*.

Yet there are young Muslims who wonder whether reformation and liberalization in Indonesia have really been effective and have really opened the door for continuing modernization. Did not reformation actually get stuck half way? Did not perhaps the reformers' path even turn off to the right again? To what extent was the work of Ahmad Dahlan afterwards overshadowed by the influence of *ulama*s such as Ahmad Hassan of Bangil? Did this development include a shift to the right comparable with developments in Cairo, where Muḥ. ᶜAbduh was succeeded by Rashīd Riḍā? In the same way as Protestant reformers called for a return to the Bible, so too Muslim reformers called for a return to the two sources of Islam, the Qur'ān and the Tradition. But did not in both cases this return result in a return to the letter of the sacred books, rather than a return to the spirit? [104]

Before hearing a member of the younger generation who has apparently been searching for radical solutions, we shall have to quote once again from the booklet by Mukti Ali mentioned at the beginning of this paragraph. Obviously Mukti Ali wants to bridge the gap between the "people of *idjtihād*" and the "people of the *madhhab*", as he calls them. According to him, the old contrast is no longer important, and a synthesis has already been arrived at. This synthesis can be described as follows. In order to find a solution for modern problems [105] the "people of *idjtihād*" operate from the Qur'ān and Tradition; afterwards they turn their attention to verdicts passed by great *ulama*s from the orthodox schools of law, and in this way they usually arrive at a decision which

---

have appeared side by side. The fortnightly *Suara Muhammadijah* has a more limited character, being the official periodical of this association. Finally the Islamic magazine *Kiblat* can be mentioned, published by "Jajasan Perdjalanan Hadji Indonesia" (Indonesian Foundation for the Pilgrimage).

[104] Compare W. C. Smith's remark in connection with reformation in Islam: "While there have been fundamentalist conservatives among those inspired by their orientation, others crying 'Back to the Qur'an!' and 'Back to the Sunnah!' have meant, 'Back to the God of the Qur'an and His commands; back to the spirit of the Sunnah and its exhilaration'." (*Islam*, p. 44).

[105] As examples we can take the questions of whether blood transfusions or lunar flights are allowed from a religious point of view.

is in agreement with the Qur'ān and Tradition and not in conflict with the opinion of one or more of the authoritative *ulama*s. On the other hand, the "people of the *madhhab*" try to answer such a question by studying firstly the opinions of the *ulama*s; from these opinions they choose the best one, that is to say, the opinion which is in accordance, or at least not in conflict, with the Qur'ān and Tradition. In this way both groups of scholars often arrive at the same decision, though by different methods.

Yet, according to Mukti Ali, the call to *idjtihād* was indeed of great significance. "With the call to return to the Qur'ān and Tradition and the call to concentrate personally on studying and analysing religious questions, a new phase in the history of modern Muslim thought in Indonesia has set in. This was where liberalism in Indonesian Islam originated... This liberalism, however, differs from the liberalism stemming from the Western Renaissance. Western liberalism considers Reason as the ultimate norm (the final judge), whereas liberalism in Islam considers Reason as only an aid in judging something, recognizing the limits put by God's revelation." [106]

With regard to the programme of the reformist movement, Mukti Ali takes over ʿAbduh's programme as summarized by Gibb in the following points: "(1) the purification of Islam from corrupting influences and practices; (2) the reformation of Muslim higher education; (3) the re-formulation of Islamic doctrine in the light of modern thought; and (4) the defense of Islam against European influences and Christian attacks".[107]

With regard to the last point, which concerns apologetics, Mukti Ali refers to W. C. Smith's "Islam in Modern History"; his explanations "can to some extent also be used for an analysis of apologetics as found in Indonesia".[108] In view of the Indonesian situation, Mukti Ali adds a fifth point to the abovementioned programme, namely the liberation from colonialism; but this has in fact already been achieved. According to Mukti Ali the remaining four points are essentially one; they can be comprised in the need to promote belief in the One and Only God.

The endeavours to reform Muslim higher education (Gibb's point 2) have already been dealt with (Chapter II, par. 5). Gibb's point 4,

---

[106] Mukti Ali, *Alam Pikiran*, pp. 31-32.
[107] H. A. R. Gibb, *Modern Trends in Islam*, Chicago 1947, p. 33. This book has been translated into Indonesian and published under the title *Aliran-aliran Modern dalam Islam*, Djakarta 1952.
[108] Mukti Ali, *Alam Pikiran*, p. 48, n. 28.

including apologetics and polemics, will come under discussion in the final paragraph of this book.

The "purification of Islam" (point 1) includes, of course, the struggle against various superstitious practices (for instance visiting graves as mentioned in Chapter II, par. 6), originating from the so-called "animistic and Hinduistic period". In this context Mukti Ali refers in particular to mysticism and its Hindu-Javanese background. According to the author the Muhammadijah showed understanding for the liking of the Indonesian people for mysticism. Hence the Muhammadijah opposed the negative aspects of mysticism leading to asceticism and renunciation of the world, but did not reject every kind of mysticism. It rather gave a new interpretation and a new tenor to mysticism by emphasizing the ethical implications of religious life. In the widest sense of the word, modern mysticism includes what could rather be called "personal piety".

One formula used by several informants was that Islam in Indonesia is developing into a religion which is indeed "rational, but not rationalistic". One informant added: "This rational character is quite different from a rationalism such as, for instance, can be found in the Aḥmadīya Movement, which for this reason can make no progress in Indonesia".

With regard to "personal piety", Mukti Ali refers to HAMKA's books, which may indeed be taken as samples of modern Muslim piety. Obviously these works are very popular.[109]

Here too one could ask in which direction Indonesian Islam is going to develop. It is clear that Islam is a "living force" in Indonesia, as one of my informants used to say, that is, a "living force" as a political, social and cultural entity. But like all religions Islam too is facing the problem of its significance as *dīn,* as "religion in a narrower sense" for the individual, that is to say, as a source of spiritual strength and an inner anchorage for the man whose traditional pattern of life is breaking up. People in a developing country such as Indonesia are losing the certitude which stems from communal life and thought, and are entering the bewildering complexity of a modern secularized world, in which everyone has to decide on his own way of life. What does religion mean

---

[109] See the List of Publications. HAMKA's book on "1,000 vital questions" has gone through 9 reprints since 1940; his book on "modern mysticism" of 1939 achieved its 11th reprint in 1961; his "philosophy of life" of 1940 a 6th reprint in 1962; and his "mysticism throughout the ages", dating from 1952, appeared in its 5th reprint in 1962.

for the personal life of its adherents, especially of the younger generation? This question also belongs to the problem of modernization. The need to pay attention to this spiritual aspect of modernization is evident from the rise and thriving condition of numerous groups based on mysticism, inner piety or a kind of moral rearmament. This area of religious life in Indonesia actually requires special research, directed to at least three phenomena. First of all, there is the area of a more or less Islamic mysticism as it is practised by means of *dhikr*, either privately or collectively in a *ṭarīka* (Ind. *tarèkat*), i.e. a mystical order. Secondly there are dozens of groups, especially in Java, which bear a more Javanese-Hinduistic character, the so-called *kebathinan* movements (Ar. *bāṭin* = inner, interior); some of these use a more or less Islamic terminology, while others have a completely Javanese appearance.[110] Finally groups can be mentioned such as the *Subud* movement, founded by the Javanese *guru* Subuh (not to be confused with the name of the movement), which also has some followers in Europe and elsewhere. This movement claims to be a movement for adherents of all religions, without making its members disloyal to their own religion. According to some of its adherents this movement could be characterized as a kind of Indonesian or Javanese "moral rearmament". Besides *tarèkat* and *kebathinan*, this third phenomenon is sometimes indicated as *kedjiwaan* (from the Indonesian *djiwa* = soul or spirit).

It is my impression that these religious movements are indeed in a flourishing condition, in spite of the government's support for more orthodox and traditional forms of religious life. To what extent does this prove that people's religious needs cannot be satisfied only by emphasizing obedience to religious precepts and the observance of religious duties? How will modern Islam in Indonesia meet these needs?

Returning to the present-day condition of modern Islam, it must be pointed out that reformism or liberalism in Indonesia has little in common with liberalism within Christianity. As has already been said, questions of doctrine are often considered speculative and therefore a luxury. To what extent are Muslim theologians aware that thinking about the "re-formulation of Islamic doctrine in the light of modern

---

[110] I have already mentioned the stencilled publication *Aliran-aliran Kebathinan* (I.A.I.N., Jogja). A recent publication by an Indonesian Christian is the doctor's thesis of Harun Hadiwijono, *Man in the Present Javanese Mysticism*, Baarn (The Netherlands) 1967.

thought" (point 3 of ᶜAbduh's programme, as given by Gibb) is a task which has to be carried on continuously? In my opinion it is not enough simply to repeat the apologetic thesis that Islam is the most rational religion, and that Islam has already accepted modern thought by accepting the true elements of evolutionism.

One of the few questions sometimes discussed is the Prophet's "ascension" or "Journey into Heaven". Educated people have difficulty in accepting this story literally. But, as far as I know, such questions are hardly dealt with in publications. In private talks theologians are wont to emphasize that this story may be taken either literally, as including body and soul (see Sura 17 : 1), or symbolically, as an elevation in the spirit (based on a tradition that according to ᶜĀ'isha the Prophet was in Mecca that night). With regard to such a story, people often act as many Christians do with regard to Bible stories: a teacher or preacher either tells the story without further comment (e.g. for children) or he simply allegorizes the story to give an edifying sermon, in both cases without touching upon questions of historicity.

Modernism or liberalism in Islam certainly has nothing to do with such critical studies of the text of the Scriptures and its historical sources as are made by Christian theologians. Even the most "liberal" Muslim theologians maintain that such a critical study is simply impossible in Islam, as the Qur'ān is the revealed Book, send down directly from God. Hence its contents may not be considered as ideas and opinions of the Prophet, who, for example, might have been influenced by his contact with Jews and Christians.

Muslim apologists are inclined to apply this "fundamentalist" belief in the Holy Book also to the "original Gospel", which according to them must have been brought in the form of a Holy Book by Jesus; this "original Gospel" is believed to have been either falsified or lost, so that the Christians afterwards could only arrive at a faulty reconstruction of the original revelation.

Anticipating the final paragraph of this book, it may be noted in passing that Muslims and Christians often talk at cross-purposes, due to their different attitudes towards Holy Scripture. For the former it is literally the Word of God, and for many among the latter it is a collection of traditions concerning the life and preaching of men who felt inspired to speak and act in God's Name. It is largely due to this different attitude towards the Scriptures that Muslim apologists and polemists are missing the target when they address non-fundamentalist Christians.

As far as the relation between the Qur'ān and modern science is concerned, in Indonesia too the usual solutions can be heard. On the one hand, apologists want to prove that the results of modern research in the field of the natural sciences are already implicitly present in the Qur'ān. On the other hand, religious belief and science are distinguished or separated, with the argument that the Qur'ān leaves room for independent research or even stimulates such research. According to general opinion a conflict between the Qur'ān (or religious belief) and scientific research is basically impossible. A seeming conflict only proves that our interpretation of certain verses has to be reviewed. In this way, also familiar in certain Christian circles, attempts are made to safeguard religious belief from possible doubts which may be aroused by modern science.

When reflecting on these developments in Indonesia, I am inclined to conclude that "reformation" has to a large extent resulted in a kind of "restoration", so that "modern Islam" in Indonesia is perhaps to be characterized as "neo-orthodox" rather than "liberal".

But Islam is primarily a practical religion. Most Muslims prefer practical solutions for daily life to theoretical speculations, so we may turn our attention from theoretical problems connected with "reformation" and "liberalization" to practical questions of "modernization".

It may first be stated that Muslims in Indonesia, generally speaking, do not feel difficulties with regard to most aspects of modernization. Some tenacious traditions which impede modern development (e.g. the use of a rice-knife, as already mentioned) do not originate in Islam but in pre-Islamic culture and are being combatted by modern Muslims. Religion in Indonesia does not actually impede technological development. Of course, religions and religious leaders often tend to be suspicious of certain novelties and especially of developments which could change the established structure of society. But the process of modernization will go on, whether some alterations are wanted or not. Religions, Islam included, will simply have to find the right reasoning in order to get the new developments accepted by conservatives. Sura 13 : 11, for example, is a fitting starting-point to combat fatalism among the people and to promote personal initiative and a feeling of responsibility. The central part of this verse can be translated as follows: "God changeth not the condition of a folk until they (first) change that which is in their hearts". According to the official Indonesian translation, the last words could be rendered with "until they change their own condition"; the following note has been added: "God will not change their condition as long as they themselves do not change what caused their backwardness".

In order to give some specific examples connected with modernization, I mention first of all the question of banking and interest. Although this question has long been debated, it is now generally accepted that modern economic development is impossible without sound banking. Formerly the prohibition on *ribā* (cf. Sura 2 : 275-276; 3 : 130; 4 : 161) was often explained as only a prohibition on usury. Nowadays the term *ribā* is often interpreted as meaning "interest in the consumer sector". That is to say, it is forbidden to lend money at interest to a poor man who needs it for his livelihood; the problem of poverty must be solved by social regulations. *Ribā*, however, does not include "interest in the producer sector"; in other words, it is not forbidden to take interest from money invested as shares in a business or other enterprise.[111]

As far as the position of women is concerned, conditions in Indonesia are probably very progressive compared with other Muslim countries. Girls and women work in offices and factories beside, sometimes above, men; they study and teach together with male colleagues at the universities. Family-planning is being vigorously propagated by the present government, in contrast with Soekarno's. Authoritative Muslims have bestowed their blessing on this propaganda. Theologians sometimes object to family-planning propaganda when based primarily on economic motives, as they consider this kind of reasoning a lack of trust in God's Providence. Some Muslim doctors oppose the introduction of "the pill" for similar reasons to those heard in conservative circles the world over.[112]

In many speeches and publications, however, it has been emphasized again and again that modernization does not mean Westernization (Ind. *westernisasi*). In particular the Islamic magazine *Pandji Masjarakat*, which aims to champion reformation and modernization, often warns against Westernization. In an article by HAMKA [113] modernization is defined as a renewal necessary for the development of the country: from a colony to a country with a truly free people, from feudalism to

---

[111] A survey of the questions and the way they have been answered is given by A. Chotib, *Bank dalam Islam*, Djakarta 1962. The author himself is of the opinion that banking in our world is a necessary evil and can therefore be compared with the case of a hungry poor man eating forbidden food; neither of the two can be interdicted.

[112] So, for example, some articles on Family Planning (*Keluarga Berentjana*) written in 1968 by the lady psychiatrist Dr. Zakijah Dradjad in *Pandji Masjarakat*, nos. 31, 32, 33.

[113] HAMKA, *Dengan Sekularisasi Pantjasila Akan Kosong*, in *Pandji Masjarakat*, no. 29.

democracy, from an agrarian society to an industrialized country, and so on. But the author warns against Westernization, which could mean the acceptance of a Western style of life based on materialism and dominated by sex (films, dancing, pornography). Moreover, the author warns against a Westernization that would result in secularization (Ind. *sekularisasi*), for instance in politics.

At the same time and in the same magazine Nurcholis Madjid, chairman of the most important Islamic student organization (*Himpunan Mahasiswa Islam,* H.M.I.), wrote a series of articles entitled "Modernization is Rationalization, not Westernization".[114] He too warned against secularism, which could destroy the religious basis of the Indonesian state ("Belief in the One and Only God") as well as against Western rationalism, humanism and liberalism. Samson reported a revealing interview he had with this student leader on April 4th, 1968. "The President of HMI (which is independent but considered close to Modernist Islam) stated that Communism is the highest point of secularism. If a person is a secularist and if he carries his beliefs to their logical conclusion, he must perforce be a Communist. If he is a secularist but not a Communist he is suffering from a split personality. Both Communism and secularism are dangers to Islam, but Communism, as the highest point, is the greater danger. When I asked him what he considered worse, Communism or Naziism, he replied that Communism was worse because Nazis believed in God." [115]

Almost two years later, however, a pamphlet by the same author appeared which took another line.[116] This pamphlet caused quite a stir and much discussion. I want to draw special attention to these recent opinions of a representative of Muslim youth. If my information is correct, the publication of this pamphlet could have had something to do with attempts by some Muslim leaders to create a union of all Islamic political parties, in view of the elections of 1971. Such a unitary party, however, would require compromises, which would automatically result in a shift towards conservatism. Such a development would estrange many educated young people from such an Islamic party. Furthermore, it could be that the author, proceeding from his earlier differentiation

---

[114] Nurcholis Madjid, *Modernisasi ialah Rasionalisasi bukan Westernisasi,* in *Pandji Masjarakat,* nos. 28, 29, 30; the articles are dated 1 Muharram 1388 H./March 29th, 1968.
[115] Samson, *Islam,* p. 1,016.
[116] Nurcholis Madjid, *Keharusan Pembaruan Pemikiran Islam dan Masalah Integrasi Ummat,* dated Djakarta, January 2nd, 1970.

between "rationalism" and "rationalization", later came to a similar distinction between "secularism" and "secularization" as discussed in recent Western publications.[117]

His pamphlet first of all states that unfortunately the idea of a renewal has often been held only by a part of the Muslim community. In the past this resulted in reactions from another part, strengthening the opposite attitude. The author stresses that in recent years an encouraging growth of the Islamic community in Indonesia has taken place. But he wants to put the question of whether perhaps this rush to join Islam means only a kind of social adaptation. Apparently many people were struck by the defeat of Communism, which suggested the victory of Islam. It seems, however, that many who now accept Islam, reject an Islamic political party or any Islamic organization ("Islam: yes; Islamic Party: no!"). So the important point is actually not the quantity of the Islamic community, but its quality.

In order to arrive at a true renewal, Muslims must free themselves from certain traditional values and search for values orientated towards the future. Putting it plainly, the author wishes to call this development the process of liberalization, and he does not hesitate to connect the process straightforwardly with present-day discussion on "secularization". Unlike "secularism", which has to be rejected as a fixed ideology and a closed world view, "secularization" must be understood as a "liberating development". Muslims must come to a better differentiation between values that are "transcendental" and those that are only "temporal". In other words, they must do away with traditional ideas which, unfortunately, have come to be considered as *uchrowi* (Ar. *ukhrawī* = connected with the world to come, Ar. *al-ukhrā*), although these ideas in fact belong to the changing cultural patterns. "Secularization", then, means that values which in fact are "worldly", ought to be considered "secular"; the Islamic community must free itself from the tendency to treat them as eternal values (*menguchrowikannja*).

Furthermore, "secularization" means emphasizing the task of man in this world, as God's representative so to speak. That is to say, man is given the opportunity and freedom to exert himself for the improvement of his conditions of life and may act creatively, in accordance with the spirit of *idjtihād*.

---

[117] This distinction goes back to the German theologian Fr. Gogarten, in his *Verhängnis und Hoffnung der Neuzeit*, Stuttgart 1953; later the discussion has been dominated by the writings of Harvey Cox, in particular *The Secular City*, New York 1965.

In other words, true belief in God as the One and Only God includes applying the idea of "transcendency" only to Him, whereas this world and all problems and values connected with this world ought to be "desacralized". It has been said that "Islam is Bolshevism plus God" (Iqbal). This means that Islamic opinions concerning this world and its problems may sometimes coincide with those of the Communists (that is to say, be "realistic"); Islam, however, adds that there is moreover a "transcendent" Being, namely God.

After this appeal for a positive appreciation of the terms "secularization" and "desacralization", the author advocates true freedom of thought and freedom of speech. New ideas which are initially considered to be wrong, can afterwards prove to contain truth, and differences of opinion can stimulate closer examination. It was not nonsensical that the Prophet considered differences of opinion within the Muslim community as evidence of God's grace. We should not fear the use of terms such as "socialism". Based on the term *sjura* or *musjawarah* (cf. Sura 42 : 38) we accepted the idea of democracy. Why then should the idea of socialism be taboo, whereas in accordance with the Holy Book Islam must champion social justice and protect the poor and oppressed? It was because the Islamic community was not prepared to take the initiative for social development that others took this task in hand, and Islam was excluded. It was lack of freedom of thought that caused this development.

It is true that Islam in Indonesia created organizations for renewal (e.g. the Muhammadijah), but the author wants honestly to face the truth that these organizations are no longer functioning as movements for renewal, because they have lost their dynamic and progressive character. On the other hand some organizations which initially bore the mark of counter-reformation (e.g. the N.U.) have been forced to take over some ideas from the former renewers, but this change does not promise much. For this reason a new, liberal movement for renewal in Islam has to be started ("liberal" in the sense of "non-traditional" and "non-sectarian").

According to the author, Muslims must realize that the values of Islam have a dynamic, not a static, character. Some basic elements of the Islamic faith (first and foremost belief in God), some principles of worship and some fundamental social values are indeed unchanging. But apart from these values, Islam does not give any definite prescriptions concerning activities in this world. The latter are determined by cultural values, which must be in a process of continuous development, in order to suit the actual situation. The struggle for improving the condition of mankind is not a monopoly of the Islamic community, but a task for all men. In this struggle the intellectuals will have to stand in the forefront, in particular the former members of Islamic student movements — "With God's help and His guidance".

Listening to independent members of the younger generation such as Nurcholis Madjid, one may indeed speak of "self-conscious Islamic youth, which is increasingly making itself felt", so that "we may have confidence and hope in the future of Islam".[118]

8. *Muslims and Christians*

Wilfred Cantwell Smith asserts: "Nowhere in the Muslim world (except perhaps in Indonesia?) do Muslims feel that a non-Muslim member of their nation is 'one of us'. And nowhere do the minorities feel accepted." [119]

Probably one point different from elsewhere is that Muslims in Indonesia cannot simply disregard the existence of Christian Churches in their country. Before 1945 Christians were often regarded by Muslims as belonging to "the other side" (Ind. *pihak sana*), that is to say, the side of Dutch colonial power. Many Christians, however, were in the forefront of the fight for freedom, together with Muslims and other nationalists. So it became clear that Indonesian Christians too could be true Indonesians and good patriots. In this way many Muslims and Christians got to know and respect each other as fellow-citizens, and thus relations between Muslims and Christians within the Republic of Indonesia turned first in a favourable direction.

After the fight for freedom, however, new dissensions arose. Beside the old contrast between various ethnic groups, four important confessional/ political groups came into being, the Muslims, the "secular" Nationalists, the Communists and the Christians. Unfortunately in the course of the years they were to confront each other more and more as closed groups, although for a time some of them made opportunistic alliances. Soekarno did see the danger of a country and a people divided against itself. Passionately he sought for new means of achieving unity and "a return to the spirit of 1945". The Dutch proffered him one, by stubbornly holding on to "Dutch New Guinea"; later the national fight could be directed against Malaysia as a neo-colonialist creation, or in general against the *Oldefos,* the Old Established Forces. As a clever phrase-

---

[118] Vredenbregt, *De Islam,* p. 10.
[119] Smith, *Islam,* p. 80.

monger Soekarno tried to bridge the gaps between the various groups by creating the NASAKOM slogan.

But in spite of Soekarno at the end of 1965 developments resulted in an attempt to exterminate one of these groups, the Communists. For the time being the extermination of Communism seemed to be furthering the unity of the other groups, but this did not last for long. Afterwards the authorities again and again warned against the subversive working of Communism, but these warnings too could not be repeated endlessly. The military way of thinking, proceeding from the doctrine of "law and order", also could not create real unity. Thus the "New Order" inherited a dissension still requiring a new ideal in order to achieve unity.

Developments after 1965 led to obvious tensions and conflicts between Muslim groups and others. The struggle for an Islamic society did have some positive results, but at the same time produced disappointments and contrary reactions. The political ideology of Islam aroused suspicion and fear among other groups, also after 1965. The Islamization of the Javanese masses was like a mirage. The belief in a Muslim victory at the elections of 1971 is probably diminishing. As far as a religious revival has taken place, it has also been manifested in a revival of Hinduism, Buddhism and Javanese mysticism (although a number of these groups are said to have been dissolved after 1965 because of left-wing sympathies among their leaders).[120] Thus after 1965 great tensions continued to exist between adherents of Muslim organizations and other groups of the population, in particular the merely nominal Muslims and non-Muslims. All these tensions, however, seemed to concentrate and find an outlet in the controversy with Christians.

It could perhaps be said that the soil for conflicts with Christians had already been prepared by an endless stream of apologetic and polemic publications. Before turning to topical problems, some examples of these Muslim apologetics and polemics must be cited.

---

[120] In the stencilled publication *Fungsi Da^cwah*, already mentioned, Muh. Natsir warned against the activities of Buddhists in Indonesia, who were using the army newspaper *Berita Yudha* for their propaganda and claimed the use of Borobudur, Mendut and other old monuments in Central Java as their places of worship. As far as Hinduism is concerned, E. Utrecht reported on articles in the Indonesian newspaper *Suluh Marhaen* (Bali edition) concerning the rapid growth of Hinduism in Central and East Java in 1968; the author himself estimated the number of converts to Hinduism during recent years as 250,000 yearly (E. Utrecht, in *De Groene Amsterdammer*, 5 October 1968, p. 5).

While respecting the efforts of Muslim apologists, it is difficult for a non-Muslim to appreciate the content of their publications (just as it must be difficult for a Muslim to appreciate what some non-Muslim authors write on Islam). "Christianity" as it is rendered in apologetic and polemic publications is sometimes almost unrecognizable to a Christian reader. Authors of such publications are, for instance, in the habit of giving quotations from all sorts of "Christian" publications without realizing to what extent the books quoted can be considered representative of Christianity. In the same indiscriminate way all sorts of critical remarks on Christianity or Christian doctrines are employed. Following a well-known Arabic expression, an apologist seems not to be interested in *man ḳāla* ("who" said something) but only in *mā ḳāla* ("what" he said). So he just quotes what he considers useful for attacking another religion and justifying his own.

Among the publications issued by Muhammadijah headquarters, two pamphlets appeared on "Christology" and on "The Old and New Testament", written by Djarnawi Hadikusumo (the first chairman of the new Islamic party, the Parmusi).[121] In these pamphlets, for example, critical remarks by Arnold Toynbee (popular in many Muslim publications) and curiosities taken from a publication of the Jehovah's Witnesses are considered equally authoritative. The author refers to "the book *Nieuwe Hemelen en een Nieuwe Aarde,* a [Dutch] translation of the book *New Heavens and a New Earth,* published by the International Bible Students' Association at Brooklyn, New York" (obviously an old publication of the Jehovah's Witnesses, who originally called themselves "International Bible Students"). With the help of this book a list covering three pages is given concerning the dates and authors of the Bible, "according to the belief of the Christians":

"After 4025 B.C. Adam wrote Gen. 1 : 1 to 2 : 4
before 3096 B.C. Adam wrote Gen. 2 : 5 to 5 : 2
circ. 2370 B.C. Noah wrote Gen. 5 : 3 to 6 : 9
after 2020 B.C. The three sons of Noah (Shem, Ham and Japheth) wrote Gen. 6 : 9 to 10 : 11."
And so on.

---

[121] *Djarnawi Hadikusumo, Sekitar Kristologi,* Jogjakarta 1965³ and *Sekitar Perdjandjian Lama [dan] Perdjandjian Baru,* Jogjakarta no date, both especially published for Muhammadijah missionaries by headquarters of the "Muhammadijah, Madjlis Tabligh".

On the basis of this exposition the author easily arrives at the conclusion that "these Christian beliefs" cannot be proved reliable by historical and scientific research.

More vehement attacks are made in a stencilled Muhammadijah pamphlet edited by Bisjron A. Wardy and intended to be a contribution to a refresher course of Muhammadijah members, in order to open their eyes to the activities of Christians, in particular in the area of Jogjakarta.[122] According to this pamphlet, the Christians (here called *Nasrani* instead of the more polite modern Indonesian term *orang Kristen*) [123] had set up a scheme to Christianize (*menasranikan*) the Indonesian people. "To begin with, they chose the island of Java as a pilot project; in Java they chose Central Java, in Central Java in particular the Special Administrative Area Jogjakarta; and within this area of Jogjakarta they chose the district of Sleman to become the centre of their activities, i.e. the area along the road to Kali Urang." [124]

This pamphlet furthermore refers to an anonymous paper which some time before had been spread in Java and had caused consternation. It had revealed "that in a joint conference of Roman Catholic and Protestant Churches held in 1962 in East Java a plan was drawn up for the Christianization (*Nasranisasi*) of Java within 20 years and of all Indonesia in a period of 50 years".[125] Some of the points on that "programme" were said to be the building of schools and the furtherance of mixed marriages of Christian girls with a strong belief to Muslim boys with a weak belief. Finally the pamphlet gives an "explanation" of the tactics of Christian strategy: based on the doctrine of the Trinity, this strategy would consist of creating a system of Christian cells, in such a way that triangles come into being when one draws lines connecting one cell (e.g. a church) with the other ones (e.g. a school or hospital). This system, then, is called the "Trinity cell system".

A well-known series of polemic pamphlets has been published by JAPI (= *Jajasan Penjiaran Islam*, Foundation for the Spread of Islam) in

---

[122] Bisjron A. Wardy, *Memahami Kegiatan Nasrani*, Jogjakarta 1964.
[123] Just as after 1965 the Chinese, unfortunately, are again being called *Tjina* instead of the more polite *orang Tjiong Hoa*.
[124] On the road from Jogjakarta to Kaliurang there was formerly a Protestant hospital at Pakem. Now on this road a huge Roman Catholic complex is being built (seminary, monastery, printing house and other dwellings). This recent display of power may have been the main origin of the abovementioned "explanation" of Christian strategy.
[125] I have not succeeded in discovering the origins of this rumour. Such a conference has certainly never been held. I was told that a leader of one of the many sectarian revivalist movements may have said something like it.

Surabaja. To mention a few titles, these pamphlets deal with The Messiah and the Cross, The Death of the Messiah and the Azhar University, Jesus in the Qur'ān, The Trumpet of Death from the Valley of Qumran ("Qumran", where the "Dead Sea Scrolls" were found, is supposed to have revealed the true origin of Christianity and therefore means the end of the orthodox Christian belief in Jesus). A somewhat higher standard is shown by the booklet by Hasbullah Bakry, entitled "The Qur'ān as a Correction to the Old and New Testament"; the same author wrote a pamphlet on "Jesus Christ according to Islam and Christianity". Finally a pamphlet by Aftabuddin Ahmad on "Woman in Islam and Christianity" can be mentioned.[126] In the same series a pamphlet was recently published by O. Hashem, entitled "A Complete Answer to Rev. Dr. J. Verkuyl", the latter being a Dutch theologian who lived for years in Indonesia and wrote a stencilled pamphlet for private use in Christian circles, intended to prepare Christians for a dialogue with Muslims.[127] There is no need to pay attention here to the content of all these pamphlets. They are samples of cheap polemics, suited to semi-intellectuals and using arguments which could have been taken over mainly from Aḥmadīya publications (although this movement itself has little following in Indonesia and is considered heretical).

A somewhat more important book was written by Hasbullah Bakry, entitled "Jesus in the Qur'ān and Muhammad in the Bible".[128] According to a Dutch reviewer, this book was written because of the author's "uneasiness about the fact that hundreds, nay thousands, of young Muslims had gone over to Christianity since leadership of Churches and Missions was transferred from foreigners to Indonesian hands". The reviewer continued: "This book contains a reaction to F. L. Bakker's abovementioned work;[129] moreover, it offers a series of quotations from the Bible which allegedly prove that Muhammad's coming was already predicted in the Old and New Testaments. According to Bakry too, it was Paul who deflected early Christianity from the true Gospel of Christ. So Paul was a false prophet according to the definition Jesus himself gave in order to distinguish a false from a true prophet."

---

[126] All these publications except the last are mentioned by D. C. Mulder, *Stemmen uit de Islam*, in *De Heerbaan*, 1968, no. 1, pp. 41-42.

[127] J. Verkuyl, *Tentang Interpretasi Iman Kristen Kepada Orang² Islam*, special issue of *Bulletin Lembaga Penjelidikan Pekabaran Indjil*, Djakarta, no date.

[128] Mulder, *Stemmen*, pp. 41-42.

[129] This refers to a Christian publication by F. L. Bakker, earlier mentioned by Mulder, entitled *Tuhan Jesus didalam Agama Islam* ("The Lord Jesus in Islam"), Djakarta 1957, the content of which is as questionable in my opinion as its title.

The Egyptian visiting professor Ahmad Shalaby also wrote a pamphlet in Indonesian on Islam and Christianity, followed by a book on Christianity intended as a contribution to comparative religion.[130] In these publications too the apostle Paul is described as the crafty enemy of Christianity, who feigned conversion in order to destroy Christianity from within by means of his theology of Trinity and Reconciliation. The emperor Constantine is said to have organized the victory of those who advocated the Divinity of Jesus at Nicaea (A.D. 325), although they in fact numbered only 318 out of 2,048 delegates.[131] The "Gospel of Barnabas", rejected and hidden by the Christians, is put forward as the only reliable Gospel.

It is not necessary to discuss the qualities of these apologetic and polemic publications. Gibb may well be right when emphasizing that "much that, on the face of it, looks like anti-Christian polemic is, in reality, an apologetic directed toward Muslim doubters"; but according to W. C. Smith we should not forget how Islam was attacked by Western critics at the beginning of this century, "attacks in the name of Christianity, rationalism, liberal progress, or the like".[132] Nowadays, however, these Muslim apologetic efforts are as naïve as some Christian attempts to explain old formulations of Christian doctrines to Muslims.[133]

A critical attitude toward apologetics is also shown by some Muslim scholars. Mukti Ali, for example, wrote that "Apologetics is a good thing, but it is not a good thing to concentrate all one's energy and strength on apologetics. Apologetics only formulates things that are already known and conditions that already exist; its character is therefore 'negative' and 'conservative'. But religion and society are changing

---

[130] Ahmad Sjalabi, *Perkembangan Keagamaan dalam Islam dan Maséhi*, Solo 1960, and *Perbandingan Agama, bahagian Agama Maséhi*, Djakarta 1960¹, 1964².
[131] Cf. Sjalabi, *Perbandingan*, p. 67. According to reliable handbooks on Church History, the number of delegates at Nicaea was about 250-300; tradition afterwards gave the symbolical figure of 318 (compare Genesis 14:14). The number of 2,048 mentioned by Sjalabi apparently originates from later Arabic sources and is perhaps based on an estimate of the total number of delegates and their following. Cf. Charles Joseph Hefele, *Histoire des Conciles*, Paris 1907, Vol. I, p. 409.
[132] Gibb, *Modern Trends*, p. 53; Smith, *Islam*, p. 86.
[133] Cf. John Crossley, *Explaining the Gospel to Muslims*, London 1967⁶; in this pamphlet there is, for instance, reference to discussions on whether the doctrine of the Trinity can be criticized by Muslims as a (faulty) addition $(1 + 1 + 1 = 1)$, or may perhaps be considered a multiplication sum $(1 \times 1 \times 1 = 1)$. The author himself prefers to give some "illustrations of the Trinity", as "no one can give a perfect explanation" (p. 24-25).

and making progress; therefore religion and society cannot be developed by negativism and conservatism. Apologetics may arouse emotions and give self-satisfaction, but they cannot produce true conviction and discernment. Apologetics cannot be practised in a scientific way, because science and scholarship have a dynamic and progressive character. They search for the 'new' and refuse to call a halt." [134]

Some basic weaknesses of polemic writings have already been mentioned, as for instance the use of worthless sources. If anywhere, Muslims and Christians could help each other here by pointing the way through each other's reading-matter, in order to find out which publications nowadays can be considered representative for Islam and Christianity, or at least for some groups within both religions, in particular modern groups.

After this survey of Muslim apologetic and polemic publications, we return to the topical problem of the relationship between Muslims and Christians in Indonesia after 1965. Since that time occasional incidents have occurred between Muslims and Christians (though they did not assume proportions at all comparable with incidents between Hindus and Muslims in India). On October 1st, 1967 Muslim youth in Makassar (South Sulawesi) caused damage to furniture in various churches. According to a Muslim reporter this incident was caused by a discussion at the home of a Christian teacher of religion who had insulted Islam by saying "that Muhammad (the Prophet of Islam) was only married to nine of his wives and lived in adultery with the others".[135] This reporter added "that the activities of the Christian community in Sulawesi show a provocative character, because almost all Christian congresses are held in Sulawesi",[136] while, moreover, "a Christian church has been built opposite the Great Mosque of Makassar, although practically no Christians live in that quarter".

These last passages may indicate things that often cause annoyance among Muslims and have sometimes led to open conflicts. They are (1) conspicuous Christian activities which take place in such a way that they can be interpreted as being provocative, and (2) the building of churches in an area or quarter where almost all people are considered to be Muslims, let alone when even a mosque has to be pulled down

---

[134] Editorial in *Al-Djami'ah*, March 1967, p. 2.
[135] *Pandji Masjarakat*, no. 19, October 1967, p. 25. Cf. also no. 20, pp. 3-8.
[136] This remark probably refers to preparations for the General Assembly of the Indonesian Council of Churches held in Makassar from October 29th to November 8th, 1967.

to make room for Christian buildings, such as an Adventist Hospital in Kebajoran-Baru (Djakarta).

At the beginning of 1967, for instance, difficulties arose about the building of a small Methodist church in Meulaboh (West Atjeh). At the beginning of 1969 even in one of the new suburbs of Djakarta a Protestant church was destroyed. Such incidents also occurred in Djatibarang (West Java) and Purwodadi (Central Java). I was told that once or twice similar difficulties arose from the other side, for instance on the island of Sangihe, where Muslims planned to build a mosque amidst the Christian community; the authorities managed to prevent a conflict by persuading the Muslims to change the plan. Christian activities considered provocative (e.g. by articles in *Pandji Masjarakat*) were mass-meetings such as those held by the American Adventist preacher Moseley in the Senajan Stadium in Djakarta. Criticism became concentrated on foreign sponsors of missionary activities (sometimes indicated as "the Rome-Geneva Axis", i.e. the Roman Catholic Church, together with those Protestant Churches that are united in the World Council of Churches in Geneva). This criticism culminated in accusing the Christians (or "the Christian West") of trying again to subjugate the world of Islam (Ind. *menaklukkan dunia Islam*), that is to say, by means of the Missions, after colonial subjugation had come to an end.

Solutions which were repeatedly suggested by Muslims during these years were the following. (1) Every religious group ought to restrict its activities to its own circle. (2) "Competition" may indeed take place between Muslims and Christians to convert those sections of the people who do not yet possess a religion (i.e. the so-called animists). (3) Religious communities, however, should be forbidden to direct their propaganda at people who do possess a religion (that is to say, Christians should not try to convert Muslims to Christianity).

One of the most important issues confusing relations between Muslims and Christians is mission work aimed at proselytizing or considered to aim at proselytizing. This problem came to a head in the developments after 1965. According to Christian reports, in recent years several hundred thousand Indonesians decided on Christianity as their religion. Some of them were former "animists" (e.g. Karo Bataks in Northern Sumatra), who actually had to choose one of the officially recognized religions. Others, however, stemmed from the millions of Javanese nominal Muslims or *abangans*.

This choice for Christianity often had little connection with mission work or Christian propaganda. Many decided to become Christians hardly knowing any more about Christianity than its name. To give one illustration, I quote the following story from a first-hand source. Some years ago a Protestant minister somewhere in Java passed the entrance to a little village and saw a notice stating that this was a "Christian Village". As he did not know any Christians living there, the pastor wanted to make their acquaintance. Then the villagers told him that actually they had not yet become Christians, but had decided to go over to Christianity and therefore had already put this notice at the entrance to their village (probably in order not to be troubled by Muslim missionaries or by Communist-hunters).

Such examples may show that a decision in favour of Christianity sometimes has little to do with direct missionary activities, and also cannot be explained as a result of bribery (by handing out food and clothing), a criticism often brought forward in Muslim publications. It would be useful if Muslims as well as Christians tried in a realistic and sober way to discover the true reasons for such developments. It might then turn out that the one side need not become too anxious nor the other too joyful. As has already been said, a Muslim author stated that since 1965 "people are now constantly wondering: what and where is the real mainstay of our souls?" [137] In such circumstances some turn to Islam, others to Christianity, and yet others to Hinduism, Buddhism or Javanese mysticism. Some of those who formerly belonged to the Communist Party or any Communist controlled organization are now searching for a new community in order to find a new spiritual home. Why do some of them decide in favour of Christianity?

The answers I collected were, for example, (1) that some nominal Muslims found it easier to choose a new religious community than to turn definitely to Islam; (2) that some considered Islam as a troublesome, foreign religion, because of its many Arabic formulas and its Arabic Holy Book, whereas for instance in Protestant churches only the national or even the regional language is used; (3) that some people feared being bothered with a number of precepts and prohibitions when becoming Muslims, e.g. religious duties such as prayer and fasting, and the prohibition on eating pork. Apart from "theological" considerations, some Christian reporters stress and generalize one answer sometimes heard from new converts, namely that "the great massacre of so-called atheistic Communists by *jang beragama* (religious people), especially by

---

[137] Amiruddin Djamil in the foreword to S. Abul Ala Maududi, *Menudju Pengertian Islam*, Djakarta 1967.

Muslim youth groups" had resulted in a choice for Christianity, as the Christians had not been involved in these murders.[138]

As far as these new Christians included ex-Communists and fellow-travellers, one Muslim informant reacted as follows: "You Christians can have them; we don't want to get a fifth column within Islam". With regard to Christian activities in prison camps, another Muslim informant said: "As for me, it doesn't matter if former Communists become Christians, if only they get a new indoctrination somehow". It can be understood that Churches did not refuse to accept these new members, although their entrance created great problems, both with regard to religious after-care and because of criticism and insinuation launched by other religious and political groups.

When trying to understand these developments and their background, I do not want to excuse or gloss over missionary practices by those people and groups which like fishing in troubled waters. Generally speaking it can be acknowledged that leaders of the "official" Protestant Churches united in the Indonesian Council of Churches do understand the difficulties and try to avoid controversy and conflict with their Muslim fellow-citizens. Present-day Indonesia, however, is being flooded by all sorts of so-called faith-missions and sects which are only interested in Muslims as objects for conversion. Indonesian Christians will have to realize that the image of a religion is often determined by the behaviour of its most fanatical representatives. In Indonesia such fanatical groups are in particular Jehovah's Witnesses and Seventh Day Adventists, who cause offense by their methods of the door-to-door selling of pamphlets. Unfortunately, Muslims consider these propagandists as representatives of "the Christian religion" and often do not realize that these visitors not only try to convert Muslims to their belief but Christians as well. In my opinion Indonesian Churches should clearly dissociate themselves from such groups and their methods. It is not enough to emphasize that "mission work" does not mean "proselytism", followed by putting a finger on the Bible to explain that even so the Gospel must be preached to all men (Matthew 28 : 19). One should not be surprised if Muslims fail to see the difference between "proselytism" and this kind of "obedience to the call to mission".

---

[138] Cf. S. C. Graaf van Randwijck, *Missiologia in loco — Een andere visie,* in *Nederlands Theologisch Tijdschrift,* October 1969, pp. 37-50, a criticism of my article *Missiologia in loco — Christendom en Islam in Indonesië,* in the same journal, October 1968, pp. 46-65.

At the initiative of the government on November 30th, 1967 an Inter-Religious Consultation was held in Djakarta, in order to improve the strained relations between the various religious communities.[139]

The meeting was chaired by the Minister of Religion, K. H. M. Dachlan. After his opening speech he requested President Soeharto "to give his important instructions and *fatwas*". The President emphasized in his address that the fundamental principles concerning religion and freedom of religion were anchored in the 1945 Constitution, inspired by the Pantjasila. According to the President all religions felt called to spread their message, but all religions also aimed at the well-being of mankind. Hence the spread of a religious message must not lead to conflicts. The government had to feel concerned when this spread turned out to be aimed only at an increase in the number of its adherents and when adherents of one religion were called on to change over to another. So the President appealed for tolerance, as tolerance was taught by every religion as well as by the Pantjasila. He warned against disunity, which would benefit the remaining followers of the "Old Order" and the Communists.

The Minister of Religion also appealed for good relations and mutual understanding between adherents of various religions. The highest ideal would be a form of co-operation as had in the past occasionally occurred, for instance when Christians helped Muslims to build a mosque and Muslims helped Christians to build a church. If this ideal were not attainable, then religious groups must at least achieve peaceful co-existence, based on tolerance and mutual respect. He reminded those present of the President's wish, expressed at a recent meeting of the cabinet, that through this Inter-Religious Consultation the following two things should be achieved. (1) Quarrels among religious people must come to an end. (2) One religious community must not address its propaganda to another religious community.

The representative of the "Hindu-Balinese community", of course, could easily agree with the idea of unity within the variety found among religions. He advocated tolerance, by telling the story of the blind men who tried to discover what exactly an elephant was like; the one who happened to touch the ear of the elephant said it was like a fan; the one who seized the tusks said it was like a stick; and the one who felt the belly said it was like a little hill; so none of them could give a complete picture.

---

[139] The speeches, but not the discussions, held at this Consultation have been published in *Al-Djami'ah,* May 1968.

The Minister of Social Affairs, Tambunan, speaking for the Protestant group, told of an informal talk he had recently had with his Muslim friend Natsir. They both wanted to acknowledge the Divine call to spread the message of their religion, and so had to face the question: how can we reach a *modus vivendi* in our multi-religious state, without each betraying his own religion? He denied that Christian Churches aimed at *la conquête du monde musulman* (the conquest of the Muslim world).

The Roman Catholic politician Kasimo reminded his audience of their unity in the struggle for freedom, as well before 1945 as after that date. The differences between the various religious and ethnic groups could be overcome at that time. He proposed that this Consultation should issue a statement calling the various religious groups to tolerance, without diminishing the fundamental freedom of man to choose a religion based on his own conviction, and without denying anyone's duty to spread the message of his own religion, although this had to be done in a proper way.

For the Muslim participants addresses were given by Lt. Gen. Sudirman,[140] K. H. Masjkur, H. M. Rasjidi and Muh. Natsir. The essence of their speeches can be summarized in two points. (1) The Christians — and in particular Protestant and Catholic Missions — were accused of aiming at wiping out Islam; Ahmad Dahlan, the founder of the Muhammadijah had been right when he warned that, although it would not be possible to expel Islam from this world, it might perhaps be expelled from Indonesia. (2) The only way to improve the relationship between the various religious groups would be an arrangement stipulating that people of one religion might not be made the object of missionary work by others.

Professor Rasjidi's speech in particular became rather sharp. In his introduction he quoted some passages from W. C. Smith's "The Faith of Other Men", criticizing the Christian view of mankind as being divided into two sections, the Christians (who would be saved) and the non-Christians (who would be damned). He then told of two Christian proselytizers who visited him at home and turned out even to be ignorant of Hugh Schofield's "The History of Biblical Literature" and the books by A. Powell Davies and Charles Francis Potter on the significance of

---

[140] This Sudirman is the younger brother of the Sudirman who was the first Chief-of-Staff of the Indonesian army in 1945. He was one of the founders of the *daᶜwa* organization P.T.D.I., mentioned in paragraph 4 of this Chapter.

the Dead Sea Scrolls. Having just returned from Jogjakarta, he wanted to report two cases of irritating missionary activities by Roman Catholics. Firstly, the family of a Communist prisoner had been able to get rice and money if he would sign a "contract" (*surat kontrak*) making him a Roman Catholic. Secondly, the Roman Catholics in Jogja wanted to build a church at a very strategic point; in order to get the land they had offered the owner a price eight times its real worth. He outlined how formerly the Missions had tried to Christianize the Indonesian people. The Dutch government, however, had resisted mission work, in spite of much criticism in Parliament. Finally the government had given in to the reasoning of the Missions that they only wanted to carry out social work in the medical and educational fields. In contrast to W. C. Smith's moderate attitude towards non-Christian religions, Hendrik Kraemer's book "The Christian Message in a non-Christian World" clearly revealed that Christians did have a plan of action to Christianize the world and in particular Indonesia. So in spite of Tambunan's words it appeared that Christians were indeed aiming at "the conquest of the Muslim world". Rasjidi ended his speech by reading out a draft for a "Charter" to be accepted by this Consultation. This Charter would lay down the principle of religious tolerance, stipulating that one religious community would not be allowed to make another religious community the object of its propaganda.

Muh. Natsir also criticized the "old recipe" of Roman Catholic and Protestant Missions to conquer the Muslim world, whereas Islam based its code and ethics on the word of the Qur'ān that "there is no compulsion in religion" (Sura 2 : 256). He appealed to the Christians to realize that Muslims do have their own religion and their own identity. Finally he expressed his optimism with regard to the future, pointing to the developments in the relationship between Protestants and Catholics. After a long religious war, now Tambunan's group and Kasimo's group obviously felt no longer "called" to make Protestants of the Roman Catholics and Roman Catholics of the Protestants. Why could not this development also take place in the relationship between Muslims and Christians?

According to oral information, the discussions unfortunately ended in an unpleasant atmosphere. The meagre result of the Consultation was a *communiqué* stating that a Committee for Inter-Religious Consultation would be set up which would assist the government in solving religious difficulties.

The failure of this Consultation produced fierce reactions in Muslim circles. The whole discussion and all the difficulties between the various religious groups were reduced to this fact: that the Christians, following in the footsteps of the Missions, appeared to be fundamentally intolerant, because they refused to accept the formula that one religious community should not address its propaganda to adherents of another religious community. Christians for their part used to explain that they disagreed with various improper methods of religious propaganda, but on the other hand simply had to be obedient to the Divine call to preach the Gospel to all mankind.

The crucial point is, of course, the question of religious tolerance, its principle and its practice. Apart from apologetic-polemic writings, a great number of publications dealt with this question of tolerance. The following examples may be referred to.

One of the older and very conservative publications was a booklet by M. Arsjad Thalib Lubis on "The Guarantee of Religious Freedom in Islam", dating from 1955 and reprinted in 1961.[141] In fact the author deals with the guarantee of religious freedom within (or under) an Islamic State. Islam divides the world into believers, unbelievers and hypocrites (*mukmin, kafir, munafiq*). Belief cannot be enforced. Therefore within or under Islam there is no compulsion in religion as far as non-Muslims are concerned (Sura 2 : 256). Further, the author explains the precepts of Islamic law concerning the various groups of non-Muslims. These groups are, (1) the *Zimmi,* who enjoy protection and freedom of worship in return for paying poll-tax (*djizja*) instead of the *zakāt* contributed by Muslims; (2) *Mu'ahad,* people with whom the Muslim government has made an alliance; (3) *Muamman,* who enjoy security while temporarily living in a Muslim state, e.g. for trade purposes, and (4) *Harbi,* enemies who may or must be combatted. Special attention is paid to precepts concerning one's attitude towards non-Muslim parents and the marriage of Muslim men to non-Muslim women. (Marriages between Muslim women and non-Muslim men could not be permitted, because according to Luke 14 : 26 a Christian husband had to hate his father and mother, wife and children, brothers and sisters). The author repeats the precepts concerning a Holy War for self-defense and the defense of religious freedom (= the freedom of Islam), which he had already explained in a publication mentioned

---

[141] M. Arsjad Thalib Lubis, *Risalat Djaminan Kemerdekaan Beragama Dalam Islam,* Medan 1955[1], 1961[2].

above (Chapter I, par. 8). He concludes, quite abruptly: so it is clear that freedom of religion is indeed guaranteed in Islam.

A leaflet by H. Aboebakar Atjeh on "Islam and Freedom of Religion" appears to be more moderate and broadminded.[142] The author proceeds from Sura 49 : 13, interpreting this verse as follows: "Mankind on earth is created consisting of various groups (*bergolong-golongan*) in order that they may know one another". Examples taken from history can prove that if anywhere it was in Muslim countries that "neutrality towards religion" and "freedom of thought" were upheld. Referring to Sura 22 : 40 the author concludes: "If freedom of religion for everyone is not realized, the result will be that churches, pagodas and mosques, where people invoke the Name of God, will be destroyed".

Part of this leaflet can again be found in a pamphlet by the same author entitled "The Tolerance of the Prophet and His Companions".[143] According to the preface, this pamphlet was handed out to *muballigh*s and Muslim youth who felt called to exterminate the atheistic "Gestapu/ P.K.I.". Basing himself on illustrations from the Tradition and the history of Islam, the author arrives at the following conclusions. (1) The Prophet was tolerant towards Muslims as far as their performance of religious duties was concerned, and he respected adherents of other religions. (2) The Caliphs were sometimes very liberal in granting religious freedom to people living in new areas of Islam. (3) Later on freedom of religion was often maintained in order to promote scholarship and development of the country. (4) The Prophet liked people to forgive and respect one another, and this attitude afterwards produced a policy which did not emphasize the importance of one's own tribe, but stressed the ideals of Islam, i.e. equality, fraternity and justice. (5) As a matter of course, we cannot advocate a kind of tolerance which would be detrimental to Islam, but nevertheless we can and must show respect for the religious convictions of others.

M. Junan Nasution has written several articles on religious tolerance in the Islamic magazine *Pandji Masjarakat*.[144] The author defines the tolerance of Islam as a "mental attitude" which must result in moderate behaviour toward others. In this way it will be possible to arrive at

---

[142] H. Aboebakar Atjeh, *Islam dan Kemerdekaan Beragama*, Tjirebon, no date.
[143] H. Aboebakar Atjeh, *Toleransi Nabi Muhammad dan Sahabat-Sahabatnja*, Tjirebon/Djakarta 1959¹, 1966².
[144] *Pandji Masjarakat*, nos. 18 and 19, September-October 1967. The latter contains a heated editorial (by HAMKA?) on the attempts to Christianize Indonesia within 20-50 years.

harmonious contact with others, (in English) "a liberality towards the opinions of others, patience with others". As basic principles of tolerance, he refers to Sura 2 : 256; 10 : 99; 29 : 46; 3 : 64; 60 : 8-9 and 16 : 125. In addition to the tolerance of Islam, the Indonesian people are aware of their common principle of Belief in the One and Only God (*Ketuhanan Jang Maha Esa*) and the other principles of the Pantjasila. This condition provides a fertile soil for the seed of tolerance.

In 1967 the influential Kasman Singodimedjo, last chairman of the Masjumi, published his "Thoughts from Prison", dating from the years before 1966, when he was imprisoned under the Soekarno regime.[145] His opinions on the first principle of the Pantjasila are as follows. "This Belief in the One and Only God may certainly not be interpreted as freedom with regard to religion (*kebebasan beragama*) ... The word of God in the Qur'ān, *Al-Baqarah* [Sura 2] verse 256 — *lā ikrāha fī 'd-dīn*, there is no compulsion in religion — is not aimed at a Muslim who has already entered Islam, but is intended to protect those who do not have a religion or adhere to a wrong religion. Those people will not be forced to enter Islam, but will be left free ... Muslims, however, who have already entered Islam, are no longer free, that is to say, they do no longer have the freedom to be religious or not, and are not allowed to apostatize (*murtad*), i.e. leave Islam. Muslims who have entered Islam are obliged to practise their Muslim belief. If they become apostates, God will punish them in the world to come with a severe judgement" (Sura 2 : 217; 5 : 54; 4 : 89). Why does Islam object to the Communist and Marxist idea of freedom with regard to religion? The reason is that those people tend to interpret such freedom as including the freedom to be non-religious or even anti-religious. Sura 2 : 256, however, has to be interpreted as follows: "This command from God means that Muslims may not force others to enter Islam. But this command also means that non-Muslims may not force Muslims to apostatize or leave Islam, that is to say, neither by means of subtle pressure nor in a crude way, for example by building a church, monastery, synagogue or temple in areas which are inhabited predominantly by Muslims. That would not be in accordance with the Pantjasila either. The Pantjasila may not be misused, may not be perverted, may not be played around with" (an Indonesian pun: *Pantjasila... tidak boleh dipentjaksilatkan*).

---

[145] Kasman Singodimedjo, *Renungan dari Tahanan*, Djakarta 1967; cf. pp. 67-68.

The summary of Kasman's pamphlet brings us back once more to the tense atmosphere after the Inter-Religious Consultation of November 30th, 1967. On the one hand, the failure of this Consultation seemed to have increased tensions. Once again a great quantity of polemic publications began to appear, for instance pamphlets by Arsjad Thalib Lubis, Abujamin Roham, Hazairin and Rasjidi.[146] It is not necessary to summarize the contents of these works as well. Generally speaking they all deal with the usual polemic themes. One new tendency is perhaps that recent publications seem to concentrate their attacks on the Christian doctrine of the Trinity. "Attempts to win Muslims over to Christianity" are now frequently typified as "attempts to win Muslims over from belief in God to belief in the Trinity".

On the other hand, however, it is worth calling attention to an official letter from the Ministry of Religion, headed "Explanation concerning the Policy and Ideology of the Government with regard to the Question of Religion and Religious Life in Indonesia", dated May 11th, 1968.[147] This letter referred to the President's speech of August 16th, 1967, in which the President clearly stated that there is no question of a majority or a minority with regard to religion. This means, according to the Ministry of Religion, that a larger religious community may not suppress a smaller community or vice versa. For the government all religious groups in Indonesia have equal freedom for worship and for carrying out their activities. All organizations for *da^{c}wa*/mission which have obtained legal recognition are allowed to exist and to continue their activities, on the understanding that they take due note of this Explanation and other regulations made by the government.

---

[146] Arsjad Thalib Lubis, *Keesaan TUHAN menurut adjaran Kristen dan Islam*, Djakarta 1968; Abujamin Roham, *Agama² Kristen dan Islam serta Perbandingannja*, Djakarta 1968; Hazairin, *Isa Almasih dan Ruh*, Djakarta 1969; H. M. Rasjidi, *Islam di Indonesia Dizaman Modern*, Djakarta 1968. The lastmentioned pamphlet shows a kind of "rehabilitation" of Snouck Hurgronje, who acknowledged that Indonesia was a Muslim country. So after all Snouck was a great man, the opposite to Kraemer who wanted to teach the Churches how to Christianize Muslims and moreover dared to compare Islam with national-socialism, the pseudo-religion of Nazi Germany (cf. Kraemer, *The Christian Message*, p. 353). The same author published a pamphlet entitled *Mengapa aku tetap memeluk Agama Islam*, Djakarta 1968, in which he repeated many of his opinions expressed in the Inter-Religious Consultation, and once again stressed the difference between Kraemer and W. C. Smith; the latter wants to be considered a Christian but not a missionary like Kraemer.

[147] *Pendjelasan Sekitar Politik dan Idiologi Pemerintah Mengenai Soal Agama dan Keagamaan di Indonesia* (unpublished stencil).

Finally President Soeharto himself may be quoted here once again. In an address given on May 29th, 1969, at the celebration of the Prophet's Birth, he used some decisive words which as far as I know had never before openly been used by an Indonesian government or its representatives. Emphasizing that the spread of a religion may not be accompanied by intimidation, the President said: "Just because religion is based on one's personal conviction and because the freedom of religion is a fundamental human right, one may not be obstructed by compulsion from outside either in choosing the religion one wants to follow or in changing one's religion".[148] The last words (in Indonesian *berpindah agama*) have always been the crucial expression in debates on the meaning of tolerance.

Some questions emerging from the concluding chapter of this book are the following. In which way are the relations between the various confessional/political groups going to develop? Who will take the initiative to arrive at a reconciliation between the various communities and groups? Will the present Indonesian government, led by President Soeharto, succeed in making social and economic development the new vehicle for the unity which Indonesia so badly needs?

Important suggestions, I believe, were made by an Indonesian informant, who summarized the conditions for successful development as follows: the Nationalists (especially those united in the P.N.I.) will have to learn to think along social lines and be aware of the necessity for social changes; the military may no longer think only in terms of "law and order", but must learn to think along political lines, so that democratic political life can develop anew; the religious groups will have to learn to think along national lines instead of being only concerned with strengthening their own positions.

With regard to the various religious groups, especially Muslims and Christians, I believe that there are more important things than winning or losing a couple of hundred thousand followers, resulting in a concentration of energy on questions of the "defense" or the "spread" of a religion. Discussions on principles of "tolerance" and the "call to mission" may be of theoretical importance, but are sometimes inopportune. Even co-operation between religious communities for the building of mosques and churches will not be of primary importance,

---

[148] *Sinar Harapan,* a (Christian) Djakarta daily newspaper, May 30th, 1969, p. 1.

and neither will co-operation in combatting Communism in a negative way, by simply rejecting its principles and aims.

In my opinion the message of the various religions becomes empty and hollow if their adherents do not involve themselves in the struggle for a just society, both nationally and internationally. The social problems of Indonesia cannot be solved by worship and preaching, supplemented with the *zakāt* of Muslims and philanthropy of Christians. These problems must be grappled with by tackling socio-economic structures in such a way that the profits of development do not only fall into the hands of the rich and powerful, but first and foremost benefit the poor and weak. I believe that Muslims and Christians should join in just this struggle for justice.

So I do not advocate exclusive co-operation between "religious people" for the sake of religion. Rather than "religion" nowadays the criterion for co-operation should be a progressive attitude towards socio-economic problems. But it would be a bad thing if "religious people" should stand aloof, while others once again took the initiative for socio-economic development. Therefore I believe that Muslims and Christians should stand in the forefront together, co-operating with all those who want to fight for a just society, by carrying out a progressive programme of development and combatting all forms of corruption and injury.

Is not this fight the order of the day for Muslims as well as for Christians? Muslims are aware of the ideal of *ḥasana fī 'd-dunyā* ("good in this world") in a *balda ṭayyiba,* a land that is good to live in (Sura 34 : 15). Christians hold that God does not want this world to become a chaos but to become and remain inhabitable for mankind (Isaiah 45 : 18). Let them together prove their belief through their works (James 2 : 18).

APPENDIX I

PIAGAM DJAKARTA [1]

Bahwa sesungguhnja kemerdékaan itu jalah hak segala bangsa, dan oléh sebab itu maka pendjadjahan diatas dunia harus dihapuskan, karena tidak sesuai dengan peri-kemanusiaan dan peri-keadilan.

Dan perdjuangan pergerakan kemerdékaan Indonésia telah sampai-(lah) kepada saat jang berbahagia dengan selamat-sentausa mengantarkan rakjat Indonésia kedepan pintu gerbang Negara Indonésia jang merdéka, bersatu, berdaulat, adil dan makmur.

Atas berkat Rahmat Allah Jang Maha Kuasa, dan dengan didorongkan oléh keinginan luhur, supaja berkehidupan kebangsaan jang bébas, maka rakjat Indonésia menjatakan dengan ini kemerdékaannja.

Kemudian dari pada itu untuk membentuk suatu Pemerintah Negara Indonésia Merdéka jang melindungi segenap bangsa Indonésia dan seluruh tumpah-darah Indonésia, dan untuk memadjukan kesedjahteraan umum, mentjerdaskan kehidupan bangsa, dan ikut melaksanakan ketertiban dunia jang berdasarkan kemerdékaan, perdamaian abadi dan keadilan sosial, maka disusunlah kemerdékaan kebangsaan Indonésia itu dalam suatu hukum dasar Negara Indonésia jang terbentuk dalam suatu susunan negara Republik Indonésia, jang berkedaulatan rakjat, dengan berdasar kepada: ke-Tuhanan, dengan kewadjiban mendjalankan sjari'at Islam bagi pemeluk-pemeluknja, menurut dasar kemanusiaan jang adil dan beradab, persatuan Indonésia, dan kerakjatan jang dipimpin oléh hikmat kebidjaksanaan dalam permusjawaratan perwakilan serta dengan mewudjudkan suatu keadilan sosial bagi seluruh rakjat Indonésia.

Djakarta, 22-6-2605.

                                    Soekarno
                                    Mohammad Hatta
                                    A. A. Maramis
                                    Abikusno Tjokrosujoso
                                    Abdulkahar Muzakkir
                                    H. A. Salim
                                    Achmad Subardjo
                                    Wachid Hasjim
                                    Muhammad Yamin

---

[1] The readings of the Charter as given in many publications show a number of small variants, in particular in the punctuation and the use of capitals. The form I give is based on Yamin, *Naskah*, I, p. 154, which may be closest to the original version, except for the use of "u" instead of a probable "oe". Compare also Yamin, *Naskah*, I, p. 401; Abikusno Tjokrosujoso, *Ummat Islam*, p. 7; Sidjabat, *Religious Tolerance*, p. 195.

APPENDIX II

BISMILLAHIRRAHMANIRRAHIM

PEMERINTAH NEGARA ISLAM INDONESIA

NOTA RAHASIA

Barang disampaikan Allah kiranja kepada
jang terhormat:
SAUDARA Ir. SOEKARNO
PRESIDEN REPUBLIK INDONESIA,
jang bersemajam di
DJAKARTA.

Assalamu'alaikum w.w.,

1. Alhamdu li-Llah!
   Allahumma! Iyaka na'budu, wa iyaka nasta'in,
     ihdinassirathal-mustaqim!
   Bismillahi, tawakkalna 'ala-Llah!
   Lahaula wala quwwata, illa bi-Llah! [1]

2. Dengan seputjuk surat jang berwudjudkan Nota-Rahasia ini, maka terkandunglah didalamnja keinginan Kami, jang — Insja Allah — tumbuh daripada hati jang sutji dan niat jang ichlas dengan penuh rasa pertanggungan-djawab atas nasibnja bangsa Indonesia pada umumnja dan Ummat Islam Bangsa Indonesia pada chususnja, serta atas nasibnja Negara Indonesia, dimasa jang mendatang.

3. Lebih dulu baiklah kiranja Kami njatakan disini, bahwa segala peristiwa jang terdjadi diseluruh Indonesia dan sekitarnja, militer dan politis, nasional maupun internasional, terutama jang langsung mengenai Bangsa Indonesia dan Ummat Islam Bangsa Indonesia, senantiasa Kami ikuti dengan teliti dan seksama. Maka bolehlah agaknja Nota-Rahasia ini dianggap sebagai hasil dan natidjah daripada pendjeladjahan dan analyse serta synthese daripadanja.

4. Mudah²an segala sesuatu jang hendak Kami rawaikan [= uraikan?] dibawah ini disertai dengan Hidajatu-Llah dan Hidajatut taufiq

---

[1] The letter is opened with the *basmala*-formula: "In the Name of God, the Beneficent, the Merciful". After the greeting, "Peace be with you and God's mercy and His blessings be upon you", the Arabic phrases following in the first point are:
Praise be to God!
O God, Thee we worship and Thee we ask for help,
   Guide us in the straight path! (Sura 1 : 5-6).
In the Name of God; we put trust in God (Sura 7 : 89; 10 : 85).
There is no power and no strength save in God.

jang sempurna, sehingga bolehlah kiranja mendjadi obor dan pelita bagi tiap² pemimpin Negara jang bertanggung-djawab. Insja Allah. Amin.

Kemudian, chusus kepada Saudara, sebagai Kepala Negara Republik Indonesia, jang dipertjajakan orang memikul pertanggungandjawab jang amat besar atas hantjur dan luhurnja Negara dan Bangsa Indonesia, maka Kami ingin sekali menjatakan persilahan: Sudi apalah kiranja Saudara suka memperhatikan isi dan maksud Nota-Rahasia ini, dengan sepertinja.

5. Dalam Nota-Rahasia ini Kami tjukupkan dengan menindjau beberapa peristiwa politik dan militer, pada masa jang achir² ini, ialah natidjah atau resultante daripada segala kedjadian (proces) dan keadaan (toestand), dikala jang telah lampau.

6. Sjahdan, maka masuknja Republik Indonesia mendjadi anggauta P.B.B. (Perserikatan Bangsa-Bangsa), seperti djuga tiap² langkah dan tindakan politik jang lainnja, pastilah membawa hasil "untung" dan "rugi", manfaat dan mudlorotnja [= mudaratnja].

7. Djika diperhitungkan benar² dan sedalam-dalamnja, terutama djika mengingat kedudukan Republik Indonesia sebagai negara muda, maka masuk dan diterimanja Republik Indonesia sebagai anggauta P.B.B. itu, nistjajalah menimbulkan kerugian jang amat besar sekali, bagi Negara dan Bangsa serta Ummat, djika dibandingkan dengan keuntungan jang ta' seberapa besarnja dan bersifat sementara itu. Lebih², djika diingati akan letaknja Indonesia di-tengah² negara² besar, jang kini lagi 'asjik menjalakan api-peperangan, jang mem-bakar² dibenua Asia.
Demikianlah pendapat daripada umumnja politici golongan "moderate".

8. Satu-dua resiko "ke-anggauta-an P.B.B." diwaktu ini, ialah:
   a. Bahwa Republik Indonesia, mau atau tidak mau, sengadja atau tidak sengadja, akan disorong kesatu arah dan djurusan jang tertentu, jang membawa dia kepada satu tingkatan: Memilih salah satu diantara dua Blok, jang lagi bertentangan.
   b. Kiranja tidak djauh daripada kenjataan (realiteit) dalam waktu jang dekat, djika orang meramalkan, bahwa Republik Indonesia akan masuk dalam Blok Amerika.
   c. Djika terdjadi jang demikian, maka "neutraliteitspolitiek" jang tempo hari dilahirkan oleh jang terhormat Saudara Drs. Mohd. Hatta, sebagai Perdana Menteri, dalam menegaskan haluan politik Pemerintah terhadap Luar Negeri, *lenjaplah,* laksana debu ditiup angin. Dan lebih landjut, Republik Indonesia akan mendjadi satu Negara jang *anti-Blok-Rusia,* atau anti Komunis. Kami jakin, bahwa semuanja itu telah masuk perhitungan Pemerintah Republik Indonesia, sebelum melakukan langkah jang "sportief" itu.

9. Berkenaan dengan jang tersebut dalam angka 8 diatas, maka Kami atas nama Pemerintah Negara Islam Indonesia menjatakan: Selamat! Terima Kasih! Dan, Alhamdu li-Llah!
Karena dengan terbukanja "topeng" haluan politik Republik Indonesia jang sesungguhnja itu, *dari politik "neutral" beralih mendjadi politik "anti-Komunis"*, maka Negara Islam Indonesia merasa mempunjai kawan jang sedjalan, dalam melaksanakan usaha membasmi dan mengenjahkan lawan jang sama (gemeenschappelijke vijand), ialah: kaum Komunis.

10. Lebih djauh, Kami pertjaja dan jakin, bahwa Pemerintah Republik Indonesia telah lebih mengetahui akan sarang² dan gerak-gerik kaum Komunis Indonesia didalam tiap² lapangan dan lapisan masjarakat Indonesia, djuga didalam tubuh Pemerintah Republik Indonesia dan alat² kekuasaannja sendiri, jang makin hari makin bertambah berbahaja bagi Negara Republik Indonesia.
Agaknja ta' perlu lagi kami tundjukkan akan perbuatan² mereka itu, dalam usahanja meruntuhkan negara, baik dalam lapangan politik dan militer maupun dalam lapangan ekonomi, keuangan, dll-nja, legaal dan illegaal.

11. Sebagai kawan sedjalan, semaksud dan setudjuan didalam menghadapi bahaja-Komunisme di Indonesia itu, maka baik djuga agaknja, bila disini kami njatakan dengan terus-terang dan dengan hati jang terbuka, kepada Saudara, sebagai Kepala Negara Republik Indonesia, kalau² — dengan tolong dan kurnia Allah pula — akan mendjadi sebab terhindarnja Negara dan Bangsa Indonesia daripada bahaja keruntuhan dan kedjatuhannja, dimasa jang akan datang.
Pertimbangan dan andjuran dari pihak kami, ialah:
   a. Tiada satu djalan lain, jang menudju kearah "Keselamatan Negara dan Bangsa Indonesia", melainkan: *"Djika Pemerintah Republik Indonesia mulai sekarang djuga, dengan tjepat dan tepat, membasmi Komunisme, dalam tiap² lapangan, terutama sekali jang melekat didalam tubuh Pemerintah Republik Indonesia dan alat² kekuasaannja, dengan wudjud dan sifat apa dan manapun djuga".*
   Lebih tjepat, lebih baik!
   b. Bilamana Republik Indonesia segan² dan terlambat dalam melakukan tindakan dan usaha membasmi "bahaja" jang selalu mengantjam-antjam itu, maka terbukalah kemungkinan jang amat besar sekali, bahwa Republik Indonesia dalam waktu jang singkat akan djatuh sebagai Negara, seperti nasibnja Tiongkok ditahun-tahun jang achir² ini, setelah kaum "merah" dapat mengusir kaum "Nasionalis", dari pusat tanah-tumpah-darahnja.
   c. Terutama djika kelambatan melakukan tindakan tersebut memandjang hingga sampai kepada meletusnja Perang Dunia ke III, maka sepandjang perhitungan sjari'at [?], nistjajalah

Republik Indonesia akan menemui djalan buntu dan nasib malang, jang sedikitnja senisbat dengan nasib Korea pada dewasa ini. Bahkan, mungkin sekali lebih djelek dan lebih buruk daripada itu.
Oleh sebab itu, maka sekali lagi Kami pertimbangkan dan serukan kepada Saudara:
"Hendaknja disegerakanlah, melakukan tindakan jang tjepat dan tepat atas bahaja nasional dan internasional tersebut, jang pada hemat kami, tindakan jang serupa itu adalah salah satu tugas dan wadjib-mutlak bagi Pemerintah Republik Indonesia, untuk menghindarkan Negara dan Bangsa Indonesia daripada antjaman marabahaja jang amat dahsjat itu!"
Adapun tentang tjara, alasan dan lakunja, maka Kami pertjaja dengan sepenuh-penuhnja atas kebidjaksanaan Pemerintah Republik Indonesia dalam hal ini.

12. Dalam pada itu, baik djuga Kami njatakan disini akan *Sikap dan Pendirian Pemerintah Negara Islam Indonesia terhadap bahaja Komunisme,* bahwa sedjak mula berdirinja — 7 Agustus 1949 — telah ditetapkan:
"*Pemerintah Negara Islam Indonesia dengan seluruh Ummat Islam Bangsa Indonesia beserta segenap alat kekuasaannja sudah, lagi dan akan terus-menerus melakukan wadjib sutjinja:
Membasmi bahaja-Negara, bahaja-Agama Allah (Islam) dan bahaja-Ummat itu, hingga sampai kepada akar^2 dan dasar^{2}nja*".
Karena dalam pandangan Islam, Komunisme itu adalah *musuh ideologi* jang amat besar sekali.

13. Lebih djauh lagi, tentulah Saudara telah mengetahui pula, bahwa "*tiada lagi ideologi melainkan hanja "Islamisme" sadjalah jang sanggup dan kuasa membendung aliran Komunisme dan menghantjur-musnakannja*".
Insja Allah.
Sedang sementara itu, bolehlah kami njatakan, dengan tiada samar^2 lagi, bahwa *Nasionalisme* jang mendjadi sendi dan dasar serta haluan Negara Republik Indonesia, *bukanlah satu ideologi* sematjam Islamisme atau Komunisme. Melainkan ia hanjalah merupakan satu tingkatan "kasih sajangnja" sesuatu bangsa kepada tanah kelahiran dan dirinja.
Dengan analyse ringkas seperti jang tertulis diatas, njatalah sudah, bahwa didalam pertentangan antara Nasionalisme dan Komunisme, *didalam masa jang lama* (longterm), terutama djika Komunisme dibiarkan mendjadi *agressor,* maka amat boleh djadi sekali Nasionalisme akan terpaksa menjerah kalah, atau patah dan terpelanting serta terpentjar dalam pertentangan tersebut.
Sebagai tjontoh dan bukti jang njata daripada nasibnja negara^2 jang berdasarkan Nasionalisme dalam "pertentangan ideologi", hendaklah Saudara suka memeriksai lembaran riwajat Eropah-

Timur dan Asia-Timur, setelah Perang Dunia ke II, teristimewa nasibnja Tiongkok Nasional jang amat tragis itu.

Djika perhitungan Saudara, dalam hal ini, tidak sesuai dengan perhitungan kami, sudi apalah kiranja suka memperma'afkan banjak-banjak!

14. Mengingat segala apa jang Kami uraikan diatas itu, maka njatalah sudah, bahwa:

   a. *Nasionalisme tidak akan mampu* dan *tidak pula kuasa* membendung derasnja arus Komunisme, karena Nasionalisme tidak dapat mengikat djiwa rakjat Indonesia, jang sebagian terbesar memeluk Agama Islam dan tidak pula mendjadi ikatan-djiwa antara Pemerintah Indonesia dan Rakjat Indonesia;

   b. Karenanja, *Negara Republik Indonesia tidak akan dapat menghindarkan dirinja* daripada mara-bahaja jang amat besar itu, jang langsung akan mengakibatkan runtuh-djatuhnja Negara Indonesia, sebagai Negara Nasional; dan

   c. Hanja *Islamisme* sadjalah, sebagai *ideologi* dan *stelsel dunia* (worldstelsel) [= socio-political system?], jang *sanggup mengatasi* kesulitan, jang boleh timbul karena datangnja bahaja Merah itu.

   Berhubung dengan itu, maka Kami berpendapat, bahwa obat jang paling mudjarrab jang akan mendjadi sebab sembuhnja Negara Indonesia dan Bangsa Indonesia daripada penjakit, jang berwudjudkan seribu satu kesulitan dalam tiap² lapangan-usaha itu, tidak lain, hanjalah:

   "*Djika Islamisme didjadikan sendi dasar daripada Pemerintah dan Negara Indonesia!*"

   Atau dengan kata² lain:

   "*Satu²nja Djalan-Selamat bagi Indonesia dan Bangsa Indonesia, ialah*:

   Djika Negara Indonesia atau Republik Indonesia dalam waktu jang sesingkat-singkatnja beralih sifat dan wudjudnja, dari "Nasional" kepada "Islam", mendjadi NEGARA ISLAM INDONESIA".

   Dengan ini Kami ingin sekali menjatakan persilahan kepada Saudara, sebagai Kepala Negara Republik Indonesia, sudi apalah kiranja Saudara suka mempertimbangkan baik² dan se-dalam-dalamnja akan pendapat Kami ini.

   Sebelum dan sesudahnja, atas perhatian Saudara itu, Kami menghaturkan diperbanjak-banjak terima kasih, dan Alhamdu li-Llah.

15. Selain daripada itu, tidak pula boleh dilupakan akan peristiwa² jang terdjadi disekitar K.M.B. [= Konferensi Medja Bundar] atau/ dan natidjah jang timbul daripadanja, jang semuanja itu makin hari makin mendekati kepada puntjak keruntjingan dan kegentingannja, jang achir-kemudiannja — lambat atau tjepat — akan

mengakibatkan "pertentangan antara Republik Indonesia dan Belanda".
Kini teranglah sudah, bahwa *K.M.B.* dengan segala sebab jang menimbulkannja dan segala akibat jang timbul daripadanja, tidaklah sekali-kali mendjadi obat jang dapat menjembuhkan Bangsa Indonesia daripada serangan penjakit *"Kolonialisme Belanda".*
Maka pada achir[2] ini, tampaklah dengan tegas dan njata, akan timbulnja kembali penjakit "Kolonialisme" itu.
Oleh sebab itu, maka *Uni Indonesia-Belanda* jang tadinja diharapkan akan mendjadi tali persahabatan antara kedua Negara itu, pada achir-kemudiannja, beralih sifat dan tjoraknja, mendjadilah *lapang pertikaian.*
Kiranja Saudara tidak menaksir rendah (onderschatten) dan terlalu "optimistis" tentang hal ini, dan baiklah agaknja, djika mulai sekarang djuga Pemerintah Republik Indonesia "bersedia pajung, sebelum hudjan".

16. Sekianlah hal[2] jang kini perlu kami njatakan kepada Saudara, sebagai Kepala Negara Republik Indonesia, jang bertanggungdjawab berat dan besar atas nasibnja Negara dan Bangsa, dimasa jang akan datang.
Sekali lagi! Sudi apalah kiranja Saudara suka menaruh perhatian, dimana perlu dan seberapa perlunja.

17. Semoga Allah selalu berkenan mentjurahkan Hidajat dan Taufiq-Nja atas kita, Ummat Islam Bangsa Indonesia, dan berkenan pulalah kiranja Ia menuntunnja kearah Bahagia-Sentausa, dunia dan achirat. Amin.

Inna fatahna laka fathan mubina... Insja Allah. Amin.
Bismillahi........... Allahu Akbar!!! [2]

Wassalam,
PEMERINTAH NEGARA ISLAM INDONESIA
IMAM:
S. M. KARTOSOEWIRJO

Mardhotillah, 22 Oktober 1950/10 Muharram 1370.[3]

Tembusan Nota-Rahasia ini
disampaikan kepada jang terhormat
Saudara M. Natsir, Perdana Menteri
Republik Indonesia.

---

[2] The letter is closed with a quotation from Sura 48 : 1, "We have given thee [= Muhammad] a manifest victory", followed by the formulas "If it be God's will. Amen. In the Name of God... God is great".

[3] The secret place from which the letter was sent is called "Mardhotillah", which is probably intended to be rendered "The place of God's *riḍā'* (favour)" or, perhaps more concretely, "The ideal Islamic State".

APPENDIX III

BISMILLAHIRRAHMANIRRAHIM

PEMERINTAH
NEGARA ISLAM INDONESIA

Nota Rahasia Kedua

Barang disampaikan Allah kiranja kepada jang terhormat:
SAUDARA Ir. SOEKARNO
Presiden Republik Indonesia,
jang bersemajam di
DJAKARTA.

Assalamu'alaikum w.w.,

1. Alhamdu li-Llah!
Allahumma! Iyaka na'budu, wa iyaka nasta'in, ihdinassirathal-mustaqim!
Bismillahi, tawakkalna 'ala-Llah!
Lahaula wala quwwata, illa bi-Llah! [1]

2. Sjahdan, maka baiklah kiranja terlebih dulu Kami njatakan kepada Saudara, bahwa telah genap hampir 4 bulan jang lalu sudahlah Kami lajangkan sebuah Nota Rahasia (jang pertama) kepada Saudara, nota mana bertarich "Mardhotillah, 22 Oktober 1950/ 10 Muharram 1370". Kiranja sementara ini, Saudara telah menerimanja dengan sempurna, serta menaruh perhatian atasnja, seberapa perlu dan dimana perlunja. Hanja bagi kepentingan Negara, Bangsa dan Agama Allah, djuga adanja. Atas perhatian Saudara jang seksama dalam hal[2] jang Kami tuliskan dalam Nota tersebut, maka sebelum dan sesudahnja Kami njatakan diperbanjak-banjak terima kasih dan Alhamdulillah!
Semoga Allah berkenan menimbulkan manfaat dan maslahat daripadanja, bagi Republik Indonesia maupun bagi Negara Islam Indonesia!
Insja Allah.
Amin.

3. Selain daripada itu, perlu djuga agaknja Kami njatakan disini, bahwa Nota Rahasia Kedua ini mengandung maksud, untuk:
   a. Memberi pendjelasan dalam beberapa hal, atas Nota Rahasia jang pertama; dan

---

[1] Cf. Appendix II, note 1.

b. Menambah sesuatu jang dianggap perlu, jang harus diperhatikan oleh tiap[2] Pimpinan Negara, teristimewa sekali oleh Kepala Negara jang bertanggung-djawab, menghadapi nasibnja Negara dan Bangsa, dimasa jang mendatang, mengarungi Lautan Merah, menghadapi Perang Brata Juda Djaja Binangun dan Revolusi Dunia, dimasa jang — Insja Allah — tidak djauh lagi.[2]

4. Bila didalam Nota Rahasia Kedua ini Kami njatakan terus terang segala sesuatu kepada Saudara, tiada lain maksud kami, melainkan hanjalah untuk kepentingan Negara dan Bangsa Indonesia belaka, jang langsung atau tidak langsung mengenai nasibnja Republik Indonesia dan Negara Islam Indonesia, mulai sekarang kedepan. Kiranja Saudara dalam hal ini sependapat dengan Kami.

5. Sebaliknja, djika didalam sual-sual tersebut ada selisih faham dan pendapat antara Saudara dan Kami, sudi apalah kiranja Saudara suka memperma'afkan banjak-banjak!
Berhubung dengan pergolakan internasional, baiklah kiranja, djika Kami njatakan sebagai jang berikut:
    a. Tentang akan terdjadinja Perang Dunia Ketiga, agaknja tidak lagi patut dipersualkan.
    b. Didalam Perang Dunia tersebut tidak mungkin Republik Indonesia akan tetap memegang haluan "Bebas" (neutral) jang mendjadi pendiriannja, baik lambat maupun tjepat.
    c. Didalam memilih Blok, dengan sukarela atau dengan terpaksa, maka amat besar sekali kemungkinan bahwa R.I. akan masuk Blok Amerika, sedang pada waktu ini politik Luar-Negeri R.I. telah menundjukkan tjondongnja kearah dan djurusan itu.
    d. Djika terdjadi jang demikian, maka segala langkah dan tindakan tentulah ditudjukan kesatu arah, ja'ni: keluar (internasional), atau/dan mengenai urusan luar. Dalam pada itu, usaha dan tindakan kedalam amat kekurangan tenaga, waktu dan sjarat (miniem).
    e. Letaknja Indonesia ditengah-tengah rantai-pertahanan Amerika di Pasifik, membawa dia kesatu arah — mau ataupun tidak mau —, terseret dalam gelanggang peperangan. Bahkan praktis Indonesia akan masuk salah satu rantai didalam "garis depan".
    f. Kiranja semuanja itu telah Saudara perhitungkan masak[2], terlebih dulu.

---

[2] The writer warns against the imminent struggle to overcome the Communists (here indicated as "Lautan Merah"?) and compares this war to the great war of the *Bhāratas*, "Perang Brata Juda Djaja Binangun", found in the Mahābhārata and in Javanese literature and *wajang*.

6. Didalam menindjau dan meneliti situasi interinsuler, baiklah Kami harapkan perhatian Saudara atas:
   a. Persiapan kaum Komunis, dalam semua lapangan, untuk melakukan perampasan kekuasaan, "coup d'etat", politis dan militer. Kiranja Saudara telah lebih mengetahui tentang hal ini dan memperhitungkan langkah dan tindakan, bagi mendjaga dan memelihara kedaulatan Negara.
   b. Persiapan pihak jang lainnja, ideologis atau tidak, didalam lapangan politik dan militer, untuk mentjapaikan maksudnja.
   c. Akibat daripada K.M.B., Konferensi Irian, dan lain² sual kenegaraan (staatkundige vraagstukken) dan ketentaraan, jang kini masih merupakan sual² jang harus penting dan kurang mendapat perhatian, maka pada saat meletusnja Perang Dunia Ketiga itu, sepandjang hitungan, akan menimbulkan bahaja jang amat besar sekali, jang natidjahnja akan merugikan kepada negara.
   d. Keadaan alat-alat negara dan pesawat-pesawat negara djauh daripada apable [= capable?], untuk menghadapi segala kemungkinan, karena:
      (1) Didalamnja telah penuh dengan benih² dan 'anasir² serta aliran "anti-negara" (anti-R.I.), terutama sekali jang merupakan: Komunisme.
      (2) Meradjalelanja kerusakan achlak dan budi pekerti, dan sepnja [= resapnja?] kesadaran bernegara, sehingga membawa akibat korrupsi, tidak boleh dipertjaja, sabotage — dengan sengadja atau tidak —, menentang usaha Pemerintah, melakukan tindakan dan perbuatan sehingga rakjat dan masjarakat anti kepada pemerintah, dan lain² sebagainja.
      Kiranja tentang hal ini, Kami tidak perlu menundjukkan tjontoh² jang njata.
   e. Oleh sebab itu, maka disaat jang kritik nanti, Kami chawatirkan, bahwa Republik Indonesia akan mengalami nasib jang tragis, seperti jang telah Kami gambarkan dalam Nota Rahasia terdahulu (pertama).
      (1) Djika terdjadi jang demikian, bukanlah negara lain jang akan menjerang dan membunuh Indonesia, melainkan alat² dan pesawat² R.I. sendiri-lah jang akan menjerang dan membunuh R.I., bagi kepentingan dan keperluan sesuatu ideologi, ialah: Komunisme.
      (2) Djika R.I. "bunuh diri", karena "sendjata makan tuan", maka pergolakan politik dan militer serta huru-hara di Indonesia tidaklah akan berhenti sampai dibatas itu. Karena proces ini hanja merupakan pangkal dan bukan udjung daripada revolusi dunia didaerah Indonesia, nanti. Lebih djauh, dengan hantjur-leburnja R.I. sebagai negara,

maka Nasionalisme Indonesia akan mengalami perpetjahan jang hebat; sebagian mungkin beralih tempat, masuk golongan Komunis, dan jang sebagian lagi akan menggabungkan diri dengan golongan Islam.

(3) Sudah boleh dikira-kirakan dan dibajangkan terlebih dahulu, betapakah gerangan kelak sikap, langkah dan pendirian Ummat Islam, jang hingga kini masih mempunjai sikap Nasional-Islamistis-parlementer itu. Karena tusukan dan tekanan kaum Komunis — dengan tjara dan sifat apa dan jang manapun djuga — maka Ummat Islam akan disorong kesudut "memilih pihak".
Dan, Insja Allah, kelak kemudian mereka akan masuk Blok Islam, tegasnja: Negara Islam Indonesia.

(4) Djika dengan idzin Allah terdjadi jang serupa itu, maka didalam lapangan dan gelanggang perdjuangan di Indonesia hanja akan ada dua golongan, jang ber-hadap²an sebagai musuh dan lawan jang ta' kenal damai, antara satu dengan jang lain, ialah: Komunisme lawan Islamisme.

7. Inilah beberapa hal, jang perlu Kami kemukakan kepada Saudara, dengan harapan mendapat perhatian sepenuhnja. Dengan ini pula Kami njatakan sekali lagi pertimbangan dan andjuran daripada pihak Kami, sebagaimana jang termaktub didalam Nota Rahasia terdahulu (pertama), angka 11, berkenaan dengan sual² tersebut:

   a. Tiada djalan lain, jang menudju kearah "Keselamatan Negara dan Bangsa Indonesia", melainkan: *"Djika Pemerintah Republik Indonesia mulai sekarang djuga, dengan tjepat dan tepat, membasmi Komunisme, dalam tiap² lapangan, terutama sekali jang melekat didalam tubuh Pemerintahan Republik Indonesia dan alat² kekuasaannja, dengan wudjud dan sifat apa dan jang manapun djuga".*
   Lebih tjepat, lebih baik!
   b. ....[= etc.]

8. Kemudian daripada itu, berkenaan dengan sual *Proklamasi berdirinja Negara Islam Indonesia,* 7 Agustus 1949, dan sual² lain disekitarnja seperti jang berikut:

   a. Proklamasi 7 Agustus 1949 adalah satu tjurahan *Kurnia Illahy,* atas Ummat Islam Indonesia, satu idzin dan perkenan Allah jang berwudjudkan: *"inti-pati* (kristalisasi, realisasi dan manifestasi) *daripada pengharapan, du'a, tekad, dan 'amal-usaha perdjuangan Ummat Islam Bangsa Indonesia".*
   b. Oleh sebab itu, maka Proklamasi 7 Agustus 1949 merupakan satu *hak-sutji* daripada Ummat Islam Bangsa Indonesia, jang tidak hanja harus serta wadjib dihargai dan dihormati oleh Ummat Islam sendiri, melainkan djuga oleh tiap² bangsa diseluruh dunia.

c. Hak-sutji tersebut diatas bolehlah kiranja dibagi mendjadi dua bagian:
   (1) Jang mengenai *isi, maksud,* dan *wudjud bulat sempurna* (essensiel substantif), ialah: *Kemerdekaan Islam bulat 100 %,* seperti jang dimaksudkan dalam Pendjelasan Singkat atas Proklamasi tersebut, angka 5, sub a. hingga d. Tentang hal ini, sedikitpun tiada tawaran, tambahan, pengurangan atau perubahan apa dan jang manapun djuga.
   Lantaran, sebagaimana Saudara tentu ma'lum dan mengerti, bahwa tiap² perubahan dalam hal ini, walaupun hanja sedikit, akan membawa akibat perubahan jang besar dalam bagian² jang lainnja.
   (2) Jang mengenai technik-pelaksanaan, seperti mitsalnja: batas daerah dan lain² jang serupa itu, berbeda dengan jang tersebut dalam angka 8, sub c. (1) diatas, jang mempunjai sifat "absoluut" (pasti), maka bagian (2) ini bersifat "relatif" (boleh berubah-ubah). Boleh pandjang atau pendek, boleh luas atau sempit, dan lain² sifat 'alam dahry (materieel). Walhasil, tentang hal ini bolehlah dilakukan tawar-menawar, perdamaian, dan lain² usaha penjelesaian jang serupa itu.
d. Agaknja keterangan ringkas jang dituliskan diatas, bolehlah kiranja dianggap sebagai bantuan daripada pihak Kami kepada Saudara, kalau² dapat meringankan dan memudahkan Saudara, dalam pertanggungan-djawab Saudara, memetjahkan sual Proklamasi 7 Agustus 1949 itu dan sual² disekitarnja.
e. Dengan ini, maka atas nama Pemerintah Negara Islam Indonesia, bolehlah dengan terus-terang Kami njatakan kepada Saudara, sebagai Kepala Negara Republik Indonesia, bahwa:
   (1) Djika Pemerintah Republik Indonesia *suka mengakui dengan resmi akan Proklamasi berdirinja Negara Islam Indonesia,* maka Kami *anggap mendjamin,* bahwa *Republik Indonesia akan mempunjai sahabat sehidup-semati* dalam menghadapi tiap² kemungkinan dari luar dan dari dalam, terutama menghadapi Komunisme, jang makin hari makin bertambah tampak bahajanja, bagi Negara dan Bangsa Indonesia maupun bagi seluruh dunia demokrasi (internasional).
   (2) Sebaliknja daripada itu, djika Republik Indonesia *tidak suka mengakui* Proklamasi 7 Agustus 1949 — jang kini sudah mendjadi kenjataan (fait accompli) — maka Kami *tidak* akan *ikut tanggung-djawab* atas nasibnja Negara dan Bangsa Indonesia, baik dihadapan Mahkamah Sedjarah maupun didepan Mahkamah Allah kelak.
   (3) Dalam hal ini, Kami pertjaja sepenuh-penuhnja atas kebidjaksanaan Saudara!

9. Adapun tentang perubahan dan peralihan Republik Indonesia, kedalam maupun keluar, sebagai djalan dan obat jang lainnja, untuk menghindarkan "Negara dan Bangsa Indonesia" daripada bahaja keruntuhan, sudahlah agaknja tjukup dirawaikan [= diuraikan?] dalam Nota Rahasia jang terdahulu (pertama), angka 14. Sudi apalah kiranja Saudara suka menganggapnja sebagai bantuan daripada pihak Kami, bagi memetjahkan sual² ketata-negaraan jang sukar-sulit itu.

10. Achirul-kalam, segala sesuatu harus dilakukan dengan *tjepat* dan *tepat*. Demikianlah harapan kami kepada Saudara, bagi kepentingan Negara dan Bangsa Indonesia, djuga adanja. Dibalik itu, djika langkah dan tindakan jang diharapkan itu lambat atau terlambat, maka tidaklah boleh diharapkan akan menimbulkan natidjah jang sebaik-baiknja, bagi kepentingan Negara dan Bangsa. Bahkan amat mungkin sekali, sebaliknja.
Sekali lagi, sudi apalah kiranja Saudara suka menaruh perhatian sepenuhnja!
Sebelum dan sesudahnja, terima kasih dan Alhamdu li-Llah, Kami haturkan.

11. Semoga Allah berkenan menuntun kita sekalian kearah dan maqam jang diliputi rachmat dan ridlo-Nja [= rida-Nja], bagi kepentingan Republik Indonesia dan Negara Islam Indonesia, serta Ra'jat dan Ummat Islam Bangsa Indonesia, djua adanja.
Inna fatahna laka fathan mubina. Insja Allah. Amin.
Bismillahi............ Allahu Akbar! [3]

Wassalam,
PEMERINTAH NEGARA ISLAM INDONESIA
IMAM:
S. M. KARTOSOEWIRJO

Mahdjurah-Tegal-Luar, 17 Pebruari 1951/10 Djumadil-awal 1370.[4]

Tembusan Nota-Rahasia Kedua ini
disampaikan kepada jang terhormat
Saudara M. Natsir, Perdana Menteri
Republik Indonesia.

---

[3] Cf. Appendix II, note 2.
[4] The letter was sent from "Mahdjurah-Tegal-Luar", which may be intended to mean "the place of *hidjra* in the open fields", or "the fields of refuge".

APPENDIX IV

KANUN AZASY
NEGARA ISLAM INDONESIA

Bismillahirrahmanirrahim.
Inna fatahna laka fathan mubina.[1]

Muqaddimah

Sedjak mula pertama Ummat Islam berdjuang, baik sedjak masa kolonial Belanda jang dulu, maupun pada zaman pendudukan Djepang, hingga pada zaman Republik Indonesia, sampai pada saat ini, selama itu mengandung suatu maksud jang sutji, menudju suatu arah jang mulia, ialah: "Mentjari dan mendapatkan Mardhotillah,[2] jang merupakan hidup didalam suatu ikatan dunia baru, ja'ni Negara Islam Indonesia jang Merdeka".

Dalam masa Ummat Islam melakukan wadjibnja jang sutji itu dengan beraneka djalan dan haluan jang diikuti, maka diketemuinjalah beberapa djembatan jang perlu dilintasi ialah djembatan pendudukan Djepang dan Kemerdekaan Kebangsaan Indonesia.

Hampir djuga kaki Ummat Islam selesai melalui djembatan emas jang terachir ini, maka badai baru mendampar bahtera Ummat Islam hingga keluar dari daerah Republik, terlepas dari tanggung djawab Pemerintah Republik Indonesia.

Alhamdulillah, pasang dan surutnja air digelombang samudera tidak sedikitpun mempengaruhi niat sutji jang terkandung dalam kalbu Muslimin jang sedjati. Didalam keadaan jang demikian itu, Ummat Islam bangkit dan bergerak mengangkat sendjata, melandjutkan Revolusi Indonesia, menghadapi musuh, jang senantiasa hanja ingin mendjadjah belaka.

Dalam masa revolusi jang kedua ini, jang karena sifat dan tjoraknja merupakan revolusi Islam, keluar dan kedalam, maka Ummat Islam tidak lupa pula kepada wadjibnja membangun dan menggalang suatu Negara Islam Jang Merdeka, suatu Keradjaan Allah jang dilahirkannja diatas dunia, ialah sjarat dan tempat untuk mentjapai keselamatan tiap[2] manusia dan seluruh Ummat Islam, dilahir maupun bathin, di dunia hingga di acherat kelak.

Kiranja dengan tolong dan Kurnia Illahy, Kanun Azasy jang sementara ini mendjadi pedoman kita, melakukan bakti sutji kepada 'Azza wa Djalla [= Allah], dapatlah mewudjudkan amal perbuatan

---

[1] Cf. Sura 48 : 1, mentioned in Appendix II, note 2.
[2] Cf. Appendix II, note 3.

jang njata, dari pada tiap² warga negara di-daerah² dimana mulai dilaksanakan hukum² Islam, ialah Hukum Allah dan Sunnatin Nabi.
Mudah-mudahan Allah S.W.T. melimpahkan taufik dan hidajatNja serta tolong dan KurniaNja atas seluruh Negara dan Ummat Islam Indonesia, sehingga terdjaminlah keselamatan Ummat dan Negara daripada tiap² bentjana jang manapun djuga. Amin.
"Lau anna ahlal qura amanu wattaqau lafatahna 'alaihim barakatin min as-sama'i wal-ardli".[3]

Bab I.
Negara, Hukum dan Kekuasaan

Pasal 1.
1. Negara Islam Indonesia adalah Negara Kurnia Allah Subhanahu wa Ta'ala kepada bangsa Indonesia.
2. Sifat Negara itu Djumhuryah (Republik).
3. Negara mendjamin berlakunja Sjari'at Islam didalam kalangan kaum Muslimin.
4. Negara memberi keleluasan kepada pemeluk Agama lainnja, didalam melakukan 'ibadatnja.

Pasal 2.
1. Dasar dan Hukum jang berlaku di Negara Islam Indonesia adalah Islam.
2. Hukum jang tertinggi adalah Qur'an dan Hadits sahih.

Pasal 3.
1. Kekuasaan jang tertinggi membuat hukum, dalam Negara Islam Indonesia, ialah Madjlis Sjuro (Parlemen).
2. Djika keadaan memaksa, hak Madjlis Sjuro boleh beralih kepada Imam dan Dewan Imamah.

Bab II.
Madjlis Sjuro

Pasal 4.
1. Madjlis Sjuro terdiri atas wakil² rakjat, ditambah dengan utusan golongan² menurut aturan jang ditetapkan dengan Undang².
2. Madjlis Sjuro bersidang sedikitnja sekali dalam satu tahun.
3. Sidang Madjlis Sjuro dianggap sjah, djika $2/3$ daripada djumlah anggota hadlir.
4. Keputusan Madjlis Sjuro diambil dengan suara terbanjak.
5. Djika forum [= quorum?] (ketentuan) jang tersebut diatas (Bab II pasal 4 ajat 3) tidak mentjukupi, maka sidang Madjlis

---

[3] A quotation from Sura 7 : 96, meaning "Had the people of the towns believed and shown piety, We [= God] should have opened up to them blessings from the heaven and the earth" (see Sura 7 : 94 in Richard Bell's translation).

Sjuro jang berikutnja harus diadakan selambat-lambatnja 14 hari kemudian daripada sidang tsb., dan djika sidang Madjlis Sjuro jang kedua inipun tidak mentjukupi forum [= quorum?] diatas (Bab II pasal 4 ajat 3), maka selambat-lambatnja 14 hari kemudian dari padanja harus diadakan lagi sidang Madjlis Sjuro ketiga jang dianggap sjah, dengan tidak mengingati djumlah anggota jang hadlir.

Pasal 5.

Madjlis Sjuro menetapkan KANUN AZASY dan garis² besar haluan Negara.

Bab III.
[Dewan Sjuro]

Pasal 6.
1. Susunan Dewan Sjuro ditetapkan dengan Undang².
2. Dewan Sjuro bersidang sedikitnja sekali dalam 3 bulan.
3. Dewan Sjuro itu adalah Badan Pekerdja daripada Madjlis Sjuro dan mempunjai tugas-kewadjiban:
   a. menjelesaikan segala keputusan² Madjlis Sjuro,
   b. melakukan segala sesuatu sebagai wakil Madjlis Sjuro menghadapi Pemerintah, selainnja jang berkenaan dengan prinsip.

Pasal 7.

Tiap² undang² menghendaki persetudjuan Dewan Sjuro.

Pasal 8.
1. Anggauta Dewan Sjuro berhak memadjukan rentjana undang².
2. Djika sesuatu rentjana undang² tidak mendapat persetudjuan Dewan Sjuro, maka rentjana tadi tidak boleh dimadjukan lagi dalam sidang Dewan Sjuro itu.
3. Djika rentjana itu meskipun disetudjui oleh Dewan Sjuro tidak disahkan oleh Imam, maka rentjana tadi tak boleh dimadjukan lagi dalam sidang Dewan Sjuro masa itu.

Pasal 9.
1. Dalam hal ichwal kegentingan jang memaksa, Imam berhak menetapkan peraturan² Pemerintah sebagai pengganti Undang².
2. Peraturan Pemerintah itu harus mendapat persetudjuan Dewan Sjuro dalam sidang jang berikut.
3. Djika tidak mendapat persetudjuan maka peraturan Pemerintah itu harus ditjabut.

Bab IV.
Kekuasaan Pemerintah Negara

Pasal 10.

Imam Negara Islam Indonesia memegang kekuasaan Pemerintah menurut Kanun Azasy, sepandjang Hukum Islam.

Pasal 11.
1. Imam memegang kekuasaan membentuk undang² dengan persetudjuan Madjlis Sjuro.
2. Imam menetapkan peraturan Pemerintah, setelah berunding dengan Dewan Imamah untuk mendjalankan Undang² sebagaimana mestinja.

Pasal 12.
1. Imam Negara Islam Indonesia ialah orang Indonesia asli jang beragama Islam dan thaat kepada Allah dan Rasulnja.
2. Imam dipilih oleh Madjlis Sjuro dengan suara paling sedikit $2/3$ daripada seluruh anggauta.
3. Djika hingga dua kali berturut-turut dilakukan pemilihan itu, dengan tidak mentjukupi ketentuan diatas (Bab IV pasal 12 ajat 2), maka keputusan diambil menurut suara jang terbanjak dalam pemilihan jang ketiga kalinja.

Pasal 13.
1. Imam melakukan wadjibnja, selama:
   a. mentjukupi bai'atnja,[4]
   b. tiada hal² jang memaksa, sepandjang Hukum Islam.
2. Djika karena sesuatu, Imam berhalangan melakukan wadjibnja, maka Imam menundjuk salah seorang anggauta Dewan Imamah sebagai wakilnja sementara.
3. Didalam hal² jang amat memaksa, maka Dewan Imamah harus selekas mungkin mengadakan sidang untuk memutuskan wakil Imam sementara, daripada anggauta² Dewan Imamah.

Pasal 14.
Sebelum melakukan wadjibnja, Imam menjatakan bai'at dihadapan Madjlis Sjuro sebabai berikut:
"Bismillahirrahmanirrahim,
Asjhadu an la ilaha illa-Llah, wa asjhadu anna Muhammadar rasulu-Llah,[5]
Wallahi (Demi Allah), saja menjatakan bai'at saja, sebagai Imam Negara Islam Indonesia, dihadapan sidang Madjlis Sjuro ini, dengan ichlas dan sutji hati dan tidak karena sesuatu diluar kepentingan Agama dan Negara. Saja sanggup berusaha melakukan kewadjiban saja sebagai Imam Negara Islam Indonesia, dengan se-baik²nja dan sesempurna-sempurnanja sepandjang adjaran Agama Islam, bagi kepentingan Agama dan Negara".

---

[4] *Bai'at* (Ar. *baiᶜa*) means here and in the following article "the oath of office".
[5] After the *basmala*-formula, the oath of office includes the profession of faith: "I testify that there is no god but God, and I testify that Muhammad is God's Messenger".

Pasal 15.
Imam memegang kekuasaan jang tertinggi atas seluruh Angkatan Perang Negara Islam Indonesia.

Pasal 16.
Imam dengan persetudjuan Madjlis Sjuro menjatakan perang, membuat perdamaian/perdjandjian dengan negara lain.

Pasal 17.
Imam menjatakan keadaan bahaja. Sjarat[2] dan akibat [keadaan] bahaja, ditetapkan dengan undang-undang.

Pasal 18.
1. Imam mengangkat duta dan konsul,
2. menerima duta Negara lain.

Pasal 19.
Imam memberikan amnesti, abolisi, grasi dan rehabilitasi.

Pasal 20.
Imam memberikan gelaran, tanda djasa dan lain[2] tanda kehormatan.

Bab V.
Dewan Fatwa

Pasal 21.
1. Dewan Fatwa terdiri dari seorang Mufti besar dan beberapa Mufti lainnja, sebanjak-banjaknja 7 orang.
2. Dewan ini berkewadjiban memberi djawab atas pertanjaan Imam dan berhak menundjukkan usul kepada Pemerintah.

Angkatan dan pemberhentian anggauta[2] itu dilakukan oleh Imam.

Bab VI.
Dewan Imamah

Pasal 22.
1. Dewan Imamah terdiri dari Imam dan Kepala[2] Madjlis.
2. Anggauta[2] Dewan diangkat dan diberhentikan oleh Imam.
3. Tiap[2] anggauta Dewan Imamah bertanggung djawab atas kebaikan berlakunja pekerdjaan Madjlis jang diserahkan kepadanja.
4. Dewan Imamah bertanggung djawab kepada Imam dan Madjlis Sjuro atas kewadjiban jang diserahkan kepadanja.

Bab VII.
Pembagian Daerah

Pasal 23.
Pembagian daerah dalam Negara Islam Indonesia ditentukan menurut undang-undang.

Bab VIII.
Ke-uangan

Pasal 24.

1. Anggaran pendapatan dan belandja ditetapkan tiap² tahun dengan undang². Apabila Dewan Sjuro tidak menjetudjui anggaran jang diusulkan Pemerintah, maka Pemerintah mendjalankan anggaran tahun jang lalu.
2. Padjak dilenjapkan dan diganti dengan infaq. Segala infaq untuk kepentingan Negara berdasarkan undang².
3. Matjam dan harga mata uang ditetapkan dengan undang².
4. Hal ke-uangan Negara selandjutnja diatur dengan undang².
5. Untuk memeriksa tanggung djawab tentang keuangan negara diadakan suatu Badan Pemeriksaan Keuangan, jang peraturannja ditetapkan dengan undang².
Hasil pemeriksaan itu diberitahukan kepada Dewan Sjuro.

Bab IX.
Kehakiman

Pasal 25.

1. Kehakiman dilakukan oleh sebuah Mahkamah Agung dan lain² badan Kehakiman menurut undang².
2. Susunan dan kekuasaan Badan Kehakiman itu diatur dengan undang².

Pasal 26.

Sjarat² untuk mendjadi dan untuk diperhatikan sebagai Hakim ditetapkan dengan undang².

Bab X.
Warga-Negara

Pasal 27.

1. Jang mendjadi warga negara ialah orang Indonesia asli dan orang² bangsa lain jang disjahkan dengan undang² sebagai warga negara.
2. Sjarat² jang mengenai warga negara ditetapkan dengan undang².

Pasal 28.

1. Segala warga negara bersamaan kedudukannja didalam hukum dan pemerintahan dan wadjib mendjundjung hukum dan Pemerintahan itu dengan tidak ada ketjualinja.
2. Tiap² warga negara berhak atas pekerdjaan dan penghidupan jang lajak bagi kemanusiaan.
3. Djabatan² dan kedudukan jang penting dan bertanggung djawab didalam pemerintahan, baik sipil maupun militer, hanja diberikan kepada muslim.

Pasal 29.

Kemerdekaan berserikat dan berkumpul, melahirkan fikiran dengan lisan dan tulisan dan sebagainja, ditetapkan dengan undang².

Bab XI.
Pertahanan Negara
Pasal 30.
1. Tiap² warga negara berhak dan wadjib ikut serta dalam usaha pembelaan negara.
2. Tiap² warga negara jang beragama Islam wadjib ikut serta dalam pertahanan negara.
3. Sjarat² tentang pembelaan diatur dengan undang².

Bab XII.
Pendidikan
Pasal 31.
1. Tiap² warga negara berhak dan wadjib mendapat pengadjaran.
2. Pemerintahan mengusahakan dan menjelenggarakan satu sistim pengadjaran Islam jang diatur dengan undang².

Bab XIII.
[Ekonomi?]
Pasal 32.
1. Peri-kehidupan dan penghidupan rakjat diatur dengan dasar tolong-menolong.
2. Tjabang² produksi jang penting bagi Negara, dan jang menguasai hadjat orang banjak, dikuasai oleh Negara.
3. Bumi dan air dan kekajaan alam jang terkandung didalamnja dikuasai oleh Negara dan dipergunakan sebesar-besarnja untuk kemakmuran rakjat.

Bab XIV.
Bendera dan Bahasa
Pasal 33.
Bendera Negara Islam Indonesia ialah "Merah-Putih-ber-Bulan-Bintang".
Bahasa Negara Islam ialah "Bahasa Indonesia".

Bab XV.
Perobahan Kanun Azasy
Pasal 34.
1. Untuk mengubah Kanun Azasy harus sekurang-kurangnja $2/3$ daripada djumlah anggauta Madjlis Sjuro hadlir.
2. Putusan diambil dengan persetudjuan sekurang-kurangnja setengah daripada djumlah seluruh anggauta Madjlis Sjuro.

* * *

Tjara Berputarnja Roda Pemerintahan

1. Pada umumnja roda pemerintahan N.I.I. berdjalan menurut dasar jang ditetapkan dalam "Kanun Azasy", dan sesuai dengan pasal 3 dari Kanun Azasy tadi, sementara belum ada Parlemen (Madjlis Sjuro), segala undang^2 ditetapkan oleh Dewan Imamah dalam bentuk Maklumat-Maklumat jang ditanda-tangani oleh Imam.
2. Berdasarkan Maklumat-Maklumat Imam tadi, Madjlis^2 (Kementerian-Kementerian) menurut pembagian tugas kewadjiban masing-masing, membuat peraturan atau pendjelasan untuk memudahkan pelaksanaannja.
3. Djuga dasar politik pemerintah N.I.I. ditentukan oleh Dewan Imamah.
4. Anggauta Dewan Imamah pada waktu pembentukannja ialah:
   1. S.M. Kartosuwirjo, selaku Imam merangkap Kepala Madjlis Pertahanan.
   2. Sanoesi Partawidjaja, ,, Kepala Madjlis Dalam Negeri dan Keuangan.
   3. K.H. Gozali Tusi, ,, Kepala Madjlis Kehakiman.
   4. Thoha Arsjad, ,, Kepala Madjlis Penerangan.
   5. Kamran, ,, Anggauta.
   6. R. Oni, ,, Anggauta.

LIST OF ABBREVIATIONS AND THEIR MEANING

ABRI	*Angkatan Bersendjata Republik Indonesia,* Indonesian Armed Forces
A.D.A.R.I.	*Agama Djawa Asli Republik Indonesia,* Original Javanese Religion of the Republic of Indonesia
A.D.I.A.	*Akademi Dinas Ilmu Agama,* Government Academy for Religious (Islamic) Studies
A.P.I.	*Angkatan Pemuda Indonesia,* (Atjehnese) Brigade of Indonesian Youth
D.I.	*Darul Islam,* Islamic State Movement
	Daérah Satu, Region Number One
Gestapu	*Gerakan September Tigapuluh,* September 30th Movement
H.	*Hadji,* Alhaji
	Hidjra (A.D. 622), beginning of the Islamic era
H.M.I.	*Himpunan Mahasiswa Islam,* Islamic Student Association
I.A.I.N.	*Institut Agama Islam Negeri,* State Islamic Institute
I.P.I.	*Ikatan Pemuda Indonesia,* (Atjehnese) Association of Indonesian Youth
I.P.K.I.	*Ikatan Pendukung Kemerdekaan Indonesia,* League of Upholders of Indonesian Independence
JAPI	*Jajasan Penjiaran Islam,* Foundation for the Spread of Islam
K.	*Kiyai,* independent religious teacher
KAMI	*Komité Aksi Mahasiswa Indonesia,* Action-Committee of Indonesian Students
KAPPI	*Komité Aksi Para Peladjar Indonesia,* Action-Committee of Indonesian Secondary School Pupils
Ketuhanan J. M. E.,	*Ketuhanan Jang Maha Esa,* Belief in the One and Only God
K.N.I.L.	*Koninklijk Nederlands Indisch Leger,* (Colonial) Netherlands East Indies Army
K.N.I.P.	*Komité Nasional Indonesia Pusat,* Central Indonesian National Committee
K.R.I.S.	*Kebaktian Rakjat Indonesia Sulawesi,* Service of the Indonesian People of Sulawesi (Celebes)
Manipol	*Manifesto Politik,* Political Manifesto
Masjumi	*Madjlis Sjuro Muslimin Indonesia,* Consultative Council of Indonesian Muslims
M.I.A.I.	*Madjlisul Islamil Aᶜlaa Indonesia,* Supreme Indonesian Council of Islam
M.I.N.	*Madrasah Ibtida'ijah Negeri,* (Islamic) Elementary State School

LIST OF ABBREVIATIONS

M.P.R.S.	*Madjelis Permusjawaratan Rakjat Indonesia*, Provisional People's Congress
Murba	*Partai Murba*, Common-People's Party
NASAKOM	*Nasionalis-Agama-Komunis*, (intended unity of) Nationalists, Religious people, and Communists
NASASOS	*Nasionalis-Agama-Sosialis*, (intended unity of) Nationalists, Religious people, and Socialists
Nekolim	*Neokolonialis-Imperialis*, Neo-colonial imperialists
N.I.A.S.	*Nederlands-Indische Artsen School*, Netherlands Indies Medical School
N.I.C.A.	Netherlands Indies Civil Administration
N.I.I.	*Negara Islam Indonesia*, Islamic State of Indonesia
N.U.	*Nahdatul Ulama*, Awakening of the *Ulamas*
Oldefos	Old Established Forces
ORBA	*Orde Baru*, New Order
ORLA	*Orde Lama*, Old Order
Parkindo	*Partai Kristen Indonesia*, (Protestant) Indonesian Christian Party
Parmusi	*Partai Muslimin Indonesia*, Party of Indonesian Muslims
PELITA	*Pembangunan Lima Tahun*, Five-Year Development
Permesta	*Perdjuangan Semesta*, Common Struggle Movement
Perti	*Pergerakan Tarbijah Indonesia*, Indonesian Movement for (the improvement of) Education (in Sumatra)
P.H.I.N.	*Pendidikan Hakim Islam Negeri*, State College for Muslim Jurisprudents (at Religious Courts)
P.K.I.	*Partai Komunis Indonesia*, Indonesian Communist Party
P.M.I.	*Partai Muslimin Indonesia*, see: Parmusi (also: *Palang Mérah Indonesia*, the Indonesian Red Cross)
P.M.I.I.	*Perhimpunan Mahasiswa Islam Indonesia*, Indonesian Association of Muslim Students
P.N.I.	*Partai Nasional Indonesia*, Indonesian National(ist) Party
P.R.R.I.	*Pemerintah Revolusioner Republik Indonesia*, Revolutionary Government of the Republic of Indonesia
P.S.I.	*Partai Sosialis Indonesia*, Indonesian Socialist Party
P.S.I.I.	*Partai Sarikat Islam Indonesia*, Islamic Political Association of Indonesia
P.T.A.I.N.	*Perguruan Tinggi Agama Islam Negeri*, State Islamic College
P.T.D.I.	*Perguruan Tinggi Da^cwah Islam*, Islamic Mission College
P.U.S.A.	*Persatuan Ulama-ulama Seluruh Atjeh*, All Atjeh Ulama Union
REPELITA	*Rentjana Pembangunan Lima Tahun*, Five-Year Development Plan
R.I.	*Republik Indonesia*, Republic of Indonesia
R.I.S.	*Republik Indonesia Serikat*, United Indonesian Republic
R.U.S.I.	Republic of the United States of Indonesia (= R.I.S.)
S.I.	*Sarékat Islam*, Islamic Association
T.	*Teuku*, member of Atjehnese aristocracy

Tavip	*Tahun Vivere Pericoloso*, Year of Living Dangerously
Tgk.	*Teungku*, Atjehnese *ulama*
T.I.I.	*Tentara Islam Indonesia*, Islamic Army of Indonesia
T.N.I.	*Tentara Nasional Indonesia*, Indonesian National Army
U.I.D.	*Universitas Islam Djakarta*, Islamic University of Djakarta
U.I.I.	University/*Universitas Islam Indonesia*, Islamic University of Indonesia
USDEK	*Undang-undang Dasar 1945*, the 1945 Constitution, *Sosialisme (à la) Indonesia*, Indonesian Socialism, *Demokrasi Terpimpin*, Guided Democracy, *Ekonomi Terpimpin*, Guided Economy, *Kepribadian Indonesia*, the Indonesian Identity.

LIST OF PUBLICATIONS REFERRED TO

Abbas, Zainal Arifin, *Peri Hidup Muhammad Rasulullah s.a.w.*, Medan 1960[3].
Abduh, Muh., *Risalah Tauhid*, Djakarta 1965[2].
Abdulgani, Ruslan, *Isi Kitab Sutji Al-Qurään guna membakar semangat Mahasiswa didalam suasana sekarang*, in *Al-Djami'ah*, no. 4, 1965.
Abdul Malik Karim Amrullah, H., see: HAMKA.
Aboebakar H., see: Abubakar (Atjeh).
ABRI, see: Sutjipto.
Abubakar (Atjeh), H., *Etiket dalam Islam*, Palembang 1963.
— *Falsafah Pergaulan*, Tjirebon, no date.
— *Ilmu Ketuhanan (Ilmu Kalam)*, Djakarta 1966.
— *Islam dan Kemerdekaan Beragama*, Tjirebon, no date.
— *Pengantar Ilmu Tarekat (Uraian tentang Mistik)*, Bandung 1964.
— (ed.), *Sedjarah Hidup K. H. A. Wahid Hasjim dan Karangan Tersiar*, Djakarta 1957.
— *Toleransi Nabi Muhammad dan Sahabat-Sahabatnja*, Djakarta 1966.
Abu Hanifah, *Soal Agama dalam Negara Modern*, Djakarta 1949.
Adams, Cindy, see: Soekarno.
Ahmad, Aftabuddin, *Wanita dalam Islam dan Kristen*, Surabaja 1963.
Ahmad, H. Z(ainal) A(bidin), *Konsepsi Tatanegara Islam*, Djakarta 1949.
— *Negara Utama (al-Farabi)*, Djakarta 1964.
Al-Djami^cah, Madjalah Ilmu Pengetahuan Agama Islam, Jogjakarta, since 1962.
Alers, Henri J., *Om een Rode of Groene Merdeka*, Eindhoven (?), 1956.
Alfian, *Islamic Modernism in Indonesian Politics: the Muhammadijah Movement during the Dutch Colonial Period (1912-1942)*, 2 Vol., Wisconsin 1969.
Ali, A. Mukti, *Alam Pikiran Islam Modern di Indonesia*, Djakarta 1964.
— *Ilmu Perbandingan Agama*, Jogjokarta 1965.
Ali, Muaz, *Agama Islam*, Djakarta 1964.
Al-Qur'ān: Al-Qurään dan Terdjemahnja, 3 Vol., Djakarta 1965-1969.
— see: Bell, and Pickthall.
Amatillah, M. Sj. Ibnu, *Analyse: Mungkinkah Negara Indonesia Bersendikan Islam?*, Semarang 1950.
Amir, Dja^cfar, *Chutbah Djum^cat*, Bandung 1966.
— *Ilmu Fiqih (bagian Ibadat)*, Sala 1965[3].
— *Ilmu Fiqih (bagian Mu^camalat)*, Sala 1965.
— *Intisari Maulud Nabi Muhammad s.a.w.*, Djakarta 1964[3].
— *Seluk-beluk Perkawinan Dalam Islam*, Sala 1965.
— & Sjafi^ci Ma^carif, *Tuntunan Rukun Iman*, Sala 1966.
— see also: Wachid.
Anshary, M. Isa, *Falsafah Perdjuangan Islam*, Bandung 1949.
— *Mudjahid Da^cwah*, Bandung 1964.
ANSOR: Anggaran Dasar dan Anggaran Rumah Tangga Gerakan Pemuda Ansor, Djakarta 1964.
Anwar, H. Rosihan, *Islam dan Anda*, Djakarta 1962.

Asad, Muhammad (Leopold Weiss), *Azas² Negara dan Pemerintahan didalam Islam,* Djakarta 1964.
— *Undang-undang Politik Islam,* Djakarta 1954.
Ash-Shiddiqy, M(oh). Hasbi, *Al-Islam,* Djakarta 1964[3].
— *Baital Mal,* Jogjakarta 1968.
— *Dasar-dasar Pemerintahan Islam,* Medan 1950.
— *Kelengkapan Dasar-dasar Fiqih Islam (Pengantar Ushul Fiqih),* Medan 1953.
— *Pedoman Berumah Tangga,* Medan, no date[6].
— *Peladjaran Tauhid,* Medan 1954.
— *Pengantar Hukum Islam,* Djakarta 1963[3].
— *Problematika Hadits sebagai Dasar Pembinaan Hukum Islam,* Djakarta 1964.
— *Sedjarah dan Pengantar Ilmu Hadits,* Djakarta 1965[3].
— *Sedjarah dan Pengantar Ilmu Tafsir,* Djakarta 1965[4].
— *Tafsir Al-Qurän "An Nur",* Djakarta, since 1956.
Asjik, Nur, see: Rusli.
Atjeh: Atjeh Membangun, ed. by Pemerintah Daerah Istimewa Atjeh, 1961.
— *Darussalam,* ed. by Jajasan Dana Kesedjahteraan Atjeh, 1963.
— *Dewan Perwakilan Rakjat Atjeh ... dan Produk-produk Legislatif,* ed. by Sekretariat DPRD-GR Propinsi Daerah Istimewa Atjeh, 1968 (stencilled).
— *Kehidupan Beragama di Daerah Istimewa Atjeh,* ed. by Secretariat DPRD-GR, Atjeh 1967 (stencilled).
— *Modal Revolusi 45,* ed. by Seksi Penerangan/Dokumentasi Komité Musjawarah 45 Daerah Istimewa Atjeh, 1960.
— *Presiden Soeharto Ditengah-tengah Rakjat Atjeh,* Atjeh 1968 (stencilled).
— *Sidang Ke-IV Dewan Perwakilan Rakjat Daerah Gotong Rojong Daerah Istimewa Atjeh 1968,* ed. by Secretariat DPRD-GR Prop. Daerah Istimewa Atjeh (stencilled).
Audah, Abdulkadir, *Islam dan Perundang-undangan,* Djakarta 1965[3].
Aziz, H. Aminuddin, *Islam dan Tjetusan Revolusi Indonesia,* Djakarta 1963.
Aziz, M. A., *Japan's Colonialism and Indonesia,* thesis Leiden 1955.
Badawy, *Mutiara Tauhid,* Djakarta 1963.
Bakker, D. (Jr.), *Da^cwah, Missionarische Mobilisierung des Islams in Indonesien,* in *Evangelische Missions-Zeitschrift,* August 1969.
Bakker, F. L., *Tuhan Jesus didalam Agama Islam,* Djakarta 1957.
Bakker S.J., J. W. M., *De Godsdienstvrijheid in de Indonesische Grondwetten,* in *Het Missiewerk,* no. 4, 1956.
Bakry, Hasbullah, *Al-Qur'an sebagai Korektor terhadap Taurat dan Indjil,* Surabaja 1966.
— *Jesus Kristus dalam Pandangan Islam dan Kristen,* Surabaja 1965.
— *Nabi Isa Dalam Al-Qur'an Dan Nabi Muhammad Dalam Bijbel,* Solo 1961[2].
Bakry, H. M(oh). K(asim), *Hukum Pidana dalam Islam,* Djakarta 1954[3].
— *Peladjaran Hadis,* 2 Vol., Djakarta 1964[6]-1966[2].
— *Sedjarah Hukum dalam Islam,* Solo 1958.
Becker, C. H., *Islamstudien, Vom Werden und Wesen der Islamischen Welt,* 2 Vol., Leipzig 1924.
Bell, Richard, *The Qur'ān,* Edinburgh 1960[2].
Benda, Harry J., *The Crescent and the Rising Sun,* The Hague/Bandung 1958.
Boland, B. J., *Missiologia in loco — Christendom en Islam in Indonesië,* in *Nederlands Theologisch Tijdschrift,* October 1968.
Buchari, *Shahih Buchari,* 2 Vol., Djakarta 1964[4]—1961[2].
Buku Peringatan, see: University Islam Indonesia.

Buku Tahunan, see: I.A.I.N.
Chalid, K. H. Idham, *Islam dan Demokrasi Terpimpin*, Surabaja (1961?).
Chalil, Munawar, *Kelengkapan Tarich Nabi Muhammad s.a.w.*, Djakarta 1965[3].
— *Peristiwa Isra' dan Mi'radj*, Djakarta 1965[2].
Chotib, A., *Bank dalam Islam*, Djakarta 1962.
"Cornell Report", see: (A) Preliminary Analysis.
Cox, Harvey, *The Secular City*, New York 1965.
Crossley, John, *Explaining the Gospel to Muslims*, London 1967[6].
Dahm, Bernhard, *Sukarnos Kampf um Indonesiens Unabhängigkeit*, Mannheim 1964; (Dutch translation), *Soekarno en de strijd om Indonesië's onafhankelijkheid*, Meppel, no date.
Departemen Agama, see: *Indonesia*.
Dradjad, Zakijah, *Keluarga Berentjana*, in *Pandji Masjarakat*, nos. 31, 32, 33.
Drewes, G. W. J., *Indonesia: Mysticism and Activism*, in G. E. von Grunebaum (ed.), *Unity and Variety in Muslim Civilization*, Chicago 1955.
Encyclopaedia of Islam (The), New Edition, Leiden, since 1960.
al-Farabi, see: Ahmad, H. Zainal Abidin.
Feith, Herbert, *The Decline of Constitutional Democracy in Indonesia*, Ithaca New York 1962.
— *Dynamics of Guided Democracy*, in Ruth T. McVey (ed.), *Indonesia*, New Haven 1963.
— *The Indonesian Elections of 1955*, Cornell University 1957.
Gazalba, Sidi, *Integrasi Islam, Ilmu dan Kebudajaan*, Djakarta 1967.
— *Mesdjid — Pusat Ibadat dan Kebudajaan Islam*, Djakarta 1962.
Geertz, Clifford, *Islam Observed, Religious Development in Morocco and Indonesia*, New Haven/London 1968.
— *The Religion of Java*, Illinois 1960.
Gema Islam, Madjallah Pengetahuan dan Kebudajaan Islam, Djakarta, since 1962.
Ghallab, Muh., *Inilah Hakikat Islam*, Djakarta 1965.
Gibb, H. A. R., *Aliran-aliran modern dalam Islam*, Djakarta 1952.
— *Modern Trends in Islam*, Chicago 1947.
— (ed.), *Whither Islam?*, London 1932.
Gogarten, Fr., *Verhängnis und Hoffnung der Neuzeit*, Stuttgart 1953.
Grunebaum, G. E. von, *Modern Islam — The Search for Cultural Identity*, Berkeley & Los Angeles 1962.
— (ed.), *Unity and Variety in Muslim Civilization*, Chicago 1955.
Gunawan, Basuki, *Kudetá, Staatsgreep in Djakarta*, Meppel 1968.
Hadikusuma, Djarnawi, *Sekitar Kristologi*, Jogjakarta 1965[3].
— *Sekitar Perdjandjian Lama [dan] Perdjandjian Baru*, Jogjakarta, no date.
Hadiwijono, Harun, *Man in the Present Javanese Mysticism*, Baarn (the Netherlands) 1967.
HAMKA (H. Abdul Malik Karim Amrullah), *Ajahku*, Djakarta 1950.
— *Dari Perbendaharaan Lama*, Medan 1963.
— *Dengan Sekularisasi Pantjasila Akan Kosong*, in *Pandji Masjarakat*, no. 29.
— *Falsafah Hidup*, Djakarta 1962[6].
— *Pengaruh Muhammad ᶜAbduh di Indonesia*, Djakarta 1961.
— *Perkembangan Tasauf Dari Abad Keabad*, Djakarta 1962[5].
— *Revolusi Agama*, Djakarta 1949[2].
— *1001 Soal² Hidup*, Djakarta 1966[9].
— *Tafsir Al-Azhar*, Djakarta, since 1967.
— *Tasauf Modern*, Djakarta 1961[11].

— *Wie der Islam nach Indonesien kam*, in Rolf Italiaander (ed.), *Die Herausforderung des Islam*, Göttingen 1965.
Hanafie, A., *Usul Fiqh*, Djakarta 1965[4].
Harahap, Zainabun, *Operasi-operasi Militer Menumpas Kahar Muzakkar*, Djakarta 1965.
Harjono, Anwar, *Hukum Islam, keluasan dan keadilannja*, Djakarta 1968.
Hasbi Ash-Shiddiqy, see: Ash-Shiddiqy.
Hashem, O., *Djawaban Lengkap Kepada Pendeta Dr. J. Verkuyl*, Surabaja (1969?).
Hasjim, Wahid, see: Abubakar.
Hassan, A., *Adakah Tuhan?*, Surabaja 1965[2].
— *Kesopanan Tinggi (setjara Islam)*, Bangil 1965[6].
Hassan, A. Qadir, *U-shul Fiqih*, Bangil 1964[2].
Hatta, Moh., *Demokrasi kita*, Djakarta 1966.
— *Nuzul Quran*, Djakarta 1966.
— *Sekitar Proklamasi 17 Agustus 1945*, Djakarta 1969.
Hazairin, *Ḥadīth Kewarisan dan Sistim Bilateral*, Djakarta 1962.
— *Hendak Kemana Hukum Islam?*, Djakarta 1960.
— *Hukum Islam dan Masjarakat*, Djakarta 1963[3].
— *Hukum Kekeluargaan Nasional*, Djakarta 1968[2].
— *Hukum Kewarisan Bilateral menurut Qur'ān dan Ḥadīth*, Djakarta 1964[3].
— *Ilmu Pengetahuan Islam dan Masjarakat*, Djakarta 1951.
— *Isa Almasih dan Ruh*, Djakarta 1969.
— and others, *Perdebatan dalam Seminar Hukum Nasional tentang Faraid*, Djakarta 1964.
Hefele, Ch. J., *Histoire des Conciles*, Paris 1907.
Herder Korrespondenz, Monatschrift für Gesellschaft und Religion, Freiburg.
Hidding, K. A. H., see: Mulia.
Hindley, Donald, *Alirans and the Fall of the Old Order*, in *Indonesia*, Cornell University, Ithaca New York 1970, no. 9.
Hoballah, M. F., *Demokrasi dan Hukum Islam*, Surabaja 1966.
Hoesin, Oemar Amin, see: Husin.
Hughes, John, *Indonesian Upheaval*, New York 1967.
Husain, T(h)aha, *Djandji Allah*, Djakarta 1968.
— *Masa Muda di Mesir*, Djakarta 1967.
Husin, Umar Amin, *Filsafat Islam*, Djakarta 1964[2].
— *Kultur Islam*, Djakarta 1964.
I.A.I.N.: Buku Tahunan Institut Agama Islam Negeri 1960-1962, Jogjakarta 1962.
— *Sewindu Institut Agama Islam Negeri (1960-1968)*, Jogjakarta, 1968.
Ibn Chaldun, *Filsafat Islam tentang Sedjarah*, Djakarta 1962.
— see also: Raliby, Osman.
Idris, M. Nur & H. M. K. Bakry & Gazali Dunia: *Peladjaran Tafsir Qurän*, 2 Vol., Djakarta, 1965-1966[4].
Imron, Marzuki, *Tata Susila*, Solo 1963.
Indonesia, Departemen Agama: Agama Adalah Unsur Mutlak Didalam Nation Building, Djakarta 1962-335.
— *Agama dan Nation Building*, Djakarta 1964-407.
— *Al-Qurän membentuk manusia baru*, Djakarta 1961-304.
— *Fungsi Wanita dalam Masjarakat*, Djakarta 1960-274.
— *Islam agama untuk sekalian manusia*, Djakarta 1961-305.
— *Kembali kepada Etik dan Norma[2] Islam*, Djakarta 1964-397.
— *Mutiara Hikmah*, Djakarta 1962-330.

— *Mutiara Ramadhan,* Djakarta 1960-285.
— *Negara Harus Ber-Tuhan,* Djakarta 1964-437.
— *Pendjelasan Sekitar Politik dan Idiologi Pemerintah Mengenai Soal Agama dan Keagamaan di Indonesia,* dated Djakarta, Dec. 7th, 1967 (stencilled).
— *Penerangan Agama,* Djakarta 1950.
— *Penjuluhan Masjarakat Agama,* Djakarta 1963-389.
— *Peranan Agama dalam Penjelesaian Revolusi Indonesia,* Djakarta 1964-425.
— *Perguruan Mesir dalam Zaman Merdeka,* Djakarta 1955.
Indonesia, Kementerian Kesehatan ("Madjelis Pertimbangan Kesehatan dan Sjara' "): *Soal Pemindahan Darah* (Fatwah no. 6/1956), Djakarta 1957.
Indonesia, Ministry of Information: The Birth of Pantjasila, Jakarta 1950.
Indonesische Voorlichtingsdienst: Indonesisch Bulletin, 's-Gravenhage 1953.
Ismail, Taufiq, *Tirani, kumpulan sadjak,* Djakarta 1966.
Italiaander, Rolf, see: HAMKA.
Jahja, Muchtar, *Butir Hikmah Isra' dan Mi'radj,* Djakarta 1964.
Jassin, H. B., *Heboh Sastra 1968,* Djakarta 1970.
Junus, Mahmud, *Hadji ke Mekka,* Djakarta 1964[9].
— *Hukum Perkawinan dalam Islam, menurut mazhab: Sjafi[c]i, Hanafi, Maliki dan Hanbali,* Djakarta 1964[3].
— *Keimanan dan Achlak,* 4 Vol., Djakarta 1965[15], 1962[8].
— *Marilah Sembahjang,* 4 Vol., Djakarta 1965[15.20].
— *Puasa dan Zakat,* Djakarta, no date[9].
— *Sedjarah Pendidikan Islam di Indonesia,* Djakarta 1960.
— *Turutlah Hukum Warisan dalam Islam,* Djakarta 1962[2].
Juynboll, Th. W., *Handleiding tot de kennis van de Mohammedaansche Wet,* Leiden 1930[4].
Kahin, George McT., *Nationalism and Revolution in Indonesia,* Ithaca New York 1952.
Kartapradja, K. Kamil, *Aliran-aliran Kebathinan di Indonesia,* 2 Vol., Jogjakarta 1968 (stencilled).
Kasman, see: Singodimedjo.
Khoury, Paul, *Paul d'Antioche, Évêque Melkite de Sidon (XIIe s.),* thesis Leiden 1950.
Kiblat, Madjalah Islam, Djakarta, since 1953.
Kraemer, H., *The Christian Message in a Non-Christian World,* London 1938[1], 1947[2].
Kroef, J. M. van der, *Indonesia in the Modern World,* 2 Vol., Bandung 1954-1956.
Loebis, Ali Basja, see: Lubis, Ali Basja.
Lubis, Ali Basja, *Undang[2] Dasar R.I. 1945 (Sedjarah Pertumbuhan dan Pendjelasan Pasal[2]nja),* Djakarta 1963.
Lubis, M. Arsjad Th(alib), *Keesaan TUHAN menurut adjaran Kristen dan Islam,* Medan 1968.
— *Penuntun Perang Sabil,* Medan 1957[2].
— *Risalat Djaminan Kemerdekaan Beragama Dalam Islam,* Medan 1961[2].
Madjalah Bulanan Séri Da[c]wah Islam, ed. by P.T.D.I., Bandung.
Madjid, Nurcholis, *Keharusan Pembaruan Pemikiran Islam dan Masalah Integrasi Ummat,* Djakarta 1970.
— *Modernisasi ialah Rasionalisasi bukan Westernisasi,* in *Pandji Masjarakat,* nos. 28, 29, 30.
Masjumi Pendukung Republik Indonesia, ed. by Pusat Komité Pemilihan Umum Masjumi, Djakarta, no date.

Mattalioe, Bahar, *Kahar Muzakkar dengan Petualangannja*, Djakarta 1965.
Maududi, S. Abul Ala, *Menudju Pengertian Islam*, Djakarta 1967.
McVey, Ruth T. (ed.), *Indonesia (Survey of World Cultures)*, New Haven 1963.
Melik, Sajuti, *Undang² Dasar '45 & "Piagam Djakarta"*, in *Mahasiswa Indonesia*, Bandung, April 1968.
Mohiaddin Alwaye, A. M., *Al-Azhar University*, Cairo 1966.
Mossman, James, *Rebels in Paradise, Indonesia's Civil War*, London 1961.
Muhammadijah: Peladjaran Ke-Muhammadijah-an, Djakarta 1965.
el-Muhammady, T. M. Usman, see: Usman el-Muhammady.
Mu'in, K. H. M. Taib Thahir Abdul, *Ichtisar Ilmu Tauhid*, Djakarta, no date.
— *Ilmu Kalam*, Djakarta 1966.
Mulder, D. C., *De Islam*, in *Theologische Etherleergang der N.C.R.V.*, no. 4, September 1965.
— *Stemmen uit de Islam*, in *De Heerbaan*, no. 1, 1968.
Mulia, T. S. G. & K. A. H. Hidding, *Ensiklopedia Indonesia*, 3 Vol., Bandung, no date.
Muskens, M. P. M., *Indonesië, Een strijd om nationale identiteit*, thesis Nijmegen 1969.
Natsir, Muh., *Capita Selecta*, Vol. I, Bandung/'s-Gravenhage 1955; Vol. II, Djakarta 1957.
— *Fungsi Da^cwah dalam rangka Perdjuangan*, Jogjakarta (1968?), (stencilled).
— *Islam sebagai Ideologi*, Djakarta, no date.
Nieuwenhuijze, C. A. O. van, *Aspects of Islam in Post-Colonial Indonesia*, The Hague-Bandung 1958.
— *Islam and National Self-Realization in Indonesia* in *Bulletin d'Informations du Centre pour l'Etude des Problèmes du Monde Musulman Contemporain*, Fasc. VII, 1958.
Nota betreffende het Archievenonderzoek naar gegevens omtrent excessen in Indonesië begaan door Nederlandse militairen in de periode 1945-1950, 's-Gravenhage 1969.
Notosoetardjo, H. A., *Peranan Agama Islam dalam Revolusi Indonesia*, Djakarta 1964.
Notosusanto, *Organisasi dan Jurisprudensi Peradilan Agama di Indonesia*, Jogjakarta 1963.
— *Peradilan Agama Islam di Djawa dan Madura*, Jogjakarta 1953.
— *Sedikit tentang Peradilan Perdata di Mesir*, Jogjakarta (1953?).
Nurlela, Nj., *Etiket — Tata Tertib Pergaulan*, Medan 1957.
Omar, Thoha Jahja, *Ilmu Da^cwah*, Djakarta 1967.
Osman, A. Latif, *Ringkasan Sedjarah Islam*, Djakarta 1965[15].
Pandji Masjarakat, Madjallah Kebudajaan dan Pengetahuan — untuk Perdjuangan Reformasi dan Modernisasi Islam, Djakarta.
Perdebatan, see: Hazairin.
Petundjuk dalam Membina Madrasah, ed. by MULJA, 2 Vol., Djakarta 1966.
Pickthall, M. M., *The Meaning of the Glorious Koran* (Mentor).
Piekaar, A. J., *Atjèh en de oorlog met Japan*, 's-Gravenhage-Bandung 1949.
Pinardi, *Sekarmadji Maridjan Kartosuwirjo*, Djakarta 1964.
Pijper, G. F., *De Edelgesteenten der Geloofsleer*, Leiden 1948.
Pluvier, J. M., *Overzicht van de ontwikkeling der Nationalistische Beweging in Indonesië in de jaren 1930 tot 1942*, 's-Gravenhage-Bandung 1953.
A Preliminary Analysis of the October 1, 1965, Coup in Indonesia, January 10, 1966 (Cornell University, stencilled).

Prins, J., *Adat en Islamietische Plichtenleer in Indonesië*, Bandung 1960[4] (thesis Leiden 1948).
Qur'ān, see: Al-Qur'ān, Bell, and Pickthall.
Rafik, *Analisa Tentang Potensi Ummat Islam Sekarang*, in *Pandji Masjarakat*, no. 32, Sept. 1968 (?).
Raliby, Osman, (ed.) *Documenta Historica*, Vol. I, Djakarta 1953.
— *Ibnu Chaldun tentang Masjarakat dan Negara*, Djakarta 1963.
Randwijck, S. C. Graaf van, *Missiologia in loco — Een andere visie*, in *Nederlands Theologisch Tijdschrift*, October 1969.
Rasjidi, H. M., *Islam dan Indonesia Dizaman Modern*, Djakarta 1968.
— *Islam dan Kebatinan*, Djakarta 1967 (?).
— *Islam Menentang Komunisme*, Djakarta 1966.
— *Mengapa aku tetap memeluk Agama Islam*, Djakarta 1968.
REPELITA, Pendjelasan Presiden Soeharto Didepan BP-MPRS 29 Pebruari 1968, Djakarta 1968.
Rida, M. Rasjid, *Wahju Allah kepada Muhammad*, Surabaja 1964.
Roesli DMB, *Pakistan, the Struggle of a Nation — Perdjuangan Suatu Bangsa Menudju Republik Islam Pakistan*, Solo 1956.
Roham, Abujamin, *Agama² Kristen dan Islam serta Perbandingannja*, Djakarta 1968.
Rusli, Moh. Munir & H. M. Nur Asjik, *Peladjaran Tauhid*, Djakarta 1964.
Salam, Solichin, *K. H. Ahmad Dahlan, Reformer Islam Indonesia*, Djakarta 1963.
— *Bung Karno dan Kehidupan Berpikir Dalam Islam*, Djakarta 1964.
— *Menindjau Masalah Polygami*, Djakarta 1959.
Saleh, T. M. Hasballah, *Tgk. Thjik Pante Kulu*, in *Sinar Darussalam*, no. 5, 1968.
Samson, Allan A., *Islam in Indonesian Politics*, in *Asian Survey*, December 1968.
Sanusi, Achmad, *Islam, Revolusi dan Masjarakat*, Bandung 1965.
Sanusi, Shalahuddin, *Pembahasan Sekitar Prinsip-Prinsip Da^cwah Islam*, Semarang 1964.
Schacht, J., *An Introduction to Islamic Law*, Oxford 1964.
Seminar Pentavipan Kurikulum Pendidikan Agama Pada Perguruan Tinggi (Bahan² dan Kesimpulan), 2 Vol., Djakarta 1965 (stencilled).
Shalaby, see: Sjalabi.
Shaltout, see: Sjaltout.
Sidjabat, W. B., *Religious Tolerance and the Christian Faith*, Djakarta 1965 (thesis Princeton 1960).
Siegel, James, *Prayer and Play in Atjeh*, in *Indonesia*, Cornell University, Ithaca New York 1966.
— *The Rope of God*, Berkeley and Los Angeles 1969.
Sinar Darussalam, Madjallah Pengetahuan dan Kebudajaan, Darussalam/Banda Atjeh, since March 1968.
Singodimedjo, Kasman, *Renungan dari Tahanan*, Djakarta 1967.
Sjafa'at, Moh., *Demokrasi dan Adjaran Islam*, Bandung 1963.
— *Pengantar Studi Islam*, Djakarta 1964.
Sjalabi, Ahmad, *Perbandingan Agama, Bahagian Agama Maséhi*, Djakarta 1964².
— *Perkembangan Keagamaan dalam Islam dan Maséhi*, Solo 1960.
Sjaltout, Sjaich Machmoud, *Islam sebagai Aqidah dan Sjari'ah*, Djakarta 1967.
Sluimers, L., *"Nieuwe Orde" op Java: de Japanse bezettingspolitiek en de Indonesische elites 1942-1943*, in *Bijdragen tot de Taal-, Land- en Volkenkunde*, Vol. 124, 's-Gravenhage 1968.
Smith, Wilfred Cantwell, *The Faith of Other Men* (Mentor), 1965.
— *Islam in Modern History*, Princeton 1957 (also Mentor).

Snouck Hurgronje, C., *The Achehnese*, 2 Vol., Leiden 1906.
— *Nederland en de Islam*, Leiden 1911.
Soeharto, see: *REPELITA*, and *Atjeh*.
Soekarno, *Dibawah Bendera Revolusi*, 2 Vol., Djakarta 1963²-1964.
— *Sukarno, An Autobiography as told to Cindy Adams*, New York 1965.
— *Tauhid Adalah Djiwaku*, Djakarta 1965.
— *Tjilaka Negara jang tidak ber-Tuhan*, in *Al-Djami^cah*, special issue, Jogjakarta 1965.
Stoddard, Lothrop, *Dunia Baru Islam*, Djakarta 1966.
Stöhr, Waldemar & Piet Zoetmulder, *Die Religionen Indonesiens*, Stuttgart 1965.
Suara Muhammadijah, Pembawa Tjita Persjarikatan Dan Da^cwah Islamijah, Jogjakarta.
Sutjipto (ed.), *ABRI, Pengemban Suara Hati Nurani Rakjat*, 2 Vol., Djakarta 1966.
Ṭaha Ḥusain, see: Husain.
Ṭāhir al-Djazā'irī, see: Thahir, and Pijper.
Taib Thahir Abdul Mu'in, see: Mu'in.
Thahir al-Djaza'iry bin Shalih, *Sendi Iman, Mutiara Ilmu Kalam*, Medan 1965.
Thaib, Aziz, *Islam dengan Politik*, Boekit Tinggi, no date.
Thé, Anne Marie, *Darah Tersimbah di Djawa Barat*, Djakarta 1968².
Tjokrosujoso, Abikusno, *Ummat Islam Indonesia Menghadapi Pemilihan Umum*, Djakarta 1953.
University Islam Indonesia, Buku Peringatan 10 Tahun, Jogjakarta 1955.
Usman el-Muhammady, *Ilmu Ke-Tuhanan Jang Maha Esa*, Medan 1963.
— *Kuliah: Iman dan Islam*, Djakarta, no date[4].
— *Pembangunan Djiwa-Negara dan Kebudajaan Islam (Kultuur, Politis dan Sociologis)*, Djakarta 1953².
Verkuyl, J., *Momentopnamen van de huidige situatie in Indonesië*, in *Wending*, June 1967.
— *Tentang Interpretasi Iman Kristen Kepada Orang² Islam*, in *Bulletin Lembaga Penjelidikan Pekabaran Indjil*, Djakarta, no date (stencilled).
Vredenbregt, Jacob, *De Islam in het moderne Indonesië*, in *Oost en West*, December 1968.
Wachid, Basit & Dja^cfar Amir: *Toleransi Dalam Islam (Ditindjau dari segi Sedjarah)*, Jogjakarta 1966 (stencilled).
Wahib Wahab, *Mutiara Hikmah, kumpulan pidato-pidato*, Djakarta 1962.
Wahid Hasjim, K. H. A., see: Abubakar (Atjeh).
Wardy, Bisjron A., *Memahami Kegiatan Nasrani*, Jogjakarta 1964 (stencilled).
Watt, W. Montgomery, *Muhammad at Medina*, Oxford 1966.
Weiss, Leopold, see: Asad, Muhammad.
Wertheim, W. F., *Indonesian Society in Transition*, The Hague, 1969².
Wolf Jr., Charles, *The Indonesian Story*, New York 1948.
Yamin, Muh., *Naskah Persiapan Undang-undang Dasar 1945*, 3 Vol., Djakarta 1959-1960.
— *Pembahasan Undang-undang Dasar Republik Indonesia*, Djakarta 1960.
— *Proklamasi dan Konstitusi Republik Indonesia*, Djakarta-Amsterdam 1951.
Yunus, H. Kahrudin, *Hidup Berkeluarga*, Djakarta, no date.
— *Hidup Bermasjarakat*, Djakarta, no date.
— *Hidup Berpribadi*, Djakarta, no date.
Zarkasji, I., *Usuluddin ('ala madzhab Ahli-SSunnah wal Djama'ah)*, Gontor-Ponorogo, no date[9].
Zorab, A. A., *De Japanse bezetting van Indonesië*, thesis Leiden 1954.

INDEX [1]

abangan, 4-5, 124, 187, 193, 231
Abbas, Zainal Arifin, 201
ᶜAbduh, Muḥ., 20, 42, 49, 77, 125n, 204, 207, 211, 212, 214, 215, 218
Abdul Abbas, 37
Abdulgani, Ruslan, 14n
ᶜAbd al-Ḳādir ᶜŪda, see: ᶜŪda
Abdul Wahab, 49
ᶜAbd al-Wahhāb, Muḥ. bin, 77
Abdur Rauf, 177n
Abidin, S. M., 89n, 91n
Abikusno, see: Tjokrosujoso
Aboebakar, see: Abubakar
ABRI, see: Sutjipto
Abubakar (Atjeh), H., 9n, 193, 203, 204, 238
Abu Hanifah, 42, 43, 80
Adams, Cindy, 141n
A.D.A.R.I., 167n
adat(-istiadat), adat-law, 28, 29, 69-70, 74, 164, 168-169, 173, 176
A.D.I.A. 120-121
al-Afghānī (Djamāl al-Dīn), 77, 78, 125n, 207
Afro-Asian Islamic Conference, 112
ahli bid'ah, 50
ahli sunnah wal djama'ah, 50
Ahmad, Abdullah, 212
Ahmad, Aftabuddin, 228
Ahmad, H. Z(ainal) A(bidin), 80-81, 163
Aḥmadīya Movement, 216, 228
Aḥmad Khān, 77
Aidit (D. N.), 104, 139
ᶜĀ'isha, 218
Al-Azhar (Djakarta), 77n, 148, 192n, 201
Alers, Henri J., 55n, 57, 60n, 72, 73n, 138n
Alfian, 191n

ᶜAlī, Amīr, 126, 207
Ali, A. Mukti, 162n, 193, 206-211, 212, 214-216, 229-230
Ali, Muaz, 199
Al-Qur'ān, 200
Sura 1 (al-Fātiḥa), 28, 200
Sura 2 : 115, 211
Sura 2 : 158, 184
Sura 2 : 201, 210n
Sura 2 : 217, 239
Sura 2 : 249, 188
Sura 2 : 256, 161, 236, 237, 239
Sura 2 : 275-276, 220
Sura 3 : 64, 239
Sura 3 : 104, 110, 114, 194
Sura 3 : 130, 220
Sura 4 : 58, 80
Sura 4 : 59, 81, 133, 171
Sura 4 : 89, 239
Sura 4 : 128, 51
Sura 4 : 161, 220
Sura 5 : 2, 184
Sura 5 : 38, 37, 66
Sura 5 : 54, 239
Sura 5 : 56, 12
Sura 7 : 156, 210n
Sura 7 : 157, 194
Sura 8 : 7, 133n
Sura 9 : 71, 194
Sura 9 : 112, 194
Sura 9 : 93, 200
Sura 9 : 94, 200
Sura 10 : 99, 239
Sura 12 : 55, 82, 171
Sura 13 : 11, 77, 219
Sura 14 : 44, 190
Sura 16 : 41, 210n
Sura 16 : 98, 32n
Sura 16 : 122, 210n
Sura 16 : 125, 239

---

[1] This Index lists all proper names and a number of subjects and technical terms, but only the most important pages have been given.

Sura 17 : 1,   129n,   218
Sura 17 : 100,   59
Sura 21 : 25,   205
Sura 22 : 30,   184
Sura 22 : 36,   184
Sura 22 : 40,   238
Sura 22 : 41,   194
Sura 24,   201
Sura 24 : 35,   96
Sura 28 : 77,   157
Sura 29 : 44,   200
Sura 29 : 46,   239
Sura 29 : 64,   157
Sura 34 : 15,   83, 242
Sura 39 : 18,   202
Sura 42 : 38,   18, 81, 162, 223
Sura 45 : 23-26,   157
Sura 49 : 13,   238
Sura 58 : 22,   12
Sura 60 : 8-9,   239
Sura 66 : 8,   134n
Sura 93 : 4,   157
amar ma‑ruf, nahi munkar, 194
amāna, 80
Amatillah, M. Sj. Ibnu, 81
Amīn al-Ḥusainī, 44
Amir, Djaꞌfar, 192, 200
Amrullah, Abdul Karim, 212
Amrullah, H. Abdul Malik Karim, see: HAMKA
Anderson, B. R. O'G., 137n
Ansor, anṣār, 52n, 145
Anshary, M. Isa, 13n, 17n, 48, 78, 80n, 83, 104, 148, 194
Anwar, H. Rosihan, 2
A.P.I., 72
apologetic(s), 225-230, 240
Arifin, Zainul, 12, 96, 97
Asaat, 104, 148
Asad, Muḥ. (Leopold Weiss), 79, 163
"ascension", "Journey into Heaven", see: miꞌrādj
Ash-Shiddiqy, M. Hasbi, 81, 165, 171, 193, 199, 201
Asj'ari, K. Hasjim, 10, 12, 42, 120
Asjik, Nur, 199
Atjeh, 68-75, 174-185
Audah, see: ꞌŪda
Aziz, H. Aminuddin, 159
Aziz, M. A., 9n, 11, 12, 70

bāb al-idjtihād, see: idjtihād
Badawy, M. A., 203

al-Baiḍāwī, 116
bait al-māl, 82, 171, 183
Bakker (Jr.), D., 187n, 190n, 193n, 195n, 196
Bakker (Sr.), D., 213n
Bakker, F. L., 228
Bakker S.J., J. W. M., 47n, 107n, 133n
Bakry, Hasbullah, 228
Bakry, H. M(oh.) K(asim), 201
balda ṭayyiba, 83, 242
banking, 220
Baried, Baroroh, 132
Barnabas (Gospel), 229
baṭin, bathin, kebathinan, 167, 217
Becker, C. H., 79n, 132
Bell, Richard, 194n
Benda, Harry J., 2ff, 7ff, 15n, 16n, 17n, 25n, 26, 34n, 40n, 70
Berg (C. C.), 213n
berkat, baraka, 115
Beureu'éh, Daud, 54, 71ff, 199n
Bhagavad-Gītā, 132
Bible,
    Isaiah 45 : 18,   242
    James 2 : 18,   242
    Luke 14 : 26,   237
    Matthew 22 : 21,   133n
    Matthew 28 : 19,   233
bi-lā kaif, 202
al-Bukhāri (Buchari), 125, 204
Budha Djawi, 167

Catholic Party, 42, 88, 95, 103, 187
Chalid, K. H. Idham, 117, 148, 162n
chalifat, caliphate, 80, 81
Chalil, Munawar, 192, 201
charadj, see: kharādj
"Charter of Bandung", 92, 97
Chotib, A., 220n
Christison (Gen.), 119
comparative religion, 206-211
Communists, see: P.K.I.
Constantine, 229
Constituent Assembly, 90ff
"Cornell Report", 137n, 139
courts (religious), 171-174
Cox, Harvey, 222n
Crossley, John, 229n

Dachlan, K. H. M., 234
daérah istiméwa, 74
daérah modal, 71
Daérah Satu, 57

INDEX

Dahlan, K. H. Ahmad, 11, 212, 213, 214, 235
Dahm, Bernhard, 1, 124ff
dāʿī, 193
Darul Fallah, 195
dār al-ḥarb (darulharb), 81, 176
Darul Islam, dār al-Islām, 42, 43, 49, 54-75, 80, 81, 147n
Darussalam, 75, 176, 177
Davies, A. Powell, 235
daʿwa(h), dakwah, 54, 108, 183, 190-196, 240
dawla, see: dīn
Democratic League, 103
Departemen Agama, see: Ministry of Religion
desacralization, 223
Dewantoro, Ki Hadjar, 35n
Déwi Sri, 195n
Dhani, Omar, 138
dhikr, 217
dhimmī, zimmi, 237
D.I., see: Darul Islam, and Daérah Satu
dīn, dīn wa dawla, 3, 8, 109, 216
Diponegoro, 209
Diponegoro Division, 135, 137
dirigism (religious), 189-190
Djabrīya, 203
Djaja, Tamar, 79n
Djajadiningrat, Hoesein, 10, 24, 29, 30, 161
Djakarta Charter, 25-27, 31, 36, 82, 92ff, 100-101, 153, 159-161, 170, 175
Djalal ad-Din al-Azhari, Tahir, 212
Djalalain (Tafsir), 116
djāmiʿa, al-djamiʿah, 204
Djam'ijatul Waslijah, 75
Djamil, Amiruddin, 147n, 232n
Djamil Djambek (Sjech), 42, 212
djihād, perang sabil, "holy war", 40, 57, 71, 75-76, 78, 83, 145-146, 237
djiwa, kedjiwaan, 77, 217
djizja, 82, 171, 237
Djojodihardjo, Sumitro, 90
Djokosujono, 139n
Djuanda, 88, 91n, 96, 103, 176
doctrine, dogmatics, 198-199, 202-203, 217ff
Dradjad, Zakijah, 220n
Drewes, G. W. J., 7n, 49n, 67n, 213n
dunyā wa ākhira, 3, 109
Dwitunggal, 87, 95, 97

elections, 52-54, 82-83, 85, 154
Enthoven (Rapport), 63n

Family Planning, 220
al-Fārābī, 163
farāʾiḍ, faraid, see: inheritance
Farouk, 162n
fatwā, 40, 59, 145-146, 177, 234
see also: Madjlis Iftāʾ
Feith, Herbert, 1, 13, 15n, 42n, 43n, 47, 48n, 51, 52n, 53, 55n, 60n, 61n, 62n, 64, 65n, 73, 78, 85ff, 102ff, 108n, 135
fiʾatan ḳalīlatan, 188
fiḳh, 125
see also: uṣul al-fiḳh
freedom of religion, 18, 30, 80, 108-110, 148, 174, 234, 237ff

Gadjah Mada University, 119, 172
Gaharu, Sjamaun, 74
gamelan, 4
Gazalba, Sidi, 191n, 192n
al-Ghazzālī, 204
Geertz, Clifford, 1ff, 10n, 106, 115, 197, 200n
Gestapu/P.K.I., 140, 144, 238
Ghallab, Muḥ., 204
Gibb, H. A. R., 3, 79, 208, 213n, 215, 218, 229
Goethe (J. W.), 13-14, 211
Gogarten, Fr., 222n
golongan, 24
gotong rojong, 22, 87
Grunebaum, G. E. von, 7n, 15n, 49n, 67n, 79n, 105
Gunawan, Basuki, 138n, 144n
Gusti Kang Maha Sutji, 128

Hadikusuma, Djarnawi, 153, 226
Hadikusumo, K. Bagus H., 23, 24, 28, 31, 32, 35, 36, 153n
hadīth, hadi(t)s, 131
Hadiwijono, Harun, 38n, 217n
Ḥālī, 129n
HAMKA, 17n, 77, 78, 95, 97, 104, 148, 201, 212, 216, 220, 238n
Hanafie, A., 202
Harahap, Burhanuddin, 89, 104, 148
Harahap, Zainabun, 55n, 65, 68n
ḥarbī, harbi, 237
Hardi, 74, 176
Harjono, Anwar, 93, 153, 165
Hartmann, (Richard?), 132

Harun, Lukman, 181n
ḥasana fī 'd-dunyā, 210, 242
Hasbi Ash-Shiddiqy, see: Ash-Shiddiqy
Hashem, O., 228
Hasjim, Wahid, 9, 10, 11n, 12, 14n, 23, 24, 26, 29, 30, 32, 34, 35, 41n, 42, 43n, 45n, 46, 49n, 50n, 52n, 53, 76, 78, 107ff, 125n
Hasjmy, Ali, 69n, 72ff, 176ff
Hassan, A., 117, 192, 193, 212, 214
Hassan, A. Qadir, 117
Hassan, T. Moh., 35
Hatta, Moh., 19, 23, 24, 25, 26, 28, 34, 35, 36, 37, 41, 57, 87, 103, 118-119, 141, 152, 187, 192
Hazairin, 118, 165, 168-171, 213,240
Hefele, Ch. J., 229n
hiba, 166
Hidding, K. A. H., 43n
hidjra policy, 56
al-Hindi, 207
Hindley, Donald, 139
ḥisāb, 188
Hizbu'llah, 12-14
H.M.I., 117, 142, 145n, 221
Hoballah, M. F., 161, 163
Hoesin, Oemar Amin, see: Husin
"holy war", see: *djihād*
Hori (Col.), 10
Hughes, John, 138, 140, 141n, 149
hukum, hukōm, 70
hulubalang, see: *ulèëbalang*
Ḥusain, Ṭaha, 204
Husein, Ibrahim, 183n
Husin, Umar Amin, 201
Hyang Widi, 128

I.A.I.N., 121ff, 197
ᶜ*ibāda, ibadah, 'ibādāt*, 146, 170
Ibn Ḥazm, 207
Ibn Ḳayyim, 207
Ibn Khaldūn (Ibn Chaldun), 162-163, 204
Ibn Taimīya, 207
(*al-*)ᶜ*īd al-kabīr*, 188-189
idjmāᶜ, 20
idjtihād, 50, 126, 130, 161, 163, 165, 169-171, 202, 213-215, 222
Idris, M. Nur, 201
Imron, Marzuki, 193
(*al-*)*Ikhwān* (*al-Muslimūn*), 67n, 147n, 162
Imām, 28, 77n, 113

India, 212
infāḳ, infaq, 59
inheritance (law), 169, 170, 173
interest, see: *ribā*
Inter-Religious Consultation, 234-236
I.P.I., 72
I.P.K.I., 99, 179
Iqbāl, Muḥ. (Iqbal), 207, 223
al-Irsjad, 212
Isaq Bey, 132
Iskandardinata, Oto, 24, 30, 35
Iskandar Muda, 177n
iṣlāḥ, ishlah, 193
Islamization, see: *daᶜwa*
Ismail, Taufiq, 134
Ismuha (Ismail Muh. Sjah), 178
istiḥsān, 202
Istiqlal Mosque, 102
istiṣlāḥ, 202
Italiaander, Rolf, 212

Jahja, Muchtar, 192
Jakobites, 203
JAPI, 227-228
Jassin, H. B., 187n, 203
"Javanese-Sundanese Religion", 108n
Jefferson, Thomas, 130
Judodihardjo, Sutjipto (Gen.), 195
Junus, Mahmud, 115ff, 170, 199
Juynboll, Th. W., 189n

K., see: *kiyai*
ḳaḍā', 203
ḳadar, 203
kāfir, 237
Kafrawi, R. Moh., 107n
Kahar (Muzakkar), 10, 54, 55n, 62-68, 75
Kahar Muzakkir, (Abdul), 10, 23, 26, 32, 95, 162
Kahin, George McT., 1, 10n, 15n, 21n, 25n, 34n, 35n, 40, 41, 42, 43n, 44, 45n, 48, 55n, 58, 72n, 139n, 144n, 213n
KAMI, 142
Kamran, 56, 57
Kanun Azasy, *al-ḳānūn al-asasī*, 59, 60n
KAPPI, 142
Ḳarafī, Aḥmad al-Ṣanhādjī, 207
Ḳartapradja, K. Kamil, 167n
Kartawinata, Arudji, 45, 128
Kartosuwirjo, S. M., 42, 54-62, 65, 74, 75, 105

Kasimo (I. J.), 235, 236
Kasman, see: Singodimedjo
kaum tua/muda, 116
Kawilarang (Col.), 64
kebat(h)inan, see: *baṭin*
kedjiwaan, see: djiwa
Ketuhanan (Jang Maha Esa), 18, 22, 26, 38, 80, 93ff, 108, 188, 239
kharādj, charadj, 82
Khoury, Paul, 207n
al-Khouri, Faris, 158
Kipandjikusmin, 203
Kipling (Rudyard), 210
kiyai, 7
ḳiyās, 161, 202
K.N.I.L., 63
K.N.I.P., 37
Koiso, 16
konsèpsi (President), 86ff
Kraemer, H., 213n, 236, 240n
K.R.I.S., 63
Kroef, J. M. van der, 1

lā ikrāha fi 'd-dīn, see Sura 2 : 256
Latif (Col.), 146
Latuharhary, 27, 28, 29, 32, 33, 35, 37
Leimena (Johannes), 128, 132
Liga Muslimin Indonesia, 46-47
Lith S.J., Father F. van, 213n
Loebis, Ali Basja, see: Lubis
Lubis, Ali Basja, 16n
Lubis, M. Arsjad Th(alib), 75-76, 237, 240
Lukman, 104
Lukman, Dahlan, 91n
Luther, 77

Macdonald (D.B.), 208
madhhab, madzhab (school of law), 11, 164-165, 214-215
madhhab Indonesia/Nasional, 170-171
"Madiun affair" (1948), 40, 138n, 144, 146
Madjid, Nurcholis, 117, 221-224
Madjlis Iftā', 176, 178
Madjlis Ulama, 178, 180ff
madrasa, 113ff
"Makalua Charter", 65
Mangkusasmito, Prawoto, 13, 42, 94, 97, 103, 104, 148, 152
Mang Reng Say, B., 95
Manipol, 101, 111
Mansur, K. H. M., 23, 49
Maramis, A. A., 17, 24, 26, 27, 29, 32, 33

Marhaen, *marhaenis,* 141
marriage (law), 46, 66, 160, 164, 165, 166-168, 237
see also: woman
Marx/Engels, 157
Masjkur, K. H., 32, 98, 235
Masjumi, 10-12, 41, 42-49, 52-53, 83-84, 88, 103, 118, 148, 149, 150-151, 179n, 187n, 194
Mattalioe, Bahar, 55n, 63ff
Mawdūdī, S. Abū 'l-ᶜAlā' (Maududi), 147, 204, 232n
McVey, Ruth T., 1, 85n, 137n
Melik, Sajuti, 35
mertju suar, 102
M.I.A.I., 10-11
milla, millet, 172
M.I.N., 113
Ministry of Education, 117
Ministry of Information, 107
Ministry of Religion, 6, 10, 12, 37, 105-112, 115, 172, 188-190, 196, 205, 240
miᶜrādj, 129n, 130, 218
Mohiaddin Alwaye, A. M., 118n
Mook, H. J. van, 82
Moseley, C. E., 180n, 231
Mossman, James, 89n
M.P.R.S., 142
mu'aḥad, 237
mu'amman, muamman, 237
muballigh, 192
Muchlis, A., see: Natsir, Muh.
mudjtahid-baru, 170
mufakat, 21
mufti, 13, 59
Muhammadijah, 11, 46, 49, 78, 126, 130, 145-146, 151, 153, 165, 179, 191ff, 194, 198, 216, 223, 226-227
el-Muhammady, Usman, see: Usman
Mu'in, K. H. M. Taib Thahir Abdul, 203
Mulder, D. C., 104n, 228n
Mulia, T. S. G., 43n
mu'min, mukmin, 237
munāfiḳ, munafiq, 237
Murba (Partai), 65
murtad, 239
muṣalla, mushallah, 178
musjawarah, permusjawaratan, 18, 213
Muskens, M. P. M., 74, 107n, 108n, 117n, 138n, 144n, 145n, 155n, 186n

Muslim Brethren, see: Ikhwān
Musso, 138n
Muʿtazila, 203
Muttaqin, E. Z., 104
Muzakkar, K., see: Kahar Muzakkar
Muzakkir, Abdul K., see: Kahar Muzakkir
mysticism, 4, 14, 56n, 131, 203, 216, 217, 225

Nahdatul Ulama, see: N.U.
Nahdatul Wat(h)an, 49
NASAKOM, 41, 102, 225
NASASOS, 41
Nasrani, -sasi, etc., 227
Nasution (Gen.), 86, 89, 128, 135, 136, 141, 143, 150, 200
Nasution, Junan, 104, 238-239
Natsir, Muh. (= A. Muchlis), 42, 43, 44n, 59, 60, 61, 64, 78, 79, 80n, 84, 89, 103, 104, 148, 152, 194, 195, 225n, 235, 236
Nazir, 72, 73n
Nekolim, 146
Nestorius, 203
N.I.A.S., 55
N.I.C.A., 39, 76
Nicaea (A.D. 325), 229
N.I.I., 58
Nieuwenhuijze, C. A. O. van, 1n, 11n, 15n, 38, 55n, 56n, 57n, 58n, 60n, 107n, 108n, 112n, 159n, 213n
Nishimura, 16
Njoman Rai, Ida Aju, 128
Notosoetardjo, H. A., 159
Notosusanto, 164, 172-174
N.U., 11, 42, 45, 46, 49-54, 145, 150, 179, 187n, 213, 223
Nur Fadjar, see: Ismail, Taufik
Nurjadin, Rusmin, 87n
Nurlela, Nj., 193

Occidentalism, 208
Oldefos, 224
Omar, Thoha Jahja, 170, 194
Oni, 57
ORBA, 141
Orientalism, 208
ORLA, 141
Osman, A. Latif, 200

Pakistan, 2, 15, 105, 159, 163
Panté Kulu, Tgk. Tjhik, 178

Pantjasila, 17, 21-23, 38, 47, 90, 158, 161, 181, 182, 234, 239
Parkindo (Protestant Party), 42, 95, 103, 179, 180n, 184, 187
Parmusi, 152, 179n, 194, 226
Partai Muslimin Indonesia, see: Parmusi
Paul (Apostle), 228, 229
Paul, Bishop of Sidon, 207
penghulu, 166
perang sabil, see: *djihād*
Permesta, Perdjuangan Semesta, 67, 68, 88-90
Perti, 47, 52-53, 150, 179
pesantrèn, 7, 113ff, 129, 130
philanthropy, 242
P.H.I.N., 120, 172
Piagam Djakarta, see: Djakarta Charter
Pickthall, M. M., 129n
Piekaar, A. J., 8n, 69ff, 177n
Pinardi, 55ff
(ber)pindah agama, 241
Pijper, G. F., 199n, 213n
Pluvier, J. M., 56
P.K.I., Communist(s), 41, 42, 53, 99, 135, 137ff, 149, 167, 225
P.M.I., see: Parmusi
P.M.I.I., 145n
P.N.I., 41, 53, 99, 149
polemic(s), see: apologetics
polygamy, 66, 167-168
pondok, see: *pesantrèn*
Potjut Meurah, 177n
Potter, Ch. Francis, 235
Prawiranegara, Sjafruddin, 42, 72, 89, 104, 148
Prawoto, see: Mangkusasmito
Prins, J., 164, 169n
priyayi, 4-5, 7-8
Protestant Party, see: Parkindo
P.R.R.I., 67, 89-89, 151
P.S.I., see: Socialist Party
P.S.I.I., 26, 45, 52-53, 55, 150, 179
P.T.A.I.N., 120-121
P.T.D.I., 194-195
P.U.S.A., 69

Qumran, 228
Qurʾān, see: Al-Qurʾān

Rachman, W. A., 98
Radjiman (Wediodiningrat), 16, 28, 34
Rafik, 187
Raliby, Osman, 15n, 34n, 162

INDEX

Ramaḍān, 186, 188
Randwijck, S. C. Graaf van, 233n
rangkang, see: pesantrèn
Rangkuti, Bahrum, 144
ar-Ranīri, Nuruddin, 177
Rasjidi, H. M., 4-5, 13, 106, 157-158, 235-236, 240
ratu adil, 22
al-Rāziḳ, ᶜAli ᶜAbd, 20
"reception theory", 169
Renville agreement, 57, 58
REPELITA, PELITA, 155
revival (of religions), 225
ribā, riba, 44, 220
Riḍā, Rashīd (Rida, M. Rasjid), 15, 49, 105, 204, 207, 212, 214
R.I., 39
R.I.S., 39
Roem, Mohamad, 13, 17n, 42, 104, 148, 152, 153, 160
Roesli DMB, 163n
Roham, Abujamin, 240
R.U.S.I., 39
Rusli, Moh. Munir, 199
ru'ya, 188

Sabīli'llāh, 13
Said, Moh., 197
Salam, Solichin, 126, 127, 213n
salafīya, 126
(as-)salām(u) ᶜalaikum, 131, 175
ṣalāt, shalat, 178, 186
Saleh, Chairul, 132
Saleh, T. M. Hasballah, 178n
Salim, H. A(gus), 23, 26, 28, 29, 30, 32, 42
Samson, Allan A., 48n, 49n, 150n, 151, 152, 153, 155, 159, 221
Santoso, Ulfa, 30
santri, 4-5, 9n, 13
Sanusi, Achmad, 33, 159
Sanusi, Shalahuddin, 193
Sarbini (Gen.), 195
Sarékat Islam, 26
Sastroamidjojo, Ali, 73, 74, 86
Sastromuljono, 24
Schacht, J., 164
Schmidt, Father W., 207
Schofield, Hugh, 235
"scripturalism", 5
secularization, 221ff
serambi Mekkah, see: verandah of Mecca
serimpi, 5

shahāda, 182
al-Shahrastānī, 207
Shalaby, Aḥmad, 204, 229
Shaltout, Sjaich Machmoud, 204
sharīᶜa, sjariᶜah, sjari'at, 20, 27, 29, 83, 121, 165
shiᶜār, sji'ar, 183-184
Sidjabat, W. B., 16n, 38, 83, 108n
Siegel, James, 175
Siliwangi Division, 58-59
Simorangkir, J. C. T., 95, 180n
Singgih, 24, 29
Singodimedjo, Kasman, 35n, 37, 104, 148, 239
Siregar, Sormin, 184
Sjafa'at, Moh., 162
Sjahrir, 12, 34, 38, 40, 41, 82, 103, 106, 107, 149
Sjaichu, Achmad, 93, 96
Sjalabi, see: Shalaby
Sjaltout, see: Shaltout
Sjarifuddin, Amir, 45, 57, 106
sjauka (bissjauka?), shauka, 133
Sluimers, L., 9n
Smith, Adam, 130
Smith, Wilfred Cantwell, 2, 50n, 127n, 129n, 147n, 213n, 214n, 215, 224, 229, 235, 236, 240n
Snouck Hurgronje, (C.), 13-14, 70, 132, 179, 240n
Socialist Party, Socialist(s), 41, 53, 103, 149
Soeharto, 136, 141, 142, 150, 152, 155, 158, 159, 166, 181, 200, 234, 241
Soekarno, 17, 21-23, 24ff, 34ff, 41, 47-48, 57, 60, 61, 62, 64, 70-71, 78, 85ff, 99ff, 119, 123-134, 135ff, 159, 160, 162, 179, 187, 189, 200, 220, 224, 239
Soorkati, Ahmad, 49, 212
Stenus, Corry van, 66
Stoddard, Lothrop, 125
Stöhr, Waldemar, 114n, 115n
Subandrio, 127, 139
Subardjo (Achmad), 17, 24, 26, 29, 35n, 37, 40, 41
Subud movement, 217
Subuh, 217
succession (law), see: inheritance
Sudirman (Gen.), 195, 235
ṣuffa, supah, 56
Sujono, 138
Sukemi, 128

Sukiman, 23, 29, 30, 42, 61, 64
Sukmadi (Comm.), 195
suku, 65, 67n
ṣulḥ, shulchu, 51
Sumantri, Kusuma, 35n
Sumarsono, 139n
Sumual (Lt. Col.), 88
Sunarjo, 74
sunna(h), 50, 169
Supardjo, 138, 146
Supeno, Bambang, 146
Supomo, 17, 18-21, 23, 24, 29, 30, 31, 33, 34
surau, see: *pesantrèn*
Sutardjo, 23, 24, 34, 37
Sutjipto, 111
Suwandi, 24
Suwirjo, 99

T., see: Teuku
al-Ṭabarī, ᶜAlī ibn Sahl Rabbān, 207
tablīgh, 192ff
Ṭaha Ḥusain, see: Ḥusain
Tahir Djalal, see: Djalal
Ṭāhir al-Djazā'irī, 199
Taib Thahir Abdul Mu'in, see: Mu'in
Talsya, T. Alibasjah, 69n
Tan Malaka, 40
takdir, taqdir, 76
taklīd, taqlid, 126, 201, 202, 213ff
Tambunan (A. M.), 235, 236
ṭarīḳa, tarékat, 217
tauḥīd, tauhid, 130, 203
tavip, pentavipan, 197n
Teuku, 69
Teungku, 69
Tgk., see: Teungku
Thahir al-Djaza'iri, see: Ṭahir
Thaib, Aziz, 76
Thé, Anne Marie, 55n, 60n, 62
theocracy, *theokrasi*, 56, 163-164
T.I.I., 58
Tiro, Hassan, 67n
Tjokroaminoto, Anwar, 13
Tjokroaminoto, H. Omar Said, 55, 56
Tjokrosujoso, Abikusno, 26, 28, 31, 42, 82, 83
T.N.I., 63-64, 68
tolerance, *toleransi*, intolerance, 29, 80, 179, 181, 205-206, 210, 234, 235, 237-239, 241
Toynbee, Arnold J., 210, 226
Trinity, 76, 227, 229n, 240

Tri Sila, 22
Tuanku, 69
Tuhan, see: *Ketuhanan J. M. E.*
Turkey, 2, 19, 78, 105, 112

ᶜŪda, ᶜAbd al-Ḳādir, (Audah), 162, 204
(al-)ukhrā, uchrowi, 222
ukhūwa, uchuwah, 183, 186
U.I.D., 118
U.I.I., 119, 172
ulama, 7, 68ff
ulèëbalang, 7, 68ff
ūlū 'l-amri, wālī al-amri, 81, 131, 171
Umar (Caliph), 171
unsur, 164
Untung (Col.), 136ff, 146
Urmonotheismus, 207
USDEK, 101-102, 111
Usman, Fakih, 46
Usman el-Muhammady, T. M., 164, 203
ustadh, ustaz, 200n
uṣuluddin, ushuluddin, 121
uṣūl al-fiḳh, usul fiqh, 202
Utrecht, E., 137n, 225n

"verandah of Mecca", 68, 175, 179, 182
Verkuyl, J., 140n, 143n, 149n, 151n, 159n, 228
Vlekke (B. H. M.), 213n
Vredenbregt, Jacob, 190n, 193n, 194n, 224

wadjhu 'llāhi, wadjah Allah, 211
Wahib Wahab, 133, 186
Wahid Hasjim, see: Hasjim
wajang, 4
waḳf, waqaf, wakaf, 165, 166
Wali Alfatah, 60
wa'llāhu aᶜlam, 124, 132
Wardy, Bisjron A., 227
Washington, George, 130
Watt, W. Montgomery, 56
Weiss, Leopold, see: Asad, Muḥ.
Wertheim, W. F., 54n, 213n
Westerling (Capt.), 62, 63
Westernization, 220ff
Wibisono, Jusuf, 13, 42
Wilopo, 46, 73n
Wiranatakusuma, 35n
Wolf Jr., Charles, 25n
woman, 178, 189, 192, 220
Wondoamiseno, 45, 56
Wongsonegoro, 29, 30, 161

Yamin, Muh., 15n, 17-18, 19n, 21n, 22n, 23, 24, 25, 26, 28, 33, 35n, 86ff, 99n, 127n
Yunus, H. Kahruddin, 193

zakāt, 44, 81, 82, 165, 166, 180-181, 182, 186, 237, 242

Zarkasji, I., 117
zimmi, see: *dhimmī*
Zoetmulder, P., see: Stöhr, W.
Zorab, A. A., 12n
Zuhri, H. Saifuddin, 95
Zwemer, Samuel M., 213n